PUBLIC MEN AND VIRTUOUS WOMEN: THE GENDERED LANGUAGES OF RELIGION AND POLITICS IN UPPER CANADA, 1791–1850

Gendered images and symbols were of central importance to public debate about loyalty, political conflict, and religious participation in early Ontario. Drawing on a wide range of international scholarship in feminist theory, women's and gender history, and cultural studies, Cecilia Morgan analyses political and religious languages in the Upper Canadian press, both secular and religious, and other material published in the colony from the 1790s to the 1850s. She examines constructs and concepts of gender in a wide number of areas: narratives of the War of 1812, political struggles over responsible government in the 1820s and 1830s, evangelical religious discourses throughout these decades, and related discussions of manners and moral behaviour. She also considers the relations between religion and politics in the 1840s, pointing to the continuous struggles of Upper Canadians to define and fix the meanings of public and private and their use of masculinity and femininity to signify these realms. She suggests as well that scholars of gender and colonial history need to consider a more nuanced way of understanding social formation in the colony through an examination of the representation of voluntary organizations. The book also examines relations of gender, class, and race as they affected the cultural development of the middle class.

Morgan concludes that while seemingly hegemonic definitions of gender relations emerged over this period – with men and masculinity identified with politics and loyalty to the colonial state and imperial connection, and women and femininity linked to the home – the meanings of gender and gendered imagery differed according to their contexts. Colonial society's attempts to make sharp delineations between the public and the private were rarely successful and were marked by numerous tensions and contradictions.

CECILIA MORGAN is an assistant professor of history at Queen's University.

STUDIES IN GENDER AND HISTORY

General editors: Franca Iacovetta and Craig Heron

CECILIA MORGAN

Public Men and Virtuous Women: The Gendered Languages of Religion and Politics in Upper Canada, 1791–1850

UNIVERSITY OF TORONTO PRESS
Toronto Buffalo London

© University of Toronto Press Incorporated 1996
Toronto Buffalo London
Printed in Canada

ISBN 0–8020–0725–2 (cloth)
ISBN 0–8020–7671-8 (paper)

Printed on acid-free paper

Canadian Cataloguing in Publication Data

Morgan, Cecilia Louise, 1958–

Public men and virtuous women : the gendered
languages of religion and politics in Upper Canada, 1791–1850

(Studies in gender and history)
Includes bibliographical references.
ISBN 0-8020-0725-2 (bound) ISBN 0-8020-7671-8 (pbk.)

1. Sex role – Ontario – History – 18th century.
2. Sex role – Ontario – History – 19th century.
3. Ontario – Religion – 18th century.   4. Ontario –
Religion – 19th century.   5. Ontario – Politics and
government – 1791–1841.   6. Ontario – Politics and
government – 1841–1867.   7. Ontario – social life and
customs.   I. Title.   II. Series.

HQ1075.5.C3M67 1996   305.309713   C96-931508-2

This book has been published with the help of a grant from the Humanities
and Social Sciences Federation of Canada, using funds provided by the Social
Sciences and Humanities Research Council of Canada.

University of Toronto Press acknowledges the assistance to its publishing
program of the Canada Council and the Ontario Arts Council.

For Francis and Joan Morgan,
and for Paul

Contents

Acknowledgments

This book began its life as my doctoral thesis in history at the University of Toronto, reaching its destination as a book with the ongoing support of many good friends, helpful colleagues, and fine instructors (categories that are not, of course, mutually exclusive). Getting the chance to say 'thank you' in public is one of the pleasurable parts – perhaps the most pleasurable – of the 'thesis-to-book' process.

Those who helped with the thesis stage deserve special mention. For encouraging my academic career long before this project took place, I thank Sylvia Van Kirk. Allan Greer suggested to me that doctoral research on Upper Canada would sustain my interest – he was right, it did (and continues to do so). Ruth Roach Pierson provided critical insights that helped me see beyond the boundaries of Upper Canada, particularly in the area of feminist theory. Wendy Mitchinson and Alison Prentice suggested a number of things that I should think about as I reworked the thesis for this book; I have tried to incorporate much of this material. As a thesis adviser, Ian Radforth provided vast amounts of enthusiasm and support for this project, many constructive and helpful suggestions, and much patience with my forays into poststructuralist theory – many thanks.

The Ontario Graduate Scholarship program, the University of Toronto History Department's C.P. Stacey scholarship fund, and the Social Sciences and Humanities Research Council provided the funding that made it possible to devote my time and energy to this work. As well, I would like to thank the staff at the Archives of Ontario, the United Church Archives, the Metropolitan Toronto Reference Library (Baldwin Room), the D.B. Weldon Library at the University of Western Ontario (Regional Collection), and the Law Society of Upper Canada Archives. The staff of the

Niagara-on-the-Lake Public Library deserve special thanks for their assistance and cheerful support.

Members of the Toronto Gender History group, Lykke de la Cour, Karen Dubinsky, Nancy Forestell, Margaret Little, Lynne Marks, Kate McPherson, and Suzanne Morton, gave generously of their time and insights as they read various chapters of the thesis; they also shared their knowledge of the hazards and the pleasures of building academic careers. In graduate school and afterwards, Susan Lewthwaite has been a generous and supportive friend and fellow historian of Upper Canada. While I was revising the manuscript Paul Deslandes, Stephen Heathorn, Maureen McCarthy, and Tori Smith provided very good company on Friday mornings; this book has benefited from both their knowledge of cultural history and their friendship. Mariana Valverde has given me much encouragement over the years and critical commentaries on parts of this manuscript, reminding me that historians need not fear theory. Craig Brown, Franca Iacovetta, Ruth Pierson, and Joan Sangster provided me with badly needed employment as I revised my thesis. Lykke de la Cour and Nancy Forestell have reminded me in countless ways that our work is best sustained through a sense of humour – even if it brings many long-distance phone bills.

At University of Toronto Press, Gerry Hallowell and Rob Ferguson made the process of getting this manuscript through the publication process far easier than I had imagined; Barbara Tessman did an exemplary job of tidying up my murky prose. Thanks also to the two anonymous readers for their insights and comments that helped to improve the manuscript. And special thanks to Franca Iacovetta for her unceasing commitment to, and support of, this project.

This book has a lot to say about constructions of 'the family,' and much of what it says is very critical of that institution's manifestation in the nineteenth century. My own family, however, has given me much over the years – from encouraging my choices to providing 'homes away from home' that allowed me to complete my research. From my brother Jonathan in particular I have learnt much about the meanings of 'family' – in the best sense of the word. My father, Francis Morgan, did not live to see my doctoral thesis completed, but he and my mother, Joan, made it possible for their children, daughters and sons, to do things (such as study and write about history) that in a different time and place he might have chosen for himself. Thanks also to Hugh and Florence Jenkins for their cheerful and unstinting support expressed in a number of ways. And, finally, neither the thesis nor the book could have been completed without the loving encouragement, patience, good humour, and never-flagging support of Paul Jenkins.

Cecilia Morgan

PUBLIC MEN AND VIRTUOUS WOMEN:
THE GENDERED LANGUAGES OF RELIGION
AND POLITICS IN UPPER CANADA, 1791–1850

Introduction

Will you, men of Upper Canada, see your laws thus trampled upon; – your liberties infringed – your opinions, sacred in the bosoms of all freemen, coerced by the scimitar of power, and transgressed by men in the favour of the Government? Stand forth, thou upholder of the British Constitution – raise thy voice in defence of her laws.

'A Dialogue Between Two Farmers on Canadian Politics,' *Colonial Advocate*, 19 April 1832

Of what infinite value to society is that tenderness, compassion, and benevolence, which the Almighty has impressed on the female heart. It is a woman's exclusive gift; it is the foundation of all her virtues; the mainspring of all her usefulness.

'Female Influence,' Mrs King, *Christian Guardian*, 12 August 1835

The men of Upper Canada demanding their rights in political life; the virtuous, benevolent woman exerting her influence over society with Divine guidance: these are two of the more powerful and prevalent images gleaned from the pages of the Upper Canadian press. At first glance, these images adhere to the concept of separate spheres, which has become central to our understanding of American, British, and Canadian gender relations in the nineteenth century, particularly for white, middle-class men and women. Political life was represented as an arena dominated by men, a place of action where freedoms and rights were vigorously debated and defended. Woman's contribution to society was measured by her virtue and nurturing abilities, which emanated from within the home where she was sequestered from the rough-and-tumble male world of political and economic life.

In many ways these images dominated nineteenth-century American and British society. They shaped but also mirrored the experiences of white, middle-class, urban men and women whose lives had been fundamentally altered by the separation of production from the home in the late eighteenth and early nineteenth centuries.[1] Feminist historians have noted the prevalence of a nineteenth-century ideology that assigned women to the home, assuming their natural fitness for the domestic world of housekeeping and childrearing. This ideology justified the division of social and economic space by positing women's innate moral superiority to men. The implications of this 'cult of true womanhood' and the subsequent hardening of society into public and private spheres, each the province of one sex, have been investigated by historians who have used these tenets to analyse the development of a private female culture, the growth of women's moral reform networks, and the ideological influence of the tenets of separate spheres upon early feminist organizations, especially in the formation of maternal feminism.[2] Women's lives, it is frequently argued, have been qualitatively and quantitatively different from men's. Men's lives were taken up with the public spheres of society and workplace, while women's centred on the private world of household and domesticity. Certainly such a division corresponded to some degree to the experiences of white, middle-class women of northeastern urban America and provincial Britain, a specificity that historians of working-class, black, immigrant, and Native women have noted.[3] Yet the process by which this division took place has often been treated either monocausally or has been assumed as an evil necessary to the process of 'modernization.' In the American and British cases, it has often been seen as a result of the separation of production from the home during industrialization or of the spread of affective individualism and the rise of the nuclear family.[4] In the Canadian literature, it has been frequently presumed that this process occurred at some point in the nineteenth century and was challenged by various groups of women into the twentieth century.[5]

In Canadian historiography on women and gender, despite an ever increasing body of work that focuses on the period between 1880 and 1950, our knowledge and understanding of gender relations in the early nineteenth century is extremely limited. Women and gender have taken a distinct second place in Upper Canadian historiography to issues such as political ideology, the composition of Upper Canadian political and social élites, the cultural patterns of religion, and the development of state-sponsored education.[6] To be sure, we know something about a few groups of women: the Loyalist women of eastern Ontario; the literate pioneer women of the 'middling sort' who left diaries and letters; the élite women of York and Kingston who were members of socially and politically prominent families; and a few Native women such as Molly and Catherine Brant.[7] The work of political economist Marjorie Cohen has shed light on the changing relationship between women, agricultural production, and the development of markets in nineteenth-century Ontario.[8]

Yet much of this scholarship focuses on the experiences of discrete groups of women; with a few exceptions, no study of Upper Canadian society incorporates gender as a 'category of historical analysis.'[9] In place of informed analysis, we have inspired guesswork, fragments of information, and the supposition that the trajectory of gender relations in the early nineteenth century mirrored developments in both the United States and Britain.[10] Nor do we clearly understand how gender shaped Upper Canadian society, or the ways in which gender relations influenced and, in turn, were influenced by historical change. And, finally, without understanding the specific forms and processes in which gender relations manifested themselves in the early nineteenth century, we cannot begin to understand how gender – as a relationship of political, socio-economic, and cultural power – might itself differ as a result of its relationships with other categories: class, race and ethnicity, and religion.

This book, then, attempts to ask a number of questions that generally have yet to be asked in scholarship on this particular colonial society. Drawing upon Joan Scott's challenges to historians, it works with two definitions of gender: first, as 'a constitutive element of social relationships based on perceived relationships between the sexes' and, second, as a 'primary way of signifying power.'[11] There are a number of reasons, based on developments in women's, gender, and Upper Canadian history, why I have chosen to examine religious and political discourses in seeking to understand both 'constitutive elements' and 'signifiers of power.' For one, religion and politics have come close to being tropes for private and public, the former the province of women, who were excluded by men from the latter. It is often assumed that gender may easily be found in the study of religion but not in that of political discourse.[12] Moreover, by concentrating on social and economic factors to account for women's absence from certain areas of nineteenth-century society, historians have overlooked the political realm as an important site of gender relations in the early to mid-nineteenth century, one that should be contrasted with that of religion. The areas on which I focus – politics and religion – experienced some of the most sweeping transformations in the transatlantic world of Britain, France, and the United States in this period: democratic revolution, particularly in the latter two countries, and the rise of enthusiastic religion in Britain and North America. As a number of women's and gender historians have recently argued, shifting political and religious structures, as well as the languages of democracy and evangelicalism, had particular implications for women and gender relations that would become critically important throughout the nineteenth century. While women were excluded from new definitions of political citizenship and from official positions in the new religious hierarchies that developed within evangelical churches, they were able to use some of the tenets of evangelical language to stake out definitions of social citizenship essential – or so it was argued – to the wider polity.[13]

In Upper Canada, the relationship between these developments in politics and religion was complicated by both international and local factors. In the newly formed colony of 'white' settlement, in which western European political, social, and economic institutions were being implemented throughout the period covered by this book, the clash between democracy and conservatism, enthusiastic and established religion, was as much over what was to be as it was over pre-existing forms and structures brought by those of European descent, whether Loyalist refugees, British colonial officials, or immigrants from England, Scotland, or Ireland. This period was also one of imperial expansion, as those aboriginal peoples – particularly the Ojibwa band, the Mississaugas – already present in the colony underwent widespread dispossession because of the growing demands of Europeans and white Anglo-Americans for farmland. By the 1850s, the majority of Ojibwa in southern Ontario had ceded much of their land and had occupied reserves; their dispersal was also complicated by the growth of early-nineteenth-century missionary movements that originated in both Britain and the United States. During this period, the economy of Upper Canada was primarily agricultural, in contrast to clearer patterns of industrial development in both the northeastern United States and Britain (however chronologically uneven and regionally diverse such developments are now understood to have been); yet I have detected in Upper Canada the dissemination of some of those norms, values, and attitudes that historians identify as either 'bourgeois' or 'middle-class.' As I will argue throughout this book, they were part of larger cultural discourses that intersected with those of politics and religion. I see this colonial society as a locality with its own specific features that helped shape the discourses discussed in this book, but it was also part of a larger, transatlantic society.

In Upper Canada, gender relations structured and informed political and religious languages – in which power was contested and the future shape of the province was debated – in a number of different ways.[14] Gender relations were used by a spectrum of political figures to establish masculine legitimacy and dispute opponents' claims to power, with various symbols and images drawn from the range of British, American, and Upper Canadian political culture. Gender relations themselves were also reshaped and rethought both in the pages of the press and in other forms of public discourse, as a variety of different categories of manhood and womanhood were introduced. Notions of male and female were not monolithic and unchanging constructs but were contested sites where different groups in Upper Canadian society struggled to define masculinity and femininity, their relationship to one another, and a code of morality and virtuous behaviour. This process of definition and the establishment of these codes resulted in the creation of images and symbols: the 'virtuous woman' and the 'public man.' Furthermore, examining the discourses of gender in Upper Canada uncovers not only assumptions about relations between men and women but also helps illuminate links between gender, race, and class in a colonial society. These subjects often were enmeshed and mutually dependent. Gender, then, can serve as a window through which other systems of power may be glimpsed: in this case, the cultural formation and constitution of a white, colonial, middle class.

By comparing religious and political discourses on gender and locating the points where they intersect and diverge, this book helps delineate the formation of public and private realms in early-nineteenth-century Canada. It also attempts to deconstruct these realms, to investigate the norms and assumptions that maintained them, and to look at the ambiguities, contradictions, and tensions that underpinned them. The 'public' and the 'private' were not two distinct and separate spheres formed in complete isolation from each other. Each sustained the other, and, as I will argue throughout this book, the lines between the two were more than a little blurred. Masculinity was constructed within the home as well as on the hustings or in the workplace. Fathers, sons, and, to a lesser degree, husbands were the subject of a great deal of religious and secular discourse concerning their spiritual and moral obligations. Images of femininity were found 'in public' as well as in the home, although the nature of many of these images (those of women fund-raising for church bazaars or riding in carriages in temperance parades) forces us to rethink the concept itself.[15] It is true that, in some contexts, 'women' might appear as the signifiers of the realm of bourgeois domesticity, the epitome of the private sphere, and 'men' of the public world of politics, yet Upper Canadian society was more complex than these binary opposites might lead us to believe.

The development of gender history that has occurred over the past ten years has been eagerly welcomed by some historians and strongly denounced by others (with the vast majority outside the field having only a vague understanding of what all the scholastic fuss is about). Although the focus of this book will be on the gendered meanings of colonial discourses, certainly another way of grappling with gender relations in Upper Canada would be to examine the experiences of particular groups of women and men, an approach that, in other areas, has yielded historians a wealth of information about various groups of women.[16] Another path might be to study the effect that women had on various aspects of Upper Canadian society, such as their contribution to social welfare through benevolent and religious associations.[17] Neither methodology, it should be noted, automatically excludes the other, for exploring women's experiences has often led to a reappraisal of a variety of historical events and processes. Both approaches owe a debt to social history, in the methodologies and sources used and in the goal to rewrite history 'from the bottom up,' thereby including women as a group formerly considered marginal to historical research. By doing so, women's history has called attention to the importance of gender. Indeed, the earliest historiographical essays on women's history argued for the integration of research on women and for a comparative perspective, which would place women's experiences alongside those of their male counterparts and thus break down a 'split vision' of society.[18]

In the Canadian field, work on women's experiences and the methodologies used to recapture these, as well as studies of the impact of women's presence on well-known events and institutions, has spoken both to women's historians and to those working in labour and working-class history, urban history, immigration and ethnic history, educational history, and family history.[19] Yet although these approaches have greatly enriched the historical record, they risk leaving certain assumptions about gender untouched. At their worst, they become little more than contribution history, telling us that 'women were there,' but doing little to challenge well-worn narrative structures.[20] In the hands of more sophisticated and thoughtful practitioners, they force us to rethink the significance of accepted historical events and processes.

Yet approaches that focus on women and that concentrate on their experiences, however rich and varied their treatment – and however much attention is paid to the ways in which women's experiences were mediated by race and class – frequently fail to ask questions about the very constitution and configuration of the categories of 'woman' and 'man.' History, Scott has pointed out, tends to be a 'foundationalist discourse' in which certain categories, premises, and presumptions are taken as natural; lacking these, the discipline's 'explanations seem to be unthinkable.'[21] Historians should strive, she adds, to '"make visible the assignment of subject positions," not in the sense of capturing the reality of the objects seen, but of trying to understand the operations of the complex and changing discursive processes by which identities are ascribed, resisted, or embraced and which processes are unremarked, indeed achieve their effect because they aren't noticed.'[22] I would add that historians must take Scott's challenge one step further and pay close attention to the ways in which other relationships – race, class, and religion being those most obviously relevant here – might alter the meanings of gender identities and categories. As feminist philosopher Elizabeth Spelman has argued, 'dominant feminist theory locates a woman's true identity in a metaphysical space where gender is supposed to roam free from race and class,' treating identity 'like a tootsie roll, or a pop-bead necklace, made up of detachable parts.'[23]

Other challenges to women's history, closely related to those just outlined, are critiques of 'separate spheres' as an accepted part of the methodological baggage of historians of women and gender. Feminist historians such as Linda Kerber have called for a more rigorous hermeneutical investigation of the construction of the notion of separate spheres. Kerber urges that future investigations of gender relations use more complex tools than the notion of simple, opposed dualisms: man and woman, household and society.[24] This approach would go beyond the two different realms posited by those voices I have quoted from the Upper Canadian press to see connections between women and men, not the 'difference and apartness' of woman in the home.[25]

Yet the power of separate spheres as a paradigm in women's history cannot be dismissed too lightly. It has wielded, and continues to exert, enormous influence over the imagination of women's historians, particularly those who study the nineteenth and twentieth centuries in the United States.[26] Separate spheres has been a strategy of great significance for women's historians, one that has 'enabled historians to move the history of women out of the realm of the trivial and anecdotal into the realm of analytic social history.'[27] Women's historians over the past three decades have successfully deployed the concept of separate spheres, demonstrating its multiple uses in the past: as ideological imposition, women's cultural creation, or spatial limits that women were expected to observe. And, in doing so, they have created a vibrant and challenging body of historiography that has demonstrated the importance of asking different questions about women's historical experiences.[28]

Moreover, the nineteenth-century division of western European and North American societies into areas designated as private and public was not simply a projection of feminist historians eager to find a paradigmatic framework for their research. There is plenty of evidence that, for men and women of particular socio-economic, religious, racial, and ethnic backgrounds in this period, the division of society along the lines of public and private was an important conceptual framework; it was used in attempts to organize that society, and it also played a critical role in shaping white, middle-class identities and subjectivities. Furthermore, as historians of men and women – whether gay and lesbian, working-class, racial and ethnic minority, or aboriginal – have reminded us, the metaphor of separate spheres wielded considerable power in shaping the legal, political, social, and economic structures that affected their subjects' lives, however much it was contradicted and complicated by other factors.[29]

Throughout this book, I argue that historians should not – indeed cannot – dismiss or underestimate the power of this metaphor, even as we struggle to deconstruct it and understand the tensions and contradictions that underlay its seemingly monolithic hegemony. I share Kerber's hope that 'one day we will understand the idea of separate spheres as primarily a trope, employed by people in the past to characterize power relations for which they had no other words and that they could not acknowledge because they could not name.'[30] But one of my intentions in this book is to show that tropes were not just intriguing literary devices but were instead strategies whereby relations of power were produced, organized, and maintained. In particular, the languages of religion, manners, and mores shaped and deployed categories of virtuous manhood and womanhood that were of particular importance in attempts to colonize indigenous peoples, to reform and regulate gender relations in Native societies to resemble those of Europeans.

While women's history has alerted us to the absence of women from particular historical narratives (the dearth of women from traditional accounts of nation building, for example), it often has limited its epistemological scope with its search for 'real' women and the dismissal by some of its practitioners of those areas where women's presence and agency may be less visible than in others: 'high' politics and the military versus the home and family, to use the well-worn configurations of public versus private, masculine versus feminine. Yet gender relations have played a vital role in shaping a number of institutions, such as the military, where either the complete exclusion of women or their relegation to positions of subordination has been critically important – some might argue essential – to the formation of hierarchical structures dominated by men. And those narratives used to explain and give meaning to events and processes considered central to 'nation building' are often structured and defined by gender relations. Women may be celebrated as the 'mothers' of the nation or lauded for their contributions in times of national crises (provided that no lasting disruption in gender relations occurs). Alternatively, as I argue in chapter 1, women's helplessness when the nation is under attack may be essential to narratives of its defence by the male citizenry.[31]

Along with social history, women's history has generally tended to shun political history unless issues such as women's enfranchisement are being investigated. But the very processes by which women were excluded from the political arena in western Europe and North America – at least in its formal and legal manifestation – depended on notions of citizenship in which constructions of masculinity and femininity played a critical role. Gender has often been a signifier of relationships of power, a 'primary field within which or by means of which power is articulated. Gender is not the only field, but it seems to have been a persistent and recurring way of enabling the signification of power in the West.'[32] Even when such concepts of power are not 'literally' about gender, as in the areas of politics, diplomacy, and the military, notions of masculinity and femininity structure perceptions and become 'implicated in the conception and construction of power itself.'[33]

While historians may not always find much evidence of women's direct participation in these areas, they are extremely rich fields for the study of masculinity. But it is this latter area that appears to underlie the unease of many feminist historians with gender history. Men, it is feared, will come to dominate the field, turning gender studies into the study of masculinity and thus undermining thirty years of work by women's historians. 'Woman' will be erased 'as a category of analysis'; women's experiences will once again take second place to those of men.[34] Some critics of gender history also argue that the discipline uses 'less confrontational language' and is thus 'less politically oriented, less concerned with describing and bettering the plight of women' than is women's history. The destructive and noxious effects of gender history become directed and shaped by men who, at every level, 'become better and more authentic' at being female than the 'real woman' who should form the subject matter of feminist inquiry.[35]

While I would agree that gender and masculinity cannot and should not be conflated – with all roads leading back to men – such arguments presuppose, first, that those who study masculinity will be men and, second, that they will be a remarkably homogeneous group, interested only in asserting their dominance of the field, and notable for their own self-absorption and inattention to those 'real women' of history. To be sure, such criticisms are not entirely unjustified; historiography in the area of masculinity includes work that is celebratory of 'manliness' or, at the very least, is not informed by feminist analyses of gender relations.[36] Yet the situation so decried by these writers resonates, I would argue, much more clearly in the United States (and possibly Britain), where the culturalist focus of much work on masculinity has been most pronounced, along with the institutionalization and professionalization of men's studies programs (just as women's studies programs have flourished most in the United States). In Canada, though, the hordes of depoliticized, careerist male historians that are feared to be lurking at the gates of feminist history have yet to materialize. Just as Canadian women's historians have been less eager to embrace separate spheres than have their American counterparts, work on masculinity in this country has generally been pioneered by labour and working-class historians, who have examined the meanings of masculinity as relational, both in terms of gender and class, and whose work has been shaped by feminist theory and history.[37] Much of this work, though, like that in Canadian women's history, examines masculinity in the late-nineteenth- or twentieth-century contexts.

To be sure, studies of middle-class masculinity can fall easily into a separatist approach that examines men and masculinity as entities unto themselves and from which the politics of gender are largely missing. I suspect, though, that this problem is not just one of gender; it occurs most frequently when those studied are also white and middle-class. The absence of the analysis of gender leads us to believe that some sort of 'fit' existed between cultural constructions of masculinity and society; tensions surrounding this aspect of gender become invisible.[38] John Tosh has argued that until we begin to understand masculinity as 'social status, demonstrated in specific social contexts' and not just as a set of historical attributes, we will not be able to see the 'historical connection between patriarchy and masculinity.' And, as he points out, 'those aspects of masculinity which bear most directly on the upholding of that power are least likely to be made explicit'; men have 'seldom advertised the ways in which their authority over women has sustained their sense of themselves as men.' But it has been precisely in 'public affirmations' that masculine status and power have been most clearly displayed.[39] While Tosh focuses on home, work, and all-male associations as being the sites where such affirmations most frequently occur, I would add that other, all-male enclaves (including armies and political institutions) are equally important.

One of the most significant insights for feminist historians in studying both masculinity and femininity is that women are not the only ones to 'carry' gender. Feminists criticized the perspective that defines men as neutral and ungendered, residing at the centre of society and providing it with objective standards with which to measure women. What, then, happens when the secure foundations of the centre are called into question, when its objectivity can no longer be assumed as the basis of social, cultural, and political hegemony? The argument that centres and peripheries – while they are constructs that inform my examination of Upper Canada – may also be interdependent and that this mutuality, with its attendant contradictions and tensions, has the potential to disrupt central dominance and hegemony runs through my examination of these discourses. What I have attempted to do in this book is to bring together the insights of both feminist history and poststructuralist thought in order to delineate the ways in which gender informed particular discourses and, in turn, how society shaped and reshaped gendered categories and images.

At present, very little work has been done in Upper Canadian history specifically, and in Canadian history in general, that uses the ideas of those philosophers and literary critics that have been loosely associated with 'poststructuralism,' 'deconstruction,' and 'discourse theory.' A few notable exceptions, it is true, have appeared in the field, on topics as diverse as education and the state in Canada West, the construction of regional identity in twentieth-century Nova Scotia, the relations of class and gender in twentieth-century Ontario, and liberalism and the law in colonial British Columbia.[40] Nevertheless, Canadian historians, even those working in intellectual history, overwhelmingly appear unconcerned and uninterested in the challenge to empirical research and the concept of 'experience' that poststructuralist thought has posed.[41] Canadian history has been 'an island of empiricism surrounded by a gulf of discourse from the larger sea of social theory.'[42]

What methodological debate there is over the use of these ideas has taken place within the circles of labour and working-class historians concerned with the effect of poststructuralism on analyses of class and gender. Ironically, much of the discussion has been posed in the kinds of binary oppositions that many poststructuralists have tried to expose with deconstruction. The notion of 'discourse' has been approached in a good/bad, yes/no fashion, questioned as to its impact on the concept of 'experience,' and rejected for its apparent preference for the language (often conflated with 'words') of those who possessed the means and opportunity to leave a written record.[43] Poststructuralist analysis, with its destabilization and fragmentation of the historical subject, its insistence that experience is constituted *through* language, its apparent denial of centralized power structures and of the historical agency and subjectivity that resisted them, has appeared to historians of women and the working class to undermine the political thrust of their work. The free-wheeling relativism of some deconstructionists who dismiss notions of material forms of power and oppression stemming from hierarchical organizations has been perceived as an intellectual conjuring trick, where the struggle and suffering of the past is made to vanish into 'discourse.' Frivolous analyses of language are seen to have replaced the more solid reality of historical materialism, the former couched in terms borrowed from philosophy and literary theory, which seem élitist and obscure, deliberately designed to exclude and befuddle rather than illuminate.[44] Overall, the challenge to liberal humanist thought that some poststructuralist concepts pose is a matter of deep concern (if not anguish) to historians, including Marxists and feminists, steeped in liberal humanist tenets. What, they ask, is to be made of an approach that denies the humanist subject its existence and, by insisting upon the irrationality of knowledge, denies that we can ever 'know' our history?[45]

Certainly these arguments hold a measure of truth. Much of the debate over poststructuralism has been phrased in language that seems to revel in its inaccessibility to the uninitiated, mystifying what it was intended to clarify. Some poststructuralist writers tend to use historical evidence cavalierly and without careful consideration of the importance of context. In doing so, they disregard the warnings of others working in this field that meanings – even indeterminate ones – cannot be forced out of context.[46] Yet what is often lost in debates over this challenge to empiricism is the wide variety of methodological and philosophical approaches that have been lumped together under the heading of 'postmodernism': Saussurian linguistics, Lacanian semiotic theory, Derridean deconstruction, and Foucauldian concepts of decentred power, to name a few. Poststructuralism has become to many historians a monolithic edifice, although a closer look suggests it instead resembles a hydra. Its theories and approaches have been used in many different ways, ranging from the avowedly apolitical deconstruction that was widely received in departments of literary criticism and English in the United States to the openly feminist work in semiotics of

French theorist Julia Kristeva.[47] In Mary Poovey's words, 'There are as many deconstructions as there are feminisms.'[48] As with so many 'schools' of theory, the aims and interests of the originators have not always been followed by their disciples.[49]

If poststructuralists share one premise, however loosely, it is the desire to expose that which has been hidden or marginalized by Western philosophy and to confound its 'logocentric' and essentialist character, its commitment 'to a belief in some ultimate "word," presence, essence, truth or reality which will act as the foundation of all our thoughts, language, and experience.'[50] By examining texts for their underlying biases, ones that have often been assumed to be natural or inevitable, poststructuralists such as Michel Foucault hope to locate and expose the workings of power wherever it might be hidden: in law courts and prisons, schools and the church, the family, the medical profession, social welfare agencies, and other aspects of society.[51] Like other feminist historians, I have found that poststructuralism works best as a methodological tool-kit, particularly when studying groups – whites, the middle class, men – who have managed to naturalize their position in society, obscuring their access to specific forms of power.[52]

The concept of discourse also helps to demarcate the areas in which gender has been an issue and its definitions have been at stake. Discourses, or discursive fields, 'consist of competing ways of giving meaning to the world and of organizing social institutions and processes.' They may be found in a variety of places, and the meanings found in them may be articulated either in language or in material forms of organization, such as legal, medical, religious, or economic practices. Furthermore, they may have different meanings for different groups in society, thus becoming the site of conflict and struggle.[53] The opinions and arguments expressed in the Upper Canadian press present, not a static or monolithic 'body of opinion,' but many discursive fields in which the construction of images of masculinity and femininity, categories of manhood and womanhood, may be found. Such images and categories were not fixed and known but rather were reshaped and reformed in a variety of contexts.

The term discourse is also useful in studying gender because it connotes a greater fluidity and less rigidity than 'ideology.' To many historians, ideology connotes a well-thought-out body of beliefs espoused by either an individual or by a specific group, a cohesive body of thought not often marked by fundamental tensions or contradictions. These latter are often glossed over or explained away in a search for unity and coherence.[54] This is not always the case in studying ideas and concepts that involve either the construction of gender or gender as a signifier of power. Although gender infiltrated a variety of discourses in the past, as Poovey and other feminist historians have shown, it becomes clear that, when attempting to discuss ideas and concepts about gender, the traditional approach of intellectual history simply will not illuminate. Poststructuralist thought provides a means of thinking about gender in the past that does not reify masculinity and femininity into sex-role theory, one that seeks to probe the values and norms that maintain these constructs as natural and essential to our understanding of Western society, one that can help us understand past configurations of gender, race, and class.

But if the terms manliness and womanliness were signifiers in these discourses, they were not irrational, free-floating ones. Their use had meanings that were linked to notions of boundaries and margins, exclusiveness and inclusiveness. I would agree with historian James Vernon's argument that languages are 'multivocal' and that there are also 'conflicts and tensions between discursive systems, so that it is always possible to play at the margins of these languages, extending their possibilities, appropriating and subverting them in unanticipated ways.'[55] However, such appropriation and subversion in Upper Canada took place in a more muted, less radical fashion than I had hoped; while conflicts and tensions arose, the ways in which these discursive systems were fashioned meant that multivocalities were often suppressed, not given free rein to play themselves out. Nevertheless, I believe that we must not overlook the elements of struggle over language and discourse and that we must avoid the trap of seeing them as totalizing and all-powerful in themselves, impervious to counterclaims. As I will argue in the following chapters, the ways in which differences were constructed in language must be considered in their historical context. Virtuous manhood in the discourse of Upper Canadian reformers, for example, was not constructed in the same manner as the Christian manhood of the province's Methodists.

A British colony officially established by the Constitutional Act of 1791, Upper Canada fell between the Ottawa River in the north and east, the St Clair River in the west, and Lakes Erie and Ontario in the south.[56] White settlement began in earnest in 1783, as Loyalists in exile from the American Revolution moved north along with their Native allies of the Six Nations under the leadership of Joseph Brant. As settlers began to take up land in the areas around Lake Ontario, the British government entered into negotiations with the resident Mississaugas, purchasing land in the southern portion of the colony in order to accommodate both white and Native

Loyalists.[57] In 1812, the colony's population was around 75,000, and in 1841, when it was united with Lower Canada under the Act of Union, it had reached 480,000. By 1852, the decennial census listed the number of inhabitants of Canada West at 952,000.[58] Although during the period covered by this book the Upper Canadian economy was largely agricultural, lumbering (especially in the Ottawa Valley), saw- and gristmills, small workshops (such as tanneries, distilleries, and forges), and a number of commercial enterprises developed.[59]

The Constitutional Act of 1791 set out a political structure similar to that of the imperial government: a bicameral legislature that consisted of a seven-member, appointed Legislative Council and an elected assembly of at least sixteen members. The council members held their seats for life and in Upper Canada were appointed by the lieutenant-governor. The council itself was intended to be an advisory body, answerable to the governor and not to the legislature. As well, an Executive Council composed of men appointed by the imperial government was to act as an advisory body to the governor. Its duties were left undefined by the act, and the governor was not required to consult the Executive Council; however, this body was generally composed of prominent colonial residents whose advice was frequently sought and heeded. The assembly was composed of white men who, while not necessarily property holders themselves, were elected for four-year terms by those with either rural freeholds worth at least forty shillings per year or town dwellers who either owned property worth at least five pounds or paid a minimum of ten pounds rent per year. The lieutenant-governor's powers were quite broad and included the right to call, prorogue, and dissolve the legislature and withhold royal assent from bills passed by both branches of the legislature.[60] By 1837, the frustration of reformers in Upper and Lower Canada with political and economic conditions culminated in armed rebellions.[61] Once these had been crushed, the British government dispatched Lord Durham to study the situation in both colonies and to suggest remedies. Among the many recommendations made by his *Report* was that the colonies be united and that the Executive Council be made responsible to the legislature, so that all internal matters of government might be decided by the colonists themselves. As some historians argue, the changes that Durham helped bring about came to fruition in the late 1840s with the development of political parties both inside and outside the legislature.[62]

Religious institutions and developments were bound up with colonial political upheavals. In order to guarantee the colonists' loyalty to Britain, Lieutenant-Governor John Graves Simcoe and the imperial authorities made arrangements for the establishment of the Church of England as the colony's official religious body. To promote the church's survival and growth in an area where white settlement was sparse, the British government stipulated in the 1791 act that a portion, equal to one-seventh of every township land grant, must be set aside "'for the Support and Maintenance of a Protestant clergy.'"[63] In addition to providing for clergy reserves, the act also stated that the lieutenant-governor might endow parsonages or rectories for the Church of England. While a certain amount of confusion ensued as to whether or not an established church existed in Upper Canada, and whether that definition included the Church of Scotland, those who belonged to other denominations were convinced that such a state of affairs was neither just nor desirable. The colonial population belonged to a number of Christian denominations; there were Presbyterians, Anglicans, Congregationalists, Roman Catholics, Lutherans, Quakers, Baptists, and Methodists. To be sure, not all of the leaders of these denominations were publicly opposed to the clergy reserves specifically or to the idea of the close link between church and state that the reserves represented. British-based Wesleyan Methodists, for example, were quite willing to accept state funds, and they generally saw their church as an auxiliary and not as a rival to the Church of England. Some, though – the American-based Episcopal Methodists in particular – were convinced that ties between church and state were destructive to freedoms of conscience and worship and, allied with political reformers, they campaigned vigorously against any form of 'state church.'[64] The clergy reserves remained a problem until 1854, when their reserve funds were handed over to the province's municipalities.[65]

The clergy reserves (and their fellow-traveller, the state-controlled university) have been central themes in the narrative of religious developments in the province.[66] But the religious landscape of Upper Canada was shaped by other denominations – from the United States, England, and Europe – as well as the presence of the colony's Native people. Some members of the Loyalist Six Nations arrived in the colony as Christians, but many members of the resident Ojibwa were not. As we shall see in chapters 3 and 4, attempts to convert the Ojibwa were an important part of the Methodists' work in the colony, work that at times brought them into conflict with the colonial government. They were not alone in their attempts to christianize Native people, as the Anglicans, Presbyterians, and Roman Catholics also engaged in missionary work.[67]

Understanding the developments outlined above is, I believe, critically important in looking at the languages of religion and politics; however, race and class (like gender) are categories that are rarely deployed in Upper Canadian historiography. Historical insights into race and class in this society have, for the most part, been generated by those who study groups designated as 'other': Natives, the Irish, labourers.[68] Yet those who are the focus of this book were engaged in the task of shaping categories and identities that were part of a larger, transatlantic discourse: that of the early nineteenth-century bourgeoisie. Moreover, they were doing so in the context of a colonial society, one that struggled to define its own relationship with an imperial power as it was simultaneously attempting to colonize aboriginal peoples within its own borders. Colonialism, as in many other contexts, had a dualistic, Janus-faced nature, and the Anglo-American colonial inhabitants of Upper Canada who shaped the discourses examined in this book tried to define their own racial identities in a similar, dualistic manner.

Middle-class formation has not been given the same intensive scrutiny in nineteenth-century Ontario history as it has received in the United States and Britain, where historians and sociologists have contributed to an ever increasing body of work that probes the political, socio-economic, and cultural trajectories of middle-class formation, whether as a quantitatively measured structural phenomenon or as a matter of ideologies, identities, and consciousness. Links between evangelical religion and the development of middle-class identities have been studied by historians in the United States and Britain; this historiography also includes studies of changing workplace relations and social identities in northeastern American cities and the fashioning of codes of bourgeois behaviour.[69] In Ontario, as I will discuss in chapter 5, historians generally agree that clear signs of middle-class formation may be seen by the 1840s. While capitalist relations in commerce, manufacturing, or agriculture were by no means the dominant forms of economic production, the growth of urban centres, the development of some forms of state-regulated institutions, the consolidation of various professional associations, and the formation of a increasing number of voluntary societies point to the growing social, political, and cultural importance of middle-class values and practices.[70] Much of the province's historiography is concerned with processes that involve the formation, dissemination, and consolidation of norms, institutions, and processes that are to no small extent 'bourgeois' – whether the topic is responsible government, the expansion of transportation networks, struggles over political patronage, or the development of professional associations.

Yet literature that focuses on the process of middle-class formation in nineteenth-century Ontario in a self-conscious manner is remarkably skimpy. To be sure, educational historians' work on the development of Ontario's public schools has pointed to school reformers' attempts to inculcate Protestant middle-class values and norms through the medium of teacher training and through the use of certain textbooks.[71] Most recently, David Burley's study of self-employed men in mid-nineteenth-century Brantford tackles the question of defining membership in the middle class during this period. As he points out, the problem with using quantification to study this topic is that class has a 'temporal dimension'; identities forged at certain points in people's lives do not neatly change overnight to correspond to material changes.[72] And, just as labour and working-class historians have argued that we must treat working-class formation as just that – a process, not a static, structural given – so too, Burley reminds us, must we consider that middle-class 'men and women are in social motion, advancing and falling.'[73] Burley's central preoccupation, however, is with the issue of persistent self-employment as a measure of bourgeois status, a question that he pursues in examining Brantford's business and political circles. Burley's work also focuses on later decades than this study.

Cultural formation was also crucial to the development of the nineteenth-century middle class. Struggles over the development of manners and mores, the delineation of virtues and vices, and the coding of certain kinds of behaviours as respectable and others as improper were central to bourgeois process of self-definition. The claims of both middle-class men and women to define the moral, political, and social terrain of nineteenth-century society were based on their supposed ascendancy over both aristocratic corruption and working-class degradation. These claims were made in the face of – indeed, despite – insecure and fluctuating material circumstances, circumstances that could divide the middle class internally and create great tensions as to the meaning and persistence of membership in this group. Bourgeois cultural resources, it has been argued, played as great a role in defining middle-class identity as the financial ones invested in commercial ventures or manufacturing enterprises.[74]

The formation of bourgeois ethics and values could be investigated in a number of places in colonial society but, given the dearth of work on this topic, the press seemed a logical place to begin. A number of scholars have pointed to the critically important role played by the press of both England and America in forging the sensibilities of the eighteenth- and nineteenth-century bourgeoisie, people who came to 'visualize in a general way the existence of thousands and thousands like themselves through print-language' and were 'the first classes to achieve solidarities on an essentially imagined basis.'[75] The pages of Upper Canadian newspapers, particularly from the 1830s on, offered a wealth of information on bourgeois culture and society: international news, advertisements, advice columns on agriculture and science, government proclamations, and excerpts from novels and poetry. And it is surely no accident that many historians of Upper Canadian politics have made great use of the colonial press.[76] In attempting to trace the emergence and development of religious and political discourses, the press seemed to me to be an obvious choice. Newspapers were the site of vigorous debate about issues of importance to Upper Canadians and the means by which international literature was disseminated. Although the newspapers often were stridently partisan, their contents were not always one-sided, nor were the discourses in their pages static. The exchange of letters to the editor and running commentaries between rival papers allows the historian to see the construction of discourses as a multifaceted process marked by interruptions, discontinuities, and inconsistencies: a synchronic, as well as diachronic, process. Furthermore, the proliferation of the Upper Canadian press in the period after 1812 and the opportunity to study various papers over a period of time make it an extremely rich resource in an area where sources are often limited and fragmented.

Newspapers, however, are not the only primary sources used here. I have also consulted material written by Upper Canadians, either published or distributed in the colony during this period, that focused on religious or political matters: sermons that were printed and distributed for a wider audience, published reports of missionary work, pamphlets and books about political matters, travel literature, secular and religious reminiscences of life in Upper Canada that contain material written during this period, and collective biographies of early Methodist religious leaders. This published literature, while perhaps somewhat eclectic, helped to fill in some chronological gaps and provide counterpoints to the discourses of the press.

For a number of reasons, this book focuses on material that made up the stuff of public discourses. While women's and social historians have used materials such as letters and diaries most skilfully, I am uneasy with the privileging of private materials (which I define, in the most basic way, as those that were not produced for public consumption and exchange) to which practitioners in these fields often succumb. Letters and, in particular, diaries are often treated by women's and social historians as somehow more real, the unmediated and raw stuff of experience, as opposed to the 'cooked' and less real world of discourse and rhetoric. Particularly among those who work in the field of family history, there is a tendency to fetishize such materials and to elevate them in status because they supposedly unlock the subjectivities of those individuals who produced them, thereby placing them (at least to some degree) outside of the realm of dominant discursive practices, attitudes, and power relations.[77] Letters were not, however, always intended to be treated as private texts, and nineteenth-century diaries, even when ostensibly produced for the author's gaze alone, should not be read without some attention paid to the use of the narrative strategies or rhetorical devices available to the author. Furthermore, even those women who did not write letters to the editor or articles in the press participated in and contributed to these gendered discourses, as they penned tributes to all-male organizations, presented the products of their labour to the militia or to the church, worked in missionary organizations, and either lined the streets or rode in carriages for the temperance cause. They may not have been willing participants at all times, and their intentions may not have been conveyed or may have been distorted in some ways; nevertheless, participants in colonial discourses they were.

Chapter 1 examines the gendered meanings of patriotism and loyalty in Upper Canada, focusing primarily on the War of 1812 but looking also at the ways in which these qualities were constructed in the 1820s and 1830s. From there I shift to the arena of political discourse, paying especial attention to the conflicts of conservatives and reformers in the 1820s and 1830s and to the implications of these struggles for manliness. The third chapter discusses religious discourse, making the transition from politics to religion by examining the links between the two in debates over the political dimensions of some religious issues and then turning to religious discourse on the family and gender relations, and the meaning of masculinity for Methodism, especially the Methodist ministry. It concludes with an analysis of missionary writings about Native peoples in Upper Canada. The fourth chapter looks at both religious and secular writings about manners and mores in Upper Canada, treating matters as diverse as temperance, duelling, Sunday schools, and codes of conduct for youths and men in the workplace and at home. The focus of chapter 5 is the nature of private and public, especially during the Union period of the 1840s; it looks at both political and religious discourses, examining the shifts in them that helped to construct and constitute the two overlapping spheres and suggesting another means of conceptualizing Upper Canadian social formation. I end this book with an epilogue that suggests the possibilities of continuities and disruptions in these languages in the 1850s.

1

'That Manly and Cheerful Spirit': Patriotism, Loyalty, and Gender

For Upper Canadian society, the War of 1812 was in many ways a crucible in which concepts of loyalty and patriotism were forged.[1] The threat, followed by the fact, of American invasion heightened the urgency and immediacy of discussions and debates on these concepts. For the colonial government, mindful of the presence of a large number of non-Loyalist, American-born residents whose commitment to Britain was questionable, and charged with the defence of a militarily vulnerable colonial outpost, the task of demarcating and assigning patriotic status was no mere rhetorical exercise. So far as the authorities and certain newspapers were concerned, the colony faced a crisis, one that demanded the marshalling of all available resources, both military and intellectual. It is in this particular context of defensive action that the language of patriotism and loyalty must be understood.[2]

Loyalty to the British monarch and constitution, and patriotic willingness to defend Upper Canada, figured prominently in political discourses in the colony. Historians may differ as to the meanings of these sentiments and their influence on society, but they generally agree that an appreciation of their importance is essential in understanding Upper Canadian political culture. In the press and other Upper Canadian publications, loyalty and patriotism often were interchangeable and interlinked, one frequently buttressing the other: patriots, often the 'brave militia' of 1812, had kept Upper Canada loyal to Britain during the war and, by doing so, proved their own loyalty and patriotism. No matter that the argument was circular; possession of these qualities was an important way of legitimating and validating claims to various kinds of political power. Sometimes these qualities were discussed in relatively abstract terms, as part of the Upper Canadian 'character' and as proof of the

British connection. At other times they were used to support or undermine political positions and personalities.

During and after the War of 1812, patriotism and loyalty were not gender-neutral qualities. Male military activities and images of courageous militia men were central to the public definition of patriotic duty and service. Men and military exploits dominated the discourse of patriotism in the Upper Canadian newspapers. Few tales appeared in the newspapers or official proclamations of the gallant work of Upper Canadian civilians on the 'home front,' nor did narratives of the war produce any female symbols or images comparable to Marianne of the French Revolution or the republican mother of the American.[3] Given Upper Canadian conservatives' feelings about these events, and the fact that Upper Canada was at war with both countries early in its history, it is not surprising that Upper Canadians might eschew symbols that could be associated with republicanism. However, the image of a woman, Britannia, was used throughout the nineteenth century to represent the British Empire, as was that of the 'Great Mother,' Queen Victoria.[4] Yet images of femininity and female symbols were nonetheless essential components of government propaganda. In Upper Canada the image of the gallant militia, under the fatherly guidance of Major-General Brock, was deployed in attempts to unify the province's civilian or military population, mobilizing Upper Canadian men to defend their homes, helpless wives and children, and, ultimately, 'British' liberty. Because the war has been defined as a watershed in the development of Upper Canadian political culture, it is crucial that we understand the gendered aspects of patriotic discourse.

Loyalty and patriotic duty, it appears, were only infrequently discussed in the newspapers of York, Kingston, and Niagara prior to the War of 1812. In part, this absence is the result of a scarcity of sources, as fewer newspapers were published in this period than in the decades after the war. Those that did emerge, such as the *Canada Constellation* of Niagara (1799–1800), were either very short-lived or have survived only in fragments. These newspapers were often less concerned with Upper Canadian affairs than with distributing foreign news and reprinting government proclamations.[5] Nevertheless, there began to emerge stirrings of patriotic sentiments in the press, along with pronouncements on the importance of public duty and the concept of a public sphere in which men might act.

By patriotism, of course, these Upper Canadians meant attachment to, and willingness to defend, Britain and the British connection. The formation in August 1794 of the Loyal Association of the Home District was announced in the *Upper Canada Gazette* as an unabashed expression of anglophilia. The association would 'maintain and preserve [the] inestimable advantages' of the British link 'by every means in our power,' and members would 'exert ourselves to the utmost, in support of the General Laws of the Empire, as well as the particular Laws of our own Province.' Promising unstinting vigilance with regard to the latter, its membership believed it 'our indispensable duty, jointly or individually, to bring offenders to justice.' Such devotion would not stop at daily legal matters. The association's members saw their duties to Upper Canada in much larger terms: 'That we will discountenance by every possible means, the introduction of all seditious or incendiary opinions, whether these may be presented in writings or conversation, And we do declare our determination stedfastly [*sic*] essentially necessary to our happiness and dearest interests, by every exertion in our power, whether directed against foreign enemies or domestic foes.'[6]

Little else appeared in the press about the association; whether it carried out its self-appointed duties is difficult to determine. Yet this voluntary patrolling by Upper Canadian civilians of the boundaries of loyalty is more than an anecdote of antiquarian interest. It marks one of the earliest attempts to carve out a realm where loyal citizens could assert devotion to Crown and province, one in which right feeling and loyalty legitimated public activities by those who might otherwise be considered private individuals. Loyalty, in this case, could be a form of empowerment or legitimation, as was suggested by the association's warning to 'discountenance' any 'seditious or incendiary opinions.'

Without further documentation, we can only speculate about the association's membership and surmise that it was composed of those types described in H.V. Nelles' study of loyalism in the Niagara peninsula: Scottish merchants and government officials drawn from the ranks of the disbanded Loyalist militia.[7] Another declaration of public allegiance by 'several gentlemen of the town,' which appeared in the *Constellation* in 1799, was more explicit concerning its origins. The notice was addressed to Governor Peter Hunter upon his arrival in the colony, and told him that the 'impulses of hearts full of gratitude ... irresistibly drew the mechanics and husbandmen of Niagara and its vicinity, to beg that your excellency will accept their most profound and respectful congratulations.' Although outwardly more deferential than the association, the men of Niagara also hoped to lay claim to Hunter and the government, citing 'the easy access to your excellency by honest men of every description.' Although they might not be 'dignified,' they were 'useful' and, as such, could offer an 'apology for their humbly soliciting for a moment your excellency's attention to them.'[8] Despite their lack of social standing, their position as honest, hard-working men was an asset that could be offered as justification for an opportunity, however brief, to gain the governor's ear.

Such addresses were not, of course, uncommon, and they abounded whenever Upper Canadians welcomed a new governor. Through the appearance of their declaration in the press, these 'loyal gentlemen' claimed a relation to the imperial government and helped define a public political realm as the world of loyal male British subjects. Neither declaration explicitly excluded those who did not meet these qualifications, and, later in this period, similar addresses to various lieutenant-governors were printed from the Native peoples of Upper Canada.[9] Yet, because loyalty was an important part of public discourse in Upper Canada, it is worth noting that this quality was framed in the context of imperial ties and, in these two instances, directed at either symbolic (the law and constitution) or (in the case of the governor) embodied representatives of Britain. To what degree gender was embedded in these symbols is, in this early period, more difficult to ascertain. The Niagara 'mechanics and husbandmen,' though, felt it appropriate to couch their submission to Hunter in a style that, while respectful, invoked their gender as a symbol of unity. Honest manliness might not completely overcome their social and economic differences from the élite, but it might partially transcend the barriers of rank and status.

Honest manliness and loyalty to the British nation might also flow in the opposite direction, emanating from the ruler of the nation, mingling with that of his loyal subjects, and subsequently increasing national virtue, prosperity, and happiness. Such fond hopes for the colony's future were expressed by the Anglican rector of York, John Strachan, in his 1810 *Discourse on the Character of King George the Third*. The Scottish-born cleric and schoolmaster was a keen supporter of the colonial connection to Britain and firmly believed that the presence of an established church in Upper Canada was essential in guaranteeing the colony's loyalty and well-being.[10] In many ways, Strachan's *Discourse*, penned both in honour of the king's birthday and to warn the colony about the dangers of the United States and France, can be seen as a classic text of Upper Canadian conservatism: anchored by loyalty to 'British values and institutions,' firmly opposed to American republicanism and sectarianism, and convinced that Upper Canada's British connection brought peace, stability, and institutions 'that encouraged both private and public morality; and that cherished true liberty, personal independence, and a decent respectability.'[11] As David Mills has pointed out, for Strachan 'political dissent and opposition were equated with disloyalty,' a point made clearly and at some length in his *Discourse*.[12]

The *Discourse* also provided a framework for the envisioning and practice of Upper Canadian loyalty to king and nation, a map for the fashioning of loyal subjects in which private and public were so tightly interwoven as to be almost inseparable. This framework's explicit concern with masculine morality, particularly for fathers, has received little attention from historians of Upper Canadian political thought and culture; generally they have been more concerned with Strachan's comments on the French Revolution and his dire warnings of American designs on the colony.[13] Certainly Strachan was concerned with those matters we might call 'traditional politics,' making sure that George's magnanimous behaviour towards Catholics, the Irish, and the Scots did not go unrecognized. The king could also be credited with ending the slave trade, promoting judicial independence, and supporting the flowering of British culture.[14] But none of these 'leading points of the reign of our gracious sovereign'[15] would have occurred had it not been for the elevated quality of his domestic life and his ability to transfer this quality into the nation's affairs. Moreover, while being a 'good father' might in many ways be a natural state (being a 'good mother' was certainly 'natural'), fatherhood itself was no mere matter of biology.[16] Indeed, in Strachan's frame of reference, biology was simply not an issue, for focusing on it would have undermined his argument that the qualities of good fatherhood were not limited to those who were, quite literally, fathers and husbands. What was 'natural' was the desire of any man who had been entrusted with the care of those weaker than himself, those who might be dependent in any way on him, to care for, protect, and guide them with both affection and judiciousness, thereby ensuring their respect, love, and, consequently, loyalty.

Not only was George a 'good father' in the more abstract and symbolic sense – ruling over his people with solicitous and beneficent, as opposed to tyrannical, authority – Strachan was anxious that Upper Canadians know that the king's public virtues were the result of 'his private character, [in which] we have everything to praise and nothing to condemn.' Admitting that he 'was not among the number of those who can admit that he who is neither a good husband nor an affectionate parent, can acquit himself uprightly in a public domain,' Strachan claimed that 'our king supports and encourages the purest morals by his deportment as an affectionate husband, and tender parent' and therefore presented 'an illustrious example worthy of the strictest imitation.'[17] Strachan elaborated upon the king's happy marriage, pointing out that the 'tender regard which he has at all times manifested for his affectionate consort, has been rewarded by the most sincere love and esteem. Marriage, producing a cordial union of hearts, becomes the bond of harmony and peace, and of the most refined and inviolable friendship; and such has our beloved Monarch always found it to be.' This 'cordial union,' Strachan believed, should serve as an example to the British people: should they follow their sovereign's example and 'remain faithful to [their] vows' they, too, would find in marriage 'a mutual communication of joys and sorrows ... instead of those jealousies, heart-burnings, and indifference which poison the peace and comfort of so many families.' And because 'all the most valuable virtues begin at home, ... what terrible consequences ensue' when marriage 'is polluted or even tarnished.' Families are torn apart, 'the most implacable animosities are produced, children are brought up in vice and infamy, and the purest sources of felicity are dried up forever.' It was the duty of those 'in higher walks of life ... to enforce the practice of virtue,' an 'imperious duty which their situation and interest especially demand.'[18]

The lessons to be learned by the monarch's exemplary private life were those of both husband and father. George's attitude toward his 'numerous offspring,' Strachan insisted, was one of deep paternal concern for their morals and character, both private and public. 'Anxious to form their minds to virtue and religion, to make them useful to their country, the guardians of its honour, and the terror of its enemies,' he had been 'rewarded for his eagerness to inspire them with the purest principles of integrity, he had already seen them standing forward the stead pillars of the constitution, and the pride of the British nation.'[19] Such statements may have been wishful thinking on Strachan's part; certainly it would be difficult to see 'virtue and religion' and the 'purest principles of integrity' in George IV's marriage and extramarital affairs.[20] Yet Strachan's message was clear: the monarch's virtue in his home could be directly linked to his people's respect and veneration for both George and the monarchy itself. How, Strachan asked, could the esteem in which George was held have grown 'had his conduct been different?'

Had the outset of his life been marked with vicious dissipation, had those hours which he spent at home with his children and amiable consort been consumed in disgraceful revelry or in the arms of a mistress. No, it is impossible – it is contrary to experience, contrary to the nature of man. Virtue possesses an extensive power over the human mind; if its direct force cannot always be traced, it is easy to view it in the contrast. In vain is a man endowed with the most brilliant talents, if his morals are impure. He may speak eloquently of justice, of truth, and of virtue; – he may attack existing abuses with the most pointed energy; – he may protest the most incorruptible integrity, the most sincere love for his country, and the greatest anxiety to promote its integrity and glory. But he speaks to the winds; his words forgotten; they are never felt – they flow from a corrupt fountain, and in his mouth good appears evil.[21]

Strachan was happy to inform his fellow colonists that, just as the British people looked to their king for paternal example and guidance, in turn George himself 'regards the Supreme Being as the common Father of all, and mankind the children, the members of one family.' Fortunately for the British, the king did not see his relationship with them 'as if he were an independent being and his subjects beneath his regard.' In fact, throughout the *Discourse* Strachan went to great lengths to reassure his audience that, rather than being subjects, they should imagine themselves to be George's 'people' or 'his children.'[22] The position of subject might imply a relationship to the sovereign defined by his oppression and tyranny, by an absence of those very virtues that Strachan believed George possessed. While it was possible that fathers might rule over their children, and husbands over their wives, in a cruel and unjust manner, Strachan was adamant that those who followed their monarch's lead would never lapse into tyranny and abuse of their power. If the British – and, by extension, Upper Canadians – were to 'imitate' George successfully, 'justice and integrity would cover us as a garment; punctual in our dealings and in the performance of promises: affectionate husbands, indulgent parents, not admitting that criminal indulgence so fatal to children, but that regular and yet tender discipline which becomes the foundation of future excellence.' Strachan's hopes for the nation grew by leaps and bounds: there would then be 'unanimous obedience to the laws, a surge in Christian charity,' and an end to 'corruption and venality'; irreligion would become a thing unknown.[23]

Of course, despite a parent's good intentions, his children might end up rebelling and rejecting his wisdom and love. Strachan warned his audience that, although the late Louis XV of France had inspired 'reverence and devotion for royalty,' his children had fallen under the sway of licentiousness, immorality, and anarchy. To a large extent, the king had 'signed his own death warrant.' He had recognized America and sent French troops to that country; upon their return, they brought republican ideas to France. His actions had not been those of a prudent, wise father – in fact, Louis had behaved in a decidedly unmanly and effeminate fashion. 'He had suffered jealousy to conquer prudence, and rejoiced in the opportunity of humbling a rival.'[24] But, as Strachan pointed out in one of his many notes to the *Dis-*

course, it was the 'corruption of manners' that had been one of the most 'powerful causes' of the French Revolution, with women's influences at the root of this corruption.

Louis XV lived in open adultery. He seduced a city matron, carried her publicly from her husband to exercise sovereign authority, and this opened a channel for licentiousness. This weak prince placed his sceptre at the feet of one of his mistresses who had been chosen from among the dregs of Paris, and this meanness covered him with contempt, the certain forerunner of state disasters. Governed by women of characters so abandoned, decency fled the court. All who made professions of honour and who respected propriety of conduct, were overwhelmed by the denunciations, the licentiousness, the intrigues, and corruption of those abandoned women, who surrounded the king, with a crowd of people without morals, and enemies to virtue.[25]

'Weakening of authority' was the result of this moral turpitude. First, Louis XV's abduction of another man's wife had relied on his abuse of monarchical power; he had acted in a tyrannical fashion and for immoral personal reasons. Second, not content with overturning another man's authority in his home, Louis had then abdicated his divinely ordained role as the nation's patriarch, allowing his court and country to be ruled by women of low moral standing. Such was the familial genealogy that had led Louis's grandson, 'the virtuous and humane Louis the XVIth,' to the guillotine.[26] Strachan ended with a warning to his fellow colonists of the 'bad effects of licentious morals in the higher orders. Indeed every father of a family who has been himself guilty, sooner or later deplores it in bitterness.' In Upper Canadian society, he informed his audience, 'licentiousness has already made a most alarming progress, [and] you frequently find people living debauched lives disgraceful to themselves and pregnant with future misery.' Some of these 'keepers' might give their 'paramour the title of wife not from any affection for her' but instead for the children's sake. 'Excluded from genteel society, they drag out a miserable existence, and the vulgarity of their domestic regulations and manners reminds them every day of their folly.'[27]

Strachan thus presented messages for both familial and political life, insisting that if the former was lacking in virtue there would be serious consequences for the latter. While the *Discourse* explicitly addressed relations of power, hierarchy, and dominance between parents – specifically fathers – and children, it had less to say about how these matters affected husbands and wives. The warnings about immoral women, placed alongside tributes to Princess Charlotte, made it quite clear what a wife's responsibilities toward her husband and the nation would be: sexual chastity, affection, and an all-encompassing (if somewhat vaguely defined) purity of morals. Strachan's many comments on George's home life made it clear that husbands should show their wives tenderness and respect. That such emotions were set within a hierarchical framework in which power resided in husbands' and fathers' hands did not trouble him. To be sure, he was concerned that those who had been entrusted with leadership must be careful not to abuse their position. Rulers and élites were, after all, expected to behave in a moral fashion and thus set examples that would encourage the development of loyalty within the home and the nation. Yet in Strachan's framework of patriotism and loyalty there was a lacuna: upper-class women were not granted an active role that would allow them to behave as patriotic, loyal subjects. Instead, they might best serve king and country by their absence from affairs of state and public life in general, a relationship whose paradoxical nature was generally not noted by men such as Strachan.

Not all of his contemporaries were pleased with Strachan's pamphlet. The young law clerk John Beverley Robinson was worried that Strachan's work would stir up trouble and 'make disaffected among us loyal and contented.'[28] Robinson did not share his former teacher's admiration for the king or his family, and he wrote sarcastically to John Macaulay that 'we surely require to be the most determinately loyal to believe that the Duke of York is the pillar of state or His Royal Highness the Prince of Wales the pride of the nation.'[29] Yet, as the threat of war loomed in 1811 and intensified in the winter of 1811–12, the themes set out by Strachan – loyalty, patriotism, and the defence of Upper Canada by virtuous men – were ones that became increasingly popular in political discourses.

Such writings appeared frequently in the *Kingston Gazette*, the only paper in the colony that published continuously throughout the war.[30] As well as editorials and letters, the paper often reprinted the proclamations, general orders, and special addresses to inhabitants that were issued by the military and the colonial government. This was a more complex discourse than earlier pronouncements concerning loyalty and devotion to Britain, for both external and internal threats were perceived as imminent. The perils of the war were constructed in a language overflowing with images of chaos and violence, one in which the notion of Upper Canadian boundaries (both literal and symbolic) were seen to be under siege by the forces of chaos, anarchy, rapacity, and immorality. Throughout these discussions an 'other' hovered, threatening to undermine and overturn the stability of Upper Canadian society. Under these circumstances, patriotism was more than a mere static embodiment of British values; it was forged and affirmed in struggle and conflict with the enemy.

In the *Gazette*, Upper Canadian men were depicted as poised to battle American viciousness, a struggle that blended nationality, race, and gender. As a nation, the Americans had succumbed to the 'war faction, or democratic part of the American population,' a group led by 'patrons of slavery, and dealers in human blood; a traffic which has a natural tendency to eradicate from their minds every feeling of humanity.'[31] Righteous indignation over slavery south of the border was a common strand in anti-American sentiment.[32] By renouncing slavery, Upper Canadians had abjured the tyranny and effeminacy that marked slave-holding societies. And Upper Canadians, the press was fond of reminding its readers, could not be slaves so long as they remained British. Worst of all, the United States was co-operating with Napoleon, a 'bloody Despot, who has wantonly trampled upon the liberties of Europe, and deluged every country around him with the blood of its inhabitants.' The willingness of American enlistment 'under the banners of this fell destroyer of the human race, is a deplorable and striking example of human depravity.'[33] Consequently the American army had been degraded to the level of savages and barbarians and had lost their claim to be professional soldiers. 'No man talks lightly of war who knows anything about the matter; we may therefore conclude that those who have set up the war-whoop, on the other side of the line, have yet the trade to learn,' warned a letter in the *Gazette*, reprinted from the *Quebec Mercury*.[34] An 'Army of Savages,' declared a writer identified only as 'A Loyalist,' was set to invade the province.[35]

'Savages' not only referred to American troops who had abandoned civilized means of warfare: implicit in terms such as 'war-whoop' was the suggestion that they had become like 'Indians.' To be sure, none of these writers vilified Indians per se, and the tribes who allied themselves with the British were praised for their loyalty. Those 'brave bands of natives' who had lost their possessions in 1776 were once again, the *Gazette*'s editor reassured his readers, ready to spring to their country's defence. Although reluctant to seek a quarrel, 'they are men, and have equal rights with all other men to defend themselves and their property when invaded.'[36] Certainly respect and esteem for individual Natives existed. Tecumseh, the Shawnee chief who fought with the British during the war, was regarded quite highly by Brock. 'A more sagacious or a more gallant Warrior does not I believe exist,' was the general's description of his ally. Later, the figure of Tecumseh captured the imagination of nineteenth-century historians of the war, although it appears that their treatment bordered on the realm of the mythological.[37]

The boundary between displays of manly courage and degenerate savagery could shift at a moment's notice: today's brave warrior could be tomorrow's archetype of a rapacious savage. Brock's 'Proclamation,' issued from Fort George on 22 July 1812, reminded Upper Canadians that 'the brave bands of natives which inhabit this colony were, like His Majesty's subjects, punished for their zeal and fidelity' in the Revolutionary War, but one month later Brock wrote privately to Colonel Proctor urging him 'to restrain the Indians ... in their predatory excursions.'[38] Other private military dispatches spoke of the need to 'control' and 'restrain' Indian allies along the borders of the colony in order to prevent 'acts of outrage [on] women, children, or unarmed men.'[39] Despite their bravery, Indians were not 'troops' but 'warriors,' not trained professionals but naturally fierce fighters. They did not observe the code of honourable conduct and manly self-control in warfare, said European spectators of battles between whites and Indians. Their methods of fighting, particularly their war-whoops, were perceived by some European observers as forms of effective psychological intimidation, and the threat of Native fighters might act as an inducement to the enemy's surrender.[40] The 'stained and painted bodies' of the 'warriors' who came to Brock's funeral were covered only by loin clothes, yet these men were 'armed to the teeth with rifles, tomahawks, war clubs, spears, bows and arrows and scalping knives. Uttering no sound, and intent on reaching the enemy unperceived, they might have passed for the spectres of those wilds – the ruthless demons which war had unchained for the punishment and oppression of men.'[41] This construction of the 'warrior,' along with similar passages that dwelt on physical features such as height and muscularity, body and facial paint, hairstyles, and clothing (or lack of it), suggested that Native men's participation in the war was a matter of animalistic instinct, not the result of strategic and political reasoning.[42]

Although lauded for their support of Britain, Indian participants in the war had little chance of attaining the symbolic status of either the British regulars or the Upper Canadian militia. Denied the manly decency and status of the Christian soldier, the 'Indian warrior' was a shadowy and ambiguous figure. In many ways the Indian participants in the War of 1812 were treated much like women and children, assigned to the role of 'other' and objectified in patriotic discourse. Not all 'others,' though, occupied the same discursive position. Women and children were to be pitied for their helplessness in the face of the invaders and therefore were perceived as being in need of protection and rescue. Natives may have been fighting on the side of the British, but they did so in the context of a colonial society, one with many former American residents who feared and hated Native peoples and with an imperial administration that was often suspicious of its Native allies.[43] For the latter, race and gender – being Amerindian men – meant that being an 'other' might evoke the fear of potential violence, not the urge to protect. In patriotic discourse, this ambivalence about Native men also might help bolster the manliness of British troops and of the colonial militia and reinforce colonists' need for their protection.

Although Upper Canadians might be uneasy about their Native allies, their worst fears were saved for their invading neighbours. Rapacity, licentiousness, and wanton destruction would be unleashed in a war with the Americans. Threats of sexual chaos and brutality ran through much of the literature on the American threat. 'Our fertile plains, and the fruits of our industry are no doubt temptations every way calculated to excite their avarice, and gratify their abominable and licentious passion for plunder and rapine,' warned 'A Loyalist.'[44] When not personifying Upper Canada itself as female, these writers were quick to prophesy the 'liberties that may be taken with the weaker and unprotected sex by the unlicensed Banditti that may compose this army. I present merely an out-line, and leave it to the feelings of every husband and father to fill up the picture.'[45] The Americans were a horde of rampaging monsters, lacking the manly self-control and discipline inherent in the British army or Upper Canadian militia. Lieutenant-Colonel Mahlon Burwell, of the First Middlesex Militia, described the 1813 burning of Government House in Burlington by American troops as a 'wanton, ferocious savage proceeding ... a house, they must have known, purely for the accommodation of travellers.'[46] There was, however, an unspoken assumption about class that ran through these pronouncements: it was not American officers who were expected to act in a violent and potentially sexually vicious manner. Instead, 'troops' or 'common soldiers' were assumed to be the potential perpetrators of such repugnant acts.

It was not only the American army that assumed the role of the pernicious intruder. The threat of treason captured the imaginations of the press and of the House of Assembly, both intent on reassuring the citizens of the colony that only in Upper Canada were their lives and liberties secure. 'Private machinations' were more dangerous than 'open attacks,' declared the assembly in an open address to Upper Canadians. The enemy had spread 'their emissaries throughout the country to seduce our fellow subjects from their allegiance.' Colonists therefore were urged to watch for and 'seize upon' any 'who either by word or deed seek to stifle or discourage that ardent patriotism which at this moment animates all the inhabitants of this province.'[47] As the *Kingston Gazette* proclaimed, 'every

inhabitant of the Province is desired to seek the confutation of such inde-
cent slander.'[48] These were some of the rare occasions when duty and loyalty were discussed in terms other than military service and conceivably
were open to all Upper Canadians, regardless of gender, race, and familial
status.

If an 'other,' whether in the form of brutish American soldiers or the
creeping menace of disloyal Upper Canadians, threatened the security of
the colony, it could be met and stared down by the patriotic virtue of
Upper Canadian militia men, acting as husbands, fathers, and sons. Just as
the 'gallant militia' needed the greater numbers and experience of the British regulars, this virtue was moored to British values and institutions. Furthermore, it was constructed around concepts of manliness that were
exercised vigorously in the colony's defence. 'We have daily experienced
that bold and manly policy is the safest and the wisest,' 'A Loyalist'
reminded the *Gazette*'s readers. 'Do you suppose we are a parcel of Quakers?'[49] The prominent Kingston merchant Richard Cartwright, writing to
the paper under the pseudonym 'Falkland,' quoted Admiral Nelson and
urged 'zeal and spirit' to counter American aggression. While admitting
that war 'is certainly an evil,' Cartwright warned that 'it is not to be warded
off by indolently deploring the miseries that attend it ... [It] is magnified by
timidity and supineness ... [H]esitation and fear invite aggression.'
'"England expects every man to do his duty,"' he proclaimed, adding that
'we feel as men ought to feel when their best interests are at stake, and are
determined to act as becomes British subjects.'[50] These feelings were shared
by John Cameron, the editor of the *York Gazette*, who was pleased to
announce in July 1812 that 'all ranks of people' had offered 'flattering
encomiums' on the town's volunteer militia. Cameron quoted a 'Veteran
Commander whose opinion he had the honor of hearing yesterday, to wit,
"that the present Garrison were a set of active and well behaved young men
– whose *conduct* did honor to their King, their country, and themselves,"'
adding 'that he believes them men who would ably distinguish themselves
in preserving the Sacred rights of Religion, Property, and Liberty, which
we now under the blessings of Providence enjoy.'[51]

Cartwright and Cameron's enthusiasm for the physicality of honourable
'manly' military retaliation was shared by other correspondents to the
paper and by the military officials themselves. In an address issued from
Fort George on 1 November 1812, Major-General Sheaffe praised the
'manly and cheerful spirit with which the militia on this frontier have
borne the privations which peculiar circumstances have imposed on them.'
Their conduct, he declared, 'has furnished the best characteristics of the

soldier, manly constancy under fatigue, and determined bravery when opposed to the enemy – by a perseverance in the exercise of those noble qualities they may be assured of accomplishing the glorious task in which they are engaged.'[52] Once the war was underway, letters, editorials, and dispatches also celebrated the 'valor and good conduct' of the troops and their military exploits.[53]

However, such bold manliness, when caught up in the heat of battle, might all too easily become prey to the vicious and bestial forces that had undermined and degraded American troops. How could it be prevented from running amok and becoming 'licentious wantonness?' In a war such as this, with reluctant participants and issues that were part of a larger imperial power struggle, appeals to the colonists' personal sense of righteousness helped place the conflict in an Upper Canadian context. Lest there be any doubts concerning the superior morality of the Upper Canadian forces, the colony's leaders provided them with symbols that embodied masculine decency under the duress of war and strife: the Christian soldier and his real-life embodiment, Major-General Brock. In an address to the Third Regiment of the York Militia at an 1813 service celebrating the Battle of Queenston Heights, Major Allan instructed his troops to 'march, then, under these colours, inspired by that pure honour, which characterizes the Christian Soldier, which inspires him with reverence for religion, and loyalty to his Sovereign, makes him a devouring flame to his resisting enemy, and the humane protector of the fallen.'[54]

Allan's paradoxical portrait of duty, retribution, and solicitude was not the first public invocation of this symbol. In August 1812 Strachan preached a sermon before the Legislative Council and House of Assembly that elaborated on this paragon. Framing the war as a struggle for justice into which Upper Canadians had reluctantly entered as a result of the enemy's 'corrupt and shameful motives,' Strachan related the numerous attempts made by his countrymen to stave off armed conflict. However, since the Americans would be satisfied with nothing else, 'we may go forth confidently to battle ... for the God of battles will be with us.' 'And if,' he told his audience, 'to the justice of our cause we add the graces of the Christian soldier, we need not fear the final issue.' Thus, in the context of a divinely sanctioned struggle, military men could use as a model one who fought not for hatred or revenge but to restore 'justice and humanity.' Unlike the demoniacal American army, the Christian soldier loved his enemy, separating his 'actions' from his 'person,' and limiting himself 'to such acts of violence as shall bring him back to equitable terms of accommodation.' Not 'blustering' but 'firm and courageous,' the Christian soldier was always ready to die for his country, having God as his solace and never, therefore, becoming despondent. With a pure, sincere, and heartfelt love, the Christian soldier exemplified a virtuous patriotism, 'and it is impossible that a person of worth and integrity can be destitute of it.' The Christian soldier was not only of symbolic value but proved, Strachan argued, to be well-suited to both battle and 'the fatigues of a march and the severe privations of a campaign.' Moreover, unlike those who responded to their country's needs only when motivated by the promise of public acclaim, the Christian soldier was content to serve in obscurity. 'It is thus that the Christian Soldier softens the horrors of war,' Strachan concluded. 'He delights not in the anguish of individuals, and approves of no acts of hostility but what are necessary and conducive to the end and object of the war; in fine, he forgets not that he is a Christian amidst the slaughter of the field. Go forth then to the battle, my Brethren, clothed in the Christian armour, our cause is just ... [A]cquit yourselves like men, perform your duty with vigour and alacrity, and the calamities which the enemy are preparing for us shall return upon their own heads.'[55]

There was more than a little irony in the use of this symbol of virtuous manhood in military action by a religious leader who saw no military service himself during the war.[56] However, as an abstract symbol the Christian soldier could be an Upper Canadian military 'everyman': virtuous manhood transcending the many divisions in Upper Canadian society. The qualities described by Strachan and Major Allan might appeal to Anglican and Methodist, United Empire Loyalist and recent immigrant; they helped legitimate the military enterprise and gave it a sense of purpose. And, although the soldier could not symbolize Upper Canadian womanhood, he could reassure women and children that their persons and homes were protected by a *beneficent* patriarchal force. Wives, daughters, and sisters did not need to fear that their own troops would fall prey to the kind of vicious masculinity inherent in the American invaders.

Yet if the Christian soldier was a potentially powerful symbol, it was an abstract one. 'Vigorous manhood' demanded something more concrete; a flesh-and-blood figure was needed. The *Gazette*, and others who contributed to the discourse of loyalty and patriotism, were not slow to make use of Brock (alive or dead) as the personification of Upper Canadian military manhood. In an 1812 address to the colonists, the House of Assembly offered Brock's character as surety for Upper Canadian liberties, arguing that some degree of martial law would not result in the very despotism and tyranny that Upper Canadians were being called upon to resist. 'The good and loyal will never perceive them, except in the greater security which they will give him, for they are placed in the hands of his Excellency General Brock, a commander no less distinguished for his valor in the field than for his justice and humanity. In his wisdom and experience in war, your Representatives have the firmest reliance; and they rejoice that at such a crisis a General of so great abilities, and whose private merits gain the hearts of all who know him, should through Divine Providence, be placed at the head of this Government.'[57]

Although the 'good and loyal' might, in the assembly's eyes, not perceive military powers as abusive, others did. Throughout the war, the Upper Canadian government was plagued with militia absenteeism, farmers' reluctance to supply army provisions, and an obdurate assembly's refusal to pass wartime legislation strengthening the powers of the military.[58] None of these problems, of course, were to be solved by the veneration of one man in political discourse, but Brock, respected and in many ways aloof from the political squabbles of the prewar decade, was a potent figure. Although his premature death at the Battle of Queenston Heights deprived the imperial power of an able military commander, it also provided those involved in the construction of patriotic discourse with an unassailable symbol: the apotheosis of the Christian soldier, sacrificing himself for his country. The biographical sketch penned by the editor of the *Gazette* epitomized this approach. 'In society, mild, unassuming, cheerful, exercising the politeness of humanity, he anticipated every wish of those about him. – It is not surprising, if by such means he acquired universal esteem, love, respect, and confidence.' A 'humanizing' force on his army, Brock and his companion Lieutenant Colonel Macdonell died so that Upper Canadians could 'continue to enjoy the purest Constitution, for the preservation of which they were devoted.'[59] These 'gallant heroes,' proclaimed the author of a description of the Battle of Queenston Heights, 'died fighting gloriously in an honourable cause, but still to Canada their deaths are an irreparable loss.'[60] Self-sacrifice, modesty, courage, and humanity: all these were qualities that, in other circumstances, might be considered feminine. However, when exercised within the realm of patriotism, especially on such a public stage as a battlefield, and linked to a man dedicated to the physical protection of his country, they formed an ideal of masculinity removed from partisan politics. After the war, Brock was hailed as the saviour and father of his country – a cultural symbol constructed in poetry at school examinations, in the building of a monument at Queenston, and in memorial services commemorating the battle in which he fell.[61]

If Brock and the Christian soldier were the ideals of masculine patriotism, did any symbols of patriotic womanhood emerge to complement them? Certainly none was created during the war to rival Brock's appeal. Laura Secord did not emerge as a symbol of courage and bravery until Upper Canada itself had passed into history.[62] However, women were not completely absent from the wartime theatre of patriotism and loyalty. At an 1813 commemorative service, the 'Patriotic Young Ladies of York' presented the Third Regiment of York Militia with a special banner for which they were publicly thanked by Major Allan. In a process that illustrated the divisions created by gender in patriotic discourse, the women had made the banner, which was then passed on to Strachan, a male religious leader, to consecrate. Their work was then returned to the women's hands to be publicly presented to the regiment by Anne Powell, daughter of the future chief justice William Dummer Powell. Merging gender and national origin, Powell told her audience that the 'Young Ladies' were 'proud to imitate the example of the most distinguished of their sex, among the most virtuous and heroic nation who have always rejoiced in giving public testimony of their gratitude to their countrymen returning from Victory.' Placing women in patriotic discourse, Powell proclaimed that the banner was 'proof that they strongly participate in that generous patriotism which burns with so pure a flame through the Province.' Yet her 'short, but elegant and animated address' also positioned women as dependent on men, 'their brave and successful defenders.' The banner, rather than symbolizing women's labour as a contribution to the war, represented emotional bonds between men and women. 'And when you behold it unfurled in the Day of Battle,' Powell told the militia, 'let it become a kind remembrance of the unlimited confidence which they place in the efficacy of your protection.'[63]

The actions of the 'Gallant Young Ladies' were not without historical precedent. As British historian Linda Colley has argued, during the Napoleonic Wars upper- and middle-class women in Britain made flags and banners, organized clothing drives and other forms of relief for the troops, and sometimes made speeches and delivered public addresses citing their support for the nation. To be sure, like the banner of 1813, these activities drew upon the 'traditional female virtues of charity, nurture, and needlework.' But because these women were performing such work for 'men who were not in the main related to them by blood or marriage, [they] demonstrated that their domestic virtues possessed a public as well as a private relevance.' As Colley points out, war work also took them out of their homes and taught them the skills of lobbying and committee work (much as religious and charity work gave them experience in running organizations).[64] Certainly a similar argument could be made for their counterparts in Upper Canada, who after the war would become active participants in a number of charitable and benevolent organizations. Yet the context in which their war work took place was somewhat different from that of the women of Colley's study. Upper Canada was a much smaller society than Britain, insofar as settlers of British descent were concerned, and therefore it was much more likely that women involved in war work would be performing services for husbands, fathers, brothers, and other male relatives.[65] To some degree such family ties may have reinforced the private and emotional nature of 'charity, nurture, and needlework,' making it easier to represent women's wartime activities as acts of love and familial duty, not hard work and patriotic service.

Furthermore, while certainly Britons were concerned with the defence of their country against both external (the French) and internal (traitorous radicals) enemies, in Upper Canada invasion and occupation were not just threats. The invasion of York in 1813 and the burning of Niagara might appear to justify and reinforce the need for Upper Canadian male protection of women and children. American invasion had been so clearly predicted and so consistently imagined as a direct threat to the helpless and the weak that its occurrence – and the perceived need to evacuate women and children from areas of fighting – was treated as a self-fulfilling prophecy by colonial officials: a host of Christian soldiers then marched to protect the makers of the banner. The colonial military context of being besieged and beleaguered, particularly in 1813, may have heightened and reinforced patriarchal relations amongst the élite, making it more difficult for women to speak and act publicly as patriots unless they used the language of emotion, familial connection, and their need for protection. We should not, of course, discount the possibility of women's scepticism about such elevated sentiments. During the invasion of York, Anne Powell herself apparently greeted the return of the banner – worn by militia colonel Archibald McLean 'for concealment' – with 'bitter words of indignation and ... [the] taunt that after all their protestations the men had sent the banner back for the women to protect.'[66]

The presentation of the banner was a lone occasion on which Upper Canadian women appeared in the pages of the *Gazette*, or any other newspapers, to openly declare support for the colony. More often, women and children were grouped together as symbolic reminders to Upper Canadian men of their duty. Like Brock, they were invoked to suggest that Upper Canadians were blessed with a higher moral purpose in military combat than their opponents. However, Brock's image suggested virtue residing at the heart of male military activities; women and children became the reasons for such activities and backdrops to them, not actors themselves. As Anne Powell's appearance indicated, it was not impossible for some women to speak about their sense of loyalty and enter into patriotic discourse at a public level. If one wished to do so, it helped to belong to a prominent upper-class York family; the term 'ladies' was as imbued with assumptions about status, class, and race as it was with ones about gender. Moreover, the language of loyalty hampered any claims women might have made to equal status with, for example, members of the militia as loyal subjects of the Crown.

This construction of patriotism as an affirmation of male activities and manly virtue becomes even more intriguing when we consider that the War of 1812 was at times fought literally on the colonists' doorsteps. Militia troops were quartered in the stables and barns, as well as in the garrisons, of York, Kingston, and Niagara. In the decades after the war, citizens from across the province filed compensation claims that cited the loss of domestic and agricultural goods: furniture, homes, crops, livestock, and farm buildings.[67] In such a setting, the women of Upper Canada might be caught up quite directly in military events, provisioning troops and possibly tending to the casualties of battles that took place in nearby fields. That women and children were also present at garrisons is evident from military dispatches and letters that mention the evacuation of 'women and children' from British garrisons at Niagara, Kingston, and York, as well as discussing allowances for soldiers' wives and families.[68] These records suggest a greater complexity around gender relations and the conduct of the war than those of the public pronouncements of the press or the government. Rather than revolving around the all-male comradeship of warfare symbolized, for example, by the deaths of Brock and Macdonell, it is possible that the daily operations of the military might have been highly dependent on the presence and unpaid work of soldiers' wives and children. And wives might not have been the only women at the garrison. In his 'General Orders,' issued at Kingston, 14 July 1813, Adjutant-General E. Baynes notified the 89th Regiment that Captain Basden had been relieved of his command for allowing 'several instances of irregularity and misconduct.' Not least of these 'irregularities' was the fact that Basden, 'in violation of all regard to decency and decorum, incumbered the brigade of boats by bringing up under his protection a female of improper character.'[69] Garrisons, it is clear, were not all-male domains.

Even when women behaved in ways that conformed to the rules of patriotic conduct, their exploits were either passed over or downplayed. Such was the case of Sarah Willott, who provided intelligence regarding enemy troop movements to the British officials. Willott informed the army that the Americans were planning to attack Fort Erie and that the Pennsylvanian troops involved lacked provisions. To be sure, her 'Statement,' included in a letter from Sheaffe to General Prevost, apparently confirmed earlier information received by the general.[70] Yet Willott had acted precisely as desired by colonial officials, and her actions could have been celebrated as the service of a loyal colonist to her government. However, Willott's contribution to military intelligence excited little public commentary or commendation. Other women might fare somewhat better. Describing events on the Niagara frontier, the youthful William Hamilton Merritt, captain of a troop of provincial dragoons, credited the escape of one of his men to the work of Mrs Gessean. 'She was a perfect heroine and deserves every credit for her patriotism,' Merritt declared. Her father and son were taken by the Americans, and the former was granted a parole (a pass ensuring his liberty in return for his promise that he would not fight for the British). The son, though, was taken across the Niagara River and jailed at Lewiston. Taking it upon herself to rescue him, Mrs Gessean smuggled her father's parole to him on a trip across the border, under the pretext of selling butter to the American garrison. He then used the parole to pass through the border guards and rejoin his militia regiment. 'It was very easy and simple,' Merritt observed, 'but few would have had the invention of carrying it into effect.'[71]

Merritt also applauded the bravery of Mrs Defield, the resident of a house near Lundy's Lane in Niagara that was the scene of a skirmish between American troops and those Canadian and British forces under the command of Lieutenant-Colonel James Fitzgibbon. Mrs Defield was in her doorway holding a child when, upon seeing that an American rifleman was about to stab Fitzgibbon, she kicked the sword out of his hand. As the rifleman bent over to retrieve the weapon, she threw down the child, ran out, and 'wrenched it [the sword] completely from him and hid it in the house.' Shortly after, according to Merritt, her husband arrived and, with Fitzgibbon, succeeded in disarming the soldiers. Merritt concluded that 'upon the whole it was a most gallant, daring, and miraculous proceeding.'[72] Gallant and daring in Merritt's deployment of patriotic discourse it might have been, yet, when the incident was reported in the *Montreal Gazette* on 6 July 1813, the only woman mentioned was a Mrs Kerby who had unsuccessfully attempted to enlist the help of some men who were nearby. The paper noted that 'poor Mrs Kerby,' who was apparently 'distracted, used all her influences, but in vain.'[73] The paper then went on to commemorate the military achievements of the men involved. Not only were Mrs Defield's actions completely omitted, the paper also differed from Merritt's account of the incident in its assessment of Mrs Kerby's helplessness: he had credited her with having warned the British and Canadian troops of the Americans' proximity.[74]

Spying, smuggling, and taking up arms when faced with immediate danger: none of these activities were, of course, new to Upper Canadian women. Janice Potter-MacKinnon has shown that Loyalist women during the Revolutionary War had performed similar services for the British cause.[75] But, like their Loyalist predecessors, the bravery of Mrs Defield or Sarah Willott was not integrated into official narratives of wartime heroism. Women and children, Upper Canadians were reminded frequently, were the potential victims of American violence and bloodlust, and part of being a victim was passive acceptance of one's plight until rescue arrived. The men of the militia units were fighting to protect all inhabitants of the colony but especially 'that tender and most amiable sex who have consigned them[selves] to our hands, and who zealously hope that we shall never abandon them.'[76] The Americans were 'ruffians,' the *Kingston Gazette* proclaimed, who would bring about the 'murder of our parents, of our wives, and those dear pledges of conjugal affection which strengthen the ties of union.' In Gananoque they 'committed depredations ... in the most wanton manner,' attempting to murder women and children, not only firing upon Mrs Joel Stone but also 'uttering imprecations against her which it would be disgraceful to this paper, even to repeat.'[77] The invasion and burning of Niagara were described with outrage by Lieutenant-General Sir George Prevost, who used the image of women and children to illustrate the extent of American depravity. 'In the enlightened era of the nineteenth century, and in the inclemency of a Canadian winter, the troops of a nation calling itself civilized and Christian had wantonly, and without the shadow of a pretext, forced four hundred helpless women and children to quit their dwellings and to be the mournful spectators of the conflagration and total destruction of all that belonged to them.'[78]

The image of 'innocent, unfortunate, and distressed inhabitants' travelled beyond the boundaries of Upper Canada to appear in the Duke of Kent's address before the Society in London for the Relief of the Sufferings of the Inhabitants of Canada. Upper Canada, the duke argued, had lost its chief economic mainstay with the militia call-up, taking away 'numbers of the young and the aged men, who cultivated the land on whose exertions their mothers, their daughters, their wives and their little ones, were dependent.' 'It was apparent that the women and children would be in a very miserable comfortless state during their absence,' a theme he stressed in his appeal for subscribers for a relief fund.[79] The duke's desire to tug his listeners' heart-strings no doubt accounted to some extent for his emphasis on helpless, starving families, yet his use of this motif was by no means unique. Excerpts from Strachan's letters to friends in Kingston, written during the war and the American invasion of York, emphasized the helplessness of the town's women and children and his responsibilities as their protector.[80] During the war, Upper Canadian society was portrayed in patriotic discourse as the family writ large, with those dependent members (represented as women and children) placed under the protection of male household heads (husbands, fathers, sons, and brothers).

Yet they were not the only justifications for Upper Canadians to take up arms. Alongside the family, and closely linked to it, was the preservation of private property. 'Such a regard to the preservation of our rights both in person and in property,' the assembly told the public once war had broken out, was embedded in 'our laws and institutions.' Under the British system, it asked, 'is there any person who is not conscious that he is completely master of his own conduct – that the quiet possession of his life, his person and property, and good name are secured to him by the laws?'[81] The difference between the Americans and the British, stated the *Kingston Gazette*, was that of a 'horde of banditti' as compared to a 'nation,' and the proof of this was the former's seizure and destruction of private property, unlike the latter's behaviour during the Conquest.[82] The destruction of homes, businesses, and farms by the invading army was denounced in thunderous tones by the *Gazette*, the assembly, and the military.[83] The looting and burning of buildings deemed public were perceived as less serious and appeared to be accepted as part of the game of war. Damaging public buildings at York was not as odious a deed as the burning of the homes of Niagara. Like the family, private property was deemed off-limits to the military, even though the families and homes of Upper Canada were invoked to stimulate patriotic loyalty to the British connection.

Linking the family to private property reinforced the former's identification with a realm removed from the machinations of politics and diplomacy. In this discourse of patriotism and loyalty, women and children came very near to being private property themselves, so close was the identification of human beings with material possessions.[84] Yet, try as they might to keep home and family distinct and apart from the world of imperial politics, those who shaped patriotic discourse ensured that women and children were its central symbols. By evoking in the public realm of the legislature and newspaper these images of feminine helplessness in need of masculine military protection, and by insisting on importance of these images to notions of public duty, correspondents to the *Gazette*, as well as the military and political leaders quoted above, were also responsible for making women and children, the family and the home, objects of public attention and concern. Through their defence, Upper Canadian men could vindicate their own and their country's honour, an honour that would be celebrated with addresses, monuments, and, through the good graces of the Loyal and Patriotic Society of Upper Canada, the Upper Canada Preserved Medal.

The Loyal and Patriotic Society of Upper Canada has been one of the better-kept secrets in Upper Canadian historiography. It has attracted little attention from those who have studied the issue of loyalty in the colony, and only relatively recently have its origins and history been examined in any detail.[85] The reasons for this neglect are not difficult to determine. The society's initial burst of activity from 1812 to 1817 was followed by a long period of inertia and a failure to accomplish its long-term goals. However, the society represented an organized attempt by the colony's leaders to structure patriotic activity and create symbols of Upper Canadian loyalty.

Formed at York in December 1812, the society came into being with reports of the distress of the militia, suffering from a shortage of arms and clothing. Patronized by General Sheaffe, who gave it military legitimacy and £200, the society's directors included such York notables as acting attorney general John Beverley Robinson, provincial judge William Campbell, Crown clerk and militia officer John Small; militia commander William Chewett; militia surgeon Grant Powell, the brother of Anne; and Strachan. In order to meet the more pressing needs of the troops, the people of York raised a private subscription and, 'aided by the personal labour of [the] young Ladies of the place,' supplied the soldiers between Niagara and Fort Erie with flannel shirts. This problem solved (at least temporarily), the society turned its attention to the promotion and reward of patriotic service, which it defined as the relief of militiamen and their families and the creation of medals. The latter would be granted 'to reward merit, excite emulation, and commemorate glorious exploits, by bestowing medals, or other honorary marks of public approbation and distinction; for extraordinary instance of personal courage, or fidelity in defence of the Province by individuals, either of His Majesty's regular or militia forces, and also the seamen on the Lakes.'[86] With the assistance of subscriptions raised from York civilians and the militia of the town (who donated a day's pay), as well as money from Montreal, Quebec, and Nova Scotia, nine medals were struck. However, the silver used did not match the original design, and they were not distributed. More medals were made, but the society, besieged with nominations for recipients after the war's end, was unable to decide which of these worthy individuals merited such an honour. In the end, none of the medals were distributed. In 1822 the medals were lodged with the Bank of Upper Canada for safekeeping, following the society's decision in 1820 to sell them as bullion and to donate the remaining portion of the society's funds to a York hospital-building fund. They remained lodged in the bank's vaults until 1840 when, after a legislative inquiry into the society's funds and activities, the surviving directors decided to sell the medals to a firm of Toronto watchmakers.[87]

As the incident of the medals suggests, not all efforts to create a tradition of loyalty were completely successful. Yet the society's pronouncements on the role of the militia contributed to the mythology of Upper Canadian loyalty, a script inscribed with male military vigour. The militia's 'valour and fortitude' were not fleeting emotions but instead 'still burn with unabated vigor,' enabling 'a raw militia to suffer with patience the greatest privations, to face death with astonishing intrepidity, but also to emulate veteran soldiers in deeds of honour and glory.' In this instance, age need not be a deterrent: 'many, though exempted by age from military duty, scorn to claim the privilege, and it is not uncommon to see men of seventy leaving their homes, and demanding arms to meet the enemy on the lines.' Furthermore, as fathers and heads of households, men's connection to their country could continue even as their bodies grew weaker. 'Others too feeble to bear arms themselves, are seen leading their sons to the military posts.'[88]

Having limited the medals' potential recipients to regular troops or the military, the society apparently did not consider rewarding civilians. However, from 1813 to 1817 it combined patriotism with philanthropy, giving out relief to selected applicants who had suffered as a result of the war. In many ways, the society's charitable acts continued the pattern established in the patriotic discourse of the press and the government by defining women and children as objects of male protection. The male heads of the society made decisions concerning whether or not, and how much, relief would be given to women and their families left destitute by the loss of, or serious injury to, a male household head in the war. Women were not the only recipients of the society's charity; with the exception of 1816, when women outnumbered men by a ratio of eleven to one, men made up the majority of the applicants.[89] Some pleaded hardship and poverty as a result of disabilities suffered in the war, and they pointed to the need to support large families. A few men received money to disburse to others, whether family members or needy persons in their communities. Total disbursements fluctuated from year to year, from an 1813 low of £248 7s. to a peak of £3693 in 1816.[90] Widows, according to the society, were entitled to at least £20 for the support of their families, although the records indicate that this sum was not always given. Moreover, to be black and widowed placed a woman even closer to the margins of male protection; the anonymous 'negro woman' who appeared on the society's books in 1815 received only 15s., despite the fact that her husband had died while imprisoned by the Americans (the average disbursement to white women, with or without husbands, was £10).[91] In this instance, it seems that the woman's race confounded the binary oppositions of male/female, protector/protected in patriotic discourse, throwing expectations as to the extent of male protection into question and demonstrating that womanly dependency had a racial subtext.

On one occasion the society recognized female patriotism unaccompanied by male valour, awarding Mrs Rice of Niagara £15 since 'she was a most active loyalist and a great sufferer by the enemy.'[92] Nowhere else in the records were women compensated for their loyalty alone. The society insisted that women establish a claim on its benevolence through the patriotism of a male relative and their loss of his protection, not on the grounds of their own loyal service nor merely because of their own poverty. Once such a claim had been established, a woman might return to the society for assistance. However, for those such as Polly Spareback and Mrs McDonell, aid from the society was not forthcoming. Polly, a widow with two children, lived at Four Mile Creek in Niagara. Her grain crop destroyed by the troops and Indians who had been quartered there, she approached the society for assistance to cover the loss. (Despite earlier reassurances, the Americans apparently had not been the only threats to the safety of civilians and their property.) Unfortunately for Polly, the society felt she was 'under the protection of her family, who appear to the Society to be able to support her.'[93] Despite Polly's widowhood, the society clearly perceived her position within her family as that of a dependant, unlike male claimants whose family ties helped strengthen their case for support. Mrs McDonell, it felt, did not prove in her petition that she had suffered as a result of the war and, arguing that it was not in the business of settling compensation claims, the society refused her request.[94] With the exception of the admirable Mrs Rice, the society's work incorporated women and femininity only as they related to men. Images of femininity were an integral motivating force to masculine heroism. Women themselves had few grounds on which to establish a claim to the public arena of patriotic and loyal behaviour.

In Upper Canada, 'woman-as-patriot' was a shadowy presence in patriotic discourse, making infrequent appearances that were quickly subsumed by a chorus celebrating military vigour. Female loyalty was also represented by a much narrower range of activities than those performed by men. Many male activities signified patriotism: joining the military, serving as loyal members of the government helping to protect the colony from sedition, and acting as civilians defending home and family from the invader on their doorstep. Sometimes these acts were universalized and stripped of overtly gendered connotations, as in appeals to 'the people' in newspaper articles and government pronouncements. Others, such as military service, were quite clearly constructed as the physical deeds of valorous *men*. Women, on the other hand, were represented as performing only those activities that were tied to the household: sewing and presenting banners, clothing, and bed linen. The contributions of Sarah Willott and Mrs Defield went unrecognized. Furthermore, unlike male activities, which were often applauded for their physicality (fighting, marching, sacrificing physical comforts), the labour that went into making the banner of 1813 or clothing for the troops was downplayed in favour of the emotional bonds the objects represented and helped reinforce: the beneficent patriarchal protection of women and children by one group of men from another group of men. In these examples, those who contributed to patriotic discourse took this idealized image of the family and extended its meaning. Womanly helplessness and childlike innocence were not the only messages conveyed: the sanctity of material possessions and the protection of individual ownership also were at stake.

In the aftermath of the war, loyalty to Upper Canada and the British connection became even more important to the colony's political culture. Tory and reform ideologies were not consistently anti- or pro-American; they had 'their roots in and were sustained by a collective understanding of *both* the United States and Great Britain.'⁹⁵ Nevertheless defence of the colony during the war was a recurring theme in political discourse. Neither party wanted to cede ground to the other on this issue. Conservatives in the press justified access to patronage not just on the basis of their war service, as a reward for services rendered, but argued that such service was proof of superior moral fibre and commitment to the colony's well-being. In this attempt to occupy the high ground, they were met with the insistence of some reformers that they, too, had protected their country's interests from 1812 to 1814; they, too, had suffered and sacrificed; and consequently they, too, should have a say in the colony's political direction. Valorous military service supposedly knew no political boundaries and could be called upon to validate opinions ranging from payment of war claims to proposals for responsible government. Some of these positions, though, posed greater tactical difficulties for reformers than for others.

It did not take long for wartime service to emerge as a form of currency in the Upper Canadian market for patronage and land. In the immediate aftermath of the war, loyalty and patriotism also became part of the competition for place and position in rural Upper Canada. 'Out of the war of 1812 came a set of inter-twined beliefs that were at once an Upper Canadian patriotic mythology, a justification of extant patterns of economic and civic morality, and an ideology that implied certain general political-constitutional positions. That the actual events of 1812–14 were so distorted as to be virtually unrecognizable is irrelevant; what counts is that the historical events were malleable and could be fashioned into a past that could be used.'[96]

Donald Akenson argues that this mythology's emphasis on virtue and suffering, and the rewards and compensation they merited, was used by those Upper Canadians resident in the province during the war to justify their access to social, economic, and political gains. In the period immediately after the war, the myth centred on wartime heroism and included United Empire Loyalists, late Loyalists, and those Americans resident prior to 1812 who had not actively supported the enemy. It provided a 'bonding myth' for these different groups. Focused on the bravery of General Brock and the militia, the patriotic myths also provided as their polar opposite a convenient cast of villains: American institutions and values, especially democracy and egalitarianism. Against these demons the population of Upper Canada had fought, with much sacrifice and personal cost, and for this they deserved a favoured position in Upper Canadian society. Such a juxtaposition, and the glorification of British images that came with it, also proved useful during the period of British immigration to Upper Canada after 1815. This adherence to the imperial connection and emphasis on loyalty, though, undercut the arguments of the residents eager to exploit this mythology: many of the new arrivals had their own tradition of loyalty to Britain. Loyalty eventually became less useful as a weapon of exclusion.[97]

The value of these patriotic images fluctuated according to the claimant's gender. On 10 February 1816 the Executive Council Office announced its receipt of petitions for land grants from sons and daughters of United Empire Loyalists. Such persons, the council announced, needed certificates from the quarter sessions magistrates, signed by the chairman and clerk of the peace, testifying that their parents were loyal during the war and were not suspected of aiding or assisting the enemy; 'And if a Son, then of age, that he also was Loyal during the late War, and did his duty in defence of the Province – and if a Daughter of an United Empire Loyalist married, that her husband was Loyal, and did his duty in defence of the Province.'[98] Gender and assumptions about the family thus were proclaimed in this most 'public' form of discourse, a pronouncement of the colonial state. The council continued the wartime practice of placing women (especially married women, but also daughters) in an indirect relationship to the rewards of wartime service and loyalty, rewards they incurred from their relationship to father or husband. Sons, on the other hand, might transcend their position in the family to win recognition for their loyalty on its own terms, a strategy unavailable to married women. In this particular pronouncement the council was silent about the unmarried daughters of United Empire Loyalists, although it would appear that they were in fact entitled to land grants.[99]

It was not only the Executive Council that wanted to establish a link between male military service and land, that common form of specie in Upper Canada. Petitioning the prince regent in 1818, men of the Midland district reminded the Crown that 'the young men of this province *were encouraged to volunteer* in its defence, by a promise of their commanders, *to recommend* that land *should* be granted them, *at the termination of the war,* as a reward for their services.'[100] The tradition of rewarding men for military service had been established in Upper Canada with the coming of the Loyalists; women, in order to receive anything from the state, had to stress their helplessness.[101] Land claims, though, could be given a new urgency and legitimation with reminders of their authors' active defence in wartime service.

Yet not all agreed that the War of 1812 had been a glorious triumph for Upper Canadian masculinity. A few voices offered an alternative version of events. The author of an anonymous letter to the editor of the *Kingston Chronicle* – as the *Gazette* was renamed in 1819 – concerning wartime reparations to the citizens of Ernest Town pointed out the kinds of inducements to fight offered to Upper Canadians. 'What greater incitements to valor, what stronger appeal to a sense of duty, and a love of country were ever presented to men?' Certainly Upper Canada had been in dire need of protection but 'did we combat alone? Was not our independence purchased with the lives of thousands ... the generous youth of Britain?'[102] Seventeen years later, the editor of the *Niagara Gleaner* ridiculed the claims made by some Upper Canadians on the disposition of lands owned by the British government, claims made on the basis that their wartime activities kept the colony safe. 'Such an assertion is almost too ridiculous to deserve an answer. – WE defended the country!!! – It is true, a number of sons of the brave Loyalists came forward and did their duty as militiamen, and assisted in defending the country, but what could they have done had it not been for the aid of the powerful arm of Great Britain, both by sea and land?'[103]

These rare attempts to debunk the myth of the brave militia were framed in terms of male military exploits, not the contribution of valorous civilians, and thus excluded women. Even patriotic consumerism, an activity that might appeal to women as well as men, could be constructed as a male responsibility and tied to military bravery. 'Highlander,' writing to the *Chronicle* in 1823, advised the public to teach boys to buy Canadian, thus strengthening their pride in their country. Pride in the colony's economic progress would then be translated into pride in its ability to defend itself, instead of the situation whereby 'the rising generation being imperceptibly led to entertain an erroneous exalted idea of the military prowess of our neighbours must at the same time pave the way for a degraded diffidence of their own power to conquer.'[104] 'Highlander' was not entirely clear as to how material goods would lead to military confidence, but the letter represented another strong association of patriotism with male military deeds.

The few histories and reminiscences of the war published during this period were similar in their choices of characters and activities. David Thompson's *A History of the Late War between Great Britain and the United States of America*, first published in Niagara in 1832, was primarily a military history. It was written, in Thompson's words, for the present generation 'to review the terrific glories of those fields of blood and carnage; the widow and the fatherless will survey the transcendent achievements of their husbands and their fathers. British youth will catch that patriotic flame which glowed with an unequalled resplendence in the bosoms of their fathers, and animated to action that noble few who stepped forward to oppose a relentless enemy invading their hitherto peaceful fire sides, and evinced a willingness to endure every privation incidental to the "tented field," defence of their King, their laws, and their country.'[105] Although Thompson did not use the term specifically, the Christian soldier lived on in his glorification of Upper Canadian male virtue under fire. Moreover, in his account Upper Canadian men went to war not just to defend the monarchy and the constitution but also to ensure the sanctity of the private sphere. '"When men are called upon to defend every thing they hold precious – their wives and children, their friends and possessions,"' he wrote, quoting the House of Assembly's address to the 'yeomanry' of Canada, "'they ought to be inspired by the noblest resolution, and they will not be easily frightened with menaces, or conquered by force.'"[106]

As a political bargaining chip, patriotic service during the war was a mixed blessing. At times it was fairly easy for those men advocating change to use the language of loyal reform based on wartime participation. In British reformer Robert Gourlay's *Statistical Account of Upper Canada*, the inhabitants of the colony addressed the prince regent, reminding him of their loyalty and of men's contribution to the colony's defence. In 1812, they declared, only a 'handful' of British troops were present to assist the colonists. Once again, women and children were cast as the war's victims, having been forced to flee their homes. However, 'the second year of war saw her sons confirmed in their virtue, and still more determined to resist.'[107] The war over, though, certain promises had yet to be kept. 'The young men of this Province, who were armed in its defence, had, for their spirited conduct, the promise of their commanders, that land would be granted them as a reward for their services.' This reward had been 'unjustly withheld,' prey of those office-holders who had sunk 'beneath the dignity of men' in their desire to allocate patronage.[108] Their actions betrayed not only those 'young men' but also the founders of Upper Canada: 'the descendants of those who sacrificed their all in America, in [sic] behalf of British rule – men whose names were ordered on record for their virtuous adherence to your Royal Father, – the descendants of these men find, now, no favour in their destined rewards.'[109] That this narrative of loyal sacrifice, as well as ensuring claims to its rewards, was based on patrilineality was accepted by the petitioners without any apparent qualms. The meaning of the war and of loyalty itself was fixed in language that celebrated masculine military struggle and sacrifice.

Yet the political battles of the postwar period highlighted the problematic legacy of the War of 1812. Undoubtedly the war was coded as an event fought by men, and its conclusion was a triumph for many virtues – Upper Canadian manhood being one of them. Both tory and reformer wished to claim the war and virtuous manhood as part of their political heritage. Definitions of loyalty were subject to contestation and affirmation by a number of groups in the province, whether conservative or reform, Anglican or Methodist.[110] Yet in the context of disputes over the nature of the imperial connection, the dispensation of patronage, and the structure of Upper Canadian government, reform discourse was faced with the obstacle of conservative claims to valiant militia service in defence of home and family, Upper Canada and Britain. Those who called for changes in the colony's political structure and in the nature of political life did so in the language of eighteenth-century Commonwealth's-men, using a critique of patronage, placemen, and the corruption of the decadent 'Family Compact.' In its place, they posited an end to patronage (or at least unfairly dispensed patronage), an assembly whose wishes would be heeded by the Executive Council, and the preservation of the 'British constitution.' All of these achievements would be possible with the triumph of honest, loyal, and forthright manliness. Much of this language came from a tradition of civic humanism and, as we shall see, it was possible for Upper Canadian reformers to use it in order to critique the colony's administration. However, one of the key elements of civic humanism and the republican tradition was the armed citizen (as opposed to the standing army) poised to defend his country's interests,[111] a position that reformers found difficult, if not impossible, to appropriate as their own. Given the wartime service of the leadership of the York and Kingston élite in militia companies and in the 1820s and 1830s, how could Upper Canadian reformers claim this aspect of the legacy of the Glorious Revolution of 1688 as their exclusive property?

Things military, especially masculine virtue cast in the mould of the Christian soldier, occupied an uneasy position in reformers' rhetoric. Despite reformers' admiration for some aspects of American society, the armed republican rarely occupied centre stage in the theatre of reform symbolism. Despite the fact that a number of reformers were members of the militia either during the war or in the 1820s, conservatives too could appropriate the armed citizen manfully defending his country.[112] Reformers thus had little room to manoeuvre. Because of their opposition to standing armies and military governors, the circumstances of Upper Canadian history had played a rather cruel joke on them. They could call up the events of 1688, justifying loyal opposition to protect the country and constitution, but, while the allusion was valid, 1688 was a less useful legacy for reformers than they might have wished. Conservatives were fond of reminding them that they too had taken up arms in defence of their country, the constitution, and the imperial connection. Furthermore, many conservatives were prominent members of local militias, units that were called out, it is worth remembering, in 1837 to suppress the rebellion.[113] Try as they might, reformers found it difficult to find a place for themselves in the narrative of loyalty and patriotism as cast in male military deeds. Other kinds of masculine loyalty had to be and, as we shall see in the following chapter, were found – ones that looked back to the British constitution and forward to a better future for the colony.

It is not difficult to know *why* the War of 1812 and the concepts of public duty and loyalty that accompanied the conflict were cast as a military struggle between men, with women and children as innocent pawns. 'Patriarchy and paternalism' were central features of early Upper Canadian society. Patriarchal family structures and relationships came with Loyalist settlers, as did their view of a hierarchical society marked by deference and respect. In these forms of social, economic, and political organization, women were marginal and excluded from any kind of formal power.[114] Furthermore, it is possible that the shadows of the French and American Revolutions, which hung over Upper Canadian patriotism, influenced the ways in which the war was given meaning by the press and official bodies. The prospect of worlds 'turned upside down' in these upheavals included the threat that relationships between men and women might be re-examined and overturned. The consequences would be the abolition of the family and morality, an increase in sexual libertinism, and social and political anarchy (as had been argued in the case of the French Revolution). Although they did not go so far as to predict these things explicitly in the case of an American victory, those who shaped public discourse in Upper Canada hinted, as we have seen, at Americans' evil intentions and the maleficent influence of their French allies. Only the loyalty of Upper Canadian men, directly expressed in an open and physical manner, could prevent their enemies' encroachment. In such a discourse, masculinity signified order, hierarchy, and respect for established social and political norms and institutions.

Patriarchy and paternalism might have shaped Upper Canadian society, yet, as Katherine McKenna has demonstrated, the upper reaches of colonial society were not completely closed to women. The boundaries between social life, a recognized area of feminine power for élite women, and the male-dominated world of politics were not watertight. Upper-class women could wield a certain degree of informal political power and influence, a 'power-behind-the-throne' that upset the outwardly visible division between public and private.[115] The ways in which loyalty and patriotism were constructed by the press and in official pronouncements on the war also merged and tangled public and private, the battlefield and the home, masculine and feminine. The 'other' on which Upper Canadian patriotic virtue was built and against which it defined itself was not necessarily woman herself. It could be other kinds of masculinity gone wrong, defiled by national or political structures bereft of the civilizing influence of British values and institutions, such as the monarch, the constitution, and the rule of law.

However, these were not enough. Without the motivation of home and family to protect, the brave militia man was in danger of becoming one of those 'rampaging savages' lurking at the colony's borders (whether such savagery was that of the American soldiery or of Upper Canada's Native allies). By their insistence that men must fight to defend their families, that their homes were one of the most sacred institutions threatened by American invasion, editors, clergymen, and politicians breached the gendered bifurcation of Upper Canadian society. This is not to ignore the fact that loyalty and patriotism were located in the context of a family that, while not patriarchal in the strict sense of the term, was still male-dominated; husbands, fathers, sons, and brothers acted in the interests of wives, mothers, daughters, and sisters. It does, though, illustrate Kerber's and Scott's arguments: that as much as we might like to divide up the past in neatly arranged realms and spheres, these divisions are dependent on each other. This dependency confounds our attempts to separate the public world of politics and warfare and the private world of home and family.

The War of 1812 gave meaning and an Upper Canadian context to concepts of public duty, patriotism, and loyalty. It also was the first time that a select group of Upper Canadians conducted an ongoing, public discussion of matters of 'national' importance in which gender relations and gendered images figured prominently. Yet the war was not the only event to which meaning was given through such symbols. The political struggles of the postwar period, from Robert Gourlay's call for changes in land distribution to the struggle for responsible government, would also include highly contested notions of gender and family.

2

Ranting Renegades and Corseted Sycophants: Political Languages in Upper Canada

There have always been bad and unprincipled men who, lusting after power, merely because they wished to abuse it, and to indulge their own passions at the expense of the happiness of others, have endeavoured to disturb the constitution and laws of their country; to excite amongst the multitude a dislike of their Rulers; and to throw public affairs into confusion, that they might take advantage of the disorder.

Rev. T. Phillips, 'A Loyal Sermon,' York, 23 April 1826

Will you, men of Upper Canada, see your laws thus trampled upon; – your liberties infringed – your opinions, sacred in the bosoms of all freemen, coerced by the scimitar of power, and transgressed by men in the favour of the Government? Stand forth, thou upholder of the British Constitution – raise thy voice in defence of her laws.

'A Dialogue Between Two Farmers on Canadian Politics,' *Colonial Advocate*, 19 April 1832

The constitution and the law: for these writers, they were the cornerstones of all that was both British and manly in Upper Canadian political life. They were also in need of protection: for the Reverend T. Phillips, these fundamental elements of British governance were threatened by unscrupulous men who wished merely to overturn the social order; for the 'Two Farmers,' who symbolized Upper Canadian reform, the key elements of justice and liberty had been subverted by tyrannical and corrupt men who abused their political power. While these writers laid claim to the same features of the British political structure, neither law nor constitution, as historians of Upper Canadian political and legal history have pointed out, held identical meanings for the political groupings of reform and conservative.[1] Like loyalty and patriotism, which were often interwoven into political debates over issues such as the Alien Act or responsible government, political structures were subject to contestation and held multiple meanings.

But what historians of Upper Canadian politics have not examined is the gendered nature of debates over appropriate political structures and the types of behaviour and morality needed to sustain them. In the aftermath of the War of 1812, beginning with Robert Gourlay and continuing into the 1820s and 1830s, debates over political reform were grounded in conceptions of public and private and couched in language suffused with gendered imagery and symbols. Participants relied heavily on the notion of 'true manhood' to validate and legitimate claims to political power, while using concepts of woman and the feminine to undermine their opponents' positions. For conservatives, the patriarchal family was the basis of society; it ensured the necessary social and political hierarchy for stability and order. Truly virtuous men were those who respected such order and deference: rational, logical men who were mindful of the need to guard political institutions from selfish men who had renounced their wider responsibilities to colonial society. For the reformers, the manly virtue needed in Upper Canadian political culture was that of the honest, upright, and – most importantly – independent man, free of the private familial intrigues of his conservative opponents and thus able to enter into fraternal unions with like-minded men. Such unions would rid colonial politics of the corruption that, as the 'Two Farmers' pointed out, threatened the exercise of British justice and liberties.

Like the discourse of patriotism and loyalty in Upper Canada, debates over political issues were shaped primarily by white, literate men; only rarely was a woman's voice heard, usually on the boundaries of political discourse. Women's relationships to the Upper Canadian state and citizenry were acknowledged infrequently by conservative and reformer alike. Gender relations in political discourse were no less rigidly conceived than those of patriotism and loyalty. We might expect that reformers would provide a more flexible and egalitarian concept of gender relations than their opponents, whose outlook was shaped by notions of hierarchy and deference. However, reformers concentrated on separating what they understood to be the private sphere from public, political life and then focused their efforts on the latter. This strategy did not lend itself to rethinking the meaning of the private realm, and related social institutions such as the family – at least, not in ways that would have brought women into political culture as actors and agents. In fact, reform discourse helped shape and reinforce notions of a society that was bifurcated by gender and in which women's absence as political actors was assumed and rarely, if ever, commented upon. To be sure, the rebellion brought about a shift in reform discourse: symbols and images of femininity became even more frequently used and important in attacks on the government and Crown. However, in these attacks, women were either helpless victims of government oppression or, in the case of the queen, the fountainhead of state tyranny.

At present, the area of politics remains virtually untouched in the international historical work on masculinity.[2] This absence is curious because, after all, political institutions were exclusively male throughout the nineteenth century. Furthermore, they were the site of struggles between groups of men openly competing for power, the place where many of the lessons learned in other, all-male institutions (such as the British public school) supposedly were put to use. The importance of such political struggles and changes for women has not gone unacknowledged. Historians have examined women's participation in the American and French Revolutions and British radicalism, the different meanings that political changes held for women, and the ways in which political discourse was gendered.[3] However, historians of masculinity in the nineteenth century have yet to turn their attention to the implications of political changes for men. Nor have they addressed the ways in which forms of male power, along with the relations of class and race, have been shaped and reaffirmed in political institutions and structures.[4] Building on the insights of feminist historians, we may begin to uncover the heretofore unseen dimension of masculinity in political discourse and the influence of conceptions of political power on the formation of ideals of masculinity. By examining language, we uncover both past struggles to fix meanings to masculinity and the power relations embedded in the concept. As Scott has argued, 'gender is one of the recurrent references by which political power has been conceived, legitimated, and criticised.'[5]

Historians of Upper Canadian politics in the period between the War of 1812 and the Rebellion of 1837 have pinpointed certain issues that provided a focus for political divisions within the colony. Robert Gourlay's calls for economic and political reform in the late 1800s, the alien question and union with Lower Canada in the 1820s, and the question of responsible government and the colony's relationship to Britain have been treated as significant landmarks in colonial political developments. The formation of political parties or factions with some unifying principles, loosely known as reform and conservative, also has been the subject of a great deal of historical inquiry, especially as this development related to demands for responsible government.

In recent years some historians have argued for a more nuanced understanding of political divisions, questioning the rigidity of the labels 'reform' and 'conservative.' Paul Romney, for one, has pointed to the political beliefs and career of Charles Fothergill, a 'conservative reformer' who associated with William Warren Baldwin and John Rolph in the 1820s but who disagreed with their definition of responsible government; in the late 1830s Fothergill was an outspoken opponent of the Family Compact. Graeme Patterson has pointed to variations within the ranks of those who advocated responsible government, arguing that the term carried a number of meanings, including the responsibility of the administration to the elected legislature as well as the colonial government's accountability to its imperial masters. The career of Francis Collins, the Irish-born newspaper editor who managed to be both an outspoken advocate of freedom of the press and an opponent of reformers William Lyon Mackenzie and Jesse Ketchum and the Methodist leader Egerton Ryerson, is yet another example of the complexities of colonial politics.[6] Those we might characterize as conservatives were far from being a monolithic group. As S.F. Wise has demonstrated, neither Strachan nor Robinson spoke for all who were opposed to reformers, nor was the definition of conservative static and unchanging throughout the colony's history.[7]

Nevertheless, for our purposes, broad-based categories of reform and conservative are relevant; the finer distinctions noted by Romney, Patterson, and Wise are less applicable in considering the gendered languages of political discourses. Less relevant, too, in this context are the arguments made by Romney that cast doubt on the use of 'court' and 'country' as a means of characterizing Upper Canadian political cultures and deepening our understanding of 'reform' and 'conservative.' Certainly Romney's point – that more meaningful lenses through which Ontario politics may be examined are those of constitutionalism and legalism – is well-taken, insofar as it applies to both the '*longue durée*' of provincial politics and the specific political-legal arenas of his study.[8]

Yet in examining political discourses, I wish to propose that historians must also alter their paradigms and take on a new hermeneutical framework. As American historian Carroll Smith-Rosenberg has argued in her study of postrevolutionary debates over citizenship, if historians wish to understand the links between politics and culture, they must begin to examine not just formal constitutions but also 'the *constitution* of new political subjects'; they 'must move from political theory to cultural theory, from the history of political ideas to the history of political *rhetoric.*' In doing so, historians will become 'doubly visioned,' enriching 'one form of analysis with the insights of another.'[9] In shifting to political rhetoric and debate, to the examination of insult and invective common to the colonial press, it is clear that the terms court and country were frequently used tropes, discursive devices that spoke to the collective historical memories of those Upper Canadians who participated in political debates. These terms were not merely descriptions of eighteenth-century British political culture that bore only tenuous meanings for Upper Canadian politics. Upper Canadians who participated in political debates found them to be a way of contesting authority, establishing legitimacy, and, in this process, claiming virtue and morality.

Colonial politics had never been completely peaceful, but political debate intensified in the years after the War of 1812. In the decade before the war, controversies had erupted over the operation of the constitution, the relationship between the legislature and the executive, and the role of the judiciary. These kinds of conflicts, often based in York and Kingston, found their way into the pages of the local newspapers, along with disputes over electoral candidates' fitness for public office. The growth of newspapers in the colony after the war (from one in 1813 to seven in 1824) meant that participants in political discourse not only grew in numbers but also began to vary the kinds of political languages used. Although the secular newspapers studied here still devoted approximately one-third to one-half of their columns to international news, Upper Canadian developments became increasingly important. From the early 1820s on, colonial newspapers were the sites of vigorous discussions about domestic issues of importance to Upper Canadians; the press provided coverage of political debates both inside and out of the legislature, as well as editorial comments, letters, pieces of political satire, and other articles on colonial politics. Furthermore, while newspapers provide the historian with the most extensive coverage of colonial political debates, the smaller body of pamphlet and sermon literature written in Upper Canada also contributed to political discourses.

Linked to the growth of the colonial press was the growing tide of British immigration to the colony in the years after the Napoleonic Wars. Although it did not reach its height until the 1840s, the arrival of emigrants from England, Scotland, and Ireland provided a new cast of participants for the political arena, helping to create sharper divisions between conservatives and reformers and, as part of this process, supplying the colony with a small, yet extremely vocal, reform press. Debate intensified about matters in the colony, beginning with Robert Gourlay and reaching its zenith over reform in the 1830s.

A scientific farmer and reformer from Scotland, Gourlay arrived in the colony in 1817. He decided to 'establish a grand system of assisted emigration' and to conduct a statistical account of the province. In order to achieve both, Gourlay distributed questionnaires to the townships. Although the bulk of the questionnaire aimed at gathering information about agricultural and other material conditions, it ended by asking settlers what, in their opinion, was holding back improvements in the colony and what might be done to rectify matters. It was the last two questions that alarmed colonial officials, concerned with the extent of unrest following the end of the war and worried that Gourlay might be stirring up disaffected colonists. The fact that residents began to hold township meetings in order to discuss their replies did little to allay their fears. In 1818 Gourlay was charged with seditious libel in Kingston and Cornwall. Although he was twice acquitted by juries, his public attacks in the *Niagara Spectator* on the government led to a third arrest in December. On 20 August 1819 Gourlay was brought to trial at Niagara, having been kept in the town's jail since January. This time, the jury found for the Crown, and Gourlay was banished from Upper Canada, a sentence that was put into effect the next day.[10]

Gourlay's attempts to introduce agrarian and then political reform ignited a political hornets' nest and brought out various assumptions, perceptions, and assertions concerning the nature of participation in political life. Such political controversy was not entirely unknown to Gourlay, whose contemporaries had included the British radicals Henry Hunt and William Cobbett. Gourlay had left England just after the Spa Fields Riots, thus missing the start of the state's sedition prosecutions.[11] His political opponents missed few opportunities to draw upon his links to radicalism (regardless of how relevant these connections were to his activities in the colony). Opposition to Gourlay and his supporters concentrated on their threat to political and social stability and on the special nature of the connection between colony and 'Parent State.' Very little (in fact, almost none) of this political rhetoric looked specifically at Gourlay's plans for Upper Canada; a newcomer to colonial politics would have learned little from the conservative press about the content of the Gourlayite schemes. Instead, editorials, letters, and unsigned articles dealt mainly with personality and style. Gourlay himself and his methods of political agitation were the villains of this political drama.

Discontent and political upheaval were the worst fears of Gourlay's opponents. Although reluctant to grant Gourlay too much importance – preferring to dismiss him as simply an 'unhappy Bedlamite'[12] or ridiculing him as a 'Scotch Don Quixote'[13] – his detractors remained uneasy about the extent of the threat he and his supporters represented to political stability. Even though opponents contended that madness lurked behind Gourlay's motives, doing their best to portray his challenge as that of an individual, not a well-supported movement, the fear of things larger than one man's questionnaires was never completely absent. 'The excitement to discontent,' according to a writer for the *Upper Canada Gazette*, 'is a madman sidling ... about the country, with his pockets crammed with ready-manufactured petitions and lists of grievances.'[14] In their address to the lieutenant-governor, Sir Francis Gore, the inhabitants of Ernest Town Township protested their loyalty and described Gourlay's work as 'the malevolent intrigues of a political adventurer' who had 'seduced a number of our inhabitants.'[15] 'A man of desperate fortune,' declared the author of a 'Letter to Upper Canada,' Gourlay was an 'adventurer,' an 'active enemy of the Mother Country.' With him came the spectre of 'national conventions, a name which every European ear still admits with horror.'[16] Attempts to play down the threat posed by Gourlay were undermined by a competing desire to expose the foreign-based dangers that lurked behind him.

In this aspect of political discourse, Gourlay came to personify not just reform but revolution, symbolizing both past and ongoing upheavals in England and Europe. The township meetings that he had instigated passed resolutions that were, according to 'An Old Inhabitant' in a dialogue with 'Squire McGuin,' 'made by such idle and discontented people as meet together and call themselves a numerous and respectable body.'[17] For C. Stuart, writing to the *Niagara Spectator* in July 1819 in defence of the 'Gagging Law,' it was all too clear what Gourlay's activities would bring. 'Behold the demagogue and his partizan, seated in their newly adopted hall of power. All the corrupt and blind and for a time, perhaps some of the nobler passions support them. But all that is truly noble soon fails. They go on to canvass, to legislate, and to act, the regular bulwarks of the constitution fall before them ... [N]ew statutes and new duties ... a new order of things arises, probably through a course of anarchy, contention, and bloodshed ... Canadians, No!'[18] Similar feelings were expressed in an article taken from the *Montreal Herald* by the *Niagara Gleaner*. Asking whether

Gourlay could be so 'totally ignorant of mankind as not to know the danger of an assembly actuated by feeling alone, where reason is trampled underfoot', the author raised the spectre of 'scenes of anarchy and confusion' and criticized Gourlay's 'diabolical intention' in creating this chaos.[19]

A man who had lost both mental and moral control could no longer claim the status of 'manliness' and the social and political privileges that flowed from such a position. Moreover, in justifying their position, Gourlay's opponents were anxious that readers appreciate the fundamental political and moral difference between themselves and the Gourlayites: their loyalty to Britain and to the Crown. As we have seen, staking out loyalty was not unique in Upper Canadian political discourse, and loyalty would continue to be the nucleus of many political debates. The conservatives who trumpeted their loyalty to British institutions and their opposition to Gourlay did so by emphasizing filial ties, ones inherited through Upper Canadian traditions (the Loyalists and the War of 1812) and embedded in a matrix of history, virtue, and morality. In this matrix the meaning of these ties was stable and known, unlike the anarchic and shifting world of the unknown represented by Gourlay. Such ties were represented by the link between parents and children and the security this bond engendered. Sometimes the metaphor of family was implicit, as in the Ernest Town Township residents' address declaring that the 'protecting arm' of the government 'has ever been extended for our comfort and security.' In his reply to a similar address from the inhabitants of Glengarry County, Lieutenant-Governor Gore described the 'virtues that ennobled their ancestors ... their brotherly attachment to each other, their love of order and instruction, and for their principled submission to the laws and government of their country.'[20] Although anxious to alert readers to the evils of reform, C. Stuart also reminded them of good government's need for stability and morality. 'If you wish to be more free and happy than you are, break off your own vices. Look to the word of God primarily for your rule, and seek, more and more, and all things, to evince to it your cheerful and entire obedience ... [L]et all revelling, all violence, all spirit of party be then especially far from you, be not guided in your choice [of assembly members] by passion, or selfishness, or interest, or apprehension ... In your own families, be serious, affectionate, candid, and peaceable ... [A]void and repel every approach to turbulence.'[21] Aside from Strachan in his *Loyal Sermon*, Stuart was one of the few participants in this aspect of political discourse to use the family and its link to government so explicitly, not just as a symbol but as the very site of political morality and obedience, the place where these virtues would be inculcated.

After Gourlay's imprisonment, trial, and banishment from the colony, the *Upper Canada Gazette* ran a loyalist poem, 'John Bull and his Mother – Song for the Radicals,' which, while probably picked up from a British source, crystallized various aspects of Upper Canadian conservatism. John Bull, an eighteenth-century 'mouthpiece' for nationalist propaganda as well as satirical attacks on officialdom, was, in this period, an icon of conservative opposition to the French Revolution.[22] This particular poem held him up as the archetypal 'industrious, honest, and brave' Briton and, while proposing a toast to his health, also celebrated 'Britannia, his mother' to whom he owed his education (loyalty to king, church, and nation) and secure position in British society. Honest toil at 'plough and loom' was extolled, as was a social system that relegated some to the status of 'lords and ladies' and some to that of 'clodhoppers,' thereby guaranteeing stability of government and adequate agricultural production. Equality, levelling, and the 'rights of man' would only lead to widespread starvation. 'Half-naked and starved in the streets / Were we wandering sans-culottes / Would liberty find us in meat / Or equality lengthen our coats?'[23]

This symbol of the 'mother country,' along with others such as John Barleycorn and Peter Ploughboy, was evoked from time to time in other conservative newspapers. The colonial context in which these symbols were claimed meant, though, that certain aspects of this imagery might have had a slightly different meaning than in their original setting, with different temporal and geopolitical referents. Celebrations of an agrarian-based society with a hierarchical structure were dualistic: they spoke of Upper Canadians' hopes for the future but also of the existing example of the mother country whose past was used to justify such hopes. Furthermore, the French 'bogeyman' invoked in British propaganda had less immediate resonance in the Upper Canadian context after the Napoleonic Wars. The starving 'sans-culottes' could be decoded, though, to signify the republicans south of the border, proof of the depredations of levelling theories.

With what sort of political discourse did these editors and letter-writers contend? How did Gourlay and his supporters fix meanings to, and claim legitimacy for, their political ideas and activities? Admittedly, Gourlay's concerns were primarily with land and not with political reform in the province: he viewed Upper Canada as an area ideally suited for the emigration of the British poor. Yet his plans for economic and social reform obliged him to confront the province's political structure and the men who controlled it.[24] In this confrontation, Gourlay and his supporters employed in the province's press a language that affirmed their masculinity and fitness to act as men in political affairs and attacked that of their opponents, a language in which gender helped to channel political discourse more explicitly than in that of their conservative critics. At times Gourlay examined the norms that delineated public and private behaviour, frequently addressing the question of public and private voices and activities. In an angry letter to his erstwhile friend and relative Thomas Clark, published in the *Kingston Gazette* on 31 March 1818, Gourlay pointed to the boundaries of the public and private that had been negotiated by men in political life: 'You accuse me of exposing the President, but why should he not be exposed, in his public capacity? Enquire into the practices of our first statesmen at home, and you will find that, as public men, they abuse each other like pick-pockets, and the very next day crack a bottle together in the utmost conviviality of private friendship.'[25] In another letter at the end of that summer, addressed to his nemesis 'The Traveller,' Gourlay burst out angrily against the conventions that dictated his silence when he felt that his honour was at stake. According to Gourlay, John Strachan had attacked him in private, and his public response to these attacks had been criticized by 'The Traveller.' 'What miserable weakness is it, to think that after all this I must say nothing against such a character, merely because he never attacked me in print! I must wait, forsooth, and be attacked by the Traveller, and all sorts of blockheads, who cannot write without losing their wits in phrenzy [*sic*] – I must wait until this little fellow Strachan, stuffed into one of the compartments of my brain, to kick and sprawl, till his Reverence is delivered by a man-midwife, and then pled for as a persecuted thing – a piteous "antagonist," a miserable, misbegotten manuculus to whom nothing but the milk of human kindness should be administered.'[26]

Gourlay frequently addressed the question of public and private voices and activities. Men should not be allowed to hide behind anonymity or the fiction of privacy when attacking the character or politics of other men who were themselves acting in a public manner for the public good. When they did so, they became less than full adult men – piteous, miserable, misbegotten antagonists – and to ignore their attacks was a 'miserable weakness.' For Gourlay, strategies such as anonymity were not polite means of defusing the personal nature of political debates and lessening its acrimonious tone; instead, they were deceptions, rhetorical masks that evoked the world of courtly hypocrisy. 'The Traveller' and his use of a pseudonym came in for his fair share of attacks. 'In his character of Traveller, [he] is not known to the public; he is unseen; he is nothing but an unfeeling man of straw. Before the public, on the contrary, I stand open to view; – a real personage, not for myself, but for the public weal.' Gourlay called upon 'The

Traveller' to 'lay aside timidity, and false pride. Example is better than precept, and the Canadians will soon get over the sin which most easily besets
them, when they see the Traveller walking before them a real man, and rid
of all maiden bashfulness.' To this end, Gourlay proposed that the two of
them meet at a specified time and place in Niagara and canvass for subscribers 'in aid of the great public cause. Every man will then be liberal;
every woman will smile on us for love of the Traveller.'[27] Those men who
wished to engage in public political issues must be prepared to do so as
public citizens in order to be perceived as men.

Furthermore, they had to embody a specific kind of manliness. Despite
his detractors' claims that he preached insurrection and sedition, Gourlay
insisted that only those who were true patriots and lovers of the British
connection should come to his township meetings. 'I address myself particularly to Land-Owners because their interests are most deeply involved;
but every man resident in Canada – every man who is a lover of peace –
who desires to see this country independent of the United States – who
desires to see a worthy connection maintained between this Province and
Britain: every man in short who has a spark of sincerity or patriotism in his
soul, has now sufficient cause to bestir himself.'[28] In Gourlay's political
vision, no militia or imperial might was needed in order to keep the province loyal, nor was the Loyalist sacrifice of the 1780s or of the War of 1812
the only measure of political commitment. 'Honest men,' acting 'as brothers, in unity' were the political basis for a settlement of land problems, the
maintenance of the British connection, and social and economic prosperity.
Despite the present degraded state of affairs, 'British blood ... will learn to
flow again, and, yet sustain, on its rising tide, that generous, – that noble –
that manly spirit, which first called forth applause from the admiring
world.'[29] And – possibly as a result of his observation of state violence in
Britain itself – 'British blood' could flow in a noble and, above all, peaceful
fashion, vindicating British manhood in the colony. It did not need to be
shed on the battlefield in order to demonstrate its worth.

As Gourlay pointed out, the individual man could not single-handedly
rescue Upper Canada. Fraternal organization, in the form of political
unions, was the most effective cure for the province's ills and one that he
hoped would appeal to all. Gourlay's call for these unions attempted to
transcend divisions between men by appealing to the 'manly spirit' that he
believed would unite all men in the political realm. He constructed the
political man first as the individual, propelled by his own spirit and moral
conscience, a propulsion that caused him to merge with other men and
form a like-minded fraternity. This fraternity embodied 'that manly spirit'

Gourlay so warmly admired: a unified spirit whose singularity gave it the strength to bring about enduring political change.[30]

Yet it was not only an emphasis on the individual male as a political being and the efficacy of male political virtue that distinguished Gourlay's discourse and foreshadowed that of the reformers of the 1820s and 1830s. His assertion of manliness was premised on the unmanliness of his opponents. The insults and taunts used by Gourlay and his supporters in the press revealed the opposite side of the patriotic, upstanding, and virtuous man and exposed an 'other' that underpinned their conceptions of true manliness.[31] This 'other,' this unmanly man, was created in images drawn from Commonwealth language: a luxury-loving, degraded, and immoral creature, dependent on favour. Economic and political reforms were needed to save Upper Canada from the pernicious influences of sycophants, tyrants, placemen, and slaves. If, Gourlay replied in a letter to 'The Traveller,' absentee landholders and clergy reserves were allowed to continue until all the land was cleared, occupied, and rented, 'the rents would sustain a host of idle people placemen and intolerant priests ... [T]he evil influences, both moral and political, generated by such a system, are far more to be dreaded. They would introduce into the country domineering wealth, and cringing poverty, proud looks and bowing sycophancy, tyrants, and slaves.'[32] All these were men who had, in Gourlay's eyes, lost their claim on true manhood. They might be bound to one another, but not by the ties of manly freedom, virtue, and independence that linked Gourlay's archetypes. Nor did he concede the kinds of filial bonds that his opponents wished to claim. Instead, he perceived these men as chained by weakness, dishonour, deceit, pride, and ambition in a web of dependence, the antithesis of political fraternalism. In a letter to the editor of the *Niagara Spectator*, Gourlay contrasted the political places and processes that exemplified the activities of different types of men. 'If there is a scene upon earth on which the eye of Providence beams with peculiar love and approbation, it must be that where a free people assembled together for the purpose of raising to honor him whose individual merit has won their regard and confidence. If, again, there is a scene wherein the Devil makes himself particularly busy, I should think it lay within the purlieus of a court, when every selfish and filthy desire could be instigated to the utmost in making interest for the appointment of a provincial governor.'[33] 'Courtly' behaviour and the subsequent perversion of the political process were not limited to the governor's appointment. Gourlay claimed that C. Stuart might be a 'lineal descendant' of James II, with his 'bowing to and flattering' Sir Peregrine Maitland, the lieutenant-governor, all the while 'bursting with a passion ... beyond his control.'[34]

Yet, at times, Gourlay hoped that systems of government, not men, would become the subject of political debate. 'Your Members of Assembly are now at home: compare their characters with those around them, and you will find them equally honest – equally wise – equally independent. Now, that they are returned to society, as private individuals, I should be the very last man to call in question their worth or their probity: they are probably every way above par. It is not the men, it is the system which blasts every hope of good; and, till the system is overturned, it is vain to expect any thing of value from change of Representatives of Government.'[35] Gourlay was not alone in this belief: 'Publicola,' who wrote to the *Gazette* on 30 June 1818 in his support, declared his exasperation with the 'fuss' made about Gourlay's character. 'Canadians, the destinies of your country hang not upon the character of Mr. Gourlay, no – they hang upon the character of its Government. The character of Mr. Gourlay concerns nobody but himself, and his immediate connections, therefore need not, and ought not to be canvassed by the public, but the character of the Government concerns every British subject in the world, and ought at all times to be rigidly examined, severely criticized, for if it be bad, this is the only way to mend it, and if it be good, it is the only way to preserve it so.' Listing the accusations hurled at Gourlay – 'unprincipled, a revolutionist, a spendthrift, reedy adventurer, suspicious character' – 'Publicola' declared that his detractor had missed the point. 'Let him be all this, and more, nay let him be the vilest compound that God even permitted to tread the earth in human form, still if he preach Righteousness, let him be heard.'[36]

Despite these attempts to focus on governments and not the men who ran them, Gourlay himself consistently fell back upon the latter and their public morals. Admittedly, he venerated the British constitution, 'that beautiful contrivance by which the people, when perfectly virtuous, shall become all powerful' and in doing so drew upon the language of late-seventeenth- and eighteenth-century whig or Commonwealth interpretations of the constitution as the safeguard of liberty. However, Gourlay also suggested that, although virtue was necessary, it was not the sole ingredient for successful government: the matter came back to those men who could exercise virtue and use the constitution correctly. 'The British constitution has provided for its own improvement, in peace and quietness; it has given us the right of petitioning the Prince or Parliament, and, this right, exercised in a proper manner, is competent to satisfy every virtuous desire ... As Individuals, we have a right to petition the Prince or Parliament of Britain; and, we have a right to meet for this purpose in collective bodies.'[37]

Gourlay's discussion of petitioning left open the possibility that women,

Natives, and unenfranchised men might act as political citizens, since petitioning was a more widely available form of political participation than voting – one that, as Gail Campbell has pointed out, was engaged in by women in other British North American colonies.[38] However, the reports of the township meetings, printed in a variety of Upper Canadian newspapers from this period (*Kingston Gazette, Niagara Spectator, Upper Canada Gazette*) list only one woman, Hannah Secord, a subscriber in Niagara Township.[39] Gourlay had constructed collective organization as the activity of virtuous and independent British men, either with land or with some stake in it. It was collective organization by such men (with the exception of the vilified absentee landholders) that was the foundation of his program for effective political, economic, and social change. This particular vision of reform, and the language in which it was couched, left little room for those who could not exploit this type of political legitimacy to stake out a claim to political citizenship.

The 1820s saw the development of political discourses that relied more and more upon gender, the family, and differing concepts of public and private. Political discourses were not 'just about' gender and the family, nor were they 'just about' Burkean versus Lockean theories of government. One set of constructs informed the other. While the latter has received more attention from historians and political theorists, careful attention to the 'other' portions of these political texts, those that have been repressed and marginalized, opens up new readings and meanings.

One of the most striking themes in conservative writings about political affairs was that of self-restraint and control: the political man as a rational, civilized creature, one governed by reason. Like the Christian soldier of 1812, it was the self-controlled man who would protect the state and social order. Sometimes, conservative actors and principles were represented directly as men and their opponents as women. In the *Weekly Register and Upper Canada Gazette*'s 'Front Page Exchange' of 25 January 1823, 'One Hundred Miles From the Metropolis,' Mrs Slipslop, 'an old gossiping politician,' discussed the Throne Speech with Mr Canada, 'a plain, sensible, well-informed man.' The conversation between them focused on ministerial attitudes toward union with Lower Canada, ones that Mrs Slipslop declared to be 'ambiguous,' as the government brought the issue forward but had no 'interest' in union. By dint of a superior command of both language and political sensibility, Mr Canada led her on ingenuously to declare her faith in 'one who is labouring so hard by night and by day, for your benefit; with a view to open your eyes to the enormities of folks in power.' Having thus induced her to expose her simplistic grasp of terms such as interest and ambiguity in the political arena, Mr Canada had the final word, lecturing Mrs Slipslop on the use of criticism, 'a dangerous weapon in the hands of an ignorant and an illiterate person.'[40] Gender, of course, is apparent in this passage, which juxtaposed feminine foolishness and flightiness with solid, reasoned male judgment and exposed criticism of government policy as mere ephemera. This binary opposition of male and female was also used to parcel up a number of other cultural traits. Mr Canada was able to control their discussion and invoke its closure not only because of his rational nature but also because of his learning, using his knowledge of Samuel Johnson's *Dictionary* to point to Mrs Slipslop's faulty understanding of her own terms.[41] In contrast with his self-control, she was 'all of a titter (shaking hysterically)' and needed, in his words, 'the little bottle which you keep in your closet.'[42] In this piece of political satire, the targets were not women per se, although there was a lesson to learn about female participation in political life. This and other articles used either the figure of a woman or characteristics that, in the cultural lexicon of eighteenth- and early-nineteenth-century Britain, had become identified with femininity. Excesses of emotion leading to hysteria, the abandonment of rational, logical thinking, and the encroachment of previously inviolate boundaries: all were pressed into the service of political insult and the denigration of a particular political perspective.[43]

Conservatives frequently painted themselves as sensible, honest men combatting forces that were either innately hysterical or would lead to the release of emotions that threatened political and moral stability. This aspect of conservative discourse was, of course, not new or unique to Upper Canada, but its *gendered* nature has received little attention from historians. Identifying their opponents with the forces of hysteria and excessive emotion shored up conservative claims to be men of honour, respectability, and morality. The *Weekly Register and Upper Canada Gazette*'s editorial of 24 February 1825 'endeavour[ed] to show how far many honest, well-disposed yeomanry of this country are sullied and imposed upon by this ranting, raving, moon-struck, envious, malignant, Scottish renegade, under the pretense of advocating their rights.'[44] During a panic over the alien bill in July 1827, reports in the *Colonial Advocate* and *Canadian Freeman* about the purported arrival of troops led the *Gazette* to lay countercharges of 'demagoguery,' labelling these reports the wild, unbalanced attacks of rabble rousers. However, the *Gazette*'s editor assured his readers, 'the people of this Province are the scions of a loyal Tory stock' accustomed to meeting such challenges.[45] As political debate intensified throughout the

1820s, so did the frequency of these insults. The arrest in 1829 of the publisher of the *Canadian Freeman*, Francis Collins, prompted the *Kingston Chronicle*'s editor to declare his support for the authorities and disgust for Collins' supporters.

No man who had any respect for the authority of the law, or who esteemed good order in society as of any value or even desirable would feel otherwise than gratified to see so gross an offender suffer the just punishment ... [S]trangely, enough, men are to be found who maintain different sentiments. A seditious society composed of a parcel of insane political charlatans, denominated *'Friends of the Liberty of the Press'*!!! whose real object, if they possessed manliness enough to avow it, is, to place the press above all law, and thereby secure impunity to certain base conductors of it, in their infamous trade of calumny, on the most upright and eminent men in the colony, against whom these contemptible creatures, for obvious reasons, entertain the most inveterate hatred.[46]

The behaviour and persona of the journalist and reform politician, William Lyon Mackenzie, attracted the greatest number of political attacks. Mackenzie, according to 'John Bull' in the *Niagara Gleaner*, pitched his 'editorial drivelings [*sic*] to the worst passions of the worst classes of the community in order to gain that foetid popularity which steams from the political brothel of a prostituted press.' This image of Mackenzie as a purveyor of sexual immorality and filth apparently was not enough for 'Bull,' who went on to state that he had 'poisoned' the public mind and, full of 'egregious vanity and selfishness,' revelled in the luxury of calumny and falsehood.[47] When Mackenzie was expelled from the Legislative Assembly in 1833, the *Patriot and Farmers' Monitor*, a vocally antireform and anti-Methodist paper, described his behaviour as that of a 'madman,' who 'stamped and raved with all the fury of a maniac.'[48] Such attacks were very similar to the charges of an unmanly loss of mental control levied at Gourlay; a man who lost emotional control was not entitled to masculine privileges and prerogatives.

Collins's attacks on Mackenzie in the early 1830s accused him of that most effeminate and, ironically, 'courtly' sin: the vanity of wearing a hairpiece. In the language of Upper Canadian reformers, all things connected with the world of the court, with an aristocracy unresponsive to the British people, and with an oligarchy that supported standing armies, high taxation, and infrequent elections, were synonymous with effeminacy and tyranny. While Collins might have opposed the strategies and behaviour of Mackenzie and his cohorts, his satires on Mackenzie's wig were written to expose him as a hypocrite, a 'false reformer' whose wearing of a wig indicated all too clearly that his espousal of reform was nothing but a ploy to advance his own career. Ostensibly a 'man of the people,' this wearer of a red wig was in fact a mere seeker of social status, hoping to become precisely that which he criticized so loudly: a 'courtly' whig, possibly of the mid-eighteenth-century Walpolean stamp, who stood less for parliamentary and press liberties and more for censorship and absolutism.[49] No virtuous and honest man could approve of the 'knight of the red wig's' behaviour, Collins declared in January 1832.[50]

Over time, the 'Morgan wig,' as Collins dubbed it, took on heightened symbolism and multiple meanings. The hairpiece signified Mackenzie's unmanly vanity and his delusions of grandeur, particularly his belief that he represented the people of the colony. But it also was the epitome of fashionable hypocrisy, as it could be worn or doffed at a moment's notice, thus changing its wearer's appearance depending on his audience. The wig allowed Mackenzie to hide his lack of hair, but it also symbolized his ability to hide his true motives, fostering his deception of the colonial electorate. Mackenzie's London excursions, in May 1832, to present reform grievances to the Colonial Office, saw him accompanied by the 'Morgan wig,' as well as the 'gingerbread medal' he had received from supporters on his re-election to the legislature.[51] In November, however, the wig 'in his own absence, was returned, in preference to Mr. Small,' although 'it is probable that a new question may yet arise – namely, whether Mackenzie's wig is a fit representative for this country.' Collins was of the opinion that eventually the electorate would realize 'that after all they have done and said, a wig is nothing but a wig.'[52] Upon Mackenzie's return to the colony, Collins noted that he had exchanged the 'Morgan wig in London, for a new one, in Bashaw fashion, with two tails' – a clear sign that he had become even more pretentious and was now aspiring to the antithesis of British manliness. But a 'whig' could also represent folly, as Collins concluded with a poem from the Gore Gazette that played upon the theme of 'wigs' and 'whigs.' Here Mackenzie and other Upper Canadian reformers were equated with the worst excesses of religious hysteria and gullibility, those personified by the female visionary, Joanna Southcott.

Those brainless dolts with empty skull
Who love the ragamuffin's lore
Con all his ribald page's o'er
And call themselves reformers true
And Whigs, tho' of the noodle crew

(Weak as the followers of Southcott)
Who on Mackenzie's red wig dote.[53]

Excessive displays of emotion, the inability to maintain self-control, immorality (reformers were also accused of attempting to 'seduce' Upper Canadians), and irreligion: all of these gendered insults combined to construct reform as a potential maelstrom of feminized and debauched evil. To be sure, reformers were generally not accused of sexual immorality per se. Although he had fathered an illegitimate child in Scotland, neither Mackenzie nor his supporters were said to follow in the footsteps of the eighteenth-century radical John Wilkes.[54] But, in a society in which the symbol of unleashed feminine sexuality could trigger great fears about social and political stability, accusations of such behaviour were important weapons. Reformers were thus bent on the destruction of the moral fabric of colonial society, men who threw off all ties to society and worked merely for their own selfish, individualistic ends. This unfettered and rampaging individualism, this undoing of social bonds and responsibilities necessary for civilized society, not only differentiated the reformer from the 'respectable gentleman,' it also allowed adversaries to depict 'the reformer' as a subhuman, animalistic creature, using images of the less-appealing members of the animal kingdom. 'He sits like an owl with a fish-hook nose and great goggle eyes, and gives a hebdomadal scream to the unclean beasts who approach his haunts,' wrote 'A Contented Canadian' to the *Niagara Gleaner*, describing the *Cobourg Reformer*'s editor.[55] The *Patriot and Farmers' Monitor*, never a paper to pass up political controversy, printed letters from 'Nicolas' in 1834 that called Mackenzie the 'Weasel' and, using the language of demonology, suggested that he might be the Devil's familiar.[56] The paper's editor, denigrating Mackenzie's behaviour in the assembly, likened his debates to the wanderings of 'the hungry raven after fresh prey.'[57] Reformers sometimes retaliated in kind: a favourite characterization of Mackenzie by his supporters was the 'little terrier' who persisted in his fight against the hounds of officialdom.[58]

Like earlier attacks on Gourlay, conservative discourse in the 1820s and 1830s emphasized the destruction of family ties that reform would bring, using 'family' either in the immediate, more literal sense or as a metaphor for the 'family' of the empire. Much was made of the 'rights of Englishmen' or the 'sturdy yeoman,' terms that, as we shall see, reformers also favoured. Yet the concept of family was tied to these terms and was brought into political discourse to underscore and legitimate them. 'A Converted Alien' wrote to the *United Empire Loyalist and Upper Canada Gazette* in July

1827 to protest the effects of 'the representations of some artful and design-
ing men, who, under the cloak of friendships, have caused the aged parent,
the widow and orphan to mourn and shudder at the sad fate which they
were informed awaited them.' 'So strong has the alien cry been kept up by
a set of factious persons, that many an ignorant, but well-disposed person,
would tremble at the idea of being shortly, with his family and dependents,
turned from his property on the wide world.'[59] Here the family was
besieged, needlessly made anxious about the future by unscrupulous men.
Using the concept of family in a slightly different manner, 'John Barleycorn' characterized Barnabas Bidwell, an American-born member of the
Legislative Assembly, as hypocritical and treacherous. 'The country and
Government under which we have been brought up are naturally dear to
us; as a child loves his parent, so a good subject reveres his country and his
King ... Was it not the vivid light of allegiance that shewed to a Nelson the
paths of glory, through the deep; and that now plays over his tomb, to
guide our sons to the same honourable career?'[60] 'Barleycorn' wrapped up
Upper Canadian loyalty and opposition to incipient American republicanism in terms that united both British and patriarchal authority. Reformers'
subversion of the two was usually depicted metaphorically as a challenge to
the filial, paternal tie that bound Upper Canadians to their royal father.

Occasionally, reformers were accused of a more direct usurpation of
paternal authority. In a letter to the editor of the Niagara Spectator, Robert Jeffers complained that his underaged son had been induced to sign a
reform petition without Jeffers' 'knowledge or consent.' Arguing that his
child was his property, especially with regard to the 'exercise of his bodily
or mental powers,' Jeffers called for the passage of a law that would 'inflict
heavy fines for persuading children to disobey patriarchal authority.' Concerned lest his power be further eroded, Jeffers argued that a father's
authority should be extended. 'Ladies should not become masculine –
should not have their attention diverted away from those maternal offices –
those tender assiduities which qualify them to infuse the drop of comfort
into man's bitter cup.' The editor agreed with Jeffers and, pleased that he
spoke out against the petition, hoped 'that all fathers of families in the
Province will take advantage of a hint so opportunely and forcibly given.'[61]
Although Jeffers' was a lone voice, his jeremiad raises some tantalizing
questions about the sexual and familial politics of petitioning and about the
role of political differences in the households of Upper Canada. Were
women solicited as petitioners, or did some women actively support
reformers at the local level? Women's absence from the petitions published
in the press should not lead us to assume that they were not interested in

political affairs. More likely, women were excluded from certain forms of public records of political discourse. The editorial support given to Jeffers suggests that day-to-day family harmony was threatened by the political differences within the home.

If a patriarchal version of the family was valued and inscribed in conservative discourses, their distinctions between public and private were rather more ambiguous. As in the language of patriotism, delineations between these two 'realms' were hazy and slippery, despite some conservatives' attempts to separate them. The *Upper Canada Gazette* and *Patriot and Farmers' Monitor* were particularly fond of images and metaphors that merged both areas to highlight the iniquity of reform. An editorial that protested Mackenzie's journalistic ethics decried the possibility that he 'or any other unprincipled scribbler may take advantage of an acknowledgment ... to a correspondent, and, by making sue of the same signature, father, by insinuation, the most infamous conclusions.' Branding him a 'caterer of loathsome food for depraved appetites,' the paper hoped that he would find other work 'in a more honest livelihood than that which may be picked up from the broad and filthy highway of public detraction, or from the darker purlieus of private assassination.'[62] Responding to an attack on Henry Boulton by James King, the editor of the reform paper *The Correspondent*, the *Patriot* argued that reformers' ingratitude towards Boulton would be celebrated in a 'hellish orgy.' A 'multitude of Devils,' seated around a table and toasting their own 'particular vices,' applauded 'the shaggy Beelzebub' who led them in a triumphant salute to 'INGRATITUDE!'[63] This characterization of reformers as devils celebrating their evil triumphs at the banqueting table linked sexual licence and viciousness to their political personas. The passage also reversed one of the most popular press images of Upper Canadian male celebrations of loyalty: the members of various nationalist, political, or voluntary societies seated at a similar table, toasting such luminaries as the monarch, lieutenant-governor, the military, or political figures.[64]

Conservatives, moreover, were fond of pointing out that none of these élite figures or their families were safe from the reformers' personal libels and slanders, especially those of Mackenzie. In an altercation in 1826 between Samuel Jarvis, the son of the prominent York conservative family, and Mackenzie over Jarvis's killing of Thomas Ridout in an 1817 duel, Jarvis insisted that Mackenzie and Collins had subjected respectable citizens to personal attacks. In his *Statement of Facts, Relating to the Trespass, on the Printing Press, in the Possession of Mr. William Lyon Mackenzie, in June 1826,* Jarvis depicted York as a peaceful town before their arrivals, a town where 'many of our townswomen – aged and respectable mothers of families, had arrived on the verge of life, without having been distressed and insulted by having their names bandied about, with the coarsest abuse, in the columns of newspapers – Many of our Townsmen had here, as in all other countries, risen to independence and to respectability in character and circumstances, by their own exertions, without having drawn upon them, by their prosperity, the envy of malignant spirits – without having their wives and mothers, their daughters and sisters, and even their grand-mothers, insulted and spoken of, with coarse and unfeeling influence, in newspapers industriously circulated throughout the province.'[65] The wounded women of York being directly insulted by reformers was a recurring theme throughout this pamphlet, which had been written in response to Mackenzie's 'Patrick Swift' columns. Even when complaining about the personal nature of Mackenzie's abuse, Jarvis felt the worst aspect of this attack was its effect on his wife and children, the 'wound' and 'pain' that they would suffer from hearing their husband and father attacked.[66] Invoking their female relatives and other 'townswomen' allowed conservatives such as Jarvis to attribute their behaviour to a code of manly protectiveness, one similar to that used in patriotic discourse. According to Jarvis, throwing Mackenzie's printing press into York harbour was not the act of hooliganism that his reform critics claimed it to be. Instead, he and his companions were ensuring public order, thus making the public spaces of York fit for their female relatives.

As we shall see, reformers had a somewhat different perspective on what was 'private' and off-limits; to conservatives, though, any attack on an individual was ad hominem and potentially libellous. Yet it was their definition of manhood in political life, one that saw men as bound in various ways into their society as members of families, that brought the private into the so-called public realm. Reformers' attacks on the intermingling of the two, especially in the distribution of patronage, was part of their attempt to impose more rigid distinctions between them, something that, it seems, conservatives could never fully understand. To those such as Jarvis, family was sacrosanct: it was the cornerstone of colonial society, and it ought never to be defamed in public. 'Independent manliness' and 'manhood' appeared in the conservative press but not as frequently as in reform writings. These terms also suggested very different relationships than in reform discourse. Rejecting the kind of individualistic male virtue posited by Gourlay, those conservatives who wrote about 'manliness' tied it to connections, to moral obligations and responsibilities needed in order to guard against the kind of chaos represented by reform.

If conservatives' understanding of their place in Upper Canadian politics was shaped by the legacy of seventeenth- and eighteenth-century English history, those opposing them made even more clamorous claims on this past. Reformers were eager to use the language of the 'True,' 'Honest,' or 'Old' Whigs, a language that has been analysed by British historians Caroline Robbins, H.T. Dickinson, and J.G.A. Pocock.[67] These 'Commonwealthmen,' as Robbins calls them, less a party than the representatives of the 'country faction' in seventeenth- and eighteenth-century British politics, opposed placemen in Parliament, disliked standing armies, and distrusted the extension of government agencies, spending, and centralization. 'True Whigs' celebrated an opposition of honest, independent, and freeborn men, those who were truly loyal to the constitution and their country, who would represent the wishes of 'the people' free from the malevolent and corrupting influences of the court.[68] Although the reformers of Upper Canada did not follow the country-Commonwealth critique to the letter, their languages were so similar that any analysis of their vision of masculine political virtue must acknowledge debts to this thread of political discourse.

With the arrival of the *Colonial Advocate* in 1824, Upper Canadian reformers had a forum and voice in which to do so consistently. 'When Bad Men Conspire and Good Men Must Unite!' proclaimed Mackenzie, the paper's editor, to his readers on 7 May 1829. The 'bad men' of Mackenzie's title were, as those familiar with Upper Canadian history might expect, the lieutenant-governor of Upper Canada, Sir John Colborne, and members of his administration. John Strachan, John Beverley Robinson, Henry Boulton, Christopher Hagerman, John Macauley, 'and their sort as his [Colborne's] divan will be made use of to induce the next session of parliament to consent to severe and arbitrary militia and other laws, new and oppressive taxes, and other such strong measures as the present system requires.' Such 'bad men' and their wicked deeds, Mackenzie argued, must be opposed by the 'good men' of Upper Canada, those who possessed enough manliness and political virtue to stand alone and resist the 'divan's' inducements and manipulations.[69]

Like Gourlay before him, Mackenzie expressed a hope that new ways of discussing politics might be attempted. In his editorial address in the first issue of the *Advocate*, 18 May 1824, he told his readers that, 'like Farmer Giles, we are perfectly exempt from all unfriendly personal feelings, and if we speak of men, it will solely be in references to their public acts.' Moreover, 'we are far from saying ... that the nobleman now at the head of the Colonial Government in North America is other than an able, and a prudent ruler. It is the system we condemn.'[70] Despite the fact that Mackenzie and other writers to the paper went on to describe their rulers in precisely the opposite manner – as incompetent fools, at the very least – they did repeat these attempts to find a new way of discussing politics. Yet like Gourlay, they constantly fell back on criticizing men, not just institutions or systems. However, if unsuccessful in this area, reform discourse did point to a different way of conceiving the public realm. Reformers saw a crucial difference in the private behaviour and characters of politicians – 'public men' – and their public personas. One did not, they asserted, lead to the other, a separation of the two that would appear to mark them as classic nineteenth-century liberals. As we shall see, when Mackenzie attacked the family background of the Robinsons and their peers, it was because he believed that they had cited their exalted ancestry to justify their control of the political process – a use of the 'private' that Mackenzie and other reformers believed was odious and inexcusable. What should not be over-looked is that in reform discourse the nature of a man's public character was even more important than his private life in determining whether he possessed enough masculine virtue for public life. When reformers attacked their opponents' manhood, it was in precisely these terms of reference, not as private men.[71]

More than anything else, the reformers studied here based their claim to manhood on independence. Of course they were not alone in this for, as Graeme Patterson has noted in his study of Upper Canadian electoral politics, both radicals and tories used the word. For the former, 'it usually had reference to that manly, upright independence of choice that was said to accompany freedom from the pressures of landlord, creditor, or political patron. In tory usage, it generally meant judgement arrived at independently of the clamours of mob and party. In both instances it was a quality more commonly lauded than exemplified.'[72] Patterson's wry observation notwithstanding, for the reformers independence was tied to a vision of virtuous political manhood. Here, once again, the spectre of the Commonwealth's-man arises: he who cannot be bought by place or pension. One such paragon was Fothergill, who sat as a reform member of the assembly from 1825 to 1830. Although initially opposed to Fothergill, Mackenzie came to admire his championing of religious and civil liberty. In 1825, Mackenzie confessed that he had been mistaken about Fothergill. 'As long as he shall persevere in the manly, independent, upright course hitherto pursued by him in parliament,' he declared, 'he shall have my sincere wishes for his, and his family's prosperity.' As a representative of the people, Fothergill had acted in 'the most honourable manner, as became A

FREEBORN ENGLISHMAN.' How many men, Mackenzie wondered, would risk personal ruin, 'to preserve his independence and integrity?' Only Fothergill had displayed 'that noble independence which a virtuous government would proudly cherish.'[73]

Yet it was not just Fothergill who might be called upon to exercise such manly fortitude. 'Up, then, and be doing,' Mackenzie urged 'the electors of Upper Canada' on 8 July 1824. 'Stir yourselves, like men, and strike at the roots of corruption, in the persons of our late corrupt representatives.'[74] Eight years later, writing about his expulsion from the legislature, Mackenzie told the 'Independent Electors of the county of York' that, despite the 'sycophantic band ... who would rule the province by *mob law*,' he believed that the electors 'will, of course, come forward like men, like honest Canadians, and show those fawning parasites by your steady determined conduct at the hustings that you are worthy of the elective franchise.'[75] Throughout the 1820s and 1830s, Mackenzie's calls upon the mechanics, labourers, and farmers of Upper Canada appealed to their 'manly virtue,' 'manly independence of character,' and their 'free, manly independent spirit.'[76] Such a determined and consistent appeal to his supporters' masculinity was not merely a personal quirk of Mackenzie's; they in turn asserted their own manly independence, either directly or by questioning that of their opponents. To 'A Friend of Liberty,' 'free men' entitled to 'rights and privileges' were the catalysts of the 'moral and physical change' needed in Upper Canadian politics.[77] In the eyes of those men attending the Markham Township Meeting, Mackenzie had 'manfully and fearlessly exposed the heartless domineering faction' by acting as a 'public journalist.'[78] Manliness became a significant symbol in reform discourse, an element that would transcend the old régime's corruption and immorality. In turn, only those possessing true manliness qualified for political citizenship.

The reformers' assertion of their masculinity was shaped not only by their claim to be independent men but also by the denigration of their opponents' public characters. In order to have a full understanding of what the reformers declared they were, as men, we must also appreciate what they declared they were not – and often these were qualities associated with femininity. As the forthcoming chapters will argue, women's dependence and reliance on male protection was the hallmark of 'virtuous womanhood.' In patriotic discourse, the image of femininity reliant on male protection was crucial to the meaning of patriotic activity in Upper Canada. But for men in the reformers' discourse, dependence of any kind was the antithesis of manliness. It smacked of the court, of corruption, luxury, and sycophancy. In one of Mackenzie's many warnings to the electorate, he told them, 'if ye will, as heretofore, choose collectors and king's advocates, ambassadors, parasites, and sycophants, to manage your affairs, you will dearly rue it.' Had not Spain, Greece, and revolutionary France made these mistakes and paid for them dearly? And, even though 'the errors were in the princes in the end, [they] sprang from an effeminacy in the people in the beginning.'[79] 'Pampered placemen' – men who had prostituted their manly independence by accepting office and pension – figured prominently in many reformers' writings. Growing fat and idle on the honest toil of the people, these parasites and drones were kept in a compromised yet luxurious condition until Upper Canadian political institutions resembled a vast network of brothels.[80]

For Mackenzie, those who wanted 'to be dictated to by a despicable faction – all such as are willing to kiss the slipper of those in a little brief authority ... all such as wish every farthing of the Provincial Revenues to be squandered in pensions and sinecures for the purpose of raising a race of lordly idle drones to domineer over their supporters who furnish them with their daily bread,' had given up their claim to honest manhood.[81] Such men might be classified with our 'well corseted dandies ... a person who struts about in *frock-coat* and *corsets* and who looks down with disdain upon the vulgar herd below, who labour for a living; one whose chief pretensions to superiority arises [sic] from the emptiness of his skull and who has the good fortune to share a small part of a public purse.'[82] According to the Markham Township Meeting, the 'domineering faction' had monopolized offices 'of honour, of emolument, and of trust' while the people, the genuine source of their power, and of their wealth, 'are vilified, and traduced by them and their parasites, the base, corrupt, and mercenary hirelings of a prostituted press, with every disgraceful epithet that malice can invent, or ribaldry supply.'[83] It was not just that the men who dominated political life were, as Mackenzie believed, effeminate, fond of frippery, and prone to petty tyranny; through their ill-gotten power they perverted and degraded the whole political process.

Yet the sycophants and parasites of the government were not the only ones to have relinquished their manhood through dependence. State-supported clerics, the 'priests' of the Church of England and, later, those Wesleyan Methodists who took money from the government, had lowered themselves to become '*state servants*, and as such must please their patrons.'[84] 'No state church' was an important part of the reform platform, in order 'to detach the sacred cause of religion from the contaminating contact of politics.'[85] In reformers' eyes, the linkage of the two produced 'the priest,' a commonly used insult in their discourse. An allusion to a 'man in skirts' underlay these attacks, yet they should not be mistaken simply for anti-Catholicism or an antipathy to religious men.[86] Rather, the 'dominant priesthood' was synonymous with effeminacy and tyranny, having tied itself to official favour and subsequently immorality and corruption. 'Ye False Canadians! Tories! Pensioners! Placemen! Profligates! Orangemen! Churchmen! Spies! Informers! Brokers! Gamblers! Parasites, and knaves of every cast and description,' fulminated *The Constitution*.[87] A comparison of the 'two greatest extremes in nature ... a real gospel minister and a Church of England priest' was made in the *Advocate*. 'The former a humble, inoffensive character, despising wealth, and wholly absorbed in his spiritual duties, the latter, a furious political demon, rapacious and insolent, and luxurious. Having no fear of God before his eyes; neglectful of his spiritual concerns, waging unceasingly all his influence to promote tyranny, and enslave and debase his fellow creatures ... [W]e consider the established clergy the most iniquitous, they devour the largest proportion of the produce of industry. They are ungrateful to those who feed and clothe them, and prostitute the religion they profess, but the precepts of which they never practice, to support a political system by which they are protected in vice and indolence.'[88]

Those clerics who remained aloof from the state and its perverting influence retained a claim to independent manhood, while those who did not became as vicious and luxury-loving as their masters. After the Canadian Methodist Church united with the British Wesleyans in 1833, thereby receiving money from the Upper Canadian government and detaching itself from the reform cause, Ryerson and his clergy were no longer 'honest gospel ministers' but 'canting hypocritical priests' who had taken the 'royal bounty.'[89] 'MONEY TO PENSIONERS! PRIESTS! BISHOPS! METHODIST PREACHERS! SCOTCH SYNODS! LAWYERS! GOVERNORS! ROGUES! THIEVES! AND HYPOCRITES! Or, the Public Purse becomes a public prostitute, with a "Maria Monk" for the procuress,' was *The Constitution*'s delicate description of provincial affairs.[90]

Reformers enjoyed levying charges of sexual impropriety at their opponents, but in these particular passages sexual insults – the 'prostitution' of the early-nineteenth-century church or the suggestion that the notorious ex-Catholic nun, Maria Monk, presided over the colonial finances – were not aimed specifically at the sexual behaviour of government officials or clerics. To be sure, these attacks hinted that they might be guilty of such indiscretions, an implication that compounded their unworthiness. Work on London's 'radical underworld' during this period has shown that political radicals had inherited a language of illicit sexual activity, ranging from the 'bawdy tradition' of the eighteenth century to the anti-clericalism of the early-nineteenth-century libertine.[91] Yet to link conservatives with sexual licence was more than just a swipe at their lack of personal morality. The sexual imagery of these passages was a trope in reformers' discourse, a discursive strategy that consigned a dependent church and state officials to the realms of pollution, sloth, and degradation.

Dependence and a subsequent loss of manliness thus were seen as endemic to a political system that relied on patronage and poisoned all that it touched. Moreover, the reformers' critique of the York élite's structure opens up yet another aspect of masculinity and reform. The term 'Family Compact' has an unexplored relationship to the reformers' critique of masculinity. Their stress on manly independence of all ties, links, and bonds – other than those to 'the people' – suggests that 'family' stood for more than just the Robinsons, Hagermans, Boultons, and Jarvises. 'Family,' in the reformers' discourse, symbolized a web of intrigue. 'The triple bonds of relationships, intermarriages, a common private *interest* directly opposed to that of the country,' was Mackenzie's definition of the compact's structure.[92] It was 'a few families' who 'usurped' all the patronage of the province, 'who bestow it lavishly on their own kindred, however humble their merit, and parsimoniously only on the needy aspirants to the crumbs that fall from their corrupt tables.' As a result, 'parasites and old women' received the public revenues.[93] 'The family of dictators, who, with their still baser minions, usurp absolute dominion in this colony over king, governor, and people,' symbolized ultimate corruption, venality, and immorality.[94]

The most notorious of such writings were the *Colonial Advocate*'s 'Patrick Swift' commentaries, those 1826 satires on the York élite that sparked the Types Riot and provoked Jarvis's *Statement of Facts*. In these columns, Mackenzie launched into a full-fledged attack on his opponents. His choice of topics ranged from the Bank of Upper Canada and customs duties to the effects of nepotism on the colonial legal structure. Any person who had reason to fall 'into the dreadful gulf of the law,' would, he declared, find themselves taken by a myriad of officials, from attorneys to jurors and jailors, all of whom would charge fees for their services. Such practices had been instituted by judges of the Court of King's Bench, individuals who 'are made and unmade at the mere pleasure of the Crown, receive their salaries from a foreign country, have their sons and nephews and relations practising law and depending on it alone (or on the hope of a place) for subsistence, and they have accordingly established a scale of charges on actions in civil law, which frightens many an honest man from seeking to recover by that means his just and lawful debts.'[95]

Mackenzie also targeted the familial origins of the Robinsons, Boultons, Strachans, and Macauleys, poking fun at those who justified their power and prestige in the colony by citing their supposedly exalted backgrounds. The commentary that so enraged Jarvis offered the Robinsons as the best example of this dishonesty. Asking what that particular family had to boast of in asserting their Virginia descent, Mackenzie reminded his readers that that colony was the 'Botany Bay of the British Kingdoms, the unhallowed receptacle of thieves, rogues, prostitutes, and incorrigible vagabonds.' 'Is it a secret in these parts that many, very many such Virginian *nobles* as the Robinsons assume themselves, were descended from mothers who came there to try their luck and were purchased by their sires with tobacco at prices according to the quality and soundness of that article? And is it from such a source that we may look for the tyranny engendered, nursed and practised by those whose blood has been vitiated and syphilized by the accursed slavery of centuries?'[96]

Here, it was clear, sexual improprieties were precisely the issue: the legacy of prostitution and its corollary, an incurable sexual disease (one that might also result in madness), made it impossible for such families to rule colonial society legitimately. During and after the rebellion, reformers used the trope of sexual crime and political tyranny more thoroughly, in their attacks on the monarch herself. But what was at stake was not just the familial histories and sexual behaviour of John Beverley Robinson's female ancestors. Certainly such insults were almost guaranteed to raise the ire of the government and those associated with it, turning up the flame of political debate and focusing attention on reformers themselves, if not on their specific grievances. However, conservatives' continuous use of their backgrounds as the guarantors of their moral superiority and the justification of their claims on political power made them targets for Mackenzie and other reformers, who continued to insist that men's private lives should not enter the public realm. When their opponents breached this division, sexual insults carried a most effective sting, particularly when levelled at those family members whom men such as Robinson and Jarvis considered in need of protection. While sexual symbols, sexuality as a metaphor, and a literal use of sexual insults were threaded through reform critiques, the image of the family as the source of vice, with its ability to pervert and pollute the public realm was used most frequently. Despite the trouble the above passage created, the link between family and tyranny was not a theme Mackenzie was willing to relinquish. The 1836 elections were characterized by the 'despotism' of government officials: 'the whole tribe of silken creatures who appear to think, that they have a hereditary right to be fed and clothed at the public expense, whatever may be their worthlessness, together with relations, friends, dependents.'[97]

Unlike the discourses of republicans in the American and French Revolutions, in which the family was *at times* seen as the bedrock of the state, and women's role as mothers was thus given some attention, 'family' in Upper Canadian reform discourse symbolized everything the reformers opposed.[98] Occasionally, men were reminded as fathers and husbands to exercise their rights 'and consolidate [their] freedom.'[99] Although reformer Charles Duncombe discussed both the family and the importance of women's education in his 'Report on the Subject of Education,' his was a rare consideration of the private realm.[100] Discussions of education in reform circles usually focused on the need for men of a 'liberal background.' Yet in the press this was not a clearly defined or frequently used position. Reformers were far more likely to couch their appeal to men by reminding them of their independence, their obligation to themselves as men to act freely and without the constraint of any ties. Family, in the reformers' script of political life and the state, was rewritten as brotherhood, to signify universality. In political theorist Carol Pateman's words, 'a nice conjuring trick' was performed, whereby the patriarchal authority beloved by conservatives *supposedly* disappeared.[101] Yet even this appeal to a transcendental fellowship was cast in terms that, while not necessarily and essentially masculine, relied heavily on an ideal of masculine virtue and morality.

Furthermore, the reformers' reluctance to discuss the private realm left them without a clear position on the family's relationship to the state or its role in achieving political change. Discussions of boycotted goods in the mid-1830s, for example, paid little attention to women's contribution as managers of the domestic economy.[102] Such discussions had taken place in America during the revolution, and the postrevolutionary period saw the formation of an ideology of republican motherhood that, while problematic for women, at least brought them into political discourses.[103] Contemporary British radicalism had a number of women members, either in mixed-sex or all-women groups, and the organizational strategies of Chartism (schools and Sunday schools, for example) brought whole families into the movement.[104]

No parallel for these discussions and structures existed in Upper Canadian reform. Possibly the more confined and narrower program of the Upper Canadian reformers, in comparison with their counterparts in

France, the United States, and Lower Canada, made it less likely (or necessary) that a wide range of areas such as the family or women's contribution to a new political and social order would come under scrutiny. Upper Canadian reformers, by and large, were not interested in the reconstituting of 'society and social relations' sought by French revolutionaries who, as Lynn Hunt has pointed out, 'through their language, images and daily political activities ... consciously sought to break with the French past and to establish the basis for a new national community.'[105] Upper Canadian reformers, whether supporters of Mackenzie or the Baldwins, were mostly concerned with rooting out the corruption of a colonial élite that was perverting existing institutions. While some reformers were concerned with issues touching on the reformation and reconstitution of both individuals and families (such as temperance), they had no monopoly on such areas, ones generally the purview of evangelical religious bodies. While some reformers were involved in these groups, religious organizations (particularly the Methodists) had an ambivalent and uneasy relationship to political reform.[106] Family would eventually figure in the reformers' writings, but, as we shall see, it was used in attacks on the colonial government.

To what – if any – extent was reform's notion of masculinity a republican ideal? Certainly the elements of Commonwealth discourse as delineated in the press had strong similarities to certain features of republicanism. The reformers' desire to separate church and state, their emphasis on 'the people' as the foundation of government, their hostility to standing armies, their calls for enlightened men of liberal education to lead the province to security and prosperity, and, above all, their claims to manly virtue – all of these suggest a shared transatlantic legacy of republican sentiments. Appeals to farmers also invoked classical republican notions of agrarian values as the bedrock of civic virtue. The call for fraternal organization, the 'glue' that bound men together in republican movements, was part of the Upper Canadian reformers' discourse. When Gourlay began with appeals to the solitary upright man, writers such as 'A Friend to Liberty' urged him to form political unions 'from one end of the Province to the other – let every free man (who is worthy of the name) come forward and join them.'[107] Public meetings in Markham, Yarmouth, Bertie, and Ancaster (to mention a few) called for adult men 'of just and liberal principles' to come together 'constitutionally' to 'resist any encroachment on the liberties of the subject.'[108]

Mackenzie's calls to farmers and artisans appealed to their common position as men in Upper Canadian society. In his analysis, not only did they share an economic tie as the producers of wealth, but their independence from place and patronage made them the natural guardians of political virtue. Thus, they should unite in order to protect their own and 'the people's' interest. 'Farmers and mechanics, you must look to yourselves – be honest and united and the day is won!'[109] Once again, associations based on a shared 'manliness' would overcome differences in socio-economic position that might impede political unity. This rhetoric of shared masculine independence was frequently aimed at, and to some degree shaped by, merchants and shopkeepers as well as artisans and farmers. It was the self-sufficiency and autonomy of the developing bourgeoisie that concerned most reformers, as well as the need to make the political structure accountable to those men whose economic independence gave them a measure of self-control and disinterest in the political arena – qualities unknown to their so-called betters.[110]

Nevertheless, Upper Canadian reform owed as much to its British antecedents, and perhaps to a conception of British republicanism, as to American or French influences. For the most part, Upper Canadian reform was indebted to British constitutional history.[111] The reformers' insistence that they were merely exercising the rights of *freeborn Englishmen* was not just one-upmanship in the game of loyalty. Repeated affirmations (except during Mackenzie's republican phase) of their attachment to Crown and constitution evinced a belief in the superiority of these instruments of government.[112] In this stance, the reformers of Upper Canada used the language of British Commonwealth's-men – those 'true Whigs' who sketched a portrait of a province that was outraged and defamed and that must be defended. Loyalty was a contested quality claimed by reformer and tory alike.[113] But for reformers, the claim to loyalty to the constitution was an integral part of their masculine virtue. Both loyalty and virtue embodied true Britishness, and to be British symbolized men's freedom from the bonds of slavery and tyranny, from the 'divans' of the lieutenant-governor and the Executive Council.

As the discussion of both kinds of political discourse has shown, notions of 'Britishness' underpinned manliness for reformer and conservative alike, albeit in different ways. For conservatives, American republicanism and international currents of radicalism were generally the threatening 'others.' They pitted British identity against that of the other 'white' nations, which were found lacking in political, not racial, terms. Reformers, though, often set 'themselves off against the Orient,' or, to be more precise, their political enemies sometimes *became* the Orient.[114] They placed a critique of their opponents' manhood in a conceptual framework that identified effeminacy with race, as well as gender, reversal. Symbols of loyalty, such as the flags displayed at the courthouse where Gore district electors assembled in 1832, had become the 'rallying cry of corruption and sycophancy, and like those of Turkey are guarded and environed by the Mamelukes – Cooks – Gardeners and Menials of the Seraglio in all the frippery and ferocity becoming the lawless and pampered instruments of inhumanity and impurity.'[115] In their use of metaphors and images of the East, the reformers combined racial and cultural terms with sexual imagery to cast their opponents as 'other' and to undermine their legitimacy as public political men. Seraglios, harems, and divans, Turks and their tyrannical forms of government: these were images pulled from a stock of cultural assumptions and orthodoxies, pitting foreign symbols of luxury, cruelty, and decadence against British morality and virtuous living. Like the use of 'court and country' language, the language of 'Orientalism' linked those who used it to a larger world than that of York politics. It tapped into the realm of eighteenth- and nineteenth-century imperial expansion and, as Edward Said argues, the 'distribution of geopolitical awareness into aesthetic, scholarly, economic, sociological, historical, and philological texts.'[116]

In Upper Canadian political discourse, this 'geopolitical awareness' furnished reformers' discourse with texts and languages in which they could conduct discussions of politics, culture, and morality. The language of reform clearly implied the inferiority of opponents as well as the foreign peoples to whom they were compared. Reformers used this language as an organizing construct to define legitimately constituted authority, as well as to draw a line between those who might be entrusted with it and those who might not. In reform discourse, the relations of gender and race were closely intermingled: 'honest manliness' was given a racial meaning by invocations of the Orient; in turn, the 'Orient' could not be understood without the invocation of effeminacy.

Armed with the British constitution, and therefore with British identity, Upper Canadian men could not be reduced to the yoked vassals or pampered playthings of the profligate and degraded York élite – 'true men' would not have to kiss the slipper of colonial officials. The township meetings invoked the 'terra firma of constitutional liberty' and the 'rights of British subjects.'[117] Mackenzie attacked Allan McNab and the 'loyal itinerant Beef Eaters' of Gore District for their conduct in the elections of 1834, in which McNab's forces had attempted to block opposition candidates. Evoking the 1381 uprising of Wat Tyler's peasants, who rebelled against the 'Norman Yoke,' Mackenzie congratulated the 'ill-used peasantry [who] rose up in their might, and manfully refused to bow down their necks to the galling yoke that their taskmasters had prepared for them.' Having laid claim to the history of British liberties, Mackenzie went on to challenge his opponents' claim to British tradition. 'What is there British, what is there constitutional in your proceedings? nothing! you have done all in your power to destroy the features of both by bringing forward, as candidates, at the late elections, all the vile Excisemen – all the corrupt custom-house officers, and postmasters that you could muster.'[118]

Mackenzie and other reformers questioned their opponents' appropriation of the symbols and images that would legitimate their actions as 'true honest British men.' While such discursive strategies did not close political discourse completely to those who might not have been British or men, they did help to set the boundaries and fix the terms in which political participation was discussed. But by 1836, these terms had begun to change. Those who were not British men still had few points of entry into political debates in the press and apparently made no attempts to exploit them. However, a growing dissatisfaction with the Colonial Office and with affairs in the colony appears to have led some reformers away from Britain and the Commonwealth tradition to a greater embrace of American republicanism. This process was intensified by the failure of the rebellion and the official repression in its wake. As reformers' discursive ground shifted, so did their use of gender within the political realm. This change did not entail a dramatic restructuring of masculinity; it did, however, shift their definitions of manliness somewhat, as reformers made greater use of symbols of femininity and domesticity in challenges to British authority.

Throughout the late summer and fall of 1837, *The Constitution* and *Colonial Advocate* displayed a growing impatience with Britain, not just with the province's élite and the lieutenant-governor. In July of that year, the 'Reformers of the City of Toronto' published a declaration of grievances and a platform for their redress to their 'Fellow Reformers in Upper Canada.' The reformers' grievances with Britain were political, economic, and social. All of these problems could be traced to obstructionist and rapacious British Parliaments that, intent on plundering the colony, had thwarted its development and sent it a succession of poorly chosen and ill-advised governors.[119] By October, *The Constitution*, in an article entitled 'Uselessness of Looking in England for Justice for Canada,' summed up the drift of the reformers involved with Mackenzie.[120] After the rebellion, those rebels who were not captured by the British fled to the United States, and Mackenzie published his *Gazette* from Rochester for the 'republicans of 1838.'[121] As we might expect, in this paper British institutions were given short shrift, and American political and legislative structures were greatly admired.

As previously mentioned, the 'feminine' was never far away from the reformers' conception of masculinity. But as their impatience with Britain and colonial government grew, so did their use of political metaphors based on either actual or symbolic women. In discussing Lower Canada, the *Advocate* frequently had used the feminine pronoun, sketching a portrait of a province outraged and defamed and in need of deliverance by 'men who know to appreciate and maintain their rights.'[122] By 1835, Mackenzie's attacks on the Bank of Upper Canada depicted the institution as a 'jealous Old Lady' who guarded her monopoly by attempting to bring rivals into dispute, a tactic that only highlighted her own 'ugliness' and 'malice.' These attacks grew over the next two years.[123]

One woman in particular was targeted, for her rank, gender, age, and, at times, physical appearance. The young Queen Victoria became the symbol of the reformers' anger at Britain, as she did in Lower Canada where she was attacked with greater virulence and vitriol.[124] Calling for meetings, political unions, and the expression of grievances in August 1837, the editor of the St Thomas *Liberal* warned reformers that neither Lord Glenelg nor the Commons would listen. 'Nor can your cries ever be permitted to disturb the frills or the frolics of that young damsel that sits as Queen, and flirts her fan over the empire.'[125] In November, Mackenzie published an editorial discussing the relationship between the queen, Lieutenant-Governor Sir Francis Bond Head, and the people of Upper Canada. Although Victoria might be called 'the mother of the people ... it is a strange manifestation of maternal love, to avow hatred to her children.' Managing to take a poke at both the monarch and her representative, Mackenzie declared that 'Sir Francis cannot be said to represent her majesty's feminine nature, for in that case he would dress in petticoats.' (In other articles, Mackenzie had described Bond Head as vain, puffed up, and a fop.) Rather, Bond Head represented her 'royal prerogative, her royal feelings and pleasure.'[126] Because this power and these emotions were used to crush reformers in a cruel and capricious manner – the logical outcome when femininity was allied with monarchical power – neither Victoria nor her representative could personify either true maternal caring or honest 'manly' justice.

Attacks on the queen intensified after the rebellion. The actions of British troops and the Upper Canadian government were attributed to her personal whims and desires. 'The Queen, by her officers seized upon the late Colonel Lount's property, and took every thing, she did not even leave his unfortunate family their wearing apparel. So much for royal gentleness in America.'[127] 'Wholesale Robbery' protested the seizure of the property of those out on bail, 'the whole of their real and personal estates seized by

Miss Victoria's band of robbers.'[128] 'A Letter to the Friends of Freedom in Upper Canada' made no distinction between the executive of the province and the monarchy, composed of a 'lunatic,' a 'vile worn out drunkard and perjured debauchee and an ignorant school girl not out of her teens.'[129] 'This goggle-eyed little daughter of a pensioned Duke and pensioned Duchess,' declared Mackenzie, plunders the people with the help of her court and rules by 'cruelty, oppression, tyranny, and persecution.'[130] In 'What is a Queen?', a scurrilous poem published in *Mackenzie's Gazette* on 4 August 1838, the anonymous author described a woman who is distinguished from other mortals only by the 'diadem, and gay attire, / that witlings crave and fools admire.' And, the *Gazette* declared, the rebellion had left Victoria with a seraglio of men rotting in her jails – a far cry indeed from the conservative press's accolades to the young and virtuous queen![131] To some extent, the queen was a logical target, and the mere fact of these attacks illustrates the extent of the reformers' bitterness and disillusionment. However, in the past such attacks had been reserved for lieutenant-governors and (primarily) members of the Executive Council; reformers usually had treated the monarch with respect. In the pages of the *Gazette*, Victoria, the traditional symbol of legitimate authority, was transformed into an ignorant, unattractive, childish, and, at times, libidinous tyrant, thereby undermining British moral authority and her claim to colonial dominion.

If Victoria represented the antithesis of the upright, honest, and virtuous men the reformers had chosen as their symbols, we should note that other configurations of women and the private domestic realm existed. Up until the rebellion, reformers said little about the family, but the executions of rebels Samuel Lount and Peter Matthews and the government seizures of rebels' property brought the plight of rebels' families into the pages of the *Gazette*. This was not a 'retreat to family' brought about by the failure of the rebellion. Rather it was another form of attack on the legitimacy of Britain and the Upper Canadian government; the private was used to expose the immorality of actions taken by the public authorities. Articles recounting the meetings of prisoners' families with Head's successor, Sir George Arthur, described in moving detail their unsuccessful appeals for clemency. Such pleas were rebuffed by 'the sanguinary monster who spurned these interesting mourners from his presence, with a cold and cautious look, adding "He [Lount] must die!" O, how they sobbed.'[132] The 'Van-Demon Arthur' compounded his unnatural and tyrannical behaviour by refusing to give Elizabeth Lount 'her murdered husband's' body.[133]

Elizabeth Lount's letter to John Beverley Robinson, one of the few pieces written by a woman that appeared in the Upper Canadian reform press, exemplified the denial of the government's claim to represent the Upper Canadian people. Her husband's execution, her loss 'of home and all that could make that home pleasant,' the 'egregious outrages upon private property, and even life itself,' must, she declared, become public knowledge. Although woman 'should not lead the way' and redress the wrongs of even 'an oppressed, enslaved, and insulted people' (a position that rightly belonged to the 'lion heart and eagle eye' of the male sex), Robinson had abdicated his claim as a man to assist Upper Canada. 'Every man has his price and however unjust the remark is with regard to others, I conceive it well applies to yourself.' The 'series of hardships brought upon me and my orphan children by you, and others of the tory party in Canada ... would call the full grown tear to manly eyes.' Robinson's refusal to let the public see the 'manly corpses of Lount and Mathews' stemmed from his fear that 'the generous sympathies of a noble people ... might rise.'[134] Their bodies symbolized virtuous Upper Canadian manhood betrayed by the tyranny, despotism, and immorality of the authorities. The government's treatment of reformers' families unequivocally exposed its lack of manliness and invalidated its right to rule. The state's claim to authority was based on nothing more than military might and bullying of defenceless women and children.[135] In her evocation of the ideals of manly protectiveness unfulfilled by colonial officials, Elizabeth Lount positioned women in much the same way as did the language of loyalty and patriotism: as dependants on the paternal beneficence of both the Upper Canadian state and male heads of households. Women's voices were heard and the private realm was discussed in the postrebellion period, but these were strategic devices that allowed reformers to continue their political critique of public authority and also evoke sympathy. The letters and articles in the *Gazette* did not indicate that reformers' conceptions of masculinity and gender had changed as much as they signalled a willingness to employ gender in a variety of ways as a fundamental part of political discourse.

The reaction to the rebellion displayed by reformers' opponents highlighted many of the themes discussed above. As mentioned in the last chapter, the notion of the armed male citizen was not the exclusive property of either faction. Pro-government newspapers were only too eager to rally the men of the province in a show of military strength. Writing to the *Patriot and Farmers' Monitor* in November 1837, 'A Militia Man' appealed 'To the Men of the Home District' to counter the reports of reformers' military drills in Toronto. Not only did he doubt their experience and ability to bear arms, he argued that their support would, of necessity, be limited. 'Is it for a moment to be supposed that the owners of valuable farms in our districts, the fathers of families, young married men, or the brothers, perhaps, or orphan children, would plunge themselves into such a sea of guilt, without one real cause to drive them to it?'[136] 'The murderous gang of Rebels,' the paper declared on 8 December, was running amok in Toronto, rioting and murdering – 'intent on subverting our happy Constitution and Government.' Yet faced with these calamities, the city had transformed itself in 'a spectacle of uncommon grandeur ... one general camp, resplendent with dazzling steel, and bristling with bayonets.' This splendid display of military might was matched by the inhabitants' response: 'Governor, Vice Chancellor, Judges, Magistrates, public Officers, professors and their students, Merchants, Bankers, Shopkeepers, Mechanics – are all alike belted and armed for battle, and all alike vigilant and active.' Reformers, it would seem, did not hold exclusive rights to the notion that manly activity for a good cause might unite 'all classes.'[137]

Although some historians argue that the 'conservatism' of the Upper Canadian people accounted for the rebellion's limited support, the reminiscences of Samuel Thompson suggest that their conservatism was not simply reactionary.[138] Thompson, a young man in 1837, was a reform supporter (along, he suggested, with many friends), but the 'republican' attitudes of John Rolph and Barnabas Bidwell alienated him and many others. Bond Head's campaign for loyalty, he believed, touched a chord with his peers. 'When he traversed the length and breadth of the land, making himself at home in the farmhouses, and calling upon fathers and husbands and sons to stand up for their hearths, and their old traditions of honour and fealty to the Crown, it would have been strange had he failed.'[139] While nostalgia may have coloured Thompson's memory, it is worth noting that once again the Upper Canadian state used – possibly successfully – the symbols of the patriarchal family to maintain order.[140]

After the immediate threat has passed over Upper Canada, the *Kingston Chronicle and Gazette* congratulated the loyal citizenry for its 'energy' and the 'military ardour displayed by all ranks and occupations.' 'The farmer has forsaken his rural occupations. The mechanic has laid aside his implements of industry. The merchant has left his counting house, the professional man his study; all have pressed forward in defence of British institutions and British domination.'[141] The irony of the paper's appeal to a shared manliness and national identity that, in many respects, resembled the universal fraternity of the reformers went unnoticed. As in the calls for men to unite in defence of the colony in 1812, this conservative vision of masculine behaviour was also one that sought to transcend class divisions, downplaying their importance when the safety of the state and the imperial tie was at risk. That the farmer and mechanic might have had different motives for forsaking and laying aside their livelihoods to come to the aid of 'British institutions' was an issue the *Gazette*'s contributor chose not to address. Nor, in this passage, were the military contributions of those Natives and blacks who supported the government commented upon.

'The Scheme that Pap Built,' a poem by 'Milites' of the 65th Regiment, sought to counter any lingering support for the rebels by exposing the degradation and wickedness of exiled reformers and the disasters that sprang from their deeds. In this poem, the desire to defend the country was not the force that bound the rebels together. Instead, the rebels were symbolized as the individual 'Patriot,' his only reason for uniting with others a shared desire to loot and plunder his neighbour's goods. And, once again, threats to private property were allied with threats to the sanctity of the home and the well-being of women and children.

> This is the 'Patriot' all tattered and torn,
> Who prowls like a wolf from night to morn;
> He has joined the plundering lawless band,
> and bears the name of a 'stout brigand;'
> and he raises the cry of the 'Canadas free,'
> to seize on his neighbour's property!!
> He is one of the knaves held up by the people
> who winked at the scheme that Pap built.
> These are the widows of those who were slain
> For Albion's right, on the battle plain,
> and they slowly chant, as they glide along,
> To the shade of the dead, the requiem song;
> But they change to cry, both shrill and wild,
> As the tearless eye of the orphan child
> Is fixed on the Patriot tattered and torn.

Yet despite this gloomy scenario, hope lay in

> The 'peri' of Albion's Isles
> Ah! where the wretch that could blight that smile?
> Or plant the canker worm of care
> In the peerless bosom of one so fair!
> She sits aloft, while her lustring eye
> Beams with the fire of majesty;

While the millions around her rend the sky
With bursts of – VICTORIA – victory.[142]

Very different uses, we might note, of notions of manhood and of femininity as personified by the monarch and state.

A number of questions arise from the arguments made above. What, for
example, are we to make of the reformers' constant use of the phase 'the
people,' an expression positing universality in the midst of arguments
focused on, and addressed to, the enfranchised adult British man? Literary
critics have reminded us that language is a slippery medium and symbols
are often multidimensional. 'The people' as a discursive tactic legitimated
and enlarged the basis for the reformers' support, promising a mirror for all
members of society, while at the same time obscuring the hierarchies and
barriers inherent to the reform notion of political citizenship.[143] Yet 'the
people' also might serve as an important symbolic weapon for those who
wished to establish a claim to that citizenship from which they had been
excluded. However, in Upper Canada there appears to have been no direct,
organized, and sustained challenges by women to their exclusion from
political languages, no public attempts to challenge the discourses of either
manly fraternity or political hierarchy.

If the public discussion of political matters was shaped by men's voices
and opinions, can we draw any conclusions about women on the basis of
an apparent silence? The sources consulted above, while drawing women
into political affairs in a variety of ways, assumed their absence as actors in
political matters. Although it is difficult to know the extent to which this
division was accepted by women in Upper Canada, a few scattered sources
hint at a more complex situation. Left by women who were more literate
and better-educated and whose family situation linked them more directly
to political matters than was the case for most Upper Canadians, male or
female, the diaries and letters of these atypical women give us at least a
glimpse of the place of political affairs in their lives. If Upper Canadian
political culture of the early 1830s was a spectator sport for Mary Gapper
O'Brien, it was one in which she was greatly interested. She had arrived in
Upper Canada in 1828 to stay with family members north of Toronto and
remained in the country after marrying Edward O'Brien, a conservative
supporter, farmer, and justice of the peace. 'This Parliament amuses me,'
she wrote to her family in England, explaining her need to read both newspapers and reviews in the same day and promising to send them colonial
newspapers. Supporting an established church and a conservative govern-

ment, O'Brien's letters to England describe matters such as the Types Riot, the 'radical' nature of various assemblies and the 'grievance party of demagogues,' Bond Head's arrival in the colony, and the rebellion. Although her letters portray a gendered division of labour within the various pioneer households in which she lived, distinctions between men and women were less rigid than in the public discourse of political life.[144]

For Amelia Harris, a descendant of United Empire Loyalists and a staunch government supporter who lived in London with her husband John, a former naval master, the political upheaval of the 1830s landed (literally) on her doorstep. Writing Henry Becher, a family friend, in December 1837, Harris told of 'running bullets' with her children during Sunday's 'hours of service.' 'I was rather abashed when Mrs Cronyn came in and caught me at it but she displayed a pair of Bullet Moles [moulds] she had just borrowed and was going home to employ her self in the same way; we have been several times notified that Mr Harris was to be shot and our house burned; Mrs Cronyn was notified that her house would be burned as it was church property but she need not be alarmed as her and the children would be allowed to walk out – very civil ... Our kitchen is turned into a guard room and it appears to me it is not the same world we were living in when you left us.' Hearing of Mackenzie's defeat, Harris declared that all local 'Rads' would be arrested. 'Had I been a man and clothed with any authority they should have all been lodged in the cells to keep them out of harm's way,' she pronounced.[145] Denied a military uniform or any other signs of authority because of her gender, Harris was thus unable to undertake what she deemed best for the colony's well-being. Yet Harris, Mrs Cronyn, and their respective families (including, it is worth noting, their husbands) were also forced to participate in the rebellion, whether as objects of rebels' threats or as supporters of the colonial government. Like the War of 1812, the particular circumstances of the rebellion undermined and contradicted political writers' attempts to isolate political affairs from other aspects of Upper Canadian society. In Harris's words, kitchens became guard rooms – if only for a short time.

Although we do not know whether Amelia Harris's world returned to its former state, the political events of the 1830s had an unmistakable effect on Maria Wait's life. Married to Benjamin Wait, who was transported to Van Dieman's Land for his part in the rebellion, she travelled to England in 1839, hoping to obtain a pardon for him. Although unsuccessful, her account of these efforts is a fascinating counterpart to Harris's letters and also raises questions about the political culture of Upper Canada. While in London, Wait was apparently taken up by a circle of women who supported reform. She attended 'female prayer meetings' where women members offered up heavenly petitions for her success, and she was introduced at court to influential women, such as Lady Barham, the queen's lady-in-waiting. The latter discussed Wait's case with the queen, who professed to be 'touched' and expressed an interest in meeting her (when and if '"it should be deemed practicable"'). 'Thus had the private influence of those benevolent ladies surrounding the throne, been exerted upon the queen,' Wait observed, although she added that Victoria, 'except in matters exclusively personal,' was 'a mere automaton, to be moved by the ministers of state.'[146] While in London, Wait was a keen observer of political affairs and wrote of the transportation of Chartists, the 'odious' church rates, and of her trip to hear Daniel O'Connell.[147] She also attended an abolitionist conference, where the 'fair and benevolent ladies' of the United States were not permitted to speak. Noting approvingly that their supporters pointed to the hypocrisy of a nation that, while singing '"hosannas"' to a queen, 'doomed' these 'talented' and 'Lacedaemonian women' to 'silence,' Wait also registered her support for abolition.[148] Wait's trip was made easier by both the organized and individual support of sympathetic women, suggesting that some kind of women's culture might have been at work. These networks, though, were not confined to the private world of family and household; in Wait's case they eased her entry into the London political world. In her letters, she also displayed a keen interest in political affairs, one that went beyond her pressing personal concerns, and told her readers about the involvement of these British women in political life and matters of state.

    London, of course, was not Upper Canada, and it is unlikely that similar groups of politically minded women were formed in the colony. Certainly geographic differences would make it much more difficult for like-minded women to come together than in the urban milieu of London radicalism. What we should consider, though, is that the political realm in Upper Canada must be incorporated into any discussion of changes in gender relations in the nineteenth century, as well as those of the home, the school, and the workplace. Feminist historians have pointed out that women were excluded from formal definitions of citizenship in many Western societies just when that definition was extended to previously unenfranchised men.[149] To this observation we can add that, even in a society seeking to redefine political structures and practices and not primarily citizenship, political struggles were shaped by competing concepts of gender, where either the absence of women or the issue of their protection was central to concepts of men's participation in political life and the state.

Like loyalty and patriotism, political discourse fought an ongoing battle to separate the worlds of the ballot and the kitchen. Yet, like loyalty and patriotism, the mutual dependence of these two worlds meant that they could not be pried apart without a great deal of difficulty. Both reform and conservative writers relied on images of the feminine, but the particular use to which they were put did little to open up political discourse to women. The valorization of the patriarchal family, on the one hand, and the high price placed on manly independence, on the other, could not speak to the notion of women's participation as political actors. The first glorified a structure and relationships in which women were subordinate; the second neglected to address the problem of those who were not clearly defined as independent in Upper Canadian society. To see images of femininity and the category 'womanhood' as more than the shadowy 'others' of political discourse, we must look elsewhere.

3

Familial Celebrations: Gender and Religious Discourse

Writers who shaped religious discourses in the colony had no choice but to incorporate a wider range of images and symbols than those of political and patriotic language. The doctrine of the equality of souls, regardless of gender, helped ensure that categories of manhood and womanhood, and images of masculinity and femininity, were much more visible in the language of religion. Nowhere was this more true than in Methodism, although Anglicans also participated in a religious discourse that incorporated masculinity and femininity. Whether in newspapers, mission reports, histories, or letters, religious writers during this period displayed an intense and *overt* interest in women and men. This interest, rooted in theological concerns about the individual, helped shape categories of womanhood and manhood in religious discourse. Religious writers also attempted to fix meanings to these categories, establishing them as known entities that were then grounded within the family – although, as we shall see, the meanings of 'family' were not static or rigid but were instead mutable. Furthermore, in shaping these categories, religious writers created gendered images and symbols. Gender relations were a recurring theme in a vast amount of religious literature disseminated throughout the colony, whether the subject was the relationship of religion to politics, the role of revivals, the place of the family in religion, or the work of missionaries among the Native peoples of Upper Canada. And in this last aspect of religious discourse, the racial meanings of virtuous manhood and womanhood in Upper Canada were made clear.

While the research underpinning this chapter draws upon a number of religious sources, there are several reasons why I have chosen to focus on Methodism as a means of exploring evangelical discourses on gender.[1] For one, throughout the period of this study, Methodist churches experienced a rate of consistent growth, particularly before the War of 1812 when their expansion into Upper Canada from the northeastern United States posed the most visible challenge to British conceptions of order. To be sure, the war curtailed their expansion and complicated the spread of Methodism; it precipitated the arrival of British Wesleyan Methodists who feared possible republican influences among their American brethern. Yet the war did not mean a complete end to growth for Episcopal Methodists (as it did for American Presbyterians in the Niagara peninsula); after the war, Methodism, in its various forms, continued to spread throughout the colony.[2]

Quantitative factors, however, do not by themselves justify examining Methodism. While indices of church membership over a number of decades may indicate persistent and sustained growth, in the short term historians of religion must also consider membership not as fixed and permanent but as subject to temporary ebbs and flows. This consideration is particularly critical in studying evangelical churches that may experience spectacular bursts of growth during revivals, growth that may be followed by equally spectacular epidemics of backsliding. Methodism warrants study for a number of other reasons, ones bound up with the political and social-cultural landscape of Upper Canada.

The Methodist Church may not have been unique in its engagement with publicly debated political matters, such as the clergy reserves, the university question, and Native missions, but, unlike more pietistic groups such as the Quakers, it maintained a very high profile across a range of political matters. As we shall see, it also received a high degree of opprobrium from its conservative opponents; I have not found that Baptists, for example, were so constantly and consistently identified with the threat of anarchy as were Methodists.[3] The church's gradual assumption of a relatively high level of social, political, and cultural respectability by the latter part of the century makes it, in my estimation, all the more compelling to study during this period; we may glimpse the role played by gender relations in this process as well as some of the effects on gender relations themselves.[4] Yet another reason for studying Methodists is their involvement in Native missions and their supposed 'success' in both converting and 'civilizing' Native women and men. This work also makes them a particularly useful body for probing relationships of gender and race, especially since the church both produced and provoked a number of publicly disseminated commentaries on the process of conversion.[5] Furthermore, the Methodist propensity to discuss both religious and secular matters in print, particularly through the medium of the colony's 'most successful' religious newspaper, the *Christian Guardian*, makes it possible to explore the gendered nature of religious and secular debates in a more focused and consistent manner than is possible with other denominations.[6] I do not want to suggest in the following arguments that, insofar as gender relations are concerned, Methodists are the sole religious body that should be studied. Indeed, I would hope that historians of nineteenth-century Ontario might examine other denominations, particularly (although not exclusively) evangelical churches, to see if they displayed concerns similar to those of the Methodists. Research in other contexts suggests that evangelical beliefs concerning gender relations cut across denominational lines.[7] But, given that in Upper Canada the Methodists were the most 'active evangelicals,' I believe that examining the sources left by this group is a reasonable and logical place to start investigating questions about gender.[8]

Historians have noted the link between religious and political affairs in Upper Canada, in controversies over the clergy reserves and church control of higher education.[9] These disputes, while focused on specific issues, may be traced to a larger division over the place of an established church in the colony and to the political and social challenges that dissenting religions offered to such a religious body. Simcoe's 'founding vision' had included the importation of the Church of England because, in his mind, the lack of such a body in the American colonies had contributed to the revolution. For some members of the Upper Canadian political and social élite, an established church was not only desirable but essential. It would guarantee political and social stability, help maintain ties to Britain, and act as a bulwark against the American presence. While some denominations felt that the Church of England should not have a monopoly over state funding, they did not have a fundamental theological quarrel with the notion of ties between church and state.[10] However, the presence of many different religious groups in the colony made the foundation of an established church a focus of controversy. American-based Episcopal Methodist itinerants Calvin Wooster, Nathan Bangs, William Losee, William Case, and Lorenzo Dow posed a direct challenge to British notions of an ordered, hierarchical society, founded on obedience, inequality, patronage, and patriarchy, a challenge their conservative opponents recognized all too clearly.[11]

Unlike the highly structured doctrine of the Anglicans, the evangelical message was one of individual responsibility for salvation and a direct, intimate relationship with God. This challenge to the beliefs of men like Strachan was not limited to Upper Canada. As Nancy Christie has pointed out, the events of the 1790s made it 'clear that all through the western world established churches, and thus the once solid notion of a prescriptive constitution and social order, were under siege.'[12] Although Christie argues that the War of 1812 and a revival of conservative values 'stifled' the republican, democratic thrust of evangelical preaching, she admits that the latter lived on in other areas, such as reform politics of the 1820s and 1830s.[13] In public debates over political change in the colony, religious matters often were construed as political affairs.

The rhetoric of political discourse in Upper Canada was, as we have seen, often passionate and emotional, designed to rouse corresponding sympathies in its audiences. When religion and politics were combined, the resulting mixture was equally (if not more) emotive. Nowhere was this clearer than in conservative attacks on Methodism, a campaign that drew upon the language and structure of political discourse. These attacks often used the binary opposition of rational, pious men of the 'established' church pitted against the emotional, hysterical forces of a politically and socially disreputable Methodism. Even when it was admitted that not *all* Methodists represented the worst excesses of American republicanism, commentators still suggested that their zeal and fervour needed restraint.[14]

Methodism, warned the author of a letter to the *Quebec Gazette* (reprinted in the *Upper Canada Gazette*), could foster unknown terrors in the 'weak mind' and drive 'the miserable wretch to desperation.' In solemn tones, the anonymous author told the story of 'a man by the name of Roblin' from the Bay of Quinte. Having listened to an itinerant Methodist preacher, Roblin underwent a terrible transformation. 'From being industrious, cheerful, and contented to struggle with his large family, he became negligent, gloomy, and desponding – His affairs were consequently soon deranged – he ceased to have any satisfaction in this world and took the dreadful resolution of rushing uncalled into the next, by hanging himself.'[15] Although certainly a lurid tale, this attempt to dramatize the effects of Methodism by focusing on its impact on individuals – its ability to transform a responsible household head to a man bereft of the stability of familial ties, a lone individual who slid into madness – was a theme that others would pick up and rework. Methodism, such writers made clear, had the power to dissolve those most intimate bonds that were the bedrock of colonial society.

That Methodism also challenged such stability by its appeal to unfettered emotion was a point made many times by those papers that supported the government. Writing to the *Kingston Gazette* in 1812 under the pseudonym 'Reckoner,' Strachan lectured his readers on the pernicious effects of enthusiasm in religion. 'Enthusiasm is the fruit of deplorable ignorance, of pride and presumption,' he pronounced. 'The loud vociferations, the absurd contortions and the vehement language which many use in prayer,' were the result of weak spirituality and a desire to present a hypocritical appearance of piety. 'Reason,' he told his audience, 'must always be the guiding and ruling faculty – the affections must not lead but follow.' 'There are many respectable and holy men of cold natural tempers who feel little of that passionate zeal and heat which others of warm tempers, but perhaps of far less respectable characters, continually feel.'[16] These sentiments were shared by the members of the Bible and Common Prayer Book Society of Upper Canada (a membership that included Lieutenant-Governor and Lady Gore, William Dummer and Anne Powell, and Jesse Ketchum).[17] Linking their social order to events such as the Reformation and the Glorious Revolution, the society asserted the stabilizing effect of religion and its ability to break down divisions of party and rank. Hoping to provide a 'means of acquiring a knowledge of the essentials of our holy religion,' the society appealed to those with 'a sound intellect, a sincere affection for the truth, a humble and teachable disposition, a mind unfettered by prejudice, a spirit free from irregular and furious passions.'[18]

As well as a vague uneasiness with regard to 'enthusiasm,' writers to the *Kingston Chronicle*, such as 'A Church of England Man,' 'No Ghost,' and 'One of the People,' questioned the kinds of men permitted to become Methodist ministers. Their supposed lack of education was a favoured target because, without formal training, those who should be leaders were just as susceptible to impulse and irrationality as their flock. 'A Church of England Man' compared the Methodist preacher's approach to that of a French philosopher, whose response to a 'formidable argument' was laughter, not 'modest assent.'[19] (A French philosopher also suggested libertinism: immorality, deism, and probable sexual licence.) Although not opposed to Methodism itself, the anonymous writer who responded to 'No Ghost' called for reform of prayer, camp, and class meetings and for better-educated preachers. Without the latter, this writer insisted, and 'as long as impulses and excitement are pronounced the signs of reformation, the preachers will rant, and the people will be unstable, ignorant, and deluded.'[20] The first wave of Methodist preachers in the colony, 'One of the People' informed the *Chronicle*'s readers, had been the 'lowest of the low' – anti-British, spreaders of republicanism, and possessed with a preaching style 'as coarse, and as low, and as vulgar, and as democratic as the style of bar-room politicks [*sic*].'[21]

Although Methodist preachers might degrade religion by their lowly state, they were at their most pernicious when mingling religion with politics. Ryerson and his fellow 'wretch[es],' declared 'One of the People,' were democrats, aiming to 'convert everybody, man, woman, and child, into a race of profound politicians.' Not only were they not content to destroy 'the balance, the strength, and the peace of society,' they brought this levelling impulse into religion. 'The field of religious adventure is over-run with this wide, wasting democracy; that which was given to mankind as a thing of unity which would be lost by division is divided, and torn, and patched.' As a result, 'religion must be driven by steam, and everyone must be fireman and engineer. Religion must be trodden underfoot at camp meetings and inquiry meetings, and night meetings, and anxious meetings, and revivals. Every individual's taste and fancy must be gratified, even to the wildest and most diseased; and these outrages on truth, religion, order, sobriety, and decency, furnish unlimited indulgence to the spirit of anarchy and fanaticism, and that restless spirit of gossip so often manifested on these occasions.' During revivals, 'there is much groaning, weeping, and shouting, and the *Spirit* is miraculously poured down upon hundreds.' This was, however, not the work of a divine presence but of 'human contrivance – an artful Machinery to excite the animal passions, and disorder the intel-lect, and banish modesty and decorum.' Just like democratic politics, 'every man, woman, and child is a doctor of divinity, and has a gift, and speaks in public or some such.'[22]

Like the tale of the suicide Roblin, this passage warned that those who fell under Methodism's sway were courting, not a state of divine posses-sion, but madness. As we shall see in other writings, the physical manifes-tation of their condition – the 'groaning, weeping, and shouting' – was seized upon as both significant in itself *and* representative of other threats. The democratic, 'levelling impulse,' where 'everyone must be fire-man and engineer,' fragmented religion and reduced it to nothing more than chaos. Acknowledged social and political codes and structures were abandoned in favour of the unregulated medium of gossip, rumours often spread secretively by women whose accountability might be difficult to uphold. The reference to 'every man, woman, and child' was a sweeping attack on democracy, which the writer envisioned as challenging specific relations of hierarchy and power. Delineations of gender, race, class, and parental authority were blurred when men, women, and children, regard-less of their class or racial and ethnic background, were granted public voices.

This outburst did not go unchallenged; two weeks later, 'One of the Many' wrote to protest such anti-liberal, confused, and 'confined' views. The two kept up a debate that lasted for two and a half months.[23] Indeed, there *was* a major contradiction in one who supported an established church castigating the Methodists for mingling religion and politics. Nevertheless, although 'One of the People' might have made the Anglican tory case more forcefully than most, those opposed to Methodism shared a similar uneasiness over its 'levelling' tendencies.

There were those who saw the problem as reaching into the very heart of society, the family and home. In voicing his objections to the evangelical work of Thaddeus Osgood, 'Clericus' listed his reasons as administrative, religious, and denominational. However, his greatest ire was reserved for Osgood's proposed Female Societies. First, 'public meetings and public societies of women are at variance with the most admired privileges and the duties of their sex; contrary to Apostolic precept, and introductory, if we may believe what history records, of the most alarming subversion of social order.' Like Jeffers and his opposition to petitions, 'Clericus' believed that Osgood would subvert the power of husbands in their own homes. Wives would find husbands 'solicit[ing] their assistance contrary to the positive opinions of those who they are bound to obey.' There were other objections – women should undertake such work only within their own households, not 'in public committee with Mr. Osgood at its helm.' And Osgood had insulted the piety of Upper Canadian women by presuming that they needed incitement to charitable works. Nevertheless, the concept of evangelical work taking women into the public and disrupting the sanctity of the home was, for 'Clericus,' the most disturbing aspect of Osgood's work.[24]

It was in the pages of the *Patriot and Farmers' Monitor* that religion, loyalty, and gender relations were linked most explicitly. As the previous chapter has argued, this paper was one of the most outspoken in its opposition to reformers, Episcopalian Methodists, and Americans (often the last two were perceived as one and the same). The *Patriot*'s lengthy broadsides on those who would undermine the moral fabric of colonial society and imperil the British connection drew on the conservative stock of images of disorder and disruption.[25]

According to the *Patriot*, there was no doubt that Methodism would bring about a world turned not only upside down but inside out as well. Physical manifestations of enthusiasm were one of the culprits targeted in editorials and in letters. 'A Canadensis,' 'A British Subject,' and 'A Lover of Temperance and Sobriety' wrote of the 'grunting, groaning, twenty-night revival fudge,' 'the wolf-like howlings, the cat-like wailings, the Bull-Like bellowings, and Hyena-like lamentations, that proceed at night from their conventicles.'[26] The physical excesses, such as jumping, shouting, and rolling on the ground, permitted at camp meetings and revivals did not merely offend these writers' notions of good taste and decorum. In these attacks, the body of the revivalist (male or female, although these writers preferred the latter) represented the colonial body politic. The unleashing of physical restraints was part of a greater problem, the pernicious effects of a dismantling of hierarchy and authority in Methodist religious encounters. As these restraints were brought down, the conventions and norms upon which 'civilized' society depended were shattered. Once physical control was given up, and the body fell under the sway of an exterior power or being, the floodgates to anarchy were opened. Upper Canadians, the paper's editor and owner Thomas Dalton told his readers in 1832, were 'destined' to be the 'prey' of the 'most deadly villains.' American Episcopalians 'have sent out over all the Continent, a pack of the most deadly villains, that are to be read of in all history, to excite the ignorant, deluded people, to what they call revivals; and four days meetings – *fourteen days meetings*; where they have preached to them such devilish *stuff*, as turns the poor creatures' brains and subjects their minds absolutely to the will of these barbarous rascals, who are regularly educated and trained for this savage brutal purpose, under the name of *pious* young *men* and at the expense of the unfortunate people, whose peace they are destined to destroy.'[27]

Sedition lurked under the piety of these young men; a favourite epithet of the *Patriot*'s contributors was that of 'hypocrite.' Episcopal Methodists cloaked their malevolent intentions by ostensibly preaching the gospel and perverted their calling by mixing religion with politics. Like 'One of the People,' Dalton found this particularly repugnant. While admitting that not all Episcopal Methodists were disloyal, he insisted that a 'vast number' were.

Their lavish praise of republican institutions; their intimate connexion with, and support of those Editors of papers, and political demagogues, whose only aim seems to be to subvert the government, their constant abuse of the Magistracy and the Provincial government; their interference at popular elections; their ministers making inflammatory speeches at the hustings and canvassing, promising, threatening, and every way trying to influence the voters, lurking about the hustings for days together, and almost killing their horses in the night procuring votes for their favorites; the opening of their chapels for political purposes; their appointing protracted meetings in the neighbourhood of political assemblages for their purpose of using their influence at those times and their openly avowed declaration that religion and politics are inseparable.[28]

Again, like 'One of the People,' Dalton did not consider that his appeals for an established church contradicted these objections. And although wary of British Wesleyan Methodists, they were not targeted in the same way, nor as frequently, as their American brethern. In fact, Dalton claimed that Wesleyan Methodists' acceptance of government funds in the West Indies had improved the quality of their work, freeing them from the pressure of working for personal gain.[29] This seeming contradiction – supporting a union of politics and religion in one context, while in another decrying their mingling – derived in part from the perceived American influence exerted by Episcopal Methodists in political life. Yet it was also bound up with notions of what constituted 'political,' and, for Dalton, an established church was not political. In his editorials, politics signified a never-ending struggle between interests and factions, ones usually antithetical to the common good. The ideal of the common good was conceptualized as a state of affairs protected by an established balance of powers and a fixed order in society. Politics represented turbulence and change, wherein self-seeking men, unbalanced because of their lack of familial and social ties, assumed false identities and masked their real intentions in order to advance their own mercenary aims.

Sexual disorder and immorality also were favourite themes in the paper's war on Methodism. Like reformers, Methodists seduced their audiences by appealing to emotions and disdaining rational argument. But Methodists went even further than their political counterparts, fostering 'intemperance, obscenity, and other species of great immorality' by gathering together the 'youth of both sexes, and of all characters.' Such scenes were 'nightly prowling thicket orgies, where vice reigns triumphant in the shelter of dark concealment.'[30] Speaking of a reform petition circulated in Kingston to oppose pauper emigration, Dalton declared that 'the young Female Emigrants, will have a better sense of decency than, like those of the rabid Ryersonian Sect, frantically to expose their nudities at Camp Meetings, to debauch and corrupt the youth of the other sex; and that their Fathers, and Mothers, and Brothers will be better principled than to encourage them in any such lewd practices.'[31] Against this lack of female morals and feminine delicacy, the paper held up those qualities exemplified by women such as Mary Collins, sister-in-law of Francis Collins of the *Canadian Freeman*. In her obituary of 31 January 1834, Collins was remembered for having 'discharged the duties of a wife, a mother, and a friend, with a degree of zeal, exertion, and ability, rarely to be met with – Her first love was centred in her husband – her first affection ever riveted to her children – ... Her talents were of a very high order – yet she was humble, submissive, and unassuming.' For those who still might have missed the point, the paper added that Mary Collins 'was followed to the grave by a numerous circle of friends and acquaintances, among whom there was no hypocrisy.'[32]

It was not just unleashed feminine sexuality itself, though, that was targeted in these writings. Sexual licence (especially female sexual licence), like physical abandonment, was a favourite trope in anti-Methodist discourse, signifying a wide-ranging threat with multiple meanings. It could encapsulate a host of dangers to the political and social order, a significant one being the overthrow of familial restraints. Such a process was a serious challenge to a social and political order highly dependent on the patriarchal authority of the monarch.[33] After all, in camp meetings children were 'lured to one of these infamous brothels ... induced to denounce father, or mother, brother, or sister, as an unconverted, or in other words an *infidel*.'[34] 'Children are encouraged to judge the belief of their parents, to belie them, and to hold them up to the malicious hatred of the low, the ignorant, the vile, and the most ferociously savage.'[35] As 'R' sarcastically noted, during the prayer sessions at a camp meeting, 'it was pleasing to hear fathers praying for their children, and children praying for their parents, husbands praying for their wives, and wives for their husbands, in fact Christians and penitents, all praying with one united heart and voice *at one and the same time*! A pretty babel indeed!'[36] Ultimately, such an inversion of familial roles and patterns of authority was extended to the rest of society, breaking down respect for other forms of authority in order to propagate sedition and disloyalty.

'Wanton womanhood' and its threat to hierarchy might have symbolic uses, but the relationship of women to enthusiastic religion was a problem for these writers. Women signified the danger of anarchy, and they also represented those most likely to be at risk from Methodist wiles. Methodists who opposed the amateur theatre in York, wrote 'A Canadensis,' had managed to obtain 'a hold over the minds of a few weak, illiterate men and a number of still weaker women.' These followers were 'the very Southcottians of society,' an epithet that combined charges of weak-mindedness, hysteria, and female leadership.[37] 'R,' who was concerned about family authority, also believed that female sensibilities were at great risk in revival preaching. 'To the pure, spotless, and delicate female (I speak from personal knowledge), they represent hell as a sort of seraglio. – "How," said a certain parson W – "would you like to be dragged away to the infernal chambers, and forced to gratify the lust of the devils in hell!" – What an unexcusable, unheard of – what a hellish question! ... Who then can be surprised at the effect upon the tender and unsuspecting female? – Who can wonder that she should become pale with horror, and cry out in agony?' Such a conversion, 'R' argued, was made under false pretences and only by deceiving and terrifying the 'innocent and credulous girl.' 'Her friends reason with her, and mourn over her delusions; while the Preachers admonish her to *persevere*, and labour to keep up the unnatural excitement, until she is smuggled away from her family and united with the church.'[38] The *Patriot* also was fond of American news of charges against Episcopal Methodist ministers for various kinds of sexual misconduct such as seduction, incest, and rape.[39]

Women might be at risk from the 'Orthodox Trumpeters' and 'tract-pedlars,' but feminine figures also could be implicated in these charges. Male preachers bore the brunt of most attacks, for being licentious, ignorant, and bad-mannered, but occasionally women became symbols of Methodist hypocrisy. In a piece by 'Washington Paul Pry' (a satirist whose work was picked up by other conservative newspapers from time to time), three supposedly pious women, Mrs A, B, and C, gathered to discuss religion. Mrs B and C, both Methodists, attempted to impress Mrs A, an 'Orthodox,' with their superior religiosity. Their boasts of constant attendance at missionary, class, and tract meetings, despite their family responsibilities and the objections of their husbands, exposed the divisions created within families by evangelical religion. Not only did it distract women from their real duties, as 'Clericus' had argued, it also provided them with both motive and excuse to defy male authority. Moreover, Mrs A's and B's attempts to score points over each other by insisting on the superiority of their respective ministers led them into a vigorous argument. Mrs B's attack on Mrs A's minister, 'who talks about "his Greek translations,"' prompted a counterattack about Mrs B's minister, who indulged in card games and played the flute. From there on the conversation deteriorated into a fierce quarrel, and the three women parted, each angrily disavowing the other's church.[40] Like the dialogue of Mr Canada and Mrs Slipslop, both the characters and their words conveyed various messages; in this case, they were about Methodism and women's participation in this religious body. Here, though, there was no masculine voice of reason to intervene and settle the argument. Encouraged by their church to carry on public disputes instead of tending to their first responsibilities – their homes and families – such women managed to disturb their communities and demonstrate the latent hypocrisy of enthusiastic religion.

The *Patriot* was most vociferous in its attacks on Methodism and enthusiasm, elaborating on themes that other newspapers discussed in less heated language. Yet as we have seen in the preceding chapter, the type of rhetoric used in the paper was not unique to Dalton and his contributors. Further-more, the *Patriot* was recognized as an important participant in conserva-tive discourse.[41] The paper's editorials and letters attempted to undermine the legitimacy of evangelical religion by pinning certain meanings to it, ones that were consistent with the *Patriot*'s attacks on reformers. These articles and letters about Methodists faded away in 1834 as the paper devoted more and more time and space to its anti-reform campaign.

The paper's invective did not prompt a direct response from the major Methodist publication, the *Christian Guardian*, but various articles, edito-rials, and letters that appeared in the *Guardian* were thinly veiled rejoin-ders to its critics. 'Self Defense,' an editorial in February 1832, reminded readers of the paper's purpose, declared in its first edition in 1829: 'Our business was with *things* not *men*.' However, certain 'high Church Tories' had attacked neither the Methodists' position nor their principles but their reputations (a complaint echoing that of reformers).[42] One year later, an article entitled 'Yankee Methodists' decried the characterization of Meth-odist Episcopalians as Americans by the 'hireling press.'[43] The next month, at the height of the *Patriot*'s attacks, 'M.N.' from Lanark wrote to discuss the question of the discipline and education of those men who took on positions of responsibility within the church, as members, class leaders, and preachers. Arguing that 'class leaders are men who fill important sta-tions in the Church, they therefore ought to be men of much piety and wis-dom, upon whom great and important duties do evolve,' 'M.N.' went on to elaborate: 'To them is committed ... the arduous task of feeding the babe, the young man and the father, to train up spirits for the skies. And does not the state of the Church greatly depend on them? Let them ever remember that an awful responsibility rests upon them for the manner in which they discharge the duties of their function; which are more clearly set forth in Discipline. They require a *face of steel*, a *heart of love*, and a mind in which are laid up the *treasures of wisdom* and *knowledge*.'[44]

This letter, which proceeded to discuss the importance of preachers, may be interpreted as part of a more general urge for 'respectability' felt by Wesleyan Methodists of this period.[45] By no means did the letter represent a consensus, as we shall see later in this chapter. What is worth noting, though, is that the question of respectable church leadership was posed in terms of *male* class leaders and preachers and, what is more, *educated* men who would pass on their knowledge and spiritual inspiration to others of their sex. It is not clear to what extent this letter was a direct reaction to the conservative press's gendered images of disorder and disreputability but, nevertheless, the writer felt that the buttressing of the church's authority rested on male authority. 'B.T.,' writing to the *Christian Guardian*, protested that a letter published in the *Brockville Gazette* had given a false impression of Episcopal Methodist congregations. The *Gazette*'s letter-writer had claimed that they were composed solely of women and children; 'B.T.' disagreed, stating that, at a recent quarterly meeting, the members were principally 'old soldiers of the Cross of Christ.'[46] As Elizabeth Muir in her study of Methodist women preachers in Upper Canada points out, newspapers such as the *Guardian* downplayed or ignored the work of the women preachers in this period.[47]

How did the family, gender relationships, and notions of private and public figure in Methodist discourse? Historians of both Canadian Methodism and evangelical movements in England and America during this period have noted that evangelical religion, and Methodism in particular, placed great importance on the family and familial relationships. To the late eighteenth- and early-nineteenth-century English provincial middle class, 'church and chapel' were central to the 'articulation and diffusion of new beliefs and practices related to manliness and femininity.' But for men, there were certain tensions embodied in the evangelical concept of manliness, in which self-sacrifice and emotion 'came dangerously close to embracing "feminine" qualities.' Furthermore, the institutionalization of 'enthusiastic religion' tended to limit the kinds of activities open to women.[48] In contrast, the experiences of women preachers in breakaway groups such as the Primitive Methodists and Bible Christians suggest that gender divisions within these groups were less rigid. Within these sects traditionally designated as 'marginal' in the history of Methodism, in which the division between private and public had not yet been tightly drawn, women were able to create a space in which they could preach openly.[49]

In Canada, much of the literature on gender and religion focuses on the late nineteenth century.[50] However, as Marguerite Van Die has argued in her study of the prominent nineteenth-century Methodist minister and educator, Nathanael Burwash, Canadian Methodism in the 1830s and 1840s became 'family religion.' 'Its future,' she notes, 'therefore, lay not in the first place in the hands of itinerant evangelists, preachers, and Sunday school teachers, but in the Christian training provided by the mother in the home.'[51] 'Family,' though, could have other meanings in evangelicalism. Among the New Lights in late-eighteenth-century Nova Scotia, Henry Alline's more egalitarian appeal and his rejection of church hierarchy at times threw into question accepted familial relationships based on patriarchal and parental dominance.[52]

As we have seen, Methodism first arrived in Upper Canada in the 1790s via those American Episcopal Methodists vilified by the conservative press. The first circuits, in Augusta Township and on the Bay of Quinte, were organized by American preacher William Losee in response to a petition presented to him by residents during a scouting mission in 1791. By 1804, Methodist circuits had reached the Detroit River and Niagara regions, and by 1812 Methodism was the largest Protestant denomination in the colony.[53] For this earlier period, there are no sources published in Upper Canada in the form of newspaper and periodical literature. As mentioned previously, we have no Upper Canadian forerunner to the *Christian Guardian* to show us what was published and disseminated by evangelicals. This does not mean, however, that we cannot discern some sort of religious discourse during this period. Certain sources, such as histories of Methodism and biographies of its leaders, make extensive use of letters and journals written in this period. Works such as *Case and His Contemporaries* and *Past and Present*, by John Carroll, George Playter's *The History of Methodism in Canada*, A.G. Meacham's *A Compendious History of the Rise and Progress of the Methodist Church*, Nathan Bangs' *A History of the Methodist Episcopal Church*, and Abel Stevens' *The Life and Time of Nathan Bangs*, as well as various reminiscences of less-famous Upper Canadian itinerant preachers, help outline the contours of evangelical religious discourse from the 1790s into the 1840s.

These works, mostly published in the 1860s, performed at least two roles. For their immediate audience, they created a golden age and a set of heroic 'founding fathers' who struggled against daunting material conditions to spread the gospel and lay the foundations of the church. In an era of the institutionalization and growing respectability of Methodism, these heroes may have been a reminder of the need for struggle and sacrifice in keeping the church's initial vitality and inspiration intact.[54] For our purposes, though, the material written prior to 1829, much of which has survived only in the pages of these books, allows us to examine the meaning of gender and the family in evangelical discourse and to establish both changes from and continuities with the later language of the religious press. Some of the sermons and exhortations at revivals from 1829 on also were reported in the *Guardian*. Since some of the more famous scenes of revivals and conversions appear in more than one history and are described in the same words, it appears that this material circulated widely within Methodist circles, becoming somewhat legendary in the process.

As Rhys Isaac has noted in his study of the impact of evangelical religion in colonial Virginia, the relationship between communality and individualism was complex and part of a process of spiritual development; both were prized and needed in evangelical religion. In the aftermath of conversion, the kinds of group discipline provided by the church were intended to strengthen the converted's commitment.[55] In Upper Canada, if the experience of saving grace through revealed religion, even in the communal atmosphere of a revival, was individualistic, it was not intended to lead to a type of free-will nihilism or antinomianism (notwithstanding the fulminations of the *Patriot*). For one, the kinds of 'group controls' described by Isaac and others were intended to guard against backsliding and a sense of false pride in one's spiritual state.[56] Yet another group in society, one often overlooked in the secondary literature, was used as a social and spiritual anchor: in religious discourse around revivals and the early spread of Methodism, the family was a recurring theme, one with several variations.

Although individuals' conversions were eagerly welcomed and lovingly recounted, the conversion of entire families in revivals was proclaimed as affirming the deepest tenets of Methodism. In recounting one of the earliest conversions in Upper Canada, the 'salvation' of John Roblin of Adolphustown in 1791, Playter emphasized that, not only did Roblin experience a change of heart after hearing Losee preach, he managed to convince his widowed mother, three brothers, and two sisters to kneel with him in prayer. Roblin then proceeded to renounce dancing and to spread the gospel to twenty-five other families in the area. He held prayer meetings and then became a local preacher and a 'useful man,' as well as representing Lennox and Addington in the Legislative Assembly (albeit unwillingly).[57] For Playter, revivals at Elizabethtown in 1817 were memorable not just for the frequency of conversions but also because 'whole families were made the subjects of saving grace. The numerous family of a pious widow were among the favoured; five sons and four daughters were among the subjects of grace.'[58] The union of parents with children, husbands with wives, and sisters with brothers, one demonized in conservative discourse for its unruliness, was given pride of place in Methodist writings. The family was the ideal framework in which its members might seek salvation.

Within the context of Upper Canadian society in this period, such an emphasis was understandable. The work of these early evangelicals took place, after all, on circuits composed of small villages and farms, areas in which many aspects of social and economic life presumably were organized around relationships of family and household. Certainly those who shaped religious discourse were eager to portray the Methodists as a community of individuals, brought together voluntarily through religious belief. However, the difference that religion might make to life in the more isolated areas of Upper Canada, even intermittently, as a way of bringing together families and households should be considered when attempting to assess the meanings of community in colonial society.[59] Itinerants' narratives often located the coming of 'real religion' to a community in an itinerant's presence in one house. By example and prayer, his message spread first to its inhabitants and then outward, as converts went from home to home and passed on the message of salvation to other families. Thus, as a 'unit' of conversion and as a vehicle for spreading salvation, the family might have been especially well-suited for Methodists, who, we should remember, did not yet prize educated men as ministers.

Moreover, it is worth remembering that, well into the 1830s (especially on new circuits), religious services often took place in 'non-consecrated' spaces, much like the weekly home meetings of Methodist sectarians in England.[60] Fields, barns, and, significantly, houses, were pressed into service in the general absence of permanent churches. In 1824, the Methodist itinerant Anson Green preached his first sermon in the Methodist church at Cramahe but then went on to hold services in a number of homes on his circuit. Just outside of Peterborough, he was greeted by 'a godly old Yorkshire woman' whose log house ('about fifteen by twenty feet') served as 'kitchen, bed-room, parlour, dining-room, and church. Here I preached to a congregation of eight souls, and was happy. O how those people in the bush value the Gospel, and love the messengers who deliver it to them.'[61] The Upper Canadian narratives liked to stress that religious experience could occur at any time and in any place – in the home, barn, field, or workshop. This aspect of spreading the gospel and experiencing Christ's love was stressed in the itinerants' writings. Especially in the case of houses, such a varied use of space contradicted notions of religion occupying a separate area in people's lives, hived off from the daily transactions of society. Instead, Methodist writers insisted, these physical locations were proof of the evangelical belief that religion must be an integral aspect of all experience, dissolving false, 'man-made' boundaries.

In the Methodist discourse around itinerancy, the family also was the one structure that might overcome the problem of continuity in the growth of religion. The proximity of individuals of different age groups within the family meant that it was uniquely suited to pass on religious practices and belief. Grey-headed grandparents praying with their fresh-faced adolescent descendants was a favourite image of Methodist writers, as was that of the whole family united happily through the medium of prayer. As we shall see, family prayer was favoured by both Methodist and Anglican writers in the religious press as a solution to the problems of irreligion and social disorder.[62]

Yet if the family was constructed as the bulwark of colonial society, providing an undergirding of stability and security for religion, this was not the only way in which it figured in religious discourse. The relationship of the family to Methodism was not a one-way street, for evangelical religion itself might pose a challenge to patriarchal and parental relationships within the family. The conservative newspapers were not guilty of complete exaggeration when they pinpointed disorder within households as one of the more pernicious effects of Methodism. George Rawlyk has pointed out that, while evangelicals helped create a 'strong sense of Christian fellowship and community,' they often did so by sacrificing familial unanimity.[63] Methodist itinerants' narratives took pride in pointing to the many times when the rule of domineering fathers and husbands had been overturned by the triumph of revealed religion. With great relish, Bangs recounted the story of a 'stout opposer of the Methodists.' This man, 'upon hearing that his wife was in a prayer meeting, rushed violently into the room, seized his wife, and dragged her to the door, when attempting to open it, he was himself seized with trembling, his knees failed him, and he fell helpless upon the floor, and was fain to bring an interest in the prayers of those very people whom he had so much despised and persecuted. He rose not until the Lord released him from his sins, and made him a partaker of partaking mercy.' Later, according to Bangs, the man became an itinerant preacher.[64] A similar tale of Darius Dunham's encounter with an angry husband appeared in Carroll's *Case*. Dunham, a prominent itinerant, had converted a wife on the Bay of Quinte circuit in the 1790s and aroused her husband's wrath. An 'ungodly man,' he came after Dunham with an axe but was disarmed by others in the house. The preacher's 'calmness and Christian fidelity, with the blessing of God, moreover, brought the man to reason, and penitence, and prayer at once, and issued in his conversion. His wife was no longer persecuted, and his house became a lodging place for way-faring men.'[65]

These narratives of male brutality transformed by an encounter with religion pitted good against evil in Manichaean struggles, yet they almost always ended with the man's conversion and the reformation of his ways. Not all of these stories discussed the transformative effects of religion on patriarchal authority; a few were about children's challenges to unbelieving mothers.[66] However, in the case of spousal conflict over religion, the converted was invariably female and the opposition frequently came from a brutal and violent husband. Even when the struggle was posed in less dramatic terms, as in descriptions of familial conversions, those who witnessed such scenes emphasized the questioning of authority permitted by religious experience. Children *did* pray for their parents, and wives for their husbands; none were bound by traditional constraints to respect an authority that lacked religious conviction.

It would be reading too much into these tales, though, to claim that the Methodists developed a critique of male violence and the abuse of women that pinpointed the problem as patriarchal dominance within colonial society. These narratives were placed within the context of religious choice and stressed its rehabilitating effects. The man in question almost always ended up back in his rightful place, as the loving, transformed head of a transformed, since loving, household. Moreover, it was usually only through the intercession of a male minister, invoking a higher male power, that a husband's or father's violence was put to a stop. Nevertheless, by insisting that individual choice in religion took precedence over customary forms of authority, the Methodists opened up the possibility for the confrontation of male authority within the family. Unlike much patriotic and political discourse, this kind of evangelical religious discourse featured women as important actors, not just backdrops to male authority and agency – actors, moreover, who could make choices about their own spirituality. It also insisted that gender relationships were not entirely 'natural' and immutable; the family was not outside history and could be reshaped to meet an individual's spiritual desires and needs.

The drunken, godless, and brutal men of the Upper Canadian backwoods and villages did not constitute the only images of Anglo-American male behaviour and character. Narratives and biographies, which focused to a great extent on individual ministers and their relationships with one another, presented very different images of masculinity. The men in question were a heterogeneous lot: some educated, some not, some charismatic and articulate, others poor speakers but indefatigable workers for Christ. However, if there was an archetype of masculinity in this discourse, it was one that combined strength with emotion, one with greater depth and complexity than the unidimensional manhood of political discourse. These men were remembered for their ability to unite those parts of their characters in their chosen calling and not, in contrast to political reformers, because they divided personal and spiritual affairs from their public personas. Moreover, even though these were the admitted leaders of the early Methodist church, their leadership was not based on superior education or class background but rather on their zeal and devotion to spreading the gospel. The images of itinerant preachers that emerge from this literature suggest a somewhat different picture of the Upper Canadian ministry than that of the American example analysed by Ann Douglas, whose portrait of antebellum Protestant ministers depicts them as largely ineffectual, even effeminate, within the context of industrializing America.[67]

Male physical strength was much admired in images of the men of the early Methodist circuits, as in the case of Henry Ryan's 'inexhaustible zeal and unfaltering energy.' Ryan's Canadian labour was 'Herculean, he achieved the work of half a score of men ... [H]e also suffered heroically from want, fatigue, bad roads, and the rigorous winters of those high latitudes.' Not only was Ryan's capacity for physical endurance remarkable, before his conversion he had been 'a practiced ... pugilist' and used his talents to keep order at camp meetings. 'He had been known to fling ordinary sized men, who were disturbing the order and solemnity of divine worship ... over the high enclosure' (a fence built around the site of camp meetings to keep out troublemakers).[68] Although Ryan's role in the 1828 split between the Episcopal Methodists and his Canadian Wesleyan Methodists followers was not viewed warmly by writers such as John Carroll or George Playter, they were unanimous in their admiration of his strength. Sammy Richardson, an Irish preacher who arrived in York in 1825, also was remembered for the way in which he brought a young man to God during a camp meeting. The son of a 'respectable yet irreligious family,' who wanted to pray but found himself unable to join the main group of penitents, was 'seized' by Richardson, who hurled him bodily into the main 'ring.'[69] Another Irish preacher, Matthew Connor, exhibited this kind of 'muscular Christianity' in which spiritual strength was buttressed with physical hardiness. Connor, who was listed as preaching in the Pembroke area in 1840, epitomized the hardy backwoods preacher. With no previous experience, Connor had become 'one of the most adroit and fearless canoemen on the river,' running the rapids 'at times when no other canoemen could be found hardy enough to do it. Great muscular power and activity were accompanied in him with a great amount of physical courage. He was a great declaimer in the pulpit.'[70]

The context of itinerant work influenced to some degree the kind of masculinity represented in religious discourse. The setting in which these men carried out their ministry meant that a certain amount of physical stamina was necessary (and the histories admit that some men's health broke under the strain).[71] Unlike many of their counterparts in provincial England, for example, or in the more settled areas of New England, travelling ministers of any denomination in Upper Canada might be faced daily with physical challenges. Such situations continued to crop up as settlement spread into the more remote areas of the province.[72] What distinguished the language of Methodism from, for example, much of Anglican discourse, was its emphasis on these heroes' merging of spiritual power and strength with physical strength in preaching and affecting conversions. Although the Anglican press used the image of the 'warrior for Christ,' the literature left by its clergy depicts a rather different picture of the Anglican itinerant, that of a functionary intent on dispensing the sacraments and diligently recording this dispensation.[73] For Methodists, corporeal toughness might provide the casing for a toughness of the soul, representing a union of body and spirit, the sacred and the profane. But evangelicals did not wholeheartedly support all physical displays of manliness. The physical power of these ministers was to be applauded since it was exercised for religious reasons, but when men's bodies and masculine strength were used in other arenas – such as the duelling field or the tavern brawl – evangelicals were quick to condemn such behaviour as vicious, irreligious, and evidence of lack of self-control.

The kind of rugged manliness of a Ryan or a Connor was also mingled with an emotional sensibility that in any other context might have been viewed as effeminate. As preachers, men like the Reverend John Dempster, who travelled the Bridgewater circuit in 1819, were expected to rouse the emotions of others and to display their own. A former tin pedlar, Dempster when preaching 'was in a perfect flame every moment, and when he was not speaking to some one on the subject of religion was breathing out prayer, or weeping and sighing over the perilous condition of sinners.'[74] The religious symbolism of tears washing away sin, of course, was part of this particular form of emotional display. However, given Methodist discourse's emphasis on the 'frontier' conditions of these circuits, where we might expect 'rugged manliness' to predominate, it is illuminating that the shedding of tears by Dempster and others did not signify a loss of manliness and self-control.[75] Instead, it was a sign of manly virtue and holiness, as when those men ordained by the Genesee Conference in 1820 at Lundy's Lane closed the ceremony by being 'locked in each other's arms, shedding tears of fond affection.'[76] These and other displays of affection between men were not only recorded unquestioningly but often were celebrated, whether they occurred in a camp meeting or in the more private setting of small prayer groups. These writers also emphasized that preachers might share beds and come into various kinds of close physical proximity with each other as they travelled throughout the province, conditions that cemented their affections for each other.[77]

The all-too common equation of Methodism with dourness and restriction, and the belief that it can be held responsible for the joyless puritanism of nineteenth-century Ontario, must be questioned in light of the celebration of religious masculinity in evangelical discourse. Michael Gauvreau has argued that the very experience of conversion was a joyful release from a state of sinfulness, and evangelicalism itself was 'a passion, a living force, a pulsating energy infusing the individual soul and human communities.'[78] Furthermore, the attention paid to the details of physical appearances in contemporary works must temper the belief that Methodist preaching taught only self-loathing for the body and advocated a Calvinistic plainness in appearance to the point of fetishizing ugliness.[79] Writers like Carroll, Playter, and Bangs, and the letter-writers and diarists they consulted, lovingly described their subjects' clothing and hairstyles when they found them appealing. Ezra Healy, an itinerant on the Ottawa circuit, was a 'portly muscular' man, with 'handsome, masculine features [and] hair with a little tendency to curl.'[80] Henry Pope, a preacher whom Carroll encountered in Toronto in 1820, 'made at that time a very respectable appearance. He and his good lady were handsome in person, and well dressed.' Carroll was quick to reassure his mid-nineteenth-century audience that 'well dressed' did not mean ostentatious, as 'their beauty was enhanced by the elegant simplicity with which they habited themselves.'[81] Franklin Metcalf, a well-known preacher on the Hallowell and Belleville circuits at the same time, possessed a 'manly beauty.' Just under six feet tall, Metcalf had a 'straight, symmetrical, lithe, and graceful' build, 'an abundant covering of brown hair, inclining to auburn ... and the whole countenance lighted-up with a genial smile – a pair of large, sparkling, dark eyes.' Thus, Carroll playfully added, 'you have some idea of the young preacher's looks, to whom the ladies flocked in troops – not so much to hear, as to "see." So they phrased it themselves. But this beautiful person was not vain, or flirty, or impudent; but pure as the virgin snow, prudent – devout to a degree, going alone, and pouring out his soul to God by the hour.'[82]

The highest accolades were reserved for Samuel Coate, a preacher on the Quinte circuit in the late 1790s, whose appearance and preaching 'captivated' the 'plain, farming people' of the area. In Playter's words, 'He wore long hair, which flowed down on his shoulders, turning up in graceful curls. Every night, with his garters, he would tie up his beautiful locks, and every morning he would untie and comb them out, then allowing them repose on his shoulders and back. Besides, his countenance was handsome, his complexion fair, and his person finely fashioned and well proportioned. Indeed, he was the Absalom of the people, attracting the eyes and winning the admiration of all. His wife, too, was like Abigail – "of good understanding, and of a beautiful countenance (Samuel, XXV, 3)." When the husband and wife were together, they were called the handsomest pair in Canada.'[83]

A touch of romanticism, not uncommon to evangelical language at the turn of the century, tinges these descriptions.[84] These accolades to male and, at times, female beauty focused on supposedly natural attributes, such as Coate's hair, or on the elegance of plain dress. Frivolity in dress or behaviour was not applauded or encouraged. After all, Mrs Pope's dress was of '"Quaker silk"' and her headgear a '"Methodist bonnet" ... much prettier than those feathery "hats" which now disfigure the crowns of some ministers' ladies.'[85] And it could have been the indirect influence of romantic thought that led writers like Carroll, Playter, and Stevens to discuss so easily expressions of affection between men.

Yet all-male friendships and the homosocial environment shared by itinerants while travelling together were only one part of Methodist discourse. Relationships between the itinerant and the families to whom he ministered were recurring themes, whether they involved the reformation of recalcitrant men or the celebration of those women, the 'mothers in Israel,' who welcomed the itinerant in their homes.[86] And, as the above quotes indicate, writers were not reluctant to acknowledge the potential heterosexual attraction and power of the itinerant. The question of marriage, though, was not a straightforward one. Despite Methodists' glorification of the family, the structure and claims of an itinerant's work created a tension between the demands of spreading the gospel and heading a household. Unlike those late-nineteenth-century Canadian missionaries who travelled to Japan, China, and India, and for whom a family was often viewed as a necessary sign of respectability, travelling preachers in Upper Canada were perceived as possibly jeopardizing their work by marriage.[87] To Methodists, wives and children were seen as a burden on the circuits, adding to financial responsibilities for men who were expected to merely survive on the money paid to them by the New York Conference.[88] Moreover, the presence of family members on the circuit might impede the itinerant, slowing him down and preventing him from devoting himself to his task.

Celibacy, of course, was an ideal not always realized. As their biographers admitted, ministers did marry. Caleb Swayze, a preacher on the Westminister Circuit in 1817–18, had married when he converted and became an itinerant, but, as Carroll admitted, 'the exigencies of the work forced the authorities of the Church to employ labourers with these drawbacks.'[89] In such cases the choice of a partner was crucial. If a man was fortunate, he might find a Miss Oria Colt, who married Nathaniel Reeder, an

American preacher on the Cornwall Circuit, in 1820. 'She had few equals either in faith or prayer, exhortation, or womanly heroism. She shared largely in all the toils and trials, sacrifices and labors of a zealous husband ... one of a thousand. She could labor in public or private, at the altar or the bedside of the sick and dying, but especially in the nursery, where she gave a theological training ... to her older children, who, being occasionally cate-chized by the good Bishops of the church, received their encomiums and blessings.'[90]

Other Miss Colts existed and were recognized as assets to their hus-bands' work, but an itinerant's marriage always posed the danger of his being enticed into the security of domesticity. The dowry of Elijah War-ren's wife included a 'valuable farm by which prospect of worldly comfort he was lured from the then incredible toils and hardships of the itinerant ministry to enter into secular life.' After serving as a local preacher for a few years, 'he was observed to decline spiritually' and became a Universal-ist, opposed to temperance.[91] So far as women preachers were concerned, their work was rarely granted any official recognition and was seldom dis-cussed in these sources. As Eizabeth Muir argues, those women who did marry while working in the Methodist Episcopal Church often found their work downgraded and their public voices silenced. They also lost their salaries as independent workers.[92]

If conventional family ties posed a problem for those who were suppos-edly the church's spiritual guides, Methodist discourse in Upper Canada did not pose an either/or choice between family and celibate loneliness. The meaning of 'family' was flexible and mutable. As we have seen in terms of revivals, it could be viewed as an important means of spreading religion and, in that process, undergo significant changes itself. However, it also might signify the relationships of those brought together in religion. By positing the church as the family writ large, all members – but especially ministers – were thought to enjoy the benefits of family ties: affection, companionship, and emotional sustenance while under spiritual duress. In turn, this particular connotation had important implications for the height-ened form of religious masculinity constructed around itinerants. Not only were they said to experience 'family' among church members (lodging in their houses, praying with them, and sometimes holding services), their friendships with other preachers were portrayed as the epitome of male comradeship and fraternity. Carroll, an itinerant himself, rhapsodized that 'among the various relationships that subsist among men, whether civil, social, domestic, or ecclesiastical, none is more peculiar than that which exists between ministerial colleagues in a Methodist circuit. There is something like it, perhaps, in the "joint partnership" which sometimes, though rarely, takes place in other communities.'

Carroll admitted that frictions might arise. 'It is a relation calculated to afford each other a great deal of pleasure and assistance; or a great deal of pain and annoyance, if not injury.' Although he had experienced both, his fellow ministers were generally 'good and amiable; men from whose society I derived both pleasure and instruction, as well as spiritual profit.'[93] Carroll's description of a conference of ministers in the 1850s highlighted the 'footing of familiarity and fraternity not to be found among any other call of men.' Common spiritual purpose, augmented by shared training and work experiences, created a brotherhood that, like political fraternity, supposedly transcended diverse educational, occupational, and professional backgrounds. Like the fraternity of reformers, though, this community of brothers also defined itself either by women's absence from its ranks or by denying their presence in the ministry.[94]

Entering into a different kind of family might have seemed a straightforward solution, but, as some of the surviving memoirs and letters attest, it did not dissolve a certain degree of ambivalence between work and family. James Evans, a Methodist missionary who had been stationed at the Credit Mission and at Fort William, wrote to his wife and daughter from the latter post in February 1839 of his commitment to a spiritual life and of his work in the North. 'The world,' he told them, 'is losing its charms. I would just as soon be buried in the depth of these wilds, as to be in the populous city ... [H]eaven is just as near the wilderness as Toronto.' 'I have no home but heaven and I desire no other, but hope God will enable me to wander about these dark regions until he calls me home.' Yet, echoing other letters in which he had stressed his devotion to them, Evans assured them that 'you may, however, depend on my being down as soon as ever I can, consistent with the duties of my mission. These I must attend to, so long as I consider you safe; if otherwise, my duty is clear, – to care for you first, – next for the heathen.'[95]

As the correspondence of Samuel Rose indicates, family duty certainly was not a clear-cut issue. The claims of his biological family might follow an itinerant over the many miles of poor roads and Upper Canadian forests. Rose, born and raised in Prince Edward County, became a Wesleyan Methodist itinerant in 1831, and until 1874 he travelled a variety of circuits, including the Toronto and Niagara areas and Middlesex and Elgin Counties, as well as serving at the Yellowhead Indian Mission. Although he saw his parents and siblings sporadically once he became a minister, Rose kept up a regular correspondence with his brother John during the 1830s. What is striking about these letters is the language of brotherhood and fraternal affection that runs through them, one that was, however, fraught with tension and ambiguities. Rose was eager to stress that, even though his calling had forced a separation from his family, he had found a new one through his fellow itinerants and church members. He constantly referred to them as his 'brothers and sisters,' telling John that 'I have found them all along the road those that have taken me by the hand and led me on and have administered to my wants.'[96] Yet despite their kindness and sustenance, Rose remained keenly interested in his family's emotional, spiritual, and material states. He reassured John constantly of his love for him and the others, chiding him when he despaired of ever seeing him again. 'My Brother do you think that one month absence has robed [sic] me of all the kindred feelings that I ever possessed? So! my brother you all lay as near my heart as ever.'[97]

At times Rose desired only to be left 'to do the Lord's work,' as he told his father in November 1831. After hearing that his father's illness sprang partially from anxiety at not seeing him, Rose could not contain himself: 'My father this pains my weary soul. Can you not give me up and let me labour and spend my days for, and in the service of the Lord? It would be more acceptable to me to live and spend my days with you if it was the will of the Lord.' But that was not to be. Rose went one step further, reminding his father that 'I have found fathers and mothers sisters and brothers and, houses where I go, to dwell in: and food to eat, with all the necessarys [sic] of life.' In a more practical vein (his letters often combined lengthy emotional passages with reminders of postage costs), he hoped 'if nothing should interfere and providence permit to come down soon; but not before sleding [sic].'[98] Rose frequently reminded his family of the heavenly reunion waiting for them should they not meet again in Prince Edward County, and with this in mind he would ask about their spiritual state.[99]

Rose's repeated explanations about his reasons for leaving home may have served to reassure himself as much as his brother, yet his outpourings to John are also consistent with the kinds of emotional and personal effusiveness encouraged in Methodism. His letters, and the other sources quoted above, not only raise the question of masculine spirituality and all-male relationships but also bring into question the construction of masculinity through their chosen work. 'Manly labour,' for those men called to the ministry, did not mean a lessening of social relationships, for religious experience and service were constructed as an intensification of these relationships (albeit those deemed appropriate to the religious life). Nor was such labour separated from the household. When we compare developments in New England, where the meaning of ministerial work changed from 1815 onwards and had become a 'profession' by the 1840s, the discourse of Upper Canadian Methodist itinerancy continued to construct its preachers' work as 'manly labour' into the 1840s.[100] Furthermore, in Methodist discourse, masculinity did not mean Victor Seidler's 'lack of connectedness,' nor did it entail the kind of split between the individual and the community documented by Anthony Rotundo in his analysis of shifting types of American manhood during the nineteenth century.[101] Methodist itinerants in Upper Canada were faced with the task of integrating sacred and secular, the individual and the community. If any kind of work in Upper Canada was constructed as epitomizing a preindustrial merging of household and economy, it was that of the itinerant preacher.

Nevertheless, becoming a minister might mean a transformation of a certain kind of youthful masculine culture. In the memoirs of both Carroll and Joseph Hilts, a 'backwoods preacher' who began his itinerancy in the early 1840s, the kinds of companions and leisure activities they enjoyed as young men were identified as contributing to the dangers in which they placed their unconverted souls. Carroll's autobiography, *My Boy Life*, was dedicated 'To all the Self-Made Men (Both Lay and Clerical) in our wide connexion; and to all the Noble Boys, Who Intend to be such Men as are Men.' It was intended to serve as an 'improving tale' for these youths. As a child, Carroll had joined a boy's gang in York, fighting regular battles with other boys in a quasi-military fashion.[102] He then spent his adolescence working first on his brother's farm and then as an apprentice in Jesse Ketchum's tannery. Although Ketchum and his wife were devout and temperate, many of their employees were not. 'None of them were a safe copy to follow; and those whose age and size gave them a claim to natural manhood, and whose company as an aspiring boy, I affected, were more likely to lure me to wider fields of indulgence than I had yet explored. Alas! these explorations were mostly made on Sunday, including sometimes the garrison, among the soldiers, not excluding the military canteen, where the older ones treated the younger to drink.'[103] Once Carroll decided to mend his ways, attending chapel regularly and swearing off alcohol, he found it necessary to avoid his workmates, keeping to himself and reading his Bible for support.[104]

Similarly, Joseph Hilts left his childhood home near Acton upon his father's second marriage and became a drifter, falling prey 'to every bad influence and follow[ing] every inclination to run into sinful ways.' By the age of twenty-two he had narrowly escaped death a number of times through his own or others' carelessness, and so decided to join the church and 'seek and serve the Lord.' Having worked in the bush around his home, he and his brother decided to work 'in the woods,' but he was talked out of this by Mr Guybeson, a former hotel keeper and lumberman. 'An older Christian than you are would find it very hard to keep from backsliding in a shanty among the kind of men that you would have for associates there,' Hilts was warned. So, having been more fortunate than Carroll in this regard, he took up part-time work as a carpenter and schoolteacher.[105]

The kinds of youth-related temptations faced by these young men were not, of course, unique to Upper Canada.[106] Nor can we call them strictly 'working-class.' As Carroll's account of his boyhood companions indicates (some of them from 'respectable' York families and patrons of Strachan's school), this aspect of masculine culture may have had a strong cross-class dimension to it – or, as was the case in other areas, masculine culture may have been idealized as cutting across class divisions. What is clear is that in Methodist discourse, these kinds of relationships between men were to be transformed by the power of religion. As we shall see in the prescriptive literature of the press, young men in particular were perceived as being at risk from social pressures. Yet the obverse ideal was not passivity or effeminacy but rather the 'wrestler' for God, a combination of spiritual and physical strength and tenderness that was, in Methodist discourse, the mark of Christian manhood.

If concepts of the family and gender helped shape discourses around revivals and itinerancy in Upper Canada, they also ran through prescriptive literature, especially in the Upper Canadian Methodist press. While it would be an exaggeration to claim that the Methodists were the only group in Upper Canadian society to be so openly concerned with these relationships, Methodist discourse devoted huge amounts of space to them. Editors of secular newspapers usually did not expend the same energy discussing the social face of religion as did the *Christian Guardian* or, in the 1840s, the papers of the New Connexion and Episcopal Methodists, the *Christian Messenger* or the *Canada Christian Advocate*. While the secular press participated in a discourse on manners, mores, and morals, as we shall see in the next chapter, these subjects were not always tied to religion or given the kind of spiritual intensity that the evangelicals brought to the discussion.

The customary division in Canadian religious historiography between the 'theological' and the 'secular' has led to 'an opposition that has obscured rather than explained the meaning and role of religion in the intellectual world of Victorian Canada.'[107] Methodism, lacking the kind of theological debates and the 'metropolitan university traditions' of, for example, the Presbyterian Church, was not marked by this opposition. Methodists placed a greater value on experiential religion than on theological systems and a rigid church structure.[108] In founding the Methodist movement, Wesley had made the Bible the basis of his theology but had granted his followers room for 'experience, reason, and truth.' Once experience had been granted such an important role, it was difficult to separate religious precepts from the daily lives in which experience occurred, to see where notions of 'theology' (as a complex and abstract body of metaphysical beliefs) ended and secular beliefs began.[109] The evangelical fear of backsliding once a state of spiritual grace had been achieved made it imperative that constant vigilance over everyday behaviour be maintained.[110] Moreover, if there was one area in which sacred and secular merged in Methodist discourse, it was that of the family. Although newspapers such as the *Guardian* ran pieces that discussed theological matters, it was in the advice columns – such as 'Youth's Department' and 'Family Corner' – that the lessons of religion were situated in social settings, one of the most recurring and significant being that of the home.

As much of the work on women and religion in American, British, and Canadian history has noted, the growing identification of women, especially white, middle-class women, with religiosity throughout the nineteenth century tended to culminate in a huge number of all-female voluntary associations. Religion has been perceived by many historians as having helped bring women into the 'public sphere.'[111] Certainly some of the voices that contributed to the discourse of religion, gender, and the family in Methodism were eager to claim that women, by virtue of their higher nature and morality, had a 'special mission' to contribute to society. Yet, although ostensibly about 'woman' or 'women,' much of this literature used these all-encompassing terms to smuggle in their real subject: the special spirituality of wives and mothers exercised within the home.[112] It was not the attributes of single women that were celebrated in paeans to those whose 'empire is the heart' and who were in the best position to convert irreligious husbands.[113] 'The Female Prayer Meeting' brought religion and female family members together, depicting old mothers, youthful sisters, and a mother with a young family in a pastoral setting, all asking God for guidance. 'O, if there is aught on earth that can elevate the female character and render it truly amiable, lovely and useful, it is to be engaged in scenes like these.'[114] 'The influence of a Christian Mother' was straightforward: writers called it a 'public blessing ... an instrument of exalted good' and an 'irresistible influence.' 'Confined by duty and inclination within the walls of her own house, every hour in her life becomes an hour of instruction, every feature of her conduct a transplanted virtue.'[115] These idealized women might possess valuable qualities, but it was only through the heterosexual rites of marriage and maternity that they were able to exercise their 'special' and 'irresistible' influence. Even when the question arose of 'Women Speaking and Praying in Social Religious Meetings,' their challenge to authority was framed within the context of marital or familial relationships. 'D,' writing in support of women praying and exhorting, asked: 'Is it not supposed consistent with all due subjection, that the wife whose eyes and heart have been opened to receive the truths of the gospel, to instruct her enquiring husband in the way of life?'[116]

Reading this literature, an historian might easily think that these articles were the bricks and mortar used to construct, in the words of Mary Ryan, the 'empire of the mother,' a discursive space where wives and mothers might indirectly wield enormous influence in society. Here, it would seem, we may see the first stages of the development of a language of separate spheres. Certainly such an observation would not be completely misplaced. Much of the literature printed in the *Guardian* originated in the United States or Britain, where the 'theory of women's domestic influence' helped create an entire publishing industry.[117] But, as Ryan and other historians have reminded us, it was not woman as an autonomous individual abstracted from social relations that religious discourse celebrated.[118] The image of the pious woman was anchored in family relationships, ones that had, moreover, been created by the tie between husband and wife.

For all their talk of women's special mission, the writers in the *Guardian*, the *Canada Christian Advocate*, and the *Christian Messenger* did not grant women unequivocal control of religious life within the home. The leading role in family prayers, for example, was delegated to husbands. In 'Family Prayer,' a piece reprinted from the *Primitive Methodist Magazine* in the *Guardian* in 1832, a 'pious tradesman' told his minister that he had initially conducted such devotions but that the demands of both home life and his business had caused him to neglect such services. However, a letter from a former apprentice, telling him that his time in his household brought him back to Christ and begging him never to end family prayers, shook the tradesman out of his spiritual lethargy. Feeling, he told the minister, as though he'd murdered his children, he resumed the services, determined that he would give up part of his business rather than drop family prayers.[119] This and similar articles provided a counterpoint to the notion that the home was women's spiritual domain. Such articles spoke of many concerns, but an important one was that of male religiosity and the position of men as heads of households.[120]

It was up to men, as husbands and fathers, to see that 'family altars' were erected. However, when men were delinquent in this duty, women were urged to step in. As we have seen earlier, male authority could be challenged in the name of religion, a theme that many writers in the religious press highlighted. The story of Clara Morland, printed in the *Guardian*, was typical. Clara became a Methodist, despite her father's threats of expulsion from the family home. To support herself, she became a governess and had a rather pathetic existence in which her religion was her main sustenance. The narrative followed Clara through to her deathbed, where she expired forgiving her family, which had refused to reconcile with her.[121] A similar tale told of a wife's persecution by an irreligious husband, who often locked her out of the family home at night. For six months she prayed in a nearby field for his conversion. At the end of this period, her prayers were answered. Her husband came home realizing that he was a sinner and (in a process dizzying in its rapidity) prayed with her and became renowned for his piety. He invited ministers to their cottage and, when it began to overflow with such visitors, the neighbours built a chapel in the convert's garden and then eventually a larger one in the village. To crown all this, the once-immoral husband became a deacon.[122] Certainly, in this and in many other anecdotes, there was no doubt that the power of an irreligious husband could be subverted. Yet the purpose of this subversion was to bring him to religion and thus work towards more harmonious relations within the household, not to cast him out completely. Although the woman no longer had to resort to the fields to pray, it was her husband who, after all, became the deacon.

The question of authority within the family was not as clear-cut as those Methodist writers who glorified the power of the mother might have liked; some writers insisted on the dominance of men over women and children. However lovingly this power might be exercised, 'the man is the head of the woman, even as Christ is the head of the Church.' Such relations must not become sullied with either tyranny or stubborn resistance: men must use kindness and reason, and women must 'obey with a willing mind' and 'cheerfulness.'[123] Structure and respect for order, according to Samuel Bingham of Beamsville, must mark even Methodist society. 'In order for the existence of society, whether civil or religious, there must be governments, laws, officers, as well as subjects. The father of a family, the constituted authorities of a nation, and the ministers of the Church of God, must all have a sufficiency of power invested in them to enjoin and enforce obedience to such laws and regulations as are necessary to the peace, good government, and prosperity of the community over which they are placed.'[124] Not exactly, we might note, a celebration of women's power in the domestic realm!

If religious power or influence was not always constructed as an all-female domain, what did these writers of literature on domesticity have to say about religion and masculinity? A large number of religious writers saw masculinity as integral to familial spiritual order. Irreligious and violent husbands were not the only images used by these writers, and not only in family prayers was the power of the father important. The *Guardian*'s 'Youth's Department' of 23 October 1830 featured the patrilineal passing of religious belief with a description of a father's dying words to his son: 'Serve God, keep your thoughts on the next world, and remember hell.'[125] Sometimes this relationship might be reversed, as in the *Canada Christian Advocate*'s 'The Good Boy and Wicked Father.' Set in New York City, the story tells of a son rescuing his father from damnation by pointing out to him the evils of working on the Sabbath.[126]

Yet, as we shall see in the next chapter, and as other Methodists argued, youthful manhood might become a problem. 'Fifteen Young Men,' reprinted in the *Advocate* in 1849 from the American *Zion's Herald*, told the story of a group of residents in a boarding house. At the Sunday breakfast table, six of them were always to be found 'shaved, dressed, and prepared as to their apparel, for attendance on public worship.' They attended services all day long and predictably went on to become 'highly respected, useful citizens.' The other nine failed to make an appearance until noon and did not go to church. With one exception, they all turned out 'vicious,' disgraces and business failures. Their early deaths ('untimely and tragical end[s]') were warnings of the failure to observe the Sabbath.[127] Along with the injunction of Sabbath-keeping, this article contained a message about the potentially iniquitous effects of boarding houses and homosocial environments. Boarding houses, no matter how clean and well-ordered, could not replicate the 'real' family relationships – those of husband, father, son, and brother – in which men should be embedded.[128] This piece, and others, highlighted the dangers young men might face as they grew into Christian manhood.

For the most part, masculinity in religious discourse was thus shaped by two premises: the importance of men's presence in religious life and the need for religion to keep young men from going astray. At times there appeared a different image of men, especially young men, as 'soldiers for God.' Writing from Whitby to the *Advocate* in 1845, the Reverend E.S. Furman argued that the Methodist church should be able to claim an equal place with other denominations in Canada West. 'I trust also, Sir, we have a number of young soldiers, rising to fill the ranks of Fathers in the Ministry when they shall "have fought the good fight," finished their course, gained the victory through the blood of the everlasting covenant, and laid their armour by, to receive the crown.'[129] 'Isaac,' in his letter to the paper's editor later that year, used a similar symbol in his title, 'A Soldier to Stand, Must Stand Like a Soldier.' However, 'Isaac' did not address his message exclusively to young male ministers, claiming that 'all God's people' were soldiers and therefore had to fight.[130] The *Christian Messenger* used Biblical images of men engaged in a holy struggle to demonstrate the power of faith. It cited Abraham, Isaac, and Jacob and quoted St Paul to show how through faith Gideon, Samuel, Daniel, and the prophets '"subdued kingdoms, wrought righteousness, obtained promises, stopped the mouths of lions, quenched the violence of fire, escaped the edge of the sword, out of weakness were made strong, waxed valiant in fight, turned to fight the armies of the aliens: women received their dead raised to life again: and others were tortured not accepting deliverance, that they might obtain a better resurrection.'"[131]

Yet this image of men striding into the heart of the battle for Christ was less popular than that of men within the home. Fondness for the latter may be linked to a certain ambivalence toward the military, especially in the context of Upper Canada where 'war' meant that of 1812, an event that had contributed to the precarious position of American Methodists. George Playter, for one, described the War of 1812 as 'cruel' and saw, not glorious Christian soldiering, but terror and destruction on both sides. War meant that men forsook their place in the home and family, and those relationships that made them virtuous, and proceeded to 'fire, stab, cut, beat each other; to separate legs from the body, arms from the side, and heads from the neck; to pluck out the eyes, knock out the teeth, and slash away the face; to cut away the flesh, break the bones, and scoop out the very vitals of the body.'[132] Male bodies were thus doubly degraded: first, by being used as the instrument that mutilated the bodies of other men and, second, by the mutilations of warfare itself.

Playter's statements may be contrasted to those of the Anglican paper *The Church*, in which the figure of the Christian soldier was prominent. 'The Religious Soldier' was 'a lawful, necessary, and honourable profession; yea, God himself may seem to be one, free of the company of soldiers, in that he styleth himself "a *man of war*."' The opposite of a 'religious soldier' was a 'vicious' man with 'an ambush within [him] ... of fleshy lusts.'[133] This particular piece aimed at rehabilitating the reputation of the soldier, a man sometimes targeted in religious discourse as being particularly likely to fall prey to moral degeneration. Others, though, celebrated the merging of martial prowess with Christian devotion, as in testimony to Sir John Colborne submitted by 'The English Layman.' 'Religion,' the 'Layman' argued, 'when she animates the warrior, girds him with a sword of irresistible temper.' Moreover, 'it has taught men, battling for their altars and hearths, to gather fresh courage from disaster and defeat.' This writer linked religion, soldiering, and the home, characterizing religion as a feminine principle that motivated and guided the 'Christian Warrior' to protect the home (also designated as feminine). The 'Layman' also tied nationalism to this, declaring that 'the holy influences of this powerful and enduring impulse are most largely showered upon the British warrior.'[134]

This piece, along with others such as 'The Good Soldier' and 'The Religious Soldier,' steered The Church's discourse on gender and religion away from the immediate setting of home and family. At the same time, though, as in patriotic discourse, the meaning given to the 'Christian Warrior' was anchored in the domestic realm. Other pieces in the paper touched on themes that were familiar to Methodist discourse: the sacredness of family religion, the mother's sway and influence in the confines of the home, and Christian manhood. The Methodists were not the only religious group to construct categories of manhood and womanhood that were mutually dependent but also relied on religion to achieve their full spiritual and social potential and meaning. Yet, in Methodist discourse, these categories were elaborated upon to a much greater degree and helped provide the very underpinning of religious life. And, although William Westfall has characterized the religious landscape of early Upper Canada as being divided between religions of order (Anglicans) and experience (Methodists),[135] we can see in Methodist discourse around the family more fluidity and complexity than this division implies. Certainly the Methodists valued experience as a central tenet of religion, but it was the family that lent structure and 'order' to this experience. That the family itself could be challenged, its 'chain of command' shaken, did not mean that Methodists failed to see it as an important location in which gender relationships were organized and maintained. Its basic structure was not an issue; what was questioned was the exercise of power that shaped gender relations within the family.

With a few exceptions, much of the literature that we have been discussing was imported from the American and English religious press. Yet there was one facet of religious discourse that was not produced elsewhere. Although they were based on evangelical models from outside the colony, the obituaries of Upper Canadian Methodists provided a 'home-grown' discourse on gender and religion. Obituaries might serve many purposes:

commemorating their subjects' lives, providing inspirational examples of piety and holiness, and constructing the moment of death as a glorious reunion with Christ.[136] Those who died unrepentant provided lessons concerning the mistake of being unprepared to meet death. Temperance literature, in particular, emphasized the terrible consequences of dying unprepared (drunkards seldom wasted away but instead frequently met sudden and violent deaths).[137] Social and spiritual themes merged in these notices, as the individual's position in the community was duly noted and discussed. Occupation, family membership and history, place of birth: all of these categories were used to set the person being memorialized in some kind of social context. As we might expect, their religious history also was important, and much time was given to the story of their awareness of sin, search for and acceptance of Christ's salvation, and the subsequent benefits to both individual and community.

As in the prescriptive literature, gender was woven into the fabric of these notices. Commentators remembered their subjects as having fulfilled the duties of Christian manhood and womanhood, especially within the home. Jemima Perry, for example, who died in Ernest Town in 1830, aged seventy, had been a wife, mother, and friend, her 'doors always open' and her house a 'chapel.'[138] James Willson's death at the age of thirty-six was remembered as the passing of a devoted family member. 'In his domestic circle, the relations of private and social life, he was adorned with many virtues, as a husband, a parent, and a friend.'[139] Minerva Spencer, whose obituary appeared in the *Canada Christian Advocate* on 20 February 1845, had experienced a lengthy religious struggle that culminated not only in personal 'victory' but in the opening of her home to 'God's people.' In this she was accompanied by her husband, who also 'partook' of this blessing.[140]

Although the dead were placed in a network of social relations structured around gender and the family, the accounts of their final moments on earth departed from clear-cut gender-based norms. Certainly the family was important at the scene of the deathbed, and obituaries seldom failed to note the presence of husbands, wives, parents, children, and siblings. The last moments often were marked by assurances from the dying person that their separation from family members would be brief and that they could foresee a heavenly reunion in the not-too-distant future. The images of triumphant departures and glorious victories – images that relied upon military metaphors, which we might expect to be associated with masculinity – appeared in both women's and men's obituaries. Apparently the rhetoric of 'courage' and the 'good fighter,' reserved strictly for men in political and patriotic discourses, might cross the divisions of gender in evangelical discourse. Betsey Frigatt from West Gwillimbury, who died at forty-one after a certain amount of suffering, was called upon in her last moments to 'fight the good fight,' and 'her final conflicts were crowned with victory.'[141] Mrs Margaret German, of Fredericksburgh, 'suffered and died with the fortitude of a conqueror.' Despite having some spiritual 'conflicts,' she was able to reconcile herself to death and, giving her children up to God's mercy, provided an example of a 'most triumphant' death.[142]

If exaltation and triumph cut across gender and were used as ways of imaging the departure of both sexes, calmness and serenity also featured in accounts of men's and women's deaths. Either sex might fall 'asleep in the arms of Jesus.' Sometimes this state was reached after a lengthy struggle. As Jacob Morden's obituary shows, triumph might culminate in calm acceptance. Morden, who died at Ameliasburgh at age twenty-three, had worn himself out praising God and shouting 'aloud for joy.' Eventually, his memorialist wrote, he 'quietly submitted himself into the arms of the Lord.'[143] The narratives of conversion contained in obituaries usually did not rely on gender-based models. Members of either sex might be depicted either as struggling to come to salvation or as finding it a relatively easy state to attain.[144] Thus, although to some extent the obituaries of Upper Canadian Methodists displayed the same gendered patterns as other evangelical discourses, spiritual regeneration was an area in which the categories of male and female might be blurred. The language of gender was not always the sole means of discussing virtue and holiness.

The notions of 'public' and 'private' that emerged in the languages of Methodism were no less contradictory than those of patriotic and political discourse. Many of the writers discussed above certainly made an effort to identify the home and family as private, marked off from the rest of society, and to locate 'woman' or 'women' within the sheltering walls of the home as the religious monitors of society. Yet many contradictions were involved in this attempt to distinguish gender by using these concepts of social and physical space. For one, as we have discussed, there was no consensus about the religious power of the wife and mother. For another, religious discourse was concerned with masculinity, connecting the importance of religion to men as husbands, fathers, and sons. These were relationships that could not exist without a connection of some sort to women. No matter how hard those who concentrated on 'woman in the home' as the repository of religiosity in society might try, it was extremely difficult to lock men out of this discursively constructed dwelling. And herein lay the paradox of attempts to establish categories of manhood and womanhood in religious discourse. Just as the meaning of 'manhood' in religious discourse was grounded in relationships with women and children, as well as with God, 'womanhood' as a symbol and women as a category were defined in relation to men and children. Moreover, the frequent use of the home as an important symbol in public religious discourse makes it difficult to see it as a location clearly removed from the vicissitudes of social change.

Images and symbols of women were used much more extensively and directly in the language of Methodism than in those of politics or patriotism. However, the ones that we have discussed were not the only representations of womanhood. In Methodist missionaries' letters and reports from Native communities on Grape Island and at Rice Lake and the Credit River, we may see the construction by white Upper Canadians of different, yet related, meanings for manhood and womanhood. Their desire to reshape gender relations within Native communities tells us, though, less about Native peoples themselves and more about the powerful, if not always explicitly stated, racial meanings attached to the categories of gender that we have been discussing.[145]

If there was one theme that connected the Native women of Upper Canada to their white counterparts in the missionaries' language, it was that of the elevated position of women under Christianity. This tenet was, of course, not unique to Upper Canadian evangelicals; for many Christians their religion was supposed to uplift women from the enslavement, degradation, and oppression of their 'heathen' sisters.[146] Explicitly or implicitly, this argument ran through the religious discourse on women and gender relations. It was made directly in a frequently quoted article entitled 'The Infidel Mother' by the French writer Chateaubriand. This piece bemoaned the unhappy lot of those who, living without religion, were forced into such practices as infanticide. These crimes arose because of their society's lack of appreciation of the bond between mother and child, one that could only be inculcated by religion. This article was often followed by 'Advice to Christian Mothers,' which both celebrated religious maternity and spoke of the need to preserve it.[147]

Some of this material was drawn from the ever-increasing body of writings on missionary work in 'faraway lands.' Articles such as 'Heathen Females – Licentiousness' and 'Missions – Paganism' placed Upper Canadian religious discourse in an international context of imperial expansion.[148] Tales of cannibalism, polygamy, suttee, infanticide, and female slavery (the latter category laden with hints that such a condition involved more than economic bondage) had many meanings and purposes. One was an attempt to make the category of sex transcend that of race for Christian womanhood. One report in the *Guardian* proclaimed that 'these scenes of oppression and cruelty and death ought to excite the pity and sympathy of all Christian women and elicit their assistance.'[149]

Such tales also made the discourse of imperial expansion multifaceted and gave it a social face, one that might soften and humanize the implications of political and economic conquest. They also helped to justify and rationalize imperial expansion, arguing that 'British' or 'white' culture brought emancipation from 'barbarism' and 'savagery' for women, a group that in eighteenth-century British culture had come to symbolize those most in need of, and likely to benefit from, the humanitarian impulse embodied in Methodism.[150] In the colonial context of Upper Canada, where missionary work was not as geographically removed as in Britain, the language of Christian uplift brought these issues very close to home. Although much was made of the effect of Christianity on Native men, especially men degraded by alcohol, in Upper Canadian missionary discourse it was the symbol of the enslaved Native woman that was used to represent the triumph of moral regeneration.[151] The York Female Missionary Society stressed this point in their 1830 report, commending 'the instrumentality of a few pious and indefatigable females who, touched with a feeling sense of the untold sufferings to which their sex are exposed in the barbarism of savage life, have spared no pains to meliorate their condition, and open to them the door of present comfort and everlasting life.'[152]

In making the connection between themselves and Native women the primary bond, and attempting to downplay, if not write out completely, the racial differences that separated them and that also might make the meanings of womanhood for Native women quite different, the society used the category of 'Christian womanhood.' Like the reformers' universal brotherhood, this category permitted generalizations about the essential nature of familial – especially maternal – ties, while simultaneously exposing the socially and culturally constructed nature of these bonds. Such an approach was exemplified in the 1833 report of the Cramahe Female Missionary Society, which highlighted the need for missions in Upper Canada by relating the tale of a mother whose son won a prize from the missionaries. With great pathos, she expressed the wish that they had arrived sooner, for their coming would have prevented her from murdering her other son.[153] Tales of the transformation of Native homes and families, while to some degree resembling accounts of domestic happiness in white families after accepting Christ's love, made it clear that the journey from degradation to uplift was one of crossing the borders of both religion and race. Not only were irreligious activities and beliefs denied – Native society and culture (or what the missionaries perceived Native society and culture to be) were also expected to be renounced. Native women, like white women, might be encouraged to speak out against the brutality of Native men, but – unlike white women – in doing so they were also expected to shoulder the cultural, social, and economic customs and values of a colonial power.

Turning the unnatural and dangerous mother into the model of loving, Christian maternity was not the only way in which Christianity would benefit Native people. According to religious discourse, the transformation of gender relations within the family was also badly needed. Like many of their contemporaries, Methodist missionaries in Upper Canada saw the transition from a nomadic life of hunting and gathering to a settled life of agricultural production as central to the redemption of Native people.[154] In religious discourse, transformed gender relations were perceived to be essential to this shift. Native men were, of course, implicated in these relations, for turning men from hunters into farmers involved reshaping the meanings of men's work and manliness in general in Ojibwa society. 'Fatherhood,' for example, in missionary discourse was no longer synonymous with teaching children (particularly sons) the skills of hunting or trapping; instead, fatherhood was to be associated with areas such as agricultural cultivation (formerly the province of women).[155] But it was on the figure of the Native woman that many of the missionaries' hopes were pinned. Men, the missionaries argued, would become industrious and sober with Christianity, supporting their wives and children and becoming the heads of stable households.[156] However, it was up to Native women as wives and mothers to provide the motive and inspiration, by their dutiful and industrious management of the home. Their hopes for the progress of Christianity and civilization did not acknowledge – and, generally, *could* not recognize – the ways in which patriarchal familial relationships would undermine Native women's economic independence and subject them to the dominance of both white society and that of their own husbands and fathers.[157]

The success of the Native women's work, missionary letters and reports insisted, was to be seen in the neatness and cleanliness of their homes. The triumph of civilization and Christian morality was represented not only by the abolition of infanticide and matricide but also by the presence of household furniture, tea-kettles, and clean, European-style clothes. All of these objects were placed within the four walls of a warm and sheltering home, a Western-style building that had replaced 'weg-ke-wams.'[158] D. McMullen, writing from Rice Lake to the *Guardian* in March 1830, noted such 'improvements' as the habits of industry and economy and the fight against alcohol, but he was especially impressed by the homes of the Native residents. 'The furniture of their houses, consisting chiefly of bedsteads, tables, benches, etc., is principally of their own make; and the females begin to keep their houses in tolerable good style.'[159] In November, the missionary Philander Smith described in glowing terms the Grape Island mission's farms, crops, buildings, and schools, but he was especially interested in the Ojibwa homes: 'I felt a desire to examine their domestic economy in their *houses*, accompanied by Mrs. Hurlburt we visited most of the females.' Here Smith saw moccasin- and clothes-making and some wood-working. 'In most cases the homes were cleanly, and their little stock of furniture in its proper order. Some cupboards, the make of Indian Mechanicks, were neat, and handsomely set off with plates, basons [*sic*] etc., in decent style.' Smith was most impressed by the Island hospital, run by Peggy Mekigk and her sister 'whose manners a few years since were well known about Bath and Hay Bay. Their virtuous deportment, and industrious habits now commend them to the care of the sick. There was a decency about the house, that no white woman need be ashamed of.'[160]

The concern with homes and household objects that ran through missionary and other religious discourses on Native people should not be mistaken for support for consumerism: in the missionaries' understanding of contact between whites and Native people, the lure of cheap finery and trinkets had led to alcoholism and moral degradation. James Evans, a Methodist missionary from England, and one of the first missionaries to speak and preach in Ojibwa, told the readers of the *Christian Guardian* about an encounter between two Christian native women from the Credit and the wife of the St Clair chief Joshua Wawanosh. The latter, being interested in Christianity, remarked on the women's plain style of dress. Upon being told that it was the sign of a Christian woman, she proceeded to take the ostrich plumes and silver bands off her hat, and, noted Evans, 'both her person and her mind are evidently brought under the sacred influence of Divine grace.' That Methodists would frown upon 'ostrich plumes and silver bands' might come as no surprise. Such objects, however, were particularly dangerous when their wearers were perceived as being untutored in Christian morality, lacking a clear sense of the dangers involved in wearing finery.[161]

Natives' acquisition of private property was an important objective for the missionaries, but it was to be limited to those essentials obtained through industry and thrift. Many of the items that were so admired in these homes were, it was stressed, the product of Native men's own manual labour. The beds and cupboards they had made signified their assumption of Christian manliness and their acceptance of the Western model of gender relations. For men, this labour was represented much more concretely than for women, whose conversion to Christian womanhood was signified by the order of their homes. The labour that went into keeping a home neat and an engaging picture for visitors' comments was downplayed or rewritten as female piety and morality. Like the banner of 1813, it was the emotional bonds of gender that a shiny tea-kettle signified, not the hard work that a woman had performed to keep it spotless.

This representation of emotional connections in material objects becomes even more intriguing when we consider that, in the religious discourse of the press, such images appeared alongside homilies on femininity and womanhood that highlighted and praised mothers' and wives' contributions to gender relations as *emotional*, not physical, 'housekeeping.' The articles and letters that make up the religious discourse on gender in Methodism did not single out neat and tidy cupboards as the primary signifier of women's contribution to morality within the home. Rather, they spoke in abstract terms of female 'influence' as exercised by wives and mothers and of the delights of feminine piety. Native women, it seemed, represented a stage in the evolution of Christian civilization. Unlike some white women, they could never aspire to the status of 'ladies,' but perhaps in the future they would reach the point where social relations could become more abstract and would take precedence over the material apparatus of Christian morality. Converted Native women were 'pious Indian women,' a designation that mingled both class and racial status. Even a supporter of Native women's reputation, like 'Otho,' who wrote to the *Guardian* in response to Bond Head's assertion that Native women in mission villages were bearing mixed-race children, did not grant them the status of ladies, although he claimed they were 'examples of chastity worthy of imitation.'[162] The term 'lady,' as Evelyn Brooks-Higginbotham has pointed out, was not coterminous with that of 'woman'; instead, it was a trope in which race, class, and gender were 'discursively weld[ed].'[163] By linking 'progress' to the symbol of the 'domesticated' Native woman, religious discourse underscored the supposedly natural and inevitable position of white women within Christian society. Furthermore, the images of gender and family relations that ran through the rest of religious discourse – images that were understood to apply to white men and women – provided an important subtext for any discussion of gender relations in Upper Canadian Native society.

Was there any other discourse about Native people that countered that of the missionaries? In the sources consulted, the voices of Native women are, unfortunately, heard only through the filters of missionaries' reports and letters. In these sources, the narrative devices and tropes used by the missionaries, the discursive strategies (such as the uplifted Christian Native mother) that constructed Native women for a predominantly white audience, obscure these women's own agency and subjectivity. It is difficult, if not impossible, to uncover what sort of language they used to discuss the meaning of Christianity in their own lives.[164] However, in the letters and reports of those Native men who worked as missionaries and missionaries' helpers, we may see a rather different perspective on religious matters. Men such as John Sunday, chief of the Mississaugas at the Bay of Quinte and a Methodist preacher, focused on the spiritual importance of religion to his people. While Sunday saw the benefits of moral discipline as important, he did not tie morality to domestic relations but rather linked it to the abolition of alcohol and its attendant vices.[165] Peter Jones, although not uninterested in the reshaping of gender relations under Christianity, stressed the need for spiritual regeneration as his people's first and foremost concern.[166] The Ojibwa chief and Methodist preacher George Copway, while noting the importance of his family in his conversion, identified his people's need for religion as a spiritual matter and a means of giving purpose to lives that had been violently disrupted by white contact. 'King Alcohol,' in Copway's memoirs, was pinpointed as causing their problems, having been brought to them by 'those fiends in human shape,' 'merciless, heartless, and wicked white men' – men who were only interested in using Indians to snatch their hunting grounds.[167]

Certainly Methodist missionary work in Upper Canada had other aspects, such as trying to prevent Bond Head from removing the Ojibwa to Manitoulin Island, a move ostensibly designed to ease the last years of a 'dying people' but also, some historians suggest, meant to free up land for white settlers.[168] And religious discourse was not the only language to employ images of Native men, women, and children. They figured in stories and anecdotes run by various newspapers, sometimes as Rousseauian archetypes who welcomed the white settler to the new land, in other cases as a pathetic warning of the brutal consequences of American democracy.[169] In Methodist discourse, the centrality of, as well as the meanings given to, gender and family relations in Native society tells us as much about this particular group of white Upper Canadians as they do about the objects of their concerns. Their conceptions of gender and race underscored, rather than undermined, other discussions of gender, the family, and religion. At the same time, the language of the missionaries exposed the extent to which the dominant images of Methodist discourse were white Anglo-American men, women, and children.

Far more than patriotic or political discourse, the language of Methodism was prepared to discuss the position of women and use images of virtuous womanhood. Moreover, the meaning of virtuous manhood was grounded in men's relationships with God and their families, not in the political arena or in relation to the monarch and state. Evangelical conceptions of society that valued the religious well-being of the individual helped shape this language. Yet individualism was not the only tenet of Methodism, as spiritual grace also was anchored within the framework of the family. Such an entity did not have to be a woman or man's biological relatives; 'family' could be the metaphor used to understand and order relationships with other, likeminded souls. However, unlike the masculine fraternity of the reformers or the shadowy female family members in conservative discourse, the Methodist definition of 'family' was heavily dependent on the presence of all traditionally understood to be members: husbands and wives, mothers and fathers, brothers and sisters.

The tensions and contradictions around gender and the family in evangelical discourse were extensive. In some contexts, familial relationships could be a site of religious solidarity, but they also might be challenged by those who were most likely to experience subordination and domination within families: women and children. Such challenges were not limited to the period of radical evangelicalism prior to the War of 1812; we cannot, for example, construct a linear chronology, a narrative of radicalism being overturned and vanquished by the forces of patriarchal domestic conservatism. Instead, evangelical discourses on the family and domesticity fell into synchronic patterns; calls for husbands and fathers to take the lead in family religion at times overlapped and co-existed with tales of women's victorious triumphs over brutal and irreligious husbands. And although the morals of these tales were meant to convince Upper Canadians of the need for family religion and not to wholeheartedly legitimate women's resistance to patriarchal authority, nevertheless these narratives not only condoned but also applauded such resistance. In doing so, they helped recuperate the figure of the 'disorderly woman,' who had been satirized by conservatives for disobeying her husband and father and assuming a public voice in religious matters.

Yet there were a number of contradictions surrounding the disorderly woman. Methodist discourse attempted to identify public and private even more explicitly with male and female. As we have seen, this was in sharp contrast to those attacks on Methodism that tied familial disorder and hysterical femininity to sedition and political upheaval.) The home, though, was not a private space, notwithstanding attempts to portray it as such. It was central to the prescriptive literature that was an important part of religious discourse, a literature that insisted, furthermore, that religion was not something that could be separated from daily life or other aspects of society. Moreover, in the Methodist discourse around missions and Upper Canadian Native peoples, the home was anything but 'private'; it became the site of public concern and curiosity, the measure of Christianity and civilization. As we shall see in the following discussion on manners, mores, and the literature of domesticity, the desire of various groups in Upper Canada to work out codes of behaviour and morality was based on notions of masculinity and femininity and would result in the articulation of a socially defined space that was neither distinctively 'public' nor 'private,' one, moreover, that could not be identified as the sole province of either 'man' or 'woman.'

4

Manners, Mores, and Moral Behaviour

Manly ministers, their pious followers, and the Christianized Native people of Upper Canada were not the only studies in character and behaviour offered as moral examples to Upper Canadians. From the 1790s to the 1830s, the colonial newspapers provided hints and advice and, at times, railed about the correct forms of behaviour for men and women. Ranging from anecdotes scattered throughout the pages of the press to weekly columns devoted to appropriate conduct for men, women, and children, and articles warning of the evils of duelling, this literature formed a discourse on manners, mores, and morals that relied heavily on gender as a given in social organization. It also took as its task the reformation and regulation of gender relations. Like much of the religious material discussed in the previous chapter, a great deal of this literature originated outside the colony, in Britain and the United States. In the absence of a widespread publishing industry devoted to Upper Canadian work, this material helped shape a public discourse on codes of behaviour in the colony. In both the religious and secular press, literature on domesticity, the problems of the workplace, the need for temperance, and Upper Canadian opposition to duelling shaped a discourse that, as much as it relied on the binary opposites of public and private, and attempted to identify men with the former and women with the latter spaces, hinted at a more complex way of conceptualizing social formation.

'Manners,' writes American historian John P. Kasson, must be seen as 'inextricably tied to larger political, social, and cultural contexts ... [T]heir ramifications extend deep into human relations and the individual personality.'[1] Kasson and other cultural historians of nineteenth-century American society have pointed to a number of changes linked to the growth of the antebellum American middle class, particularly in the urban northeast: the growth of conduct literature and advice books, the elaboration of rules of etiquette, the development of the sentimental 'cult of mourning,' and the formation of rules and regulations governing behaviour in public spaces, such as streets, parks, and theatres.[2] Linking these new forms of conduct for white, middle-class men and women were ideals of sentimentality and sincerity, in which expressions of inner feelings were lauded as the signs of the truly virtuous, and hypocrisy (no matter how well-disguised as virtue) was condemned as the mark of immorality. This desire to distinguish between sincere, heartfelt expressions of morality and those counterfeit gestures of – to use Karen Halttunen's immensely influential phrase – 'confidence men and painted women' grew, Halttunen argues, out of the immense social, economic, and political dislocation of this period. The American experience of urbanization, industrialization, and a massive growth in the electorate was accompanied by intense anxieties and fears about increased mobility, whether social, economic, or geographic, and the erosion of the familiar ties of community and kinship that had characterized much of colonial society. Middle-class Americans' concerns about these changes were frequently channelled toward the figure of the 'stranger,' who might deceive and dupe the innocent citizens of the new republic, luring them from the virtues of hard work, thrift, and morality to the corrupting and vicious enticements of idleness, luxury, and crime. Only by developing ways of behaviour that were guided by the principles of sincerity, ones that clearly demonstrated an individual's innermost character, could the middle class come to terms with itself and the mobility that had helped create it.[3]

As Kasson points, out, however, the elaboration of bourgeois codes of conduct 'cannot be understood strictly within national boundaries.'[4] Indeed, the work of cultural historian G.J. Barker-Benfield has demonstrated that, a century earlier, British society underwent a series of similar shifts in the transformation of manners and social conduct, from the rough, crude, and often violent behaviour of the farmer-warrior to the middle-class, humanitarian ethos of 'sensibility.' This ideology, which valorized the expression of spiritual and moral values and encouraged the expression of empathy for others (most notably women), permeated, Barker-Benfield argues, much of British literature, religion, education, politics, and domestic relations. Sensibility was particularly influential in articulating middle-class women's subjectivity and helping to shape their culture, giving them a language in which to express their desires for an end to male domination within the home. The rise of the 'cult of sensibility' in Britain came about because of developments in the new science of sensational psychology and the growth of commercial capitalism and consumerism during the eighteenth century. These forms of economic exchange, Barker-Benfield argues, in which men were dependent on the goodwill and patronage of their fellow traders, necessitated a shift in men's behaviour towards each other, leading to greater attention to the sensitivities of others and a decline in physical violence.[5]

Languages of sensibility and sentimentality, as well as a general concern with social behaviour, thus came to Upper Canada from across both the ocean and the colony's southern border. It is difficult, if not impossible, to gauge the relative weight of either British or American discourses on colonial developments. Nor can it be stated that the kinds of social and economic changes that occurred in either Britain or the United States fuelled the development of discourses on manners and mores in Upper Canada. The colonial language of moral conduct was less concerned with the specifics of public manners and behaviour (how to use cutlery in the correct manner, for example) than with general standards of virtue and righteousness. But given that this was a colonial society with a white population that was mostly descended from, or directly connected to, Britain or the United States, it should be far from surprising that these codes of behaviour and morality were reiterated in Upper Canada. Moreover, because such codes were articulated by the British and American middle classes, it is reasonable that they should appear in the pages of the Upper Canadian press and then be elaborated upon by a number of voluntary organizations.

The behaviour of men and women towards each other, in the home specifically and in society generally, was a theme that fascinated the colonial press. Although such behaviour was of special interest to religious writers and editors, who focused on it as they elaborated a code of domesticity in the 1830s and 1840s, other writers also were eager to discuss gender and familial relations. Yet, especially in its earliest manifestations, not all of this discourse subscribed to the glorification of home and family, nor did it always see relations between men and women as founded on ties of love and affection.

Although his appearances were infrequent, the predatory male surfaced from time to time in the pages of the press.[6] In 'The Seducer, addressed to the fair daughters of America,' which was run by the *Upper Canada Gazette* in 1800, the sad tale of the lovely yet unfortunate Juliana was recounted for edification. Having fallen a victim to her anonymous seducer's 'solemn declarations of constancy ... intended only to conceal his internal intreagues [sic], and to effect her ruin,' Juliana had her life destroyed. Finding it 'astonishing that rational beings should so far forget the dignity of their natures, as to give themselves over to the controul [*sic*] of their passions,' the anonymous writer called for the exposure of the 'author of all these miseries.' Such a man 'poisons all the social enjoyments of life, to gratify his brutal lust ... [H]e sports with the fair victim ... and prides himself on his ignoble exploits.' 'Such a one is a monster in creation; and ought to be treated with universal contempt. The injury done by the thief and the robber, may be repaid: but the vile seducer does an injury, for which he can never make restitution ... Such are more dangerous to meet, than bears bereaved of their whelps. They ought like ravenous wolves to be hunted from civilized society.'[7]

While making it clear that the man in question undoubtedly had committed a most serious and reprehensible act, this particular article did not focus solely on him, or on the possibility of his reformation. Much was made of the destruction of Juliana's life, the 'shame and sorrow' she brought upon her parents, and the 'fear and derision' evoked by her company. The 'miseries' brought upon a woman who had lost her honour, who was forced to leave 'the circle of mirth and gaiety, to drag out the remainder of her existence of her life ... in gloomy solitude,' could result in her 'seek[ing] relief from her misery, by destroying her own life.' This, the author hinted quite broadly, was the tragic result of young women being unable to resist youthful temptation and the blandishments of evil and corrupt men. Juliana's tale thus was as much about the need for women to protect their honour from such men as it was about male sexual licence.

Although 'Eusebius,' writing to the *Gazette* in 1823, argued that 'the degree of female chastity existing in a nation might serve as almost a certain rule by which to estimate that nation's moral, religious, and political character,' the burden of protecting this chastity was not placed on women's shoulders alone. 'Eusebius' hoped to expose the wrongdoings of a certain magistrate who had committed a 'gross breach of the seventh commandment.' This 'husband of a virtuous and faithful wife, the father of a numerous and promising family of children ... clothed with magisterial authority ... a conservator of the public peace, and a guardian of the public morals,' had seduced and impregnated, according to 'Eusebius,' a friend of his daughter, an action that was doubly immoral since the young woman was also a near relative of the magistrate. Reaching even greater heights of moral outrage, 'Eusebius' asked rhetorically whether the magistrate should be treated like a 'monster in vice and depravity, whose right to the common courtesies of life, and the privilege of friendship was fairly cancelled by his misconduct? – Do we suppose his brother magistrates would sit down with him to the solemn discharge of their important duties?' Not only should the offender be shunned by his peers, 'Eusebius' also insisted that they must feel obligated to report him to the governor, 'in a true spirit of allegiance to their Sovereign and, as fellow subjects, to the community at large.' In this correspondent's view, the governor was the appropriate official to whom this problem must be brought. He would listen, 'Eusebius' felt, since 'he hath taken his station by the side of religion and virtue; and our Capital bears honourable testimony to the weight of his example; and it were to be wished that the Province at large would go and do likewise.'[8] The solution to this particular breach of both private and public morality lay in invoking the political powers of the imperial representative as the guardian of the colony's morals.

The code of moral conduct set out by 'Eusebius' for men, especially those in positions of respect and trust, generally was not elaborated upon as much as were the perils of seduction for women. Articles that discussed the dangers of the fashionable life often hinted at the snares that might underlie its heady excitements, ones that could lure impressionable and foolish young women into moral danger. The *Kingston Gazette*'s 'Reckoner' column offered the edifying example of Mariana, the sheltered and uneducated daughter of a colonel whose regiment was posted to Montreal. Introduced into the 'best company ... in a few weeks Mariana was transformed from a smart but bashful country lass to a leader of the fashions.' Moreover, the 'Reckoner' noted drily, 'the Colonel was as giddy as his daughter, and delighted to indulge her in all her whims.'[9] Women, as we shall see later, were not the only sex accused of foolishness and susceptibility to the blandishments of the world, but they were most likely to pay a higher price than men for such weaknesses. Unlike American conduct literature's warnings about the 'confidence man,' it was not just the influence of devious strangers that was to be feared – women's own moral weaknesses, particularly their susceptibility to blandishments and flattery, might cause their downfall.

Relations between the sexes were shot through with the possibility of danger for women, underscoring the need for the security of marriage. Yet if this particular discourse on sexuality and seduction constructed women as potentially beleaguered creatures with weaknesses and vulnerabilities, there was no consensus on 'woman's nature.' Other writers took delight in poking fun at certain aspects of behaviour that were considered typically female, gossiping and scolding in particular. These traits were mocked in pieces such as the untitled poem run by the *Kingston Gazette* in 1810, its subject being a woman who took delight in scolding. From the minute she awoke, the anonymous poet declared, her neighbours could hear her 'clack a mile hence.' After describing the stream of annoyances and irritations this woman visited upon her family and servants, the poem ended in her own voice:

> At night, when I retire to bed, I surely fall a weeping;
> For silence is the thing I dread, I cannot scold when sleeping;
> But then my pains to mitigate, And drive away all sorrow;
> Although tonight may be too late, I'll pay them off tomorrow.[10]

This poem hints that the same tongue that a woman used to harangue her family and community might become a weapon of considerable potence and give the woman some influence, though not popularity. The gossip, however, was a figure who did not invoke the same kind of grudging respect. Instead, she signified feminine foolishness and untrustworthiness. Some writers held up the gossips themselves as figures of fun, while others managed to work this supposed trait into their writings about women in general. The obituary of Mrs Jane Beaton, who died in England at the age of eighty-eight, exemplified such stereotyping. She supposedly was a Freemason and had attained this singular achievement for a woman by having learned the lodge's secrets while hiding in its meeting room. Her memorialist noted sardonically, 'It is said she was a very SINGULAR old woman, as the SECRET died with her.'[11] 'Learning for Ladies,' reprinted from a London paper, created a conversation on women's education between a 'learned Lady' and a 'Gentleman.' Upon asking him why arts and sciences were thought to be 'incompatible with a woman's situation,' she was told that, while learning was not 'entirely unbecoming,' women needed only a small dose of these subjects in order to 'answer the purpose.' 'In my opinion, a woman's knowledge of chemistry should extend no farther than a thorough acquaintance with every hole and corner of her house; her algebra to keeping an exact account of the expenses of the family: and as for tongues, Heaven knows that one is enough in all conscience, and the less use she makes of it the better.'[12]

Womanhood often was represented as a foolish and irrational state of being, a discursive strategy that was not unique to Upper Canada. Intellectual and cultural historians have pointed to a tendency in Enlightenment thought to link foolishness to femininity, part of the process whereby rationality was constructed and understood as a masculine trait and also perceived as essential to the very definition of masculinity itself.[13] At times these qualities might be mediated by factors other than gender, as in the anecdote of the young Dublin servant who found herself pregnant by a Dutch sailor. Advised by a friend to pin the baby's paternity on her master, as he was the richer of the two men, the servant replied that she had considered this strategy but believed that 'the child will discover all, when it begins to speak Dutch.'[14] As a servant, this young woman's class might invest her with a kind of cunning and slyness. Her own credulity, symptomatic of her gender and also of her nationality (the childish foolishness of the Irish was a recurrent theme in newspaper satire), undercut any real harm to the social order that such a woman might pose.

Another popular figure was that of the spinster, desperate to marry. One article, 'The Old Maid's Register,' charted one woman's evolution from fifteen to fifty, demonstrating that her own false pride and stubbornness had led her to her state. From refusing, at the age of twenty-two, 'a good offer because the gentleman is not a man of fashion,' by thirty she 'betrays the dread of being called an old maid.' Between the ages of thirty and forty-six she becomes obsessed with men, alternating between 'rail[ing] against the entire sex' and seeking out quite unsuitable liaisons (including 'exhibit[ing] a strong predilection for a Methodist person'). At forty-eight, according to this chart, the 'old maid' 'attunes her sensibility to dogs and cats' and, having 'adopt[ed] a dependent relation to attend to this menagerie,' by fifty she 'becomes disgusted with the world, and vents her ill-humour on the unfortunate keeper of animals.'[15] As unmarried and childless women, spinsters stood outside the 'natural' order of marriage and represented a type of womanhood that was defined as deficient because of absences, those of husband and child. The stereotypes of unmarried women that appeared in the press were tinged with uneasiness concerning their position in society, an uneasiness signified by the use of humour and satire.

Although this discourse portrayed marriage as the symbol of women's fulfilment, matrimony itself was not necessarily presented as being synonymous with happiness and harmony between men and women. To be sure, a happy marriage was held up as an ideal. Nevertheless, writings on family relations warned that some marriages might be made in a place other than heaven. As in the religious discourse examined in the last chapter, here too can be found depictions of marriages made miserable because of a husband's domineering ways. Sometimes marriage was treated as an institution shaped by the behaviour of those concerned and thus subject to change and improvement. Such was true in the case of the woman who, ill-treated by her husband, saw a drastic improvement in his ways after he overheard her reasons for her cheerful forbearance. Upon being questioned by his friends as to why she put up with his bad temper, she admitted that she wanted to make him as comfortable as possible in this world since she believed that he would be miserable in the next. This remark prompted him to change his ways, whereupon 'she received the fruits of his "labours of love" in his vital reformation.'[16]

But unlike irreligious behaviour within the family, which was often blamed on men, discord within the home was less often attributed to husbands alone. Although the 'Reckoner' used the edifying tale of Drusus, whose bad temper terrorized his family until an injury to one of his children made him realize the error of his ways, the author hastened to warn his readers that wives too might make similar mistakes. A 'greater number of families are disturbed by the perverseness of the Lady, than by the sullenness of the Gentleman,' he wrote, and then proceeded to elaborate upon the virtues of wifely obedience and submission. Not only would a husband be pleased by his wife's 'softness' and 'tenderness,' but he would be induced to obey her wishes and anticipate her desires.[17]

Other writers also recognized the power relations involved in marriage, taking a more cynical perspective and characterizing marriage as an ongoing struggle between men and women. This outlook was most often found in the conservative *Upper Canada Gazette,* but it was not limited to that paper. Similar articles, often with strong misogynist tones, appeared in reform papers as well, especially in *Mackenzie's Gazette.* Some writers believed that wives held the winning cards and argued that, no matter what men achieved outside the home, 'woman ruled' within its boundaries (sometimes dominating men by nagging or scolding, sometimes by the 'bonds of love').[18] 'Captain Rock,' though, writing in the *Canadian Freeman* in 1832, saw marital relations as negotiable, at least at the outset of a couple's relationship. In 'The Marriage Ring,' he observed that the way in which a husband placed the ring on his bride's finger indicated what was to come. If he placed the ring on the fingertip, then she would be 'the queen and mistress of every thing in the household.' However, if he was 'ungentle enough to push the ring up to the root of the finger,' then he would be the 'lord and master.' The captain advised his readers that 'for this very reason, well-bred ladies take care to bend the ring finger at the moment they receive the marriage ring, so as to stop it at the first or second joint, and it is to this little artifice that they still owe the pleasure of governing their husbands, who always, however, boast that they guide their own vessels.'[19]

This concept of women's 'hidden power' ran through much of the secular literature on marriage and domesticity, bolstering the notion of marriage as a state of never-ending contractual negotiations. It also was used to poke fun at the seeming dominance of husbands, a position that, while enshrined in common law, nevertheless could be undermined in the give and take of daily relationships. Such was the case in the story of Solomon Swallow and his attempts to draw up a plan of 'Matrimonial Observations.' His system of marital rules and regulations was thwarted by his wife, who refused to follow his guidelines and, in retaliation, threw crockery, tore up his shirts, attempted to escape the marriage, and, finally, became the dominant partner. The moral of this 'authentic tale,' the anonymous author advised readers, pointed to Swallow's own foolishness. If he had treated his wife properly in the first place, ruling her with love and not by formal rules and regulations, she would not have needed to behave 'like a Tartar.' The jocular tone of the story invited the reader to sympathize with Swallow's wife and share a laugh at his expense, poking fun at the Swallows' deviation from the norms of marital relations: a dominant (albeit affectionate) husband and a submissive, loving wife. From the outset, Swallow's failure as a husband was predestined and known.[20]

Others saw marital relations from a less jaded perspective. At least as early as 1811, in the *Kingston Gazette*'s 'Reckoner' column, marriage was praised as a blessing, especially for men. Responding to a bachelor's diatribe against the institution, the 'Reckoner' told him that man's 'natural' energy needed the softening influence of woman's 'delicacy and sweetness.' The 'Reckoner' also delivered a short sermon on the joys of fatherhood. 'It is impossible for a father to spend his leisure hours in the company of his children without becoming a better man. In them, he perceives more solid happiness ... than from the possession of all those objects which mankind are striving to obtain.' This oblique critique of materialism was followed by the observation that 'those who [do] not delight in the society of children were seldom remarkable for the delicacy of their feelings; the strength of their affections; or the stability of their virtue.'[21]

The *Gazette* was fond of teaching bachelors about the redeeming qualities of married life and the importance of being husbands and fathers. Such men, it seemed, needed instruction and a certain amount of cajoling; women, on the other hand, were all too eager to enter into the 'holy bonds.' We should note, though, that writers on domesticity could not come to an agreement as to whether women were more 'naturally' suited for marriage than men. Womanly tenderness and sincerity often were prized as fundamental to a happy home life, the assumption being that women could be expected to provide the emotional furnishings in the domestic realm. Nevertheless, women might be in need of advice on marital conduct.[22] For those who wished to shape domestic affairs, it was too important a subject to be left to chance or to concepts of natural feminine inclination.

The subject of domesticity and familial relations was not the sole province of any one faction or group in Upper Canada, but it was the religious press that discussed these matters most fully. 'Clergy,' as Leonore Davidoff and Catherine Hall have pointed out, 'were in the vanguard of formulating rules of male and female behaviour,' although lay writers also 'played a vital part in establishing the social codes which informed middle-class propriety for many generations.'[23] In the colonial press, happy family life was often tied to the benefits of religion. Animated and guided by the love of Christ, husbands and wives would act lovingly towards each other; acceptance of God's love would be the catalyst for a great transformation of these particular social relations. Religious themes were worked into the discourse on marriage, and religion was often pinpointed as the agent of change.

The question of character formation ran through this material; neither sex was exempt from the need to constantly monitor and modify its nature and behaviour. These beliefs were not unique to Methodists in Upper Canada; rather, they were part of a transatlantic Methodist discourse that emphasized free will in embracing Christ and in choosing to live a life of holiness.[24] The sooner individuals began to prepare to recognize their sinfulness and receive Christ's love, the better. This state of spiritual awareness could best be brought about within the family. Both girls and boys needed the kind of upbringing that would prepare them for Christian adulthood, including marriage and relations with the opposite sex. Mothers should be ready to train their daughters in practical household matters. Articles such as 'Housewifery,' which reminded mothers of the need to let their daughters take on a certain amount of responsibility and learn by making mistakes, were common.[25]

Training in emotional matters was equally important. In preparing for marriage, 'Female Temper' argued, girls needed to learn to 'command' their emotions. 'Much of the effect of their power of reasoning and of their wits, when they grow up depends upon the gentleness and good humour with which they conduct themselves.' After all, 'a woman who should attempt to thunder with her tongue, would not find her eloquence increase her domestic happiness.' Furthermore, 'a man in a furious passion, is terrible to his enemies, but a woman in a passion is disgusting to her friends; she loses all the respect due to her sex, and she has not masculine strength and courage to enforce any other kind of respect.'[26] This literature not only stressed the need for women to shape their behaviour in relation to others, it also represented the ways in which the discourses of sensibility and sentimentality tended to deny the expression of anger as a legitimate emotion for middle-class women.[27] While men's anger was not to be encouraged, at least it would be respected and might be a way of subduing opposition. Women, though – particularly if they wanted to be considered 'ladies' – would lose all social approbation if they expressed feelings of anger. Ultimately the angry woman would damage only her own dignity, since she lacked 'masculine strength and courage' and therefore did not pose a serious social threat. Yet this passage demonstrates that the spectre of the disorderly woman was never far removed from the image of the respectable wife and mother; without emotional restraint and repression, one could easily become the other.

Such messages reinforced the notion of marriage and family life as a site of constant work for women (although, as we shall see, it was one for men too). 'Economy in a Family' epitomized this perception of wives and mothers as engaged in useful toil. Although man might be the household's financial mainstay, a wife was not idle; instead, she directed the affairs of the household. The pinnacle of her ambition should be wise management and savings. She 'acts not for herself only, but she is the agent of many she loves, and she is bound to act for their good, and not for her own gratification. Her husband's good is the end to which she should aim – his approbation is her reward.'[28] Time and again those who shaped the discourse on domesticity in both the religious and secular press stressed that, while the home was the special province of women and one in which she might be enthroned, her temperament and activities within this supposedly enclosed empire had to be modified to suit the needs of, first, her husband and then her children. To be sure, daughters needed her guidance, but it was in her position as a mother of sons that a woman might be called upon to perform her most sacred tasks, ones essential to the future of the nation and to Christianity. 'Mothers, Read This,' proclaimed the author of a homily reprinted in the *Guardian* from the *Quarterly Christian Spectator*. 'Let the Christian mother arm the mind of her son with the truths of the gospel, and she need not fear to send him forth to the conflict with the world and the powers of darkness. Let it be the glory of the Christian matron to be the mother of Christians. Let her clothe her son with the whole armour of God. Let her give him the sword of the spirit, and the shield of faith, and send him forth to fight, not fearing that his sword will turn back in the day of battle, or that his shield will be ingloriously thrown away.'[29]

Not all such exhortations to Christian mothers were couched in militaristic language. Much of this literature was romantic in tone, becoming increasingly sentimental by the late 1830s and into the 1840s.[30] Whatever the tone, the basic message was clear: a woman's position within the family was determined by the nature and intensity of the moral housekeeping she was expected to perform. In the discourse of domesticity, mothers might be granted 'empires,' but they were realms that were obtained through hard work and the effacement of the female ego; they were not to be taken for granted.

Moreover, as in discussions of religion, the notion of the home as women's domain was not an uncontested concept. 'Vidi,' writing to the *Guardian* in 1837, asked that the importance of fathers not be overlooked. Reminding his audience of the 'peculiar and commanding influence' of Abraham and Zacharias, he told them that 'the father has his proper place, and if he stands right with God and his child, in loveliness and holiness of example, though the mother may have the pre-occupancy [*sic*] in sowing the good seed in the earlier days of their offspring, he from pre-eminence in strength, will raise the higher and stronger wall, to keep and control that child when youth is lost to manhood.' A family with a 'deeply devoted Christian father' was 'privileged' to have such a 'viceregent.' Tying the father to the state and the marketplace, 'Vidi' asked, 'Upon whose shoulders rests the government, and who stands as example of the many whose eyes are turned upon him, for leading moral influence? the father. Who holds in his hands the resources that administer to the comfort, convenience, and happiness of the family? the father.' Such power, of course, might easily be abused, and guidelines for its exercise had to be set out. The difference between those families governed by Christian and those by wicked fathers was that 'while the one governs and controls the family, under the lawful enactments of heaven's high King and within the protecting influences of the reign of grace; the other owning no higher authority than self, sways the sceptre under the defenceless reign of sin.'[31]

Although some historians have argued that this literature was part of a growing women's culture in British North America, the discourse of domesticity that we have been discussing was as much about fathers and sons as it was about wives and daughters.[32] Masculinity, when defined by marriage and fatherhood, was central to writings about family life. Men were advised to spend more time at home with their wives, learning how to govern and manage the household and in this process becoming its true head. As illustrated in Strachan's tribute to George III, such governance was not to be conducted without concern for the feelings of those subordinated to the rule of the husband and father. 'To enable you to live as a Christian husband, in how many instances will the exercise of an enlightened prudence be found necessary! By this you are to ascertain the temper, the excellencies, the foibles of your associates. This is to teach you, how to accommodate. This is to show you, when to see as if you saw not, and to hear as if you heard not. This is to tell you how to extinguish the touch of discord; how even to prevent the kindling of strife – when to give up – when to recede from a lawful claim for the sake of a great good. This is to teach you also when you are NOT to yield.'[33]

The authors of this literature attempted to downplay potential conflicts with wives and sometimes would go on to discuss the importance of the mother's influence in the home, attributing her position to different, yet equally necessary, qualities. Many of these writers, especially those in the evangelical press, promoted an organic vision of the family, and of society in general, that attempted to ignore or write out conflict or differences. At other times, though, the images of men and women clashed, and there was more than a hint of competition over whose domain the home really was and whose influence would prevail.

If there was one figure over whom men and women, as fathers and mothers, might have to exercise their influence, it was that of the young man. Girls and young women were, it was admitted, in need of parental protection and guidance. Fathers were perceived as having a part to play in their daughters' lives, but mothers were seen as more likely to influence them on a daily basis. And, although daughters might be at risk from seducers and libertines, young men were equally in peril (if not more so) from the dangers of the world. After all, it was young men who might become the vicious rakes.

As we have seen in the previous chapter, youthful masculinity was constructed as a potentially perilous time, one when the guidance of religion was particularly important. Literature on domesticity was full of improving tales and anecdotes about the need for moral guidance in young men's lives. In his letter to the 'Reckoner,' 'Vernon' told the sorry tale of a young man's 'wasted life.' Willful and selfish, spoiled by his parents, and expelled from various schools, this individual went to work for the North West Company. The hoped-for reformation that such an experience might have brought about did not occur. 'He that is virtuous, Mr. Reckoner, may become depraved among the savages, but he that is vicious will never reform. He was quickly initiated in all the low degrading vices common in that wretched country.'[34] This assessment of life in the fur trade reversed the customary pattern of discussing cultural contact between whites and Native peoples: much of the literature in the Upper Canadian press depicted immorality as emanating from 'depraved' Europeans. Nevertheless, the letter highlighted the theme of the perils faced by young men, which was to become increasingly common in the Upper Canadian discourse on morality.

Young men, warned an anonymous author in the *Guardian*'s 'Youth's Department' in 1830, were often unaware of the 'The Beginnings of Evil.' 'No one becomes suddenly abandoned and profligate,' and, because of the gradual nature of the slide into depravity, it was extremely difficult to convince a youth of the danger. Social drinking in particular was offered as an example of this process. Although a young man might consider such drinking a small sin, 'soon his bonds are made strong and he becomes the slave of a sottish vice. Thus it is with all vicious practices.'[35] Drinking was a favourite example of the kinds of temptations waiting for the unsuspecting youth, but other equally lethal diversions, such as gambling, idleness, and swearing, might lie in wait. Evangelicals were fond of pointing out that visiting the theatre might mean the end of a virtuous existence, a stricture that was brought home in pieces such as 'Cautions of Young Men' and 'Theatrical Amusements.'[36] The dangers of such an institution were assumed to be self-evident, and writers provided few arguments to shed light on the reasons underlying their antipathy to the theatre. Their opposition probably stemmed from the theatre's appeal to sensations and emotions (unfettered by religious principles) and the presentation of fiction as representative of reality. Methodists were not alone in their opposition to 'plays and players.' In 1824, Mackenzie warned the residents of Queenston that 'a company of play-actors have been wiling the villagers of Niagara out of their money and time – we hope they may not come here, and wish them no good luck, if they do come.'[37]

Women were frequently perceived as the arbiters of male behaviour. For all their lampooning of the female gossip, Upper Canadian editors and writers often cited women's opinion as a kind of courtroom of morals in which male character and behaviour might be judged.[38] While the opinions of other men, especially fathers, were seen as important to a man (and that of God was the most significant), women's judgments and their ability to shape male behaviour were given a great deal of weight. This influence did not translate into the power to make independent decisions; it was to take the form of tact and persuasion. Moreover, the purpose of the mother-and-son bond was to prepare young men to handle future power (as husbands and fathers) judiciously, to ensure that they would not become petty domestic tyrants. Women also would be providing moral guidance to the nation's future leaders. A daughter's education, 'Poor Robert' told the *Kingston Gazette*'s readership, was not just for the girl's own happiness 'but as it respects the character of our country. Your daughters are to be the mothers of the next generation. Can a race of heroes and statesmen, men of vigourous minds and strong constitutions, be produced from a pale, weakly, soft mother? Such were not the mothers of the Grecian heroes of whom our parson used to tell us.'[39]

Evangelical literature in particular liked to stress the link between mother and son, using this form of female influence to underscore the centrality of wives and mothers to social stability. A review of *The Mother at home; or, the Principles of Maternal duty familiarly illustrated*, by the American writer John S.C. Abbott, enthused about Abbott's discussion of familial duties. While making clear that, for Abbott, 'the family' included fathers, the reviewer was quite taken with the author's characterization of mothers' influence over their sons. A Christian mother, according to Abbott, would raise Christian sons; having learnt virtue and patriotism in the home, they in turn would take these qualities out into the world.[40]

The influence of mothers and fathers might be harder to exercise once a young man left home. Young men, without the ties of home and family to act as moral ballast, were prone to making unsuitable friendships and, as we have seen in the previous chapter, falling into bad habits in residences such as boarding houses.[41] Much of this literature was imported from the United States and often used the 'discourse of the city' common to much evangelical literature, wherein the urban environment was represented as the site of sin, filth, and immorality, overcrowded and teeming with vice.[42] The extent to which this might have been a social problem in towns like York and Kingston, which grew into cities in the period covered here, is somewhat beside the point for our purposes. What is significant is that this stage in a young man's life was *perceived* as being problematic. The solution lay partly in young men's moral efforts, especially through the formation of voluntary societies.

A concern for, and celebration of, youthful masculinity appeared in reports on these groups' activities in York. The 'Report of the York Young Men's Society,' published in January 1832, established a program for this group that included working at Sunday schools, visiting jails, and conducting inquiries into young men's boarding houses. The members of the Young Men's Society executive included men such as its secretary, Thomas Ford Caldicott, a twenty-nine-year-old Baptist clergyman, teacher, and storekeeper (stationery and books). Caldicott was born in England and in 1827 came to Canada where he was active in various York voluntary societies: the York Mechanics' Institute, the Upper Canada Religious Tract and Bible Society, and the York Auxiliary Bible Society, and the York Young Men's Society. Another executive member was James Lesslie, publisher, politician, and merchant, a well-known supporter of reform and of Mackenzie (in 1842 he succeeded Francis Hincks as the editor of the *Examiner*, a Toronto reform paper). Like Caldicott, Lesslie was active in the Mechanics' Institute and also worked for the establishment of a House of Industry in Toronto.[43] Adopting as its motto 'let all things be done in love,' the Young Men's Society announced its intentions to be neither polemical nor denominational.[44]

In 1833 the *Guardian* reported the address of reformer and doctor John Rolph to another group, the York Young Men's Temperance Society. Rolph's speech, applauding the young men's 'Christian and patriotic philanthropy,' traced the history of the group. Although the society was founded out of a feeling that 'the elder society in this town had become a little *torpid*, and deficient in that ceaseless activity, which is the natural attribute of the noble spirit of *doing good*,' its young men nevertheless 'wore their laurels meekly,' wanting to honour their seniors. Tying male youthfulness to a celebration of the producing classes in society, Rolph declared: 'It seems a delightful characteristic of the age in which we live, that not only all *classes* but that all ages should be taught to think, and act a part in the great Theatre of moral and religious duty, and prepare the world for regenerating changes which perhaps the youngest amongst us may even live to see. Temperance Societies began without the aid of the Law or the patronage of the great. A few farmers and mechanics, lamenting the excesses which were humiliating and demoralizing a wide range of society, combined in the bold project of suppressing them by the power of persuasion and the influence of example.' Their own 'Christian and patriotic philanthropy,' Rolph told the members of the society, would help vanquish the problem of drunkenness, a menace to young men that Rolph blamed on the activities of the 'cold-blooded calculator.' Such a man 'looks like a spider in his corner, which has spread his net to catch the first thoughtless beings that may chance to flitter by; and then, having got them into his toil, he assiduously infuses into them for their destruction the very venom of his decorated barroom.'[45]

Underlying this particular aspect of moral discourse was the assumption that young men would someday become husbands and fathers, and thus they would have to learn now how to conduct themselves. Much of the advice proffered to youths and young men stressed the need for education and criticized fathers for overworking their sons. The 'Reckoner' offered his readers the sad example of fathers who neglected their sons' education and took no interest in instructing them in 'virtuous principles.' Instead, they 'drive them to work like slaves, and force them to labour at a time when neither their bodies nor their minds enable them without the greatest injury to bear the fatigue.' Farming families were especially prone to neglect their sons' training. One such family had educated their five daughters but put their son to arduous farm work; his awareness of his own ignorance led to his departure to become a raftman in Quebec.[46] Other articles warned of the need for the colony to develop its own educational institutions in order to keep youths and young men from leaving the province and to offer them more useful training that suited the needs of a developing society.[47] While these writings did not explicitly deny the rights of girls and women to an education, nevertheless they must be seen as part of a wider set of discursive attitudes and practices that prized the education of men (particularly higher education) over that of women. It is also possible that, in these passages, writers attempted to counter the growing number of arguments in support of women's education.[48]

Once in the workplace, the real test of masculine virtue began: that of balancing the demands of work with those of home and family. The literature on this aspect of moral conduct produced a certain amount of ambivalence around the code of masculine virtue. On the one hand, young men were urged to choose a 'profession' and strive for excellence in it. Try to be 'distinguished,' urged 'James's Father's Present,' even if you become a tradesman. 'It will give you weight in society, and thus, by increasing your influence, augment the means of your usefulness.'[49] In this and in other pieces, young men were exhorted to devote themselves wholeheartedly to their work, establishing patterns of behaviour that would become lifelong habits. This devotion was not, though, the unfettered pursuit of profit for its own sake. Morality in the shop or office was, men were told, a duty, one that was as important as morality in the home. Businesses must be run with honesty, probity, and prudence. 'Honest hard work' would be rewarded not just with material success (this, these writers were fond of warning their readers, might well be modest) but with the emotional and moral rewards of self-esteem and community respect.[50]

A code of moral conduct in the workplace was not to be pursued strictly for its own sake. No matter how single-mindedly a young man was to devote himself to business, it could not be forgotten that eventually he also would become a husband and then a father. And, although wives and mothers were important arbiters of morality within the home, men too were expected to pull their moral weight. Certainly religious discourse realized that the demands of work and home might be contradictory and pose problems for men. Some writers saw the solution in men's recognition that their family obligations came first. This point was pressed most forcefully by those who advocated male leadership in family prayers.[51] For these writers, the workplace did not exist for itself or only on its own terms.

Instead, it was the place where young men put into practice the lessons learned within the family, the church, and the voluntary association. Later in life, the workplace was perceived as significant not just as a testing ground for men and the site of all-male relationships but as the place where men might make good their claim to be the head of the household by supporting their families. Articles such as 'A Good Husband,' which advised women to choose men who might be found both in the home and in 'the place of business,' hammered home the point that the ideal spouse was not a man of fashion but a good, steady provider.[52]

In the Upper Canadian religious press, gender relations were as central to the discourse of social mobility and economic advancement as they were to that of the family and domesticity. Yet it is important to note that in this literature men were seen as actors in both home and workplace, and women were constructed as active only in the former. While their relationships with men were an important motivation for male behaviour, there was little possibility that women might enter the workplace as heads of households. Pieces such as 'The Rights of Woman,' which desired to bring to the public's attention the injustices suffered by poorly paid working women, especially widows with children to support, were extremely rare.[53] The absence of wives and mothers from the paid labour force was not merely assumed by those who shaped the discourse of domesticity, it was an essential aspect of attempts to reform gender relations. Husbands and fathers were to become breadwinners, the mainstay of the family economy.

Running through this discourse on morality was a critique of 'fashion,' of the allurements of the world that might cause both men and women to deviate from the moral life. Youth was especially vulnerable to being enticed by fashionable society, where 'foibles, silliness, the scandal, and the absence of rational conversation' reigned.[54] Young men and women were perceived by both religious and secular writers as falling prey to worldly amusements, wasting their lives in idle pleasures, and forgetting their obligations to God, their souls, and society. Dress was a favourite topic in advice to young women, who were warned to avoid any appearance of 'wantonness' and 'love of finery.' They were told to choose sensible clothing and to dress 'for circumstance.' Such practicality would allow them to spend more time in charitable work, such as organizing Dorcas Societies that would dispense sensible clothing to those less fortunate.[55] Young men were also the target of advice about finery and 'dandyism.' Like the 'honest manliness' of the reform movement, 'virtuous manhood' in this particular discourse could not countenance anything smacking of foppishness, although contact with women was not the problem. Men were advised to seek out the company of 'virtuous, intelligent, and refined females,' who would 'smooth down the natural brusqueries of man and give a high polish to his mind and manners.' However, there was a fine line between seeking female companionship and 'becoming that contemptible THING, a ladies' man or dandy – an animal despised by every man or woman of sense, though sometimes tolerated by the latter, as they answer all the purposes of a pet poodle.'[56]

As we have seen, while evangelicals were in favour of reforming gender relations and, in the process, detaching masculinity from brutishness, they were also concerned that polite behaviour might become merely a matter of adherence to form and ritual, masking inner corruption and providing a vehicle for hypocrisy. In the fashionable world, polished manners could easily be mistaken for true virtue.[57] Evangelical literature therefore took a very solemn view of such a weakening of 'honest manhood.' Although the secular press saw male vanity and love of fashion as a threat to masculine dignity, it often chose satire as a weapon. 'Power of Fashions' held up to ridicule a wealthy gentleman who, upon falling in love with a woman much poorer than himself but 'far his superior in intellectual talents,' was told that he must make a great sacrifice before she would marry him. He told her he would leave all his money, 'wage war with giants, or fight the fierce lions of the desert,' or travel to the 'Indies,' China, or Japan to satisfy her. '"No," she replied, "it is no less this ... that you shave off your monstrous whiskers, that I might have the pleasure of beholding your face!" – "*My whiskers*!" cried he in astonishment! "my whiskers! O heavens! No madam, be it known to you, I will not part with my whiskers, to obtain the heart and hand of any daughter of Adam now existing on the face of this earth."'[58]

'Lucinda' complained to the *Kingston Chronicle* in December 1824 that gentlemen about town had fallen prey to a 'whim which is becoming fashionable in some Gentlemen, of appearing singular in their dress.' Although she did not specify exactly what this 'singularity' involved, she asked the editor how she should react on being 'beset' by these types in the streets. The editor, while sympathetic to her complaint and agreeing that this habit was becoming 'quite common,' replied that nothing could be done directly to prevent them 'from making themselves ridiculous.' However, it was quite acceptable for 'Lucinda' and her friends to make these men 'feel by their deportment towards them, that their company is irksome and unpleasant. A single glance from offended female dignity is enough to put to flight a host of these warriors of ignorance.'[59]

Leisure and the world of fashion thus undermined the dignity of 'virtuous manhood' and 'true womanhood,' especially in youth. Both sexes might make themselves look foolish by following the dictates of fashion in dress, a point made many times by the secular press.[60] 'An Old Fashioned Countryman,' writing to the *Colonial Advocate* in 1832, went so far as to call for an end to tight lacing in women's dress, condemning it on a number of grounds. Such a practice was injurious to female health (a point the 'Countryman' elaborated on at great length) and was an affront to religion (because it interfered with woman's natural and God-given shape). The 'Countryman' ended with a call for societies 'for the preservation of our females,' similar to temperance organizations formed to prevent 'the destruction of the male part of our species.' The article was followed by an editorial reminder that 'a great many effeminate dandy fops of young gentlemen' also tight-lace. 'This contemptible piece of effeminacy in our young dandies' demonstrated that women were not the only sex to follow customs that were silly and harmful.[61]

It was the religious press, though, that tied fashion and luxury most clearly to immorality, either in symbolic ways or directly in prescriptive literature. In 'The Trial of Truth – An Allegory,' female characters symbolized both truth and falsehood. The former, having been disgraced and expelled from society, ran into 'Lady Lye,' who was sitting in a splendid chariot, 'dressed in a changeable silk, with a canopy of clouds over her head, and adorned with a rainbow. Perjury was her gentleman usher, Impudence and Hypocrisy were her supporters, and Calumny and Detraction served her as guards.' Despite the worldly accoutrements of Lady Lye, Truth's humble but morally superior character and mien triumphed.[62] In literature on the family and domesticity, men were warned to shun the worlds of ballrooms and other frivolous entertainments and, in business, to be unashamed of humble origins and 'solid' trading practices. Trade in luxury goods, it was often suggested, was frequently linked to credit because demand for them was fickle and ephemeral, and borrowing became a indispensable way of staying in business. Furthermore, those who traded in luxury goods often found it necessary to imitate their patrons' dress and way of living, turning their own lives into a kind of theatre that bore little or no relation to their 'real' situation. In doing so, such tradesmen became even further entangled in debt and were dragged down to ruin.[63]

Women also might succumb to the lure of fashion and personal vanity; some writers suggested that they were even more prone than men to these temptations. 'Fashionable Follies' described the 'five thousand young ladies' in Upper Canada who spent their time on music, algebra, Paleyite doctrine, novels, and the theatre, instead of being instructed in household matters. 'Display, notoriety, surface, and splendour: these are the first aims of the mothers,' the author complained.[64] Women, the *Guardian* pronounced, were especially tempted by fine dress and must curb their propensity to indulge themselves at the expense of others in society. 'What,' the paper argued, 'will afford you the most pleasure when you come to die – the recollection of the property you employed in clothing the naked, or of that which you expended in costly apparel? What satisfaction resulting from the applause of finery can equal the joy of benevolence a female feels, while moving among the tears, prayers, and benedictions of gratitude?' While 'cleanliness, neatness, and good taste' were admirable, 'finery, or show' clearly were not.[65]

Certainly male vanity was admonished as well, but, especially in advice columns aimed at men in business, women's desire for fashionable clothing and home furnishings was perceived as a force that could lead men down the path of financial ruin. As was illustrated in the story in Genesis, wives might influence their mates to make rash and profligate decisions, a point that buttressed the arguments of those who were fond of declaring that, whether for good or evil, women had significant influence over men.[66] Thus, it was important for men to choose their future partners carefully, but it was equally important that girls and young women be taught to shun fashionable amusements and affluent company. In this critique of fashion, women of the leisured classes were the antithesis of the virtuous housewife and mother. Thrift, hard work, and prudent behaviour were the province of the latter. Unlike many images of womanhood in American periodical literature in the 1840s, this symbol of femininity in Upper Canadian discourse was not synonymous with consumerism.[67] Frugality, rather then conspicuous consumption, was the hallmark of the wife and mother at home. Lessons to this effect were offered to readers, such as the tale of Elizabeth, the little girl who wasted crumbs until rebuked by her more careful sister (their mother acted as the arbiter of their dispute.)[68] The material details of housekeeping management were not quite as popular in the religious and secular press during this period as was advice on women's emotional management of their families. This literature repeated the message that women should practise self-effacement even as it reminded them of their importance as managers of the home. The emotional sacrifices women were told to make were constructed as work by these writers, an ongoing struggle of moral negotiation and mediation on women's part that the lazy, selfish women of the upper classes were too idle to practise.[69]

Much of this discourse was deeply concerned with notions of shifting class formation, and a great deal of the literature originated in countries that were experiencing such changes in a variety of material and ideological ways.[70] So far as the discourse of domesticity and moral propriety in Upper Canada was concerned, we can discern the lineaments of a bourgeois moral code that identified respectability and morality with the home, a realm whose values would provide a moral influence on the marketplace. Inasmuch as the literature of both secular and religious presses spoke of concepts of class, it was defined in relation to a leisured aristocracy or gentry and contained an explicit critique of consumerism and unnecessary consumption. In this critique, gender and class relations were difficult to untangle and often were presented as mutually dependent forms of social organization.[71]

By vilifying consumerism and pointing to the moral consequences of fashion and finery, the discourse of domesticity and familial relations engaged in a discussion of class relations that, paradoxically, attempted to write out class or social rankings. As we have seen in discussions of gender relations in Native communities, the acquisition of objects (except as a means of inculcating thrift and hard work) was downplayed; work was highlighted as a form of moral regeneration and a badge of virtue, not as a means of social mobility. If work were engaged in honestly and with cheerful submission, it could not fail to benefit those who toiled and laboured, whether in the office or the home, no matter if they profited materially from it or not (although it was hoped that they would). The maxims set out in the discourse of the family were offered as advice that all could follow, no matter what their position in life. This universality and tendency to homogenize traits characteristic of bourgeois ideology were the hallmark of dictates concerning moral conduct.[72] Class differences were posited as the gulf between those with independent incomes, men and women who did not have to work at any kind of 'useful labour' (whether in a shop or at home), and those without such means. These distinctions were then rewritten into the realm of morality, affection, and sentiment. Moral conduct and behaviour, not the possession of wealth and its often attendant frivolity, would determine a person's real value to society. True virtue, whether male or female, would thus transcend the mundane details of daily life and could be practised no matter what a man or woman's social and economic circumstances might be. Like the universal brotherhood of the reformers, reconstituted gender relations would help bring about these changes.

Furthermore, much of the literature on family and gender relations transcended religious and political boundaries. Although it was taken up and elaborated upon most fully by the Methodists, such prescriptive literature could not be pinned down to any particular political perspective or social institution. Much of this literature was shared by the religious and secular press, going beyond some of the customary divisions in Upper Canadian history (in particular, those of British versus American and reform versus conservative).

If discussions of the family and domesticity strove to present an idealized version of gender relations, literature on temperance in Upper Canada took as one of its central themes the family in moral peril, endangered by alcohol abuse. Temperance, practised both within the family and in society generally, would rescue families from degradation, as well as improving social, economic, and political conditions. Like the Methodist discourse on the family, gender, and religion, temperance literature focused first on the individual but then extended its analysis of the problem to those with whom he (the drunkard was usually male) was intimately involved. Although only the strength of the individual's will could bring about a reformation, this change could be assisted through the exhortation and example of other family members. The language of temperance advocates in the Upper Canadian press and in temperance societies relied upon the symbols, images, and codes of the language of domesticity and must be viewed in this context. Temperance literature, insofar as it pertained to the family and gender relations, was in many ways the other side of the coin of domesticity, a discourse that provided temperance advocates with a kind of shorthand in which the horrors of drink might be fully revealed.

Although temperance as a province-wide movement was strongest from the 1840s to the mid-1850s, literature extolling the benefits of temperance emerged much earlier, and the first temperance society in Upper Canada was founded in 1828, in Leeds County.[73] As early as 1810, the *Kingston Gazette* decried the effect of drinking on men's home life in a piece entitled 'Intoxication.' Alcohol abuse, the author declared, led husbands to ignore their 'help-mate[s]' and 'tender offsprings.' 'What can be more abusive to the understanding of human nature, than beholding a young man in the prime of life, bowing his neck to the tyrannical yoke of intoxication?' The solution lay in the example set by parents for their children, but, not content to warn young men, the author closed with an observation concerning women: 'I would fain pass, unnoticed, one class, but duty forbids it, that is the fair sex. Alas! we find some of this sex walking hand-in-hand with the sons of intemperance. The sex which is the flower of human nature, has some attached to it which frequently swallow the bitter draught – who have left all claim to that rank which the sex are justly entitled to. Oh! reader the subject is too delicate for my pen. I will leave you to make your own remarks.'[74] Despite this self-professed delicacy, this author made a point about 'the drunkard' that was seldom taken up in the later discourse around temperance. The drunkard was rarely constructed as female; instead, women were usually perceived as the victims of alcohol abuse and often as men's helpmates in the battle against strong drink.

In the early 1830s, more articles began to appear in both the religious and secular press about the evils of alcohol. Often these accompanied announcements of the formation of temperance societies, such as the York Young Men's Temperance Society. Gender was not always the sole concern of this material, as an article accompanying the proclamation of the Kingston Temperance Society indicated. The 'Magistrates,' the paper informed the city, had resolved to co-operate with the society, since they were aware of the causes of 'breaches of the peace, and promot[ion] of discord and contention among the lower orders of society.'[75] 'The Effects of Teetotalism,' a cheery Samuel Smiles-like ditty run by the *Kingston Chronicle and Gazette* in 1842, predicted the wholesale economic and social improvement of Upper Canadian society that moderation would bring:

> More of good than we can tell,
> More to buy with, more to sell,
> More of comfort, less of care,
> More to eat and more to wear,
> Happier homes with faces bright,
> All our burdens rendered light,
> Conscience clear, minds much stronger,
> Debts much shorter, purses longer,
> Hopes that drive away all sorrow,
> And something laid up for tomorrow.[76]

When the question of 'who' was doing the drinking arose, both in literature from outside the colony and in material written by Upper Canadians, the answer was invariably the same: husbands, fathers, sons, and brothers. Young men, as we have argued, were especially at risk, for a supposedly innocent social drink might be the beginning of a slide down the 'slippery slope' to full-fledged alcoholism.[77] Yet young men were not alone in falling prey to this temptation, as the anonymous essayist whose work was read at a meeting of the Whitby Temperance Society argued: 'How often have we known an industrious farmer, an ingenious mechanic, and a thriving tradesman with a happy wife, an endearing family, with a prosperous business ... how often have we known such a one from a moderate drinker to become a drunkard, lose his property, his trade, and his credit, reduced to want, to misery, and ruin – his children made beggars, and wanderers; perhaps obliged to seek a morsel of bread from the charity of their more fortunate fellow mortals – and himself the inmate of a gaol, a poorhouse, and or lunatic asylum – nay, more.'[78]

This dire picture of the fate awaiting those who, as small-scale producers, were paragons of thrift and industrious habits was typical of the frequently made argument that even those who signified masculine stability could be ensnared. Once men had fallen prey to alcohol, the results might be even more tragic than the loss of business and property. Death, frequently a violent and terrible one, might await the drunkard. William Lyon Mackenzie, writing in 1824 of the many recent accidental deaths in York, drew his readers' attention to the state of intoxication of the deceased. Calling this 'an unusual number of warnings to the living,' he advised members of the public 'to shun the intoxicating draught, as they would the plague of pestilence, or the dagger of the midnight assassin.'[79]

The death of the drunkard himself was not the only means by which the 'demon dram' worked its pernicious results. Far from being a sign of manliness, alcohol 'unmanned' men, causing their worst passions to be unleashed and releasing the inhibitions of civilization and masculine virtue. Tales of drunken men who became 'vicious' towards their families were told in the pages of the press. 'Slander, abusive language, vilest passions are connected with it, a man will waste his property, insult his friend, and disgrace himself and family under a fit of intoxication. Lying, swearing, cursing, profaning God's name, ridiculing sacred things and hellish language frequently take place in a fit of drunkenness.'[80] Like the worst excesses of war, alcohol gave free rein to men's basest tendencies, producing temporary fits of madness in which they might commit the most terrible crimes. Such was the story of 'Sovereign' (Henry Sovereen), executed in the London District for murdering his wife and six children. In this pathetic narrative, Sovereen's road to the gallows was linked to his drinking: an occasional dram had led to drunkenness, and from there it had been a short journey into the depths of poverty, cruelty, madness, and murder.[81]

This particular aspect of the discourse of drink was augmented by missionary writing about Native people and alcohol, especially the effects of drink on Native men. Although Upper Canadian missionaries were quick to admit that Native women (unlike the majority of their white counterparts) might fall victim to alcohol themselves, much was made of its effects on their men (who, it was often suggested, had led them into this vice).[82] To be sure, the ultimate triumph of Christianity was the Native women in the home, but her husband, father, brother, and sons had to swear off alcohol in order for this to happen. Reporting to the Methodist Conference in 1825, the Canada Auxiliary Missionary Society emphasized the renunciation of alcohol by the Mohawks at the Grand River as effecting their moral uplift. 'Comfort,' the society proclaimed, was promoted, and women were no longer abused by their 'drunken husbands,' nor were they 'made unhappy by excessive toil.' 'By the industry of their husbands, they are better provided for; and the cleanliness of their persons, and the neatness of them are a handsome comment on the change which has taken place in their husbands and fathers.'[83]

If Native men could redeem themselves through the aegis of religion and civilization, how were their white counterparts to guard against the moral perils of intemperance? Female influence was important, but equally so were the efforts of men themselves. As John Prowls told the Thirty-Mile Creek Society at its founding meeting in 1830, alcohol must be recognized as the enemy of peace and prosperity. 'Was our country invaded, our lives, properties, and families, endangered, you would all despise those who would remain in apathy and indifference – yet, when a moral enemy is destroying the health, and taking the lives of thousands, depriving families of property, of peace, and of happiness, and rendering the morals of many loose, how many startle at the idea of making a bold and manly stand against the fell-destroyer?' Prowls called for the banishment of alcohol, telling his listeners 'to take a firm and manly stand, and break off from its use altogether, unless it be for medical aid.'[84] In response to the formation and work of various societies in York, the anonymous author of a letter to the *Guardian* expressed the great 'pleasure' this person derived from these events, especially the labours of young men. 'In witnessing the exertions of the young men of our community, coming forward with so much manliness and courage, I was highly gratified ... I trust that the young men will receive the support and approbation which they justly deserve, and that they may be abundantly successful in preventing many of the rising generation from the great evil of intemperance, and thus prove a blessing to themselves, their families, and the public at large; and set an example worthy of imitation.'[85]

Masculine strength and bravery, then, were the foundation stones for a new moral order of sobriety and domestic bliss. But if the onus was on men to begin the process of reformation, women were urged to exercise their 'special influence' in order to assist them. As much of the literature addressed to young women was so fond of stressing, they could be a 'force for good' on youthful male character development. If 'young ladies' objected strenuously enough, their male companions would renounce vices such as intemperance, gambling, and duelling.[86] Not only was it part of women's mission as wives and mothers to act as moral arbiters, it was also in their own interest. As 'Anti-Bacchus,' writing to the *Guardian* from Chinguacousy, pointed out, drunkenness added to the distress of poor families, especially to a wife's hardships. Her sorrow, in seeing 'the husband of her early affections going fast to the drunkard's grave,' would be even clearer at the resurrection, when 'the tens of thousands of immolated wives will be a swift witness against the cruel assassin, who, drop by drop, has drained the last drop of blood from the palpitating heart of her whom he had sworn to love and cherish throughout life.'[87] As Jan Noel has pointed out, temperance literature of the 1840s, such as the Montreal-based *Canada Temperance Advocate*, not only depicted women as suffering from the abuse of drunken fathers and husbands, but consistently pointed to the 'hallowed social role' of women in working for the cause.[88] Furthermore, as we shall see in the following chapter, women's public support for temperance was greeted with approval by writers and editors in both religious and secular newspapers.

Like religious discourse, which it strongly resembled, temperance literature, in making the link between male violence and drunkenness, opened up a forum in which male behaviour could be stringently criticized. There was little doubt in the discourse around drunkenness that women and children were its victims, and that, theoretically, they might challenge male cruelty. Yet, unlike evangelical discourse on revivals and the need for women to defy male tyranny to gain religious freedom, temperance literature was less concerned with creating symbols of female defiance than with manipulating the image of the abused and victimized woman. It was not impossible for women and children to bring about a change in the behaviour of their husbands, fathers, sons, and brothers. However, women were counselled to take up the temperance cause either within organizations or to use their 'gentle influence' with their male kin; seldom were they advised to use more direct measures such as throwing out either the whiskey bottle or the drunken husband.[89] While legitimating women's opposition to alcohol, this language of indirect moral suasion tended to overlook and, at times, directly suppress women's agency and their work for the temperance cause. It also helped construct womanly support for temperance as being white and middle-class, as it relied on an idealized 'woman' who, as we have seen, did not express anger directly or in a physical manner, even when her target might be a drunken and abusive husband. Nor did a divine thunderbolt usually strike down the drunkard in the literature of the 1830s and 1840s (although this might happen within the context of a revival). Instead, his wife's moral suasion and the pitiful appearance of his children would make him realize the error of his ways. The literature on temperance drew upon a language of domesticity that, as we have argued, became increasingly sentimental by the mid-nineteenth century. This literature embraced images and symbols that, no matter what they implied about women's influence, were insistent that households were headed by men.[90] Strong drink disturbed the 'natural order' of the home and, like irreligious behaviour, came between a man and the expression of his natural affections for his wife and children. It also interfered with his ability to provide for them and act as their leader and representative.

Temperance, however, was not just about gender relations and the family, although supporters frequently insisted that temperance would inevitably benefit husbands and wives, parents and children. Woven through the Upper Canadian discourse on drink was an understanding of economic and social relations and the way in which alcohol signified downward mobility. In literature on domesticity that identified luxury and consumption as a threat to morality, drink was one of the many allurements of 'high society' that would lead to a young man's moral ruin. As a glass of wine offered at a ball or reception, alcohol might appear as one of the accoutrements of gentility, consumed in the presence of 'ladies,' its evil nature thus cloaked. However, it also might be drunk within the walls of the tavern, in the context of an all-male group that could as easily be composed of disreputable 'young rakes' as of labouring men.[91] In the temperance literature, though, excessive drinking was often identified as a threat to the small producer as well as the honest but poor workman.[92] The rhetoric of the dangers of alcohol was not pitched at one specific class, and the results of dissipation were the same for both aristocrat and artisan. Disgrace, illness, poverty, and, sooner or later, a pauper's grave could be found at the bottom of either a crystal wineglass or a whisky bottle. Alcohol, in the discourse of temperance and in warnings about the temptations of fashion, was a means of downward social mobility, dragging to the same level of degradation all those who fell into its clutches. In Upper Canadian temperance literature, strong drink became the colonial equivalent of the American archetype of the confidence man. It might be found everywhere, even in polite society, its influence all the more deadly and contaminating than that of the confidence man because it was able to trick and seduce both youthful honesty and adult male reason.[93]

Like writings on the family, support for temperance was most likely to appear in the religious press, missionary reports, and those secular newspapers that either looked kindly on reform or were less stridently conservative. The *Patriot and Farmers' Monitor* stood out most clearly in its opposition to temperance as an organized movement. This might take the form of satirical commentary on its organization, as in an 1833 letter from 'A lover of Temperance and Sobriety.' This person objected to the sex-segregated seating arrangements at a recent meeting of the 'young men's' society run by the Episcopal Methodists, and found fault with the speaker and the 'loud discordant bawling' that passed for music. The letter concluded with hopes that 'this Young Mens [sic] Temperance Society, which consists of old men and maidens, widows and wives, will make arrangements for a more uniformly rational entertainment at their next meeting.'[94] Usually, though, the paper based its objections to temperance organizations on the grounds that such societies might encourage hypocrisy, their members advocating public godliness while simultaneously practising private wickedness and cruelty. Although certainly opposed to drunkenness, Dalton told his readers in 1842 that he found the membership of women and children in temperance groups 'repugnant.' Just because 'that odious spectacle, a drunken female, may occasionally be seen, are upright matrons, spotless maids and artless children to exhibit themselves to the public as bound together by a solemn compact, [not] to commit what their ostentatious renunciation proves that they consider a deadly and debasing sin?'[95] Dalton's well-established dislike of 'hypocrisy' may very well have spurred him to scorn temperance societies, but, as Sean Cadigan has pointed out, the *Patriot* also opposed anything so closely identified with reformers and Methodists as the anti-drink societies.[96] Certainly it was clear in his editorials that Mackenzie was a strong supporter of temperance. As Cadigan argues, one of the reformers' targets was the use of alcohol during elections, a bribe that robbed voters of their 'manly independence.'[97] Ironically, though, Mackenzie was accused of circulating the *Colonial Advocate* in taverns, in order to gain a wider audience for his 'licentious' abuse.[98]

If drinking was constructed primarily as a masculine activity, conducted outside the home and causing men to forget their familial obligations and ties, it was often accompanied by another vice that also was practised by men: duelling. Part of the opposition to duelling may be traced to a more generalized dislike of open displays of male violence, whether on the hustings at election time or in general 'rowdyism' on Toronto streets during the 1840s.[99] A special opprobrium was reserved for a type of hand-to-hand combat, known as 'gouging,' imported from the southern states. A letter to the editor of the *Weekly Register and Upper Canada Gazette* decried gouging as having 'long been the custom of the Blacks in the Southern States, but now practised by white men in this country, on the persons of the subjects of George, the King.' It was called 'rough and tumble' by 'wicked men from the United States' and involved 'knawing flesh like wild beasts; and tearing eye-balls out of sockets, biting noses and ears off, and laying hold of a certain part of the outward man which it is a shame even to speak of.' Calling this custom 'a thing which corrupteth our youth, endangereth our persons, and bringeth disgrace upon this fair portion of the British Empire,' 'Ebenezer' called for legislation imposing prison terms or banishment on any found guilty of such practices.[100] Edward Talbot, the author of *Five Years' Residence in the Canadas*, also expressed disgust with this kind of fighting. He had seen 'the modern style of rough and tumble' in the Ottawa Valley and called it a 'detestable practice.' The men involved 'attack each other with the ferociousness of bull-dogs,' gouging, biting, and tearing each other's eyes, faces, and hair until one combatant 'is disabled by the loss of blood, or a severe invasion of his optic, his olfactory or auditory nerves.'[101]

It was the practice of men duelling that attracted the most attention from writers in the press and commentators in other public forums. While not provoking the same sort of widespread and sustained discourse as that about drink, duelling was discussed and condemned on a number of grounds as an unacceptable type of masculine activity. Certainly this discourse was not unique to Upper Canada for, as Donna Andrew has demonstrated, in England the 'code of honour' fell under attack during this period as an affront to both religious and secular law.[102] Like so much of the literature discussed in this chapter, arguments against duelling had a wider, transatlantic reference. Duelling was linked to excessive drinking, the temptations of luxury, and the dangers of uncurbed and vicious, rather than honourable, masculinity. Like the writers of obituaries of Upper Canadians, those who shaped the 'discourse of duelling' could use specific examples of duels that occurred on their doorsteps (or, as was more likely, in their wheat fields).

One of the earliest and most famous duels in the colony took place in 1800, between the first attorney general, John White, and John Small, a former friend of White's. White had apparently insulted Mrs Small during the Christmas season of 1799, and her husband issued a challenge to meet behind the government buildings at the foot of Berkeley Street in York. The duel ended with White sustaining a wound that, in the *Upper Canada Gazette*'s rather terse report, was feared to 'prove fatal.'[103] Thirty-six hours later, the *Gazette*'s predictions were borne out and White died. Small was tried for murder on 20 January 1800, the jury and Justice Allcock finding him not guilty.[104] Although duelling was technically illegal in the colony, participants in duels (survivors and their seconds) were seldom convicted by juries if the duel had been conducted fairly, according to the 'code of honour.'[105] While perhaps not as common as its detractors liked to claim, duelling was practised by certain members of the York élite and by less-famous men in other areas of the colony.[106]

In Upper Canada, the notion of 'affronted honour' defended in a duel might signify that of the upper-class patriarchal family, as in those duels (such as the White–Small encounter) that were ostensibly fought over insults to a woman's chastity. Yet 'honour' might also mean the defence of a more bourgeois ethos and standard. Such was the case when lawyer William Warren Baldwin challenged Attorney General John Macdonell. Macdonell's behaviour in the courtroom had become a constant source of irritation to Baldwin; in April 1812, the attorney general's 'wanton and ungentlemanly' words resulted in his being challenged by Baldwin (the affair ended with Baldwin firing aside and no physical harm being sustained). As an institution and practice that encompassed various social and political situations, duelling involved in many ways a multifaceted and protean code of masculine honour. Duelling 'intertwined itself with politics, and love, and with social habits like drinking and gambling'[107] (a point that was not lost on the Methodists).

However, in Upper Canada the flexibility of the code of honour was limited by both race and gender. While it is difficult to tease out the racial meanings of duelling, for the most part it was understood as the province of men of European ancestry. Furthermore, the central, unifying tenet of this code was the right and responsibility of certain men to defend their reputations, and that of their family, with a public display of physical courage, an option that was not open to women of the same class and racial group. The code of honour made a clear distinction between male and female bodies within the upper class: by fighting a duel, male bodies might attain and signify the honour of their gender and class, becoming momentarily detached from sexuality and incorporating broader, public meanings. The bodies of their female counterparts, however, were potentially sources of sexual shame, dishonour, and disorder – the reason why the duel was fought in the first place. This public valorization of upper-class men's bodies that were engaged in physical combat should also be contrasted to the threats often signified by the bodies of working-class and plebeian men, when engaged in activities such as strikes, riots, and crime (the exception being the service of those bodies to the state in the military). And, as we have seen in chapter 1, Upper Canadians' ambivalence about Native peoples – even as their military allies – was often expressed as an uneasiness about the physical appearances of Native 'warriors.'[108]

Critics of the kind of masculinity embedded in the code of honour, though, stressed physical and emotional self-control for men, arguing that duelling meant physical abandonment and a lack of emotional restraint. In succumbing to these weaknesses, duellists forfeited their claims on the political, social, and economic prerogatives conferred by 'manliness.' Instead, their bodies sank to the level of those of an hysterical woman or a tavern brawler.

In the Upper Canadian discourse around duelling, issuing a challenge was frequently perceived as nothing less than a declaration of intent to murder. Opposition to duelling in both Britain and Upper Canada was based on its subversion of God's law and that of the state. A satirical letter, written by 'Sam Sober' to the *Upper Canada Gazette* in the aftermath of the White–Small duel, noted that 'in ordinary disputes, doubtless, everyone will confess, [dueling] ... is an equitable, summary, and easy mode of decision, far preferable to the tedious judicial forms of obtaining redress.'[109] An editorial comment on duelling three year later commended the Quakers for knowing that they had no right to take another's life and that there could be 'no evasion, no exception, no permission given to men to murder each other under this or that pretence.' The 'unhappy man' who had done so 'must stand a poor miserable, convicted, despairing contemner of thy insulted GOD – in need of all the treasures of HIS MERCY, for his JUSTICE must condemn thee!'[110] The Reverend W. Taylor, in a sermon preached from a Montreal pulpit in 1838 about a recently fought duel in that city, condemned duelling 'as a system' and duellists 'as a class' on the grounds that they offended divine law and were remnants of ignorance and feudal barbarity.[111]

The notion that duels were private means of settling scores that, if truly important, should have ended up in the public courts was a recurring theme. Of course, there were those who thought that duels were fought over such trivial and negligible matters that the offended party should simply 'turn the other cheek.' Duellists were mocked by writers such as 'Sam Sober,' whose comments on the White–Small affair ended with a suggestion that the 'art' of duelling might be improved by using 'blunderbusses' instead of pistols. 'Would it not,' he mused, 'have a warlike appearance and raise a noble air?'[112] At times, editors presented accounts of duels in a straightforward manner that stripped these encounters of their participants' motives and intentions, thereby divesting the duel of its social and cultural meanings and holding it up to ridicule. Such was the tactic employed by the *Kingston Chronicle and Gazette* in 1836, when the paper retold the story of two duelling doctors in Brantford. Dr Dowding had called in Dr Digby to treat a difficult childbirth case, and, when words were exchanged over the patient's treatment, Dowding had challenged his colleague. Presented as a comic opera, unlike the tragedy of the White–Small duel, the affair ended to the satisfaction of both parties. Two shots were fired, and, with the seconds' intervention, both men retracted the words that had led to the duel. Dowding took back his description of Digby as a 'liar, scoundrel, and coward' and Digby his equally unflattering 'liar, villain, scoundrel, and fool.' 'Thus ended the whole affair in smoke! and we hope the past case will be the last of a similar kind to raise an excitement in our community.'[113] By omitting any discussion of the doctors' prior relationships or exploring the reasons for the dispute, and instead focusing on the fairly ridiculous exchange of epithets, the article's author neatly skewered both event and participants.

A critique of the gender politics involved when men defended their honour in such a fashion was also part of the attack on duelling. Male 'honour,' according to these writers, did not need to be consistent with violence; duelling, though, forced such a connection. A term of praise when discussing men's patriotic defence of their country or the imperial connection, 'honour,' when used in the context of debates over duelling, was one of derision and condemnation. 'Go to, now, thou *foolish* one, thou man of *fashion*, thou man of *honour*,' admonished the *York Gazette*. 'Stained with the blood of thy brother, and who shall be thy counsellor and who shall be thy advocate in that dark and terrible hour when the crash of the universe is in thine ears, and returning chaos, illumined by the conflagration of an expiring world yawns at thy feet? – Alas! Alas! unhappy man that thou art – the painted bauble of this world's honour will retain its shadowy forms no longer.'[114] Although he did not reach the heights of the *Gazette* editor's apocalyptic language, the frequent contributor 'Eusebius' devoted an entire letter to the concept of 'honour' and the duel. While aware that 'polite life' would call him 'not a man of honor,' but neither would accuse him 'of entertaining low and vulgar ideas,' 'Eusebius' outlined the way in which honour 'which imposes upon the mind the idea of something noble and exalted' was associated with duelling and thus masked its true character. Describing the potential reactions of a stranger to the news that a 'man of honour' had gone 'to settle an affair of honour' and risked either killing or being killed, 'Eusebius' claimed that the stranger would assume the matter was an affair of state, such as the defence of the sovereign, the realm, or his countrymen, and would admire and respect him.

But on being informed that the man of honor was a gay young spark whose gallantry had been called in question by another saying he could despoil him of his mistress by only administering a few potions of high seasoned flattery; that the invidious and hateful words had caused his whole soul to boil with rage and his eyes to dart the fierce fires of fell revenge, the stranger would reply, 'Contemptible and pitiable wretches ... why do you thus madly and wickedly rush upon your own destruction? Why do you disgrace your honourable appellation, under which you would profanely cover a deed of darkness, that would stain the name of a savage? Why are you suffered to run at large, and insult the laws of the land and publish your own infamy by daring to make an unreserved profession of such diabolical principles?'[115]

A correspondent to the *Kingston Gazette* wrote that duelling 'originated in heathen darkness and it has been propagated by infidelity.' Duellists were 'supremely selfish. He who can take God's holy name in vain, and trample on all laws Divine and human, cannot brook an insult from his equal, his fellow, his friend! And is this man of blood really, himself, so immaculate, so virtuous, so honourable? No, so base are his actions, and designs, that rather than have them exposed to the world, he will lose his own life, or, take that of his fellow ... This *man* of honour, this *painted* sepulchre, not having the fear of God before his eyes, being instigated by the Devil, and setting up his own perverted judgement as the standard of right and wrong, would browbeat the world, and shut the mouth of every preacher of righteousness.'[116] The duel therefore perverted the whole notion of manly 'honour,' whether it was fought to uphold a man's own reputation or the good name of a wife or female relative. (Male reputation, it should be noted, might encompass a wide range of characteristics, while women's 'good names' were reducible – indeed, essentialized – to one element: chastity.) Male honour became synonymous with lawlessness, excessive pride, and murder, and male bodies signified fashion, frivolity, and sexual licence. 'Eusebius' saw the problem as a failure of emotional control, manifested physically by such features as darting eyes, but ultimately attributable to uncontrolled male sexuality. Critiques of duelling were also structured around a distaste for aristocratic and courtly codes of behaviour, in which human life was held cheaply, and men were expected to defend public insults both personally and by means of violence. Those who were most supportive of the colony's imperial connection, such as the editor of the *Upper Canada Gazette*, overlooked the practice's link to British aristocratic behaviour; instead, they did their best to construct it as a 'heathen' and 'barbaric' act that may have originated in the feudal past but had been superseded by the rule of British law.

Yet terms such as 'heathen' and 'barbaric' had other meanings, ones related more directly to the context of Upper Canada where an aboriginal population was simultaneously experiencing dispossession and assimilation. By discursively linking the practice of duelling to 'heathen darkness,' a term that evoked the past but was understood by more than one Upper Canadian as signifying the state of unconverted Native peoples, those who spoke out against duelling may also have buttressed their own claims to be both respectable and 'white.' While so-called 'savagery' might be part of the European past, some colonists feared that the perceived loosening of forms of authority in a colonial setting, coupled with proximity to those who were constructed as 'heathens,' could result in a regression to these earlier forms of behaviour. Such fears may be glimpsed underlying this righteous rhetoric and the attacks on gouging. Moreover, for those who were eager to convert Native peoples to Christianity, the examples set by duellists were very poor ones.

Others, such as the Methodists, included duelling more or less automatically in their lists of upper-class vices that a true 'Christian gentleman' would shun.[117] While those whose attacks on duelling were part of a more general critique of upper-class morality may have overlooked its appeal to the middle classes, certainly the practice of physical combat to uphold manly honour was incompatible with the notions of manly virtue propounded by others in the colony. For those influenced by evangelical discourses, or the related ideas of sensibility, male physical violence could not be reconciled with male virtue. Many proponents of duelling believed that virtue was possessed primarily by women. Their opponents insisted that men were just as capable of possessing virtue and of expressing it through their relations with others, not by engaging in acts of physical violence that could end in death.

In some of the solutions that were proposed to stop men from threatening to kill one another, we may see the same sort of discourse at work that proposed the substitution of harmony and affectionate relationships for class conflict. Heavily indebted to early-nineteenth-century literature on the importance of bourgeois domesticity, drawing upon many of its images and metaphors, opponents of duelling proposed a different kind of familial model than that defended by duellists. While men were still the heads of families, it was as husbands and fathers that they were to refrain from physical violence. Those who discussed duelling in a more abstract and literary context suggested that men's relations with wives, mothers, sisters, and children should be the catalyst for an end to violence.[118] The distress their loved ones would suffer was a recurring theme in warnings to would-be antagonists. 'A Good Lesson for Duellists' recounted the happy tale of two men who concluded their dispute by refusing to fight, shaking hands, and becoming good friends. Such a felicitous state of affairs occurred because one man refused to participate, bringing his wife and children to the site of the duel and citing them as the reason.[119]

Yet sometimes not even the images of such tender scenes were enough to overcome men's pride. 'The Duel,' printed by the Anglican paper *The Church*, extracted by the *Boston Witness and Advocate*, and written by the editor of the *Zion's Herald*, Mr Stephens, was told in the voice of a minister who came upon the scene of a duel just about to be fought. Invoking God's law, the minister came close to stopping the duel, yet could not persuade 'Y' to retract his statement concerning the character of 'X,' a 'stout, ruffian-like' man, with a 'countenance easy but sinister and heartless.' The minister reminded Y of his 'probable domestic relations,' and 'the allusion touched his heart. He suddenly wiped a tear from his eye. "Yes, sir," said he, "there are hearts which would break if they knew I was here."' However, he could not 'sanction [X's] villainous character' and the duel was fought, with the predictable result that Y was killed, X fled, and Y's body was taken home to his widowed mother and unmarried sister. Deprived of the support of their son and brother, their sad fates of economic destitution and heartbreak were elaborated upon. The story concluded with a call for women to exert their influence to prevent duelling, since 'so many hearts of mothers, sisters, and wives have been made to bleed by this cruel and deadly custom,' based on a 'fictitious sense of honour.'[120]

'We may guess,' V.J. Kiernan writes, 'of a suppressed wish in men for women some day to intervene and rescue them from their own folly.'[121] Whether or not we wish to make such speculations in the realm of 'psycho-history,' the image of the heartbroken women affected by a duellist's conduct was pressed into service to prevent the practice, even though men's relations with female family members might have been the rationale for the duel itself. As one writer pointed out, truly virtuous women and their 'honour' should be the last 'objects' over which duels should be fought. 'Were she endowed with that virgin modesty, that chaste and retreating timidity, that meekness, gentleness, and compassionate tenderness which impart such peculiar and overpowering charms to their possessor, she would blush with the deepest confusion, and shrink back from the idea of tender attachment for him who could act thus! She would shudder at the thought that her name should be in any way associated with such a transaction, and turn with horror from the miscreant who would fain lay his bloodstained laurels at her feet, as the genuine tokens of his love and affection!'[122] As this passage demonstrates, the image of womanhood constructed by supporters and opponents of duelling was remarkably similar. Whether she was evoked to ignite or to douse the impulse to duel, the virtuous woman had to be constructed as compassionate, tender, meek, timid, retiring, blushingly modest, and – the most critical category of all – sexually chaste.

Thus, as a socially constructed matter involving both class and gender relations, duelling, in Upper Canadian discourses, concerned men's behaviour towards one another and also implicated them as family members, as husbands, fathers, sons, and brothers. While the popular image of duelling may have reduced it to a dispute between two men, standing at dawn in a field with pistols pointed at each other and accompanied only by their seconds and their respective horses, those who spoke out against duelling believed that the law, the church, and the family – particularly their wives, daughters, and sisters – also stood at the sides of these 'men of honour.'

Manners and social mores have not always appeared of great importance to historians, concerned with seemingly larger questions of political and economic power. Yet conceptions of the ways in which human beings behave towards one another may have great historical relevance, forming an important part of shifts in power relations, whether of class, religion, race, ethnicity, or gender. The kinds of literature that we have been discussing may be deeply implicated in such changes. Through media such as the press, historians may link the formation of codes of behaviour to changes in political formation or in the means of production.[123]

Manners could mean more than simple politeness. As we have seen in the previous chapter, some writers in the colony equated enthusiastic religion with political sedition. Those same writers then proceeded to seize on the lack of refinement and rough manners of itinerant preachers as symbolic of republicanism and the destruction of the imperial bond. In a description of the American Methodist preachers who presided at the first chapel in York, in 1818, the *Patriot and Farmers' Monitor* revelled in their 'vulgarity' and the shock suffered by the British members of the chapel upon seeing their 'spiritual leaders.' 'They had never been accustomed in England to see ragged and dirty preachers with beards "that shewed like a stubble at harvest home," nor had they ever been outraged and disgusted, by seeing their minister put his finger on his nose, and lean over the pulpit first on one side, and then on the other, and blow like a snorting horse, and then wipe with the cuff on the lap of his coat, and after vociferating nonsense for over an hour, sit down in the pulpit and cram his hands into his waistcoat pockets, and bring out of one a plug of tobacco, and a short pipe, and out of the other a Jack knife, and deliberately cut his plug, and fill his pipe, then light it at the pulpit candle and come down puffing away to salute his brethern.'[124] It is also worth remembering that the uncontrollable, passionate, and vulgar behaviour of some reformers came in for similar criticisms. That these men might be concerned with reforming behaviour as well as political institutions did not protect them from the jibes of the conservative press, which drew attention to their unkempt clothing and disruptive behaviour both on the hustings and in the assembly.[125]

Although discourses around the family, temperance, and the 'code of honour' were not completely monolithic and could be as full of contradictions and tensions as the codes of behaviour that they sought to replace, they shared one common element. These concepts of morality were to be engaged in voluntarily; the impetus would come from the individual who would attempt to change her or his behaviour, with family members and friends providing guidance and support. Although editors and writers might call for institutions such as the assembly or the judiciary to suppress duelling (and, by the 1850s, drinking), they also agreed that the onus was on men, first and foremost, to change their behaviour. The type of reformation in gender relations that these discourses envisaged was one that would take place, not under the aegis of the state or by ecclesiastical fiat, but through the union of men and women outside these institutions. Certainly there was a place for church and chapel since, as we have seen, these discourses owed a debt to religious belief. Middle-class appeals to the religiously sanctioned nature of writings on the family, drink, and the 'code of honour' not only acknowledged a very real debt but also gave the writers of this material an important claim to some kind of legitimacy.

Furthermore, the voluntaristic appeal that ran through moral writings poses some challenging questions about conceptions of the state in Upper Canada. In his work on Bond Head and the election of 1836, Cadigan has characterized reformers as wanting to replace paternalistic relationships in Upper Canada with, as he calls it, the more impersonal 'rule of law,' as in the case of municipal ordinances in Cornwall and Brockville that were directly concerned with behaviour in public spaces. Reformers thus became the harbingers of middle-class formations concerned with moral regulation in mid-nineteenth-century Ontario, a point also made by Noel, who links temperance to middle-class reformers and 'radical mechanics' and points to the temperance movement's reliance on the doctrine of self-help.[126] Yet, while reformers may have wanted to use the state at a local level to implement a platform aimed at improving conduct (and, in Cadigan's essay, it is not entirely clear that such by-laws were the work only of reformers), we must remember that reform publications also came to speak freely and at great length about the need to liberate certain aspects of Upper Canadian society from the heavy hand of the colonial state.[127] And, as chapter 2 has argued, reformers also attempted to set boundaries in political discourse between private and public, hoping to divorce political life from the entanglements and corruption of the former. 'Manly,' virtuous independence would be brought to political life and institutions, reforming and rejuvenating them in the processs. Overall, the discourse of the Upper Canadian press did its best to locate such matters as gender relations and the family as outside the purview of the state.[128]

It thus might be tempting to characterize the discourses examined above, especially those around the home and family, as concerning private behaviour and to see women as synonymous with the private sphere, but such a schema oversimplifies dramatically. As in religious literature, many who wrote about relations between husbands and wives wanted to reassure their readers that these were, in some sense, 'private' and personal matters, to be worked out by individuals within the confines of their homes. Yet, as indicated by George IV's attempts to divorce his wife, a domestic 'squabble' that became known as 'the Queen Caroline affair,' matters concerning domestic life could turn public *and* political very rapidly.[129] The *Upper Canada Gazette*, admittedly not a paper likely to support the queen's cause, observed rather huffily that 'the general sympathy at first excited in her majesty's favour was quickly dispelled by her making common causes with a set of factious demagogues, whose debasing maxim seems to be that whatever is, is wrong; and who seek to overturn all constituted authority; guided by these men, she has sanctioned their intemperate and inflammatory productions; by allowing them to appear as answers to addresses made to her. Indeed her whole conduct appears too much the appearance of daring, unblushing effrontery, rather than the dignified modesty of calumniated female innocence; we repeat that her own conduct, since the commencement of the investigation, has injured her cause far more than all the assertions of her accusers.' Not content with its pronouncement on the queen's morals, particularly her transgression of the codes of modest, chaste womanhood, the paper also wanted to reassure its readers that any reports that the British government had brought in foreign troops to protect itself were absolutely false. Even if such assistance were needed (which was highly unlikely), 'the real friends and staunch supporters of their country, would rise in their strength, and crush the reptiles who are now malignantly using the Queen's cause, to involve the country in anarchy and bloodshed.'[130]

The domestic life of the British monarchy was not likely to be perceived as a private affair, and, in any case, the quarrel between George and Caroline was more than just a common domestic 'spat.' The 'dignified modesty of calumniated female innocence' that Caroline might represent became, as Davidoff and Hall have argued, part of 'the rejection of aristocratic moral standards,'[131] a rejection that reverberated across the Atlantic, drawing the colony into its ambit. Moreover, it was not easy to equate the private world of the home with women and children for, as we have seen, the discourse of the Upper Canadian press was as much about family relations that involved men as ones that involved women and children. And when other matters, like drinking and duelling, came under scrutiny, men and women were told that they must work together to reform social mores: men by exercising self-control, women by their 'moral influence.'

These public affairs (for what could be more public than the socio-economic destruction foretold by temperance advocates or the killing of one man by another?) would be resolved using a code of behaviour and morality taken from writings on gender relations in the home and family. Later in the century, as the British North American state began to rigidify gender distinctions and to fragment the category of 'woman' along the lines of class, ethnicity, and race, it drew upon the types of gendered languages that developed during first three decades of the nineteenth century. These archetypes of femininity and masculinity provided a cultural and moral framework for the legal and administrative reformation and regulation of gender relations.[132]

Furthermore, although the voluntary impulse clearly relied on the ethos of individual responsibility, voluntarism also meant the development of a number of organizations and groups. Although voluntarism in Upper Canada deserves its own study, one that goes beyond reports of these groups in the press, for our purposes it is worth noting that many of the themes discussed in this chapter also ran through the public pronouncements of the voluntary organizations. Groups such as Female Benevolent Society, Young Men's Temperance Society, and the Dorcas Society, and other organizations associated with missionary work, carved out social spaces, using gender as a means of defining the social space and setting its boundaries, but we should note that these boundaries were not impermeable. The 1825 report of the Kingston Female Benevolent Society regretted that the organization's operations were less extensive than in other years (a common theme in many charitable societies' reports) but was pleased to note that this condition had 'compelled' members 'to be less limited in their exertions in consequence of the lowness of their funds' for the support of the town's hospital. To this end, the report noted that the society had received donations from the military – the Thirty-Seventh Regiment, the Officers of the Royal Artillery, the non-commissioned officers, the gunners, and the drummers – as well as various individuals, doctors, and the clergy (including the archdeacon).[133] Two years later, the society, still experiencing financial problems, printed a subscription list that noted the contributions of men and women, married and single.[134] Whether or not the society was able to continue its work because of the support of male representatives of the imperial government and the church is difficult to determine. What is important here is that, while headed by women and purportedly about 'female' concerns, this organization also involved men and publicly acknowledged their involvement. Similarly, while many temperance and Sunday-school societies were headed by all-male boards, the subscription lists printed in the paper sometimes included women's names and acknowledged the contributions made by women's unpaid labour.[135]

Certainly the predominance of the York and Kingston élite in many of these groups must be considered as well; it was not uncommon for the same surnames to show up in the executive lists of both male and female societies. Class or social rank, in this case, might crisscross with gender in these organizations' self-representation in the press, in their lists of members such as Kirby, Herchmer, Molson, Markland, and Macauley. Nor should we overlook the power relations at play in colonial society whereby a woman's access to economic resources was invariably mediated by her relationship to male family members. Economic necessity and the need for social legitimacy in all likelihood led to the inclusion of the regiment or the archdeacon in women's organizations. By acknowledging that these associations represented a particular group of women, one whose class, racial, and ethnic background defined them and their goals as inherently respectable, the inclusion of élite men may have deflected (or even suppressed) any concerns about the desirability of women's voluntary work.

The situation was somewhat different in the case of missionary reports. In reports of the activities of Dorcas Societies, members' pious sisterly concern for their Native counterparts was a predominant image. Replete with womanly feeling, white women were presented as collecting clothes and taking up donations for Mississauga women at Grape Island, Rice Lake, and the Credit River, in order that the Native women might make and sell household objects such as brooms and baskets.[136] The symbolism of the female sex working together for the uplift of all women amounted to an attempt (more so than in other reports of benevolent voluntarism) to portray women in relation to one another, making men far less important in their work.[137] But, as in the missionary reports, racial differences underlay the coverage of Dorcas Societies. Clearly these white women were perceived as being in a position to offer Christian charity, and Native women in a position to receive it. White women, through such charitable activities, were the recipients of something equally precious: their own spiritual and social redemption. Yet the relationship between Native and white women was not perceived as being one of exchange and agency for both parties, in which Native women might help shape the terms of white women's spiritual regeneration. Instead, in the sentimental language employed by Protestant missionaries, Native women became the 'human scenery before which the melodrama of middle-class redemption could be enacted, for the enlightenment of an audience that was not even themselves.'[138]

Voluntary organizations frequently shared in and contributed to the gendered languages of manners and morality of the press. Together, these societies helped create a space in Upper Canadian discourse that might be most usefully described as social.[139] A place that to some degree escaped the binary oppositions of male and female, workplace and home, public versus private, it was an area in colonial society inhabited by both men and women. Supposedly divorced from the squabbles and conflicts of the political realm, social life (which could be defined as home and family, the church, and the voluntary association) was given meaning by its voluntaristic nature, by the fact that, supposedly, no institution intervened to regulate and shape the behaviour of the men and women who inhabited this space. The threat of conflict might loom, as in the case of the drunkard, but it was one that could be resolved by self-control and the influence of others; social life drew its strength from its perceived distance from political and sectarian power struggles. That power relations, such as race and class, were implicated in the construction of 'the social' was seldom directly acknowledged, nor were the dynamics of power that underpinned gender relations. Such relationships were coated with the language of affection and sentiment, a tendency that would become more pronounced as the colony moved into the 1840s.[140]

5

Party, Parades, and Bazaars in the 1840s

The decade that followed the rebellion has been characterized as one of political transformation, with the union of the Canadas, the attainment of responsible government, the growth of parties, and the expansion of the state in Canada West.[1] So far as religious developments are concerned, some issues remained unsettled. Debates over the future of the clergy reserves, for example, continued throughout the 1840s; the issue was not resolved until 1854.[2] However, as a state-supported church became less and less popular, voluntarism was gradually accepted as a guiding principle for Anglican and Methodist alike. Along with other denominations, these churches entered a period of institutional consolidation and equilibrium in the more settled areas of Canada West.[3] The decade also saw the growth of a province-wide temperance movement, one that spread alongside other forms of voluntary activity in the growing cities and towns of the colony.[4]

To date, gender has figured hardly at all in most historians' understanding of the 1840s. Yet, certain historical events and processes in Upper Canada and Canada West – whether debates over the notion of party, the meaning of patriotism, or the spread of religious organizations – are only partially understood if we do not incorporate gender into our analysis of historical change. The meanings given to various aspects of political, religious, and social life, as they were developed in the pages of some of the more significant newspapers and by certain voluntary organizations of this period, relied on many of the notions of gender that have been explored in the previous chapters. Moreover, as scholars as diverse as J.M.S. Careless and Bruce Curtis have argued, by the 1840s the formation of an Upper Canadian middle class was well under way.[5] In this particular aspect of social formation, gender, class, and, frequently, race meshed while simultaneously producing a number of tensions, contradictions, and ambiguities.

Middle-class discourses continued to divide Upper Canadian society into the realms of private and public, using masculinity and femininity as the signs of these divisions. But various aspects of political and social change in the 1840s also indicate the development of interstices between these seemingly monolithic categories, pointing to the need to conceptualize Upper Canadian society in less rigid ways than the dichotomies of public and private, male and female.

Patriotism in Upper Canada had long been signified by the deeds of virtuous men, loyal to the Crown and the British connection, but in the immediate aftermath of the rebellion, protestations of loyalty and patriotic zeal took on an even sharper edge.[6] The bravery of the provincial militia was, as in the War of 1812, commemorated in editorials and letters to papers such as the *Patriot*, the *British Colonist*, and the *Kingston Chronicle and Gazette*. 'A Freeholder, in Port Sarnia' wrote a glowing account of the loyalty and bravery of the First Regiment of the Huron Militia, which had recently gone home after defending the border from the 'assemblage of rebels and pirates' threatening to invade from the United States. 'To any man,' wrote the 'Freeholder,' 'who has never had to plough, dig, swim, and wade his way from the known parts of this Province, to Port Sarnia, through Adelaide, Warwick, and Plympton, the sufferings and merits of these men who accomplished what to me appeared an impossibility, can never be known, understood, or appreciated.' This journey into the heart of the colony's 'wilderness' was the source of the local inhabitant's gratitude and provided proof of the militia's loyalty to queen and constitution. The people of Port Sarnia apparently knew 'from much lighter and far less painful duties this winter, what it is for three hundred farmers at one day's notice, to leave their wives and children, their cattle and farms, themselves without greatcoats or blankets, many nearly barefooted, without a change of shirt or socks, and march one hundred and twenty miles – remain on actual duty for ten weeks; and they will ever bear testimony to the kindness, civility, sobriety, and good discipline of these loyal men, than whom no body of officers and men ever left a place more respected and beloved.' These paragons of loyal manhood, like the virtuous militia of 1812, were God-fearing men. Although quartered in the new Methodist church of Port Sarnia, 'while they were in it, they had it so clean and neatly arranged, that we had divine service every Sunday, at which they gave the most general and decent attendance, and I regret to say that since their departure we have not been able to use the church that way.'[7]

As was the case with militia activities during the war, it is a moot point whether the colony was actually 'saved' from chaos and invasion by its own citizens' military activities or by the colonists' lack of support for an armed uprising.[8] Whatever the militia may have actually accomplished, there were those who were eager to portray the events of the winter of 1837–38 as the triumph of virtuous and loyal Upper Canadian manhood, ever-vigilant in its defence of crown, constitution, home, and family.[9] Other political developments necessitated that this vigilance be maintained. As 'Tecumseth' told the *British Colonist* in 1838, 'good men' down through the ages had been obliged to put themselves in peril. Upper Canadians, threatened by either 'wicked men' such as Lord Brougham or the 'selfish and weak men' of the Imperial parliament, had recognized their danger and 'crushed the monster at his birth.' Now Lord Durham was in danger of being 'waylaid' by 'men of lofty station, who call themselves patriots' but were really dishonest and self-seeking. 'Tecumseth' continued:

To arouse ourselves, in the pride of Britons, and with the spirit of our forefathers and, with assistance of the few gallant troops among us, let us sacrifice every man who shall dare to set a hostile foot upon our territory from without. That we are fully equal to this task, let no stout-hearted loyalist for one moment doubt. – Prepare yourselves, every one of you, fathers and sons, brothers and husbands, and make your wives and your daughters proud of you. On the 7th of December last, when we crushed a rebellion in one short hour, near this city, I had my sons at my side in the field while my wife and my daughter and my sister were agitated with fear for our personal safety, but they were at the same time animated with the proud confidence that we should acquit ourselves like men, defending the rights, and all that could be dear to Christian men. And such were the feelings of every mother and daughter and sister of every loyal man that day in our city. Yes, Sirs, my eyes filled with tears on the morning of that day while I glanced over the face of many gallant youths of sixteen standing proudly by the side of his senior.[10]

It is worth noting the irony of the correspondent's choice of pen-name, at a time when Native peoples were entering a period of isolation and stagnation on reserves. The choice of 'Tecumseth' might have been intended to invoke a history of colonial courage and devotion to the British Crown, qualities so intense that they transcended racial differences. This passage also continued to link the masculine protection of home with that of country, as we saw earlier writers do in chapters 1 and 2. Loyalty to the Crown and to British political traditions were offered to the paper's readers as more than abstractions; instead, they lay at the heart of men's most intimate social relations, that of familial relationships. As fathers, husbands, sons, and brothers, loyal British (and Christian) men would rush to take up arms, and, in doing so, they too might transcend other divisions (specifically those of age, although other, unspoken barriers might also be dismantled or overlooked). This passage also continued the pattern of linking women to the realm of emotion – fearful for the safety of their male relatives – while at the same time relying on their presence and their need for protection in order to give meaning and appeal to this scene of patriotic fervour. Men could shed tears of pride over the sight of their compatriots, but, given the context, such an expression of emotion would in no way expose them to charges of effeminacy. While wives and daughters could also experience feelings of 'proud confidence' in the patriotic activity of their husbands and fathers, female loyalty could not be expressed in marching and drilling. Instead, women's commitment to Crown and country would be channelled through the bodies of men who undertook physical activities generally forbidden to women.

Loyalty, as we have seen in chapter 2, could not be taken for granted in the colonial context. It was worth remembering whose loyalties had measured up to conservative standards during the troubled times of 1812 and 1837.[11] While other political events eventually dominated the pages of the press, the rebellion and its leaders hovered at the edges of political consciousness, useful reminders of the precariousness of colonial government. Mackenzie, the *Patriot*'s editor Thomas Dalton reminded his readers in February 1841, had been 'totally deficient in morality, uprightness, honesty, candor, manliness, decision, and physical courage.'[12] Six years later, the organization of a petition for his pardon drew forth a suitable amount of ire from *The Church*. He had been 'an apostle of discontent and sedition,' the paper pronounced, and Upper Canada was 'happily relieved of his evil presence.' Questioning the loyalty of those men who had signed the petition, the paper later ran a poem that described Mackenzie as 'Lucifer's elite,' satirized his courage and patriotism, and called him a 'blood-stained poltroon.'[13] While more consensual discussions of patriotism and loyalty took place over the 1840s, at the start of the decade vilifying rebels was important to those self-appointed guardians of the British connection.[14]

Political discourse in the province's press became caught up in defining and shaping a code of political morality. Much of this code was related to the political changes brought about by union with Lower Canada and by the formation of political parties. This latter development was the subject of some discussion and not a little anxiety and ambivalence. Although, as chapter 2 has demonstrated, political divisions and factions were familiar to the colony, 'party' (in the sense of organized voting blocks within the legislature, a recognized leadership that, if in the majority, might be expected to assume cabinet positions, and an extraparliamentary organization that could be rallied in an election) was a relatively new phenomenon. A necessary component of responsible government, the organization of political parties was by no means a fait accompli in the early 1840s.[15] Carol Wilton has argued that the decade saw their development and that political parties were eagerly embraced by many Upper Canadian politicians, but this observation needs some qualification. Political parties may have been a fact of political life by 1849, when responsible government had been attained with the passage of Rebellion Losses Bill, yet they were not developed without debate and discussion.[16] In arguing over the meaning and morality of 'party,' political essayists and journalists offered another symbol loaded with a variety of implications, that of the 'public man.'

Such an image was not entirely new to political discourse in Upper Canada. Declarations of political candidacies in elections had earlier employed this term. However, its use in the context of debates over party and the strife it brought (at a time when the strife of the late 1830s was all too fresh a memory) meant that 'the public man' would be the saviour of a fragile political system. Like his counterpart in domestic literature, the mother and wife in the home, the public man of politics could exercise a much-needed moral suasion and influence, not least because of his own moral probity. And, like the wife and mother, the public man represented harmony and consensus. He presided above the clash and din of party strife and rescued Upper Canadians from the venality of these political divisions. As a 'Correspondent' wrote to the British Colonist in 1839, the coming of responsible government was an occasion for rejoicing. The previous 'irresponsible government' of the province had 'created a mighty and independent power, linked together by the strongest ties that can bind man to his fellow man, of self-interest, pride, ambition, love of power, family connexions.' Consequently, the irresponsible members of the government of Upper Canada 'have placed their foot on the neck of the Lieutenant Governor of this province – thrown around him the chains of party, which no effort of his could throw off.' Those who had just defended the province, the British constitution, and the sovereign were the same men who demanded responsible government, as 'men attached to our Native or adopted country.' The choice was clear, the 'Correspondent' informed the paper's readers: British freedom or despotism and slavery.[17]

'Let the people of the Canadas mark the conduct of every one of their public men on the great measure of the Union,' declared 'Milesius' regarding this political change. Those perceived as 'ready to cast aside every feeling of present personality and every recollection of the unhappy animosities of the past' also must be men who would not sacrifice the country to their narrow personal interests.[18] Although directed at a different kind of activity than voluntarism or religiosity, addresses to young men about the development of a 'public spirit' and the need to work for the 'public good' bore many similarities to those discussed in the previous chapter. As 'An Old Man' told 'the Young Men of Canada,' they must cultivate a knowledge of 'our Public Men, that thereby you may exercise your own minds in the truth of all things, and in a sincere and ardent desire to do good to one another.' The political struggles of the last two decades – the Family Compact versus the reformers – were dismissed as nothing more than selfish wrangling over patronage and nepotism, a pattern of public outrages that young men must be prevented from repeating. However, although an interest in political matters was fundamental to the 'public good,' young men should not be 'ambitious for office.' It would come to them if their ability and circumstances warranted. They should 'train their minds to look upon every man who pushes himself forward for the sake of office as more or less an enemy to the peace, happiness, and good government of his neighbours.'[19]

Not all those who addressed the subject were as forthright as the 'Old Man,' who highlighted some of the unease felt over the issue of party formation. 'Party' might easily signify venality, corruption, and selfishness. The spoils of patronage returned once again to haunt political discourse.[20] It was crucial that the 'public man' be capable of transcending what were, after all, diversions from the real business of government. He could thus prove unequivocally his manly and virtuous independence. That quality, so prized by the reformers of the 1820s and 1830s, became, in the debates of the 1840s, the key to understanding the essence of the 'public man.' Furthermore, such independence was one of the fundamental characteristics of the very concept of public in this aspect of political discourse. Political life could easily sink to the level of the private when selfish interests were allowed to dominate men's behaviour. It was only really 'public' when these interests were transcended, when patronage was abolished and personal ambitions were subsumed. Unlike the virtuous woman, the public man was free of the intense emotional ties that might prejudice his judgment and imperil his impartiality. His whole persona was predicated on his ability to rise above such considerations. With responsibilities not unlike those of women, the self-effacing managers of relationships within the home, he was expected to navigate the shoals of party and keep his fellow politicians together and on course.

'Public' also might mean 'moderate,' as was suggested by the *Patriot*'s 1842 editorial on 'Conciliatory Policy.' Dalton advised that, rather than forming a cabinet from party leaders who were bitterly opposed to each other, a conciliatory policy should be applied to 'moderate men of all parties – to the calm and temperate mass of people who have never in any violent way manifested their utter implacability to the opposite party. Men who, belonging nominally to one party or the other, can yet regard with temper and moderation those whose views may happen to be opposed to their own.' Warming to his subject, Dalton declared: 'We conceive that under the term, "moderate men" can be comprised the great mass of the intelligence and respectability of the land – the bone, substance, and sinew of the country – the men who look more to the general prosperity and tranquility of the land in which they have made their home, than to the temporary triumph of party; and who would consider the elevation of one set of men to office, and the exclusion of another, very dearly purchased at the expense of a convulsed country and a paralyzed government.' He concluded by reassuring his readers that the governor could count on the support 'of the moderate and temperate men of all classes.'[21] Hugh Scobie, the editor of the *British Colonist*, told his readers that a 'practical spirit' would bring joy and happiness. This spirit 'lies at the foundation of political and public morality. It subordinates party to the public weal. It reduces mere party men to the true level of their real worthiness. It teaches public men their duty – private men their interest. It makes them lovers of country rather than lovers of party.'[22]

Anxieties concerning party, and suggestions that independent men of public spirit were the solution, were not limited to one particular political perspective. Conservative papers such as Dalton's, journals that cast themselves as supporters of moderate reformers (such as the *British Colonist*), and unabashed champions of the 'Reform Electors of Canada' (such as George Brown's *The Globe*) all, at one time or another, used the symbol of the public man to legitimate various political projects and attack those politicians suspected of self-aggrandizement.[23] Volleys against place-hunters and sycophants did not vanish once Mackenzie and his cohorts went into exile but instead became part of a widely shared arsenal of political taunts, insults, and attacks on the government's legitimacy. A letter to the governor general, Sir Charles Metcalfe, from 'A Friend to British Interests,' accused him of despotism, of attacks on the constitution and Canadian freedom, and of condoning 'barbarous informalities' on the part of his 'late

Ministers.' Insisting that 'manly virtue' must be summoned up when British rights were questioned, the writer then spoke of the contentious 'rewards and honours' of patronage and the governor's purported misuse of these emoluments. 'Yes, Sir, we do trust that our advocacy of the principle, "*that the executive power shall never be exercised without advice,*" will stamp us, for future life and posterity. The enlightened body of men, whose extensive influence in this province has been basely presented to you, Excellency, as a thing to be purchased, spurn the proposal with an indignant scorn, fitted to wither even the recreant Priest who has dared to put upon them such an insult.' These representatives, according to the 'Friend,' could not be bribed or threatened. The 'flame of freedom' will continue to burn brightly, the 'arm of despotic power' will be put to rest, 'and then, Sir, our children shall turn and bless that unbought integrity of their fathers.'[24]

The reformers' desire to separate public and private personae and issues continued to spark debate in considerations of the 'public man.' The reform paper of Francis Hincks, *The Examiner*, complained in 1841 of the tory press's attacks on the moderate reform leader, Robert Baldwin. It was their 'violence and malignity ... with a view of damaging not only the public but the private character of an individual,' that Hincks found objectionable. 'It is not sufficient to destroy Mr. Baldwin's character as a politician, say these vile panders to the depravity of a profligate party – we must impeach his conduct as unworthy of a gentleman and a man of honour.'[25] That *The Examiner*'s choice of language might have led the paper to walk a very fine discursive line itself was somewhat beside the point. In its defence of Baldwin, the paragon of political honour, the paper continued the reform practice of drawing distinctions between what was acceptable public debate and what was mud-slinging and character assassination.[26]

Some of the most valiant attempts to retain these distinctions were made in the pages of the *British Colonist*. An 1841 editorial, which concerned the candidacy of John Beverley Robinson's brother William in the riding of Simcoe, reassured readers that the paper had no personal animosity toward Robinson. Instead, Scobie insisted, the issue was his familial and political connections with the old party and the fact that he would probably be an advocate for their 'selfish interests.' Although Robinson's 'private' life was, of course, an issue, it was the political use to which it might be put that bothered Scobie. Rather than allowing 'family' to corrupt public life, voters should support Robinson's opponent, Captain Steele, a man of 'honest reform principles.'[27] The private, supposedly unseen links that bound Family Compact members together and that had led to corruption, disaffection, and finally armed revolt were often targeted in the *Colonist*. The desire to distance conservatism from the excesses of the York and Kingston élite was part of the changes involved in moderate conservatism's development during the 1840s. At times it was suggested that even 'honest men' must guard against a similar selfishness and lack of public spirit. An editorial on the 'state of the colony' warned the readership: 'We are now arrived at a crisis when every loyal and patriotic man in the community must be up and doing. The responsibility rests equally on one and all, and that man who may content himself with remaining quietly at home, when he ought to be at the hustings recording his vote in favour of the government, cannot fail to reproach himself hereafter, if any difficulty should arise, with being to a certain extent the cause of it. – The present is no ordinary crisis.'[28]

The home, it seemed, was no place for men to demonstrate their commitment to political stability; indeed, men who remained within its sheltering walls during a crisis ran the risk of being seen as unmanly, charged with feminine passivity. This passage also attempted to remove the taint of immorality from the political arena by suggesting that the 'hustings,' an area that to some colonists was the antithesis of domestic virtues (since its party-inspired strife might end in physical violence), was in fact a site where men could demonstrate morality. And, although Scobie did not make this explicit to his readers, there was another, implicit message concerning men's demonstration of political duty. By fulfilling their political responsibilities, they would be exercising a right granted primarily to certain adult males – property-holders of European descent – and thus would remind their fellow colonists that these categories were tied to the retention of political power.

This piece was followed by an address 'to the Independent Electors of the City of Toronto' by the Scottish-born Hamilton businessman and moderate reformer, Isaac Buchanan. A supporter of responsible government, Buchanan represented Toronto from 1841 until his resignation in 1843, believing that responsible government had been achieved. A moderate, Buchanan was opposed to Robert Baldwin, believing him to be a 'dangerously doctrinaire extremist who, while personally above reproach, was surrounded by potentially subversive influences.' Buchanan was a particular favourite of the *Colonist* during the 1840s; in his writings he underscored the theme of personal gain vs. public welfare and the separation of private lives from public service. 'I mean not,' he told the electorate, 'to impugn the private characters of the old Government Tory party, but as an independent man I shall ever raise my voice against their selfish and exclusive political need. However respectable or amiable some of them may be, as individuals, I must view them as a Compact, to be the worst enemies of their country and blind enough not to see, that they are thus the enemies of themselves and their children.' Buchanan proceeded to argue that the electorate would vote for him not because of personal reasons or party loyalty but because Toronto deserved, and would receive, 'all the adherence which independent men can give to any Government.'[29]

If at times pronouncements concerning the public man were as abstract as they were solemn, there were writers and editors eager to provide concrete examples of just who such luminaries might be. A degree of vagueness concerning his identity was necessary, because the public man was by definition modest and unassuming. Nevertheless, certain men were presented as exemplary. Baldwin, according to Brown's 'Political Portrait Gallery,' was one who had transcended his personal tastes and family background to act for the good of Canadians. Despite a liking for old books, paintings, and customs, an 'early attachment' to the members of the Family Compact, and a devotion to the Church of England, Baldwin was able to see that responsible government, civil and religious liberty, and the spread of education would bring stability and prosperity to the province.[30] In this passage, Baldwin appears as a harbinger of nineteenth-century liberal ideals, particularly those values and morals of the educated man of property that were prized by the British North American state. He combined some of the more valued attributes of 'courtly' or upper-class behaviour – taste, refinement, a love of learning, and a claim on British cultural and political traditions – with a staunch opposition to political and religious oligarchy and tyranny and a desire to improve his fellow colonists' moral and economic well-being through education.[31]

But, as Brown's other thumbnail sketches of various political luminaries demonstrated, the immorality of men in political office might throw into question the symbol of honesty and probity. Writing about two favourite targets, Solicitor General John Hillyard Cameron and former solicitor general Henry Sherwood, Brown's 'portrait' was one of wickedness and dishonesty. Observing that 'to sketch the character of a public man with certainty in such times as these it is necessary to know him personally – to know whether he is a rogue or a fool – facile, though, inclined to do right – strong of mind, though weak of purse – right in his convictions, wrong through the influence of his friends or social position – or whether his course is one of utter indifference to right or wrong.'[32]

Although this passage appeared to reject the distinctions made by reformers between personal lives and public service, for Brown the matter was more complex. 'There is a strange sentiment held almost universally in

Canada, that a man may be utterly dishonest in public life, that he may be guilty of the most unprincipled, and really disgraceful transactions, and yet be a highly honourable private citizen – estimable, and in every way a pattern of private virtue.' For Brown, though, the two areas – personal life and public service – were intertwined. Any attempt to separate the two, as he believed his opponents did, was political sophistry. Symbolic of this attitude, he told his readers, were the evaluations of the conservative politician Henry Draper. According to their authors, Draper was less than moral, but he possessed the potential to be a good judge. It was this flexibility of standards that, Brown declared, underlay a decline in political honesty. 'Differing as we do, most decidedly, from such a general doctrine, we cannot deny that the prevalence of this idea, and the relaxed code of morality to which political men are held amenable ought to be considered in weighing the guilt of individuals ... We hold the public Press amenable to a standard of morality, equally strict with private individuals, and for ourselves we are at all times prepared to vindicate the truth of our statements of opinions to the letter.'[33]

One editor's public icon might be another's example of the betrayal of such ideals. By 1844, the *Colonist* was carrying on a running feud with *The Examiner* and was openly opposed to Baldwin, Hincks, and their supporters as the antithesis of the 'moderate principle' personified by Buchanan. Scobie supported Governor Metcalfe during the province's constitutional crisis of 1843–44, a stand that 'enraged' Hincks and his supporters. According to Scobie's biographer, Hincks almost bankrupted the paper and its proprietor, but the outcome of this campaign was to raise the *Colonist* to 'new heights of influence.'[34] Baldwin 'and company,' the paper stated, had used 'coarse invective, low scurrility, meanness, malice, and falsehood' to subvert loyal authority.[35] Their opposition to Governor Metcalfe, their refusal to work towards consensus in the assembly, and their previous 'desertion' of Governor Sydenham amounted to a 'betrayal' of responsible government, one that could only be put right by a public confession of guilt. 'Let him say honestly, and like a man,' declared Scobie, '"*I erred grievously in the Executive Council, I am sorry for my offence against Responsible Government, and for the misrepresentation I have been of the Reformers of Upper Canada.*"'[36] Publicly expiating their guilt might then allow these political sinners to aspire to the status of public men, ones committed to 'responsible government' and thus to the submersion of any selfish, personal desires and programs. Such a man was Buchanan, a 'highly independent gentleman' who wanted only to guarantee his countrymen the 'birthright' of every Briton: 'true freedom.'[37]

Anxious to assert its own 'independence' as an arbiter of 'public opinion,' the *Colonist* used the term 'public man' as an award for those political figures who measured up to the paper's standards. Such was the paper's verdict on Robert Graham Dunlop, whose lengthy obituary in 1841 (chronicling his education and his careers in the Royal Navy and as the MLA for Huron) concluded with the observation that the community had lost a 'thoroughly independent man, who neither courted power, nor feared it.'[38] That the notion of 'independent' behaviour exercised by certain men in the assembly might not be the same as the 'moderation' valued by the *Colonist* was a contradiction the paper chose not to address. Furthermore, although it frequently attacked the 'Compact' as the source of political corruption, a malevolent force that prevented 'public men' from asserting their manly vigour in defence of responsible government, in its support for 'men of moderation' the paper differed from the reform discourse of the previous decade. The manly independent representatives of the people constructed by Mackenzie would have found it difficult to recognize their descendants in the moderates who supported the governor and reconciled their differences with (reformed) 'High Churchman.'[39]

Baldwin and Buchanan were not the only symbols of the public man deployed in the political discourse of the 1840s. Admittedly these two were useful representatives of this ideal, their speeches and activities a yardstick to measure others. However, the editors and writers considered here perceived political life and public duty as more than an arena in which famous (and infamous) men performed. While they might never attain the fame of members of the Executive Council, the voters of Canada West were urged to consider themselves as an integral part of the political process, important arbiters of public morality. Farmers, or 'honest yeoman,' were often called upon in this regard. Brown in particular was famous for his support of the farmers of Canada West as the bedrock of an emerging Canadian nationalism.[40] His 1844 address to the 'Electors of Canada West' was typical in this regard. 'The rotten boroughs have exhausted their strength, and the independent yeomen are now called on to take their place in the ranks, to do battle against the hosts of Tory misrule and oppression.'[41] Many of his pronouncements on farmers used the country language of reform discourse, lauding their manly independence and incorruptibility.[42]

However, the symbol of the sturdy yeomen had a wider currency in the province. As we have seen in chapter 2, both tory and reformer deployed it in debates over political legitimacy and support. Some, like writers in the *Patriot and Farmers' Monitor*, were less comfortable with the hardy farmer as the touchstone of political morality. Dalton and his contributors instead preferred to emphasize the viciousness and ulterior motives of political agitators and the need for cross-class alliances. After all, these agitators had made it their 'business ... to decoy the unlearned and contented yeomanry of the country into the belief that they are practically suffering from political grievances and disabilities, the very existence of which they knew not until they heard of them from the lips of the pedlars of agitation.'⁴³ Rather than risk leaving political decisions to those who entered politics strictly for the money, to men who will 'lie, fawn, wheedle, pimp, [and] cajole,' the paper advocated the candidacy of 'men of fixed independent fortune,' who would remain above such venal concerns.⁴⁴

Although Dalton might have been sceptical of the notion that the farmers of the province were the impregnable guardians of public virtue, Scobie agreed with Brown that 'independent freemen' were the repository of this virtue. They were called upon in an 1841 editorial that argued for support for Sydenham and told them to ensure 'the return of men at the approaching elections, pledged to support the present liberal and enlightened government.'⁴⁵ The *Colonist* did not always tie the status of 'yeoman' to those who acted for the public good as closely as did Brown. Scobie preferred the more ambiguous term 'the people.' If party voting in elections became the norm, it was 'the people' who would be prevented from 'coming forward boldly and manfully when appealed [*sic*], to express their sentiments on public questions.' Such a practice would make them the 'perpetual slaves of party.'⁴⁶ However, according to 'A Farmer of the first Riding of York,' there was little doubt who was best suited to represent the 'Farmers of Canada West.' The country needed the farmers themselves – not the lawyers who dominated politics – to represent its interests. Lawyers were trained to argue and thus might confuse their constituents. Furthermore, they were the only group to profit from the farmers' debt; merchants, mechanics, and labourers thrived when farmers did well. Thus, all such men should unite ('union is strength') and elect farmers in rural ridings. The cities could send lawyers to 'Parliament.'⁴⁷

Brown viewed lawyers more kindly, suggesting that they might be especially suited to sit in the assembly. Offering examples of 'liberal institutions' in England, the United States, and France, in which lawyers filled many positions, he argued that their education and experience made them well-suited to political life. They were particularly relevant to the situation in Canada West. 'In new countries especially, before wealth and refinement have raised up a class of men highly qualified for managing the important interests of the country, a large share of the management will necessarily fall into the hands of the lawyers.' As 'honourable' men, they 'will set themselves strenuously to support the rights and privileges of the people of Canada.'[48] Like Baldwin, lawyers were cultivated and educated men who, by representing reason and resisting emotional appeals, might uplift the electorate of Canada West.

Thus the 'public man' of the 1840s, whether as political figure or as one responsible for choosing political figures, was ostensibly not tied to any one class or occupational group. He might be the target of multiple claims of ownership, often being remade in the image of whoever had chosen to claim him. This protean quality apparently was the source of this symbol's popularity. The flexibility and the air of ambiguity that hovered around the 'public man' meant that he could be referred to by a spectrum of political commentators. Yet while he might be claimed by various groups in colonial society, it is worth remembering that not all men (and no women) could become this paragon of political virtue. Despite the talk of editors and letter-writers regarding the public man's appeal to men of all classes, the emphasis on independence posed a number of problems for that small, but significant, minority of Upper Canadians who depended on some form of waged work for their livelihood, a group that in other contexts (such as employment law) was treated as being less independent than the 'sturdy yeoman.' Moreover, for Native men, whose status was becoming increasingly defined as that of a dependant upon the colonial state, the notion of being 'public men' would likely have had little or no meaning.[49]

One quality of the 'public man' transcended the political divisions of various newspapers. It was essential that, as a symbol of political harmony and consensus building, the 'public man' not be perceived as a rabble-rouser or a demagogue. Underlying much of the writing on political conduct and public morality throughout this decade was a fear (even among those who were sympathetic to reform) of a return to the political turbulence of the previous decade. As we have seen in the appeals to 'moderate men,' the upheavals of the 1840s were to be forestalled before they developed into anything like rebellion.

The linkage of impartial and unselfish male behaviour to the concept of the 'public' continued the discursive process of collapsing the two and making them coterminous. It was highly unlikely that, within this context, the image of the 'public woman' would carry the same kind of meaning. As we shall see later in this chapter, one of the definitions of 'public woman' – that of the prostitute – was linked to illicit sexuality. While the construction of the 'public man' of political life might have served many purposes, ones rooted in the political culture of Canada West, it also helped to underline that (in *theory*, at least) public life as political life was a masculine domain. Yet, as in so many attempts to carve and appropriate certain 'spheres' as the province of one gender, class, or race, there were a number of anxieties and tensions wrapped up in the construction of this image of masculine predominance in the political sphere.

Like the virtuous independent man of reform discourse, the 'public man' was generally presented as being without family ties, an impartial being completely unaffected by private prejudices and determined to work for the 'general good.' Unlike the images of men and masculinity discussed in the previous chapter, it would appear that this symbol of masculine recti-tude was created without any reference to women. No images of woman-hood or femininity, whether as wives, mothers, sisters, or daughters, appeared in this political discourse to disrupt the public man's clear-sighted perspective. In light of the proliferation of literature that promoted the benefits of domesticity for men (and, in some papers, much of this appeared alongside columns on political matters), we must ask ourselves whether this image of the man without 'private interests' was to some extent a reaction to the discourse on domesticity. Explicit links between these discourses were rare, and this period was characterized by attempts to fix boundaries between the world of politics and that of the home. The *Colonist* urged men to get out of the house and to the hustings as part of their patriotic duty.[50] Frequent exhortations to public duty and the demand that an all-male electorate put into office representatives who would be free of private entanglements (and thus private corruption) may have been to some degree a reaction to demands from others that the home and family be placed at the centre of social organization.

If we place these discourses side by side, comparing the concepts of mas-culine identity and behaviour that they promoted, it would appear that the 1840s were marked by at least two significant competing versions of Anglo-American, bourgeois masculinity. Masculine identity, it would seem, could be grounded in the home, given real meaning and weight mainly by men's relationships with women and children. However, it also was their relation to the political arena and their unselfish behaviour in the 'public' sphere that allowed men to find true fulfilment as Upper Canadians.

Reading the texts that made up these discourses, it is possible to see the contradictions inscribed in such concepts of masculinity. It is worth prob-ing a little deeper into this question and exploring some of its other com-plexities. As we have seen, 'family' itself was a symbol that might be used quite flexibly, signifying selfishness and nepotism in one context, while being used as the basis of morality and self-sacrifice in another. In his editorials, Scobie attached the first set of meanings to family. Dalton, in his writings, frequently relied on the second. Even those who wrote endless reams about the need for young men to prepare themselves for family life were quick to applaud voluntary work in the streets of York and Kingston as exemplifying the family's influence beyond the home.[51] Given that those who wrote about the home were anxious to assure their readers that 'private' was not equated with 'selfish idleness,' they may have approved of the 'public man' because he implemented the lessons of the home in areas outside its physical boundaries. In turn, this paragon created the conditions of peace, prosperity, and good government essential for the security and sanctity of the home.[52]

What about the absence of women or the 'feminine' from this construct? If the notion of family posed certain problems for political writers and commentators, was its absence necessary to allow the public man to rise above all personal interest? In the political context, women and femininity usually signified the private and the personal. Therefore, this model of male rectitude might have derived its most fundamental meaning because of the 'writing out' of women from this aspect of responsible government. Women, it is worth keeping in mind, were excluded quite specifically by a reform government from the electoral franchise in 1849.[53] And, as we shall see later in this chapter, Upper Canadian papers published satirical articles and broadsides lampooning those in the United States who campaigned for women's rights (including the right to vote). Although it is difficult to see direct links between colonial political discourses and hostility to women's participation in political life, it would be too much of a coincidence to think that at some level these phenomena were not linked. If nothing else, the construction of the mid-nineteenth-century Canadian state as a masculine arena in which bourgeois men would be the main actors suggests that the image of the 'public man' in the 1840s may have been an important symbolic part of this linkage.[54]

The symbol of masculine virtue in political life was not the only to be used to construct political culture during the decade. Banquets, parades, and political demonstrations were important public manifestations of political and patriotic sentiments and celebrated a number of things. The imperial connection and the men who maintained it, the fitness of certain men to govern the province, or the triumph of those who opposed them: all these might be cause for a display in the streets or at an open dinner in which men were cast as direct participants and women as spectators. The reports give us a glimpse into public manifestations of political culture in Canada

West, and, through them, we are given a chance to examine the symbols and images deployed in shaping that culture.

Banquets held to honour prominent officials or to commemorate special days were certainly not new to Canada West. The 1825 Christmas dinner held by the Society for Promoting Christian Knowledge was described in the society's Seventh Annual Report and distributed in the *Christian Sentinel*. Roast beef and plum pudding 'in the true English style' had been served to the one hundred and twenty boys and one hundred and thirteen girls attending the society's schools. The food appeared after the children had completed their annual public examination, and 'general satisfaction was expressed at [their] progress ... their orderly appearance, and the precision and promptitude of their evolutions.' According to the society, the children were of the colony's poor – in contrast to those who conducted the examination and then served the roast beef.[55] The dynamics of class relations were thus intertwined with this expression of charitable largesse. In this ceremony the children were, first, surveyed (as indicated by the comments on their appearance and state of knowledge) and then constructed for the paper's middle-class readers as 'orderly,' 'precise,' and 'prompt' – in other words, worthy recipients of charity. The society's report does not mention the participation of 'the ladies':[56] bourgeois women appear to have been absent from this dinner and thus did not participate in this particular process of defining the poor, unlike those Thanksgiving dinners organized by white, middle-class women for the working-class children of New York City.

Although its correspondent did not see fit to print the menu, the *Colonist*'s coverage of the banquet to honour Lieutenant-Governor Sir George Arthur attempted to recreate for the paper's readers as many other details as were available. Held at Toronto City Hall on 10 February 1841, the banquet was given by the 'Merchants, Bankers, and others, of Toronto.' Arthur had asked that it take place on Queen Victoria's wedding anniversary, in an attempt to stress that this was an 'independent' event and not a partisan gathering. Noting that some members of that 'degenerate race,' the '"Family Compact" ... the men who fawned about Sir George during his administration of the Government,' had failed in their attempts to dissuade him from attending, the *Colonist* was nevertheless pleased to report that the celebration came off 'without reference to party.' 'There were men of [all] parties present – men who possess independence enough to think and act for themselves.' Other events commemorated were the christening of the Princess Royal, the founding of Upper Canada, and the anniversary of the prorogation of the last Upper Canadian parliament. Prominent men from politics, commerce, and the military attended (again, all 'independent' and without 'party feeling'), the band of the Thirty-Second Regiment played, and duets were sung by members of the Thirty-Fourth. A litany of toasts were drunk, including ones to the queen and other members of the royal family, to the governor, Lady Arthur, and their family, and to the constitution, the army and the navy. Toasts ended with 'The Sheriff,' 'The Stewards,' and, finally, 'The Manufacturers and Mechanics.' Arthur's speech was followed by the thanks of E.W. Thomson, representing agriculture, Colonel Mackenzie Fraser for the British forces, the vice chancellor of the London Emigration Society, and the adjutant general of the militia.[57]

More than just a glimpse of the social life of the province's élite, this record of the banquet (and others like it) not only reported their activities but also described the deployment of symbols of official power in Canada West.[58] Politics, the imperial connection, and patriotism gathered around the banquet table, as did symbols of social and economic progress and the future of the province. This event was part of a larger process whereby many aspects of what was considered the 'public sphere' were symbolically carved up. As such, there were presences and absences that merit comment. Present symbolically were the young queen, her mother, and baby daughter; the monarch's youth, gender, and virtue were used to connote hope, stability, and harmony.[59] Otherwise, women appear to have been absent from the banqueting table.[60] Middle-class women's absence from ceremonies such as public dinners and official landings may very well have signified the importance of these events (as compared to openings of parliament, which women did attend).[61] Yet what was not made clear by the Upper Canadian press was whether or not women – regardless of their class, race, or ethnicity – witnessed processionals into the banqueting hall or if they attended official landings as spectators. And as spectators, whether present at these events or witnessing them through a reporter's eyes, women may have played an important role in the spectacle's hegemonic effects. In order for these events to be an effective symbolic legitimation of certain groups' position in colonial society, spectators would have been necessary. Such an event held *without* spectators – whether watching the ceremony itself or reading about it in the paper – would ultimately have said little about the wider importance of the ceremony.[62] It is worth noting that the absence of Native men and women in the *Colonist*'s account, either seated at the table or mentioned in the toasts, was even more pronounced than that of white women.

Political distinctions might shape the way in which these occasions were presented, and such distinctions might lead to rather different kinds of public commemorations. The 'independent,' non-partisan men at the city

hall table, united in harmony around these masculine symbols of officialdom, may be contrasted with Brown's accounts of political gatherings. The
1849 parliamentary defeat of the conservative James Webster in Waterloo
by reformer A.J. Fergusson was celebrated at the end of Fergusson's first
session with a procession that ended in a public dinner in a Guelph pavil-
ion. The event was organized by those Waterloo reformers who had 'manfully battled the watch.' Fergusson and his friends were met three miles
outside Guelph by the 'stalwart yeomanry' of the county. A mile-long procession, with one hundred and twenty-seven wagons, as well as pedestrians
and riders, converged on the town. The gathering, Brown was pleased to
report, exemplified 'that array of Anglo-Saxonism of Upper Canada; the
manly independent farmers of Waterloo – the happy faces of their dames
and daughters – the substantial equipages – the sleek fat horses.' A salute
was fired at the outskirts of town, and balconies, windows, and the streets
were filled with spectators. The parade ended with various men making
speeches on the lawn in the town centre. At that evening's dinner, an
exhaustive number of toasts were drunk: The queen and the royal family;
the governor general and Lady Elgin and their son; the army and the navy;
the former reform MPP James Durand; the various government bodies of
the province; civil and religious liberty; George Brown and the press; agricultural, commercial, and manufacturing interests; the 'land left and the
land lived in'; the men of Gore; and the day's organizers.[63]

Fergusson might be a member of the Legislative Assembly, and thus a
man of the 'public,' but his relation to official power was not clear-cut. The
record of his victory was tinged not just with the triumph of oppositional
politics but with the reminder that members of the opposition had also
formed governments and had sat on the Executive Council in the past. The
concept of loyal opposition, while certainly present in reform discourse of
the previous decade, had become more acceptable by the 1840s.[64] Therefore, unlike reform gatherings of the 1820s and 1830s, which were characterized by defensiveness regarding loyalty, Fergusson and his companions
could confidently toast many groups and structures, representatives of
both the imperial power and the reform party. Furthermore, although the
main participants were men, the presence of women as wives and daughters
could be noted quite cheerfully, part of Brown's promotion of the 'agricultural interest.' Unlike the fraternity of Mackenzie's reformers, defined to
no small extent by the absence of women, the manly 'Anglo-Saxon' 'independent farmers' were given full meaning and weight as husbands and
fathers by the presence of wives and daughters (as well as by their 'sleek fat
horses'). At this particular function, the women of Canada West were of

greater symbolic value than at events orchestrated by the officials of the province. Thus, women's exclusion from public events, or the relegation of their presence to the sidelines, was not automatic. To be sure, women rarely spoke from either the platform or the banqueting table, and they were frequently presented as a homogenous group, 'the ladies,' thus defined by their class and race as well as their gender.

These glimpses of the construction of political and patriotic culture in Canada West might lead us to conclude that the binary oppositions of private vs. public and the identification of women with the former were processes well under way by the 1840s. Certainly there is a measure of truth to this argument; a growing identification of white, middle-class male dominance in political affairs cannot be denied.[65] Furthermore, in the growing sentimentalization of motherhood in other discourses, we can see attempts to identify womanhood (or at least a certain kind of womanhood) with the home and family. However, we should be careful not to reify our notions of the 'public' by limiting this realm to only politics, imperial ties, and loyalty. Other forms of activities, such as the development of charitable and benevolent work and the formation of religious institutions and temperance organizations, were discussed openly and granted 'public' status in many of the papers consulted here. Women's work and women's presence, in a variety of places other than the home, were far from ignored in accounts of these activities. The implications such coverage had for the construction of gender relations must be considered if we are to see past the traditional boundaries that have hedged in our understanding of past relations between men and women and public and private.

As argued in the previous chapter, the colony's voluntary organizations were often structured around gender. In the 1820s and 1830s, the secular press enjoyed running membership lists and reports of the meetings and fund-raising efforts of groups such as the Kingston Female Benevolent Society or the Compassionate Society.[66] Much of the former's work was done on a voluntary basis and consisted mostly of giving assistance to the poor of the city,[67] but by 1842 the society included in its report news from their directresses, managers, and other office-holders 'to whom had been entrusted the management of the funds voted by the Legislature, for the benefit of the sick and destitute of this Town.' While men were probably involved in this organization (possibly as legal advisors), only women's names were on the list of executive members.[68] According to the *Kingston Chronicle and Gazette*, the mayor of Kingston had asked the society to handle the funds in November 1841, with the re-opening of the Kingston hospital (previously destroyed by fire). The directresses were happy to report that not only had they been able to provide aid for people and organize a sewing society for 'needy Sunday and Day School pupils,' they also had supplied 'Bibles and tracts for patients.' While pleased to alleviate suffering, they could not 'forbear remarking that of those cases of disease and destitution which have come more immediately under their notice, nearly one half have originated in intemperance and vice.'[69]

Work in these interdenominational societies was not the only female activity covered by the press. As fund-raising organizers and workers, women members of Anglican and Methodist churches were shown to have laboured assiduously to support religious organizations and the construction and maintenance of church buildings in the colony. The eleventh annual report of the Society for the Promotion of Christian Knowledge, printed in an 1829 issue of the *Christian Sentinel*, noted with pleasure the funds for the 'Asylum for Female Orphans' brought in by the 'benevolent undertaking' of the 'Ladies' who looked after the 'Female School.' In a large bazaar held the week after Easter, these women had raised £560, 11s., and 11 1/2d.; £200 of this was to go to other charities, the rest to the asylum. In praise of the endeavours of the 'Ladies,' the report concluded with the wish that they 'proceed with unabated ardour in their benevolent undertaking, and do thou, O Lord, prosper the work of their hands upon them! O prosper thou their handy-work.'[70]

Such pieces appeared more frequently in the late 1830s and throughout the 1840s. 'Carrying-Place,' for example, reported a bazaar held as a fundraiser for the parsonage in that community. This event was attended by three hundred visitors from Port Hope, Cobourg, Colborne, Kingston, Belleville, and Picton. The bazaar itself was held at 'Mrs. John Wilkin's house, which she kindly gave up for the occasion, [and which] was crowded in all parts. A most attractive assortment of fancy articles was displayed at the different tables; the Dinner Table, too, allured its share of visitors.' Portraits of 'our noble Governor' were sold, and, in all, the bazaar raised £200. 'Too much praise,' it was noted, 'cannot be given to those ladies through whose exertions this handsome sum was obtained, nor too many thanks returned to those kind friends who so liberally came forward with their handiwork and their purses to aid the good cause.' The 'Ladies of the Committee were indefatigable in their exertions.' Mrs Wilkin, Mrs Wragg, and Mrs Cassidy were specifically singled out for congratulations. However, the reporter could not close without recognizing the contribution made by the Hon. R.C. Wilkin, 'mainly instrumental in setting on foot and bringing the project to a successful issue.'[71]

This tribute to women's fund-raising efforts was typical of its genre. The total amount raised was mentioned (often at least £200), individual women were thanked, and the efforts of men, whether as husbands, clergy, or as members of military regiments providing music, were acknowledged.[72] Although men were always praised for their contribution, it was women's skill and abilities that usually received the greater share of attention. Such reports deserve further consideration in any discussion of the spread of institutional religion in Upper Canada and Canada West. William Westfall has explored the cultural and intellectual issues involved in the construction of Protestant denominations' stone churches during the mid-nineteenth century, but to date we have no study that analyses the social and economic processes, particularly their gendered nature, at work in their construction.[73] Stone edifices erected for the 'glory of God' did not, we must remember, build themselves.

The public accolades and recognition granted to the women involved in their charitable work should make us tread very carefully when we entertain the concept of women's 'confinement' to the home in the mid-nineteenth century. Certainly, as chapter 4 has argued, women's separate sphere was a recurring theme in the prescriptive literature on religion and domesticity, one that became increasingly popular in this period. Yet, although women's religious and benevolent work might meet with approval from many of these writers, they disagreed as to how it might best be practised. Was the home the best place for women to meet in a Ladies' Benevolent Society? Was the well-appointed parlour (a place possibly more metaphorical than material for the majority of women in the province) the most appropriate setting for the production of charitable assistance? For some, this was undoubtedly the case, and such writers worked hard to persuade readers of their argument's soundness (although the parlour itself might not be perceived as a completely 'private' space).[74] Nevertheless, women had been granted a special relationship to Christianity and were seen as having a vested interest in the prosperity of organized religion (as we have seen in missionary writings). Thus, it was less easy to restrict their work for the church to the narrowly defined parameters of home and hearth. There were contradictions involved in women's participation in activities that took them out of their homes and into what were perceived as public events, held in public spaces (sometimes churches, but also at town and city halls).[75] However, these problems were rarely acknowledged by those who discussed 'woman's' relation to religion. To be sure, gender relationships within organized religion were far from egalitarian (running a bazaar was not perceived as the same thing as public preaching), and women's relationship to this kind of public activity was not straightforward. The presence of men was necessary to make the events social and economic successes. Nevertheless, this form of 'womanly endeavour' was not 'hidden in the household,' at least so far as those who shaped these particular forms of public records were concerned.[76]

In covering these events, the papers wished to leave no doubt that they had been organized by 'ladies,' women respected by their communities and whose gender was shaped by their socio-economic and racial position, as well as by that of their male relatives. Only occasionally was the participation of working-class, immigrant, or Native women mentioned in relation to bazaars or other forms of voluntary work. These women were often constructed in the pages of press or missionary reports as the recipients of aid or of the tools that would allow them to be self-sufficient, an approach that was most often found in the pages of the *Christian Guardian* but also appeared in the Anglican press as well.[77] Fund-raising events for mission work sometimes featured public displays of Native children singing or reciting. At these events, the middle-class home was reaffirmed as the 'apotheosis of nurture';[78] the white women who accompanied the children took on the role of their mothers, symbolizing their entry into the new family of Christ, even if they might not have borne children themselves. The maternal contributions of the Native women who had given birth to the children and raised them, or the paternal contributions of fathers, were seldom acknowledged in these reports.[79]

Although references to working-class and immigrant women as participants in fund-raising were rare, one account allows a tantalizing glimpse of a somewhat unusual situation. The 1841 consecration of St George's Church and cemetery in St Catharines, an event solemnized by the Anglican bishop of Toronto and the installation of a church bell, was marked by a configuration of gender, ethnicity, and class. Out of the £48 needed for the bell, £17 had been donated by William Caley, the director of the Welland Canal and a 'gentleman whose enterprise, intelligence, and high character, point him out as one of the most valuable settlers in the Province. The remainder was furnished, with laudable zeal, by the labourers on the Canal, a majority of whom are Irish Protestants, a class of men, on whom it has been the fashion, with late administrations in this Province, to heap contumely and injustice, except in the hour of rebellion or invasion. The Ladies of the congregation have richly decorated the Altar and Pulpit, in which appropriate and pleasing task they were assisted by a contribution of £5 from the wives of the labourers. They have also commenced a subscription for the purchase of a set of Communion Plate.'[80] Here was a reversal (albeit a temporary one) of customary gender and class distinctions in the description of the women's contribution. The image of working-class, immigrant women giving money so that middle-class women might perform the physical task of decorating reverses the familiar patterns of class and ethnic distinctions in the province. In the 'normal course' of things, it would not be unusual for the middle-class women to hire the Irish women as domestic servants.[81] Decorating the altar was seen not as hard work but as a mark of distinction.

The writer also attempted to rehabilitate the reputation of the working-class Irish men by recognizing their contribution to Protestant religious efforts and thereby placing them among the ranks of the respectable. Yet, like the treatment of their female relatives, this designation might be easily withdrawn in another context. Three years later, the *Niagara Chronicle* reported that passengers disembarking from a pleasure steamer on their way to Niagara Falls were met with the news that the canal labourers were planning an attack. Armed with muskets, pikes, pitchforks, and (of course) shillelaghs, two hundred men were supposedly amassing to meet the first group of passengers (made up mostly of women and children). Order was restored once the army was called out and the Riot Act read. The reporter, convinced that without this military intervention the labourers would have attacked unarmed men and women and children, concluded that 'it is inconceivable to us how a body of men can entertain such a feeling of deadly animosity towards their fellow-creatures as these men evidently do; it seems so unnatural, as well as so opposite to all ideas that can possibly be formed of what duty to God and man demands, that we cannot compre-hend it.'[82] Here working-class Irish men were constructed as grave physical threats to the colonial middle class, and a particular danger to the women and children of this group. Unlike the intentions of their religiously inclined counterparts in 1841, the motives that underlay such a mobiliza-tion were not discussed. The *Chronicle* omitted to mention that the Irish Catholic labourers had been mobilizing to confront members of the Toronto Orange Lodge.[83] Conflicts from another colonial society might lie behind the 'unnatural' behaviour of these labourers, not just the uncon-trolled tempers and tendency to violence of men who – as well as being Irish – performed heavy manual labour.

For middle-class women, though, hard work for charity functions gar-nered them a great deal of public recognition. Not only was their labour appreciated insofar as setting up, decorating, and running the bazaar stalls was concerned, but the work that had gone into the production of the goods sold at the stalls was applauded. The goods themselves were praised highly, and, while that might have been a strategy to tantalize the buying public, it resulted in a rarely seen appreciation of women's labour.[84] The items sold at bazaars, ones manufactured by the 'ladies' and their families and friends, might be symbolic of the so-called leisured existence of middle-class women. The 'ottomans, music stools, purses,' and other assorted 'fancy-work'[85] that raised money for church roofs and hymn books not only spoke of a gendered division of labour, they also were articles that could easily be designated as frivolous by those who criticized consumerism in religious discourse. However, they were considered appropriate for even the Methodists to sell. Both the Wesleyan Methodists in the *Christian Guardian* and the Primitive Methodists in their paper, *The Evangelist*, reported bazaars and fund-raising drives to which women's labour made a substantive contribution.[86] The strategies of the Primitive Methodists differed somewhat from those of their Wesleyan counterparts. Women and girls raised hens and geese for mission work, as well as selling needlework. 'Little Eliza's missionary hen, and Mrs Jane Nashinter's missionary goose,' brought in three dollars for the cause in Smithfield and Hainstock (near Etobicoke). *The Evangelist* was pleased to report:

The praiseworthy expedient adopted by our esteemed sisters, who cheerfully devoted the increase of their geese and hens to the increase of the Mission funds, is worthy of our admiration, and ought to stimulate others who are similarly situated to go and do likewise. Nor should I omit to make mention of those ladies in our Circuit to whom it perhaps has been impractical or inconvenient to raise goslings or chickens in aid of our Mission funds, who with zeal, industry, and good taste, not less commendable, turned their attention to the Missionary-basket and Work-box, which they tastefully furnished, with a pleasing variety of beautiful specimens of fancy needlework, wrought with their own hands, which they cheerfully devoted to the important work of supporting the gospel of the blessed God, and which when disposed of yielded a handsome revenue.

The writer John Lacy exhorted others to follow their example, as a profitable use of leisure time and a means of developing skills, knowledge, and 'habits of industry.' He could not resist adding, however, that such work would be of great use to single women. These attainments 'could not fail to commend them in the estimation of young men of enterprising talents.' They would then marry, creating 'domestic felicity,' thus doubling the good done by mission work. Here honest housewifery could be combined with the more decorative aspects of bourgeois femininity, allaying any fears that these Methodists might have had concerning the frivolity of 'fancy needlework.'[87]

Bazaars were not the only places in which women appeared in both the pages of the provincial press and in provincial society. Accounts of temperance meetings and parades invariably mentioned the participation of women members and the use of symbols of femininity on banners and decorations. In a passage similar to the pieces about bazaars, G.W. Bungay described a temperance meeting at Niagara in 1844. While appreciative of the 'maiden speech' of the politician Robert Baldwin Sullivan, Bungay also was enthusiastic about the appearance of the Temperance Hall. Decorated with evergreens, 'woven, twisted, and traced by the fair fingers of the ladies ... artificial flower-work – a cluster of fruit, the horn of plenty – flags and pictures – were gracefully arranged around the hall.'[88] This celebration of middle-class women's creative talents, ones customarily associated with the decoration and adornment of their homes, hinted strongly at the widespread social and economic benefits that temperance would bring to Upper Canadians. Yet such acknowledgments of these women's work did not automatically lead to women's assumption of leadership within the movement. Bungay might praise the women, but Sullivan was evidently the sole speaker at the meeting. Tributes to women might reinforce the symbolic nature of middle-class womanhood as a trope for socio-economic harmony and the repression of conflict.

Accounts of temperance parades pose some of the most challenging questions about the relation between the 'public' and the construction and organization of gender relations. As the temperance movement gained momentum in Canada West, and as groups such as the Daughters and Sons of Temperance were formed in the early 1850s, accounts of temperance parades were more frequent. A full account and analysis of the public manifestations of temperance support rightly belongs to the period following that covered here.[89] However, as early as 1841 *The Examiner* reported an 'impressive' procession, with possibly fifteen hundred participants. 'The ladies were, of course, in carriages,' the reporter noted, with the children 'on the sidewalks.' The procession was attended by many different political parties, religious denominations, and 'grades of respectability' all led by a 'good band.' The banners included the slogans 'Bright water for me,' 'Train up a child in the way he should go,' and 'We come to the rescue (*Ladies*).'[90]

By 1850, accounts of the Sons of Temperance and their processions were beginning to appear in religious and secular newspapers. The *Canada Christian Advocate* saw fit to report a Hamilton procession organized by the Sons and held on Queen Victoria's birthday in 1850. At 9:30 in the morning, the Sons 'mastered in full force at their Division room, to prepare to receive a Banner which was to be presented to them by the

Ladies of Hamilton.' Once assembled, one hundred and fifty Sons gathered in the square opposite Week's Hotel. Here 'a large crowd had assembled to witness the presentation of the Banner, among whom we distinguished many of the fairer portion of our race, who are always ready to lend their aid to any enterprise which has for its object the elevation of man.' In a ceremony reminiscent of the presentation of the patriotic banner of 1813, the mayor (having been deputed by the ladies) presented the banner. Written on top of it, and placed over a set of pillars, were 'Daughters of Temperance' and 'Sons of Temperance;' a globe was set between the two names with 'Redeemed' under it. In the centre of the banner were the words 'Love, Purity, and Fidelity' and, at the bottom, a drawing of a fountain, labelled 'nature's beverage.' The other side of the banner was inscribed (in gold lettering) with the name and date of organization of the Hamilton Sons (24 October 1849). It also informed the public that the banner had been presented by the 'Ladies of Hamilton' and gave that date as well.

The mayor told the Sons that they had taken a 'noble stand' and reassured them that 'should any one of your number for a moment be tempted to abandon your cause, retreat, I implore you, under the consecrated folds of this emblem of virtue.' Replying for the Sons, Mr C.H. Vannorma thanked the 'Ladies' and expressed the members' pride in placing themselves 'under this beautiful emblem of purity and virtue, presented by our Sovereign's fair representatives.' 'Love, Purity, and Fidelity is the bond that unites our brotherhood,' he told the crowd, assuring the 'Ladies' that his members would be better 'members of society, and especially better fathers, husbands, sons, and brothers.' Expressing his happiness that a Daughters of Temperance group had been formed, Vannorma, accompanied by the Sons, then marched the banner to Gore and King Streets.[91]

These accounts of the Sons and their public displays stressed a number of themes common to the temperance literature previously discussed: the social and economic benefits of a world without strong drink, the devastation wrought by alcohol, and the need to work diligently, in both public and private, in order to eradicate the use of alcohol.[92] The Sons publicly stated that they were organized around familial relationships, as husbands, fathers, sons, and brothers. Women who united with them, either as the Daughters or, like the 'Ladies of Hamilton,' in support of their work, would do so as wives, mothers, daughters, and sisters. The gendered relationships of family, not the 'selfish interests' of any one party, class, or religious organization, were thus ostensibly the structure for temperance work. Women as participants, and symbols of femininity, also provided the necessary balance to public displays by men who, as the Sons argued, might be accused of belonging to a secret and possibly subversive society.[93] As Mary Ryan has argued in terms of temperance parades in antebellum America, women became 'associated with another new entry in the vocabulary of urban ritual. They were both allies and symbolic props in a campaign to attach public value to personal habits of sobriety.'[94] With women present, the claim that improved family relationships were the goals of temperance advocates was meant to be much more convincing.

The designation of the women involved as 'Ladies' suggests once again that, in this context, gender distinctions were bound up with notions of class and race. Coverage of ceremonies and rituals where women spoke was rarer than reports of the types we have been discussing (and very well may have occurred less often). Nevertheless, women did not always fall back on designated male representatives or on the emblems of femininity inscribed on a banner. At the 1848 presentation of a banner to the Toronto Fire Brigade, the 'Ladies' who had made this emblem chose the mayoress, Catherine Gurnett, to act as their representative.[95] In her address to the city's chief engineer, officers, and members of the brigade, she equated the brigade's work with the army and navy's protection of the citizenry, describing its members as 'generous and noble-minded men' who sacrifice 'personal ease and domestic comfort' to risk life and limb. In so doing, they were preserving homes and properties. The 'Ladies' had made the banner, a possession that they were sure the brigade – '"as honourable and patriotic men"' – would value more than money. In his thanks, the chief engineer spoke of the honour of 'forming that guard upon which you rely for the protection of your peaceful and happy firesides.' He assured the 'Ladies' that the 'chaste, classical, and truly eloquent banner' would be dear to the firemen. When terrified by the flames and the sound of the alarm bell in the night, the 'Ladies' would be calmed by the cry, 'They come – the Firemen come!' And if one man, he declared, was slow to stir, the mention of the banner would revive him.[96] This record of the ceremony suggests that a few small yet crucial changes had occurred since the 'gallant young ladies of York' presented their banner to the militia in 1813. While this emblem still reminded men that the meaning of their 'manly' work was anchored in their ties to home and family and their need to protect women and children, and the banner was presented as a reminder of these emotional bonds, here the women who had made it were the ones who publicly voiced these sentiments. The banner was not taken from them to be presented by male representatives of either state or church. To be sure, these women may very well have been constrained by the language of domestic affection and sentiment and may have found it difficult to express their relationship to Toronto's civic services in any other respectable manner; these services were also, it is worth remembering, being provided only by men. Yet this instance affords us a glimpse of middle-class women as more than 'apparition[s] ... gliding through' such ceremonies as mere figureheads and spectators.[97]

The indirect relationship of the mayoress to the political power of the local state made her a fitting spokesperson in making the 'womanly' desire for protection appear to be the most important factor at play. Similarly, in 1846 a 'Ladies' Petition to the City Council' asked for a reduction in the number of houses selling alcohol. Despite Toronto's improvements, the women argued, an increase in drunkenness could be seen. They were especially concerned with the 'relief of indigent and distressed persons of their own sex.' Putting the symbols of temperance literature to work, the women asked the councillors and mayor, 'what heart does not bleed at the sight of the numerous tattered, hungry, and decrepit children, – at the many emaciated, decrepit, and loathsome objects whom we meet, or who frequent our kitchens imploring relief?' Furthermore, 'could your Worships but hear the pitiful cries of the hapless orphan, and see the aching heart of the disconsolate but affectionate wife, and know the anguish that lacerates the breast of the aged and tender mother, as each feels the present, and dreads the future, fearing that the parent, or the husband, or the child, must fall a victim to the drinking habits so common in the community,' then no arguments would be needed to rouse them to action. The petitioners asked them to consider the problem seriously 'and, by interposing your powerful authority, speedily and happily avert from this otherwise highly favoured City, the innumerable public and social evils.'[98]

That these women, supposedly protected from such 'evils,' could not be sheltered from the devastation wrought by alcohol was a loaded argument. On the one hand, it was a staple of temperance supporters that no one was safe from drunkenness. However, this petition also pointed to the contradictions within the literature of domesticity on which the 'discourse of drink' so heavily relied. The position of 'woman' in the home, theoretically a place of haven, was tied to the conduct and behaviour of male relatives and family members, a point appreciated by the lady petitioners. Because drunkenness might mean downward mobility for all, it could leave any mother, wife, daughter, or sister vulnerable to its depredations.

The bazaar workers, banner presenters, and temperance supporters were not the only women and representations of femininity to appear in the press. The records of Kingston and Toronto's criminal courts were run in various newspapers. In the reports of trials, convictions, and sentencings appeared other kinds of women, whose 'public' presence and activities were as shaped by ethnicity and class as were those of the 'Ladies' of the voluntary societies and religious organizations.[99] The 'Brigid Murphies' and 'Mary Gormans,' often convicted of offences such as prostitution, vagrancy, and petty larceny, were a reminder that 'womanhood' was by no means a homogeneous, undifferentiated category.[100] These women's confrontations with the local and provincial states underlined (however much prescriptive literature liked to use the general category 'woman') that the category 'the Ladies' was a complex mixture of relations of gender, class, ethnicity, and race. Not only was the symbol of the 'lady' as much a social construction as the 'uplifted Indian woman' or the 'public man,' it was one that was defined by these other representations of femininity and masculinity. Being perceived and treated as a 'lady' meant that delineations of respectability had been drawn between women in the streets of Toronto and Hamilton, differentiating those who presented banners from those who appeared in courtrooms.

Women's appearances in public took place in many of the same spaces as political demonstrations, events that could, and sometimes did, end in riot and violence.[101] Although the link was not made explicitly by the press, bringing middle-class 'British' women into 'the public,' and to public events, might mitigate the hostilities and rowdiness associated with 'masculine' activities in the streets and town squares.[102] Yet we should be careful to distinguish between those activities that might be considered suitable for women, such as the presentation of banners, and those that were not, such as agitating for women's political rights. Although their targets usually were American women, Canadian commentators enjoyed satirizing the 'unwomanly' aspirations of females who spoke openly about participating in areas considered the province of men.[103] 'The Rights of Woman – "A Tempest in a Tea Pot"' was the designation the *Colonist* gave to the Worcester women's rights convention in 1850. Mrs Foster, the *Colonist* declared, 'harangued' and 'demanded,' along with Mrs Mott, 'another amazon' (the paper was referring to women's rights campaigners and abolitionists Lucretia Mott and Abby Kelley Foster). The public expression of the 'foolish opinions of these qarrolous [*sic*] old women,' indicated that something was '"radically wrong" in the social system of the country where such meetings are held.' This author was convinced that these 'old' women were set on accomplishing nothing less than a revolution. Quoting the New York *Herald*, it was claimed that these meetings were designed to abolish the Bible, the constitution, the law, and the gallows and to reorganize society to permit not just equality but also the free mingling of all colours and sexes. 'What awful times are coming!' the paper warned. Even worse, men would have to stay at home with babies while the 'ladies' were out conquering or annexing. Fortunately for Canadians, 'we are happy to think that the women of Canada, as well as of most other countries, are endowed with sufficient good sense which prevents them from making themselves ridiculous, by stepping out of their proper places, they are perfectly satisfied with the rights and privileges which public opinion freely accords them ... Home is the proper sphere of woman, and to make home happy will always be the chief desire of every woman of sense.'[104]

Writing of events closer to home, *The Church*'s editor spoke to his readers of the efforts of the 'young ladies' at the Burlington Ladies' Academy to publish a student paper, *The Calliopean*. Such efforts, he warned, would detract from their education and could not be recommended as a 'safe' experiment. 'Every one knows that some women have excelled in authorship; but they were remarkable women; and if their position in life was peculiar, we have reason to believe that God – who endowed them with their unusual talents – gave them also a counterbalancing strength – stability of mind.' He doubted that, as a general educational principle, 'our young women should be encouraged ... to walk in the public, and conspicuous paths of literature.'[105] The women's paper came to Brown's attention, and he too questioned its usefulness. Although not pinpointing the issue of women writing per se, Brown's attack on the paper's style amounted to much the same thing. The articles, he believed, were too 'weak' and the subjects were 'not well enough chosen even to effect much toward the rather ambitious object of raising the standard of female education in Canada.' He also disliked the 'minced oaths,' such as '"goodness"' and '"mercy,"' as well as 'unladylike exclamations' such as '"humph."'[106]

Some writers in the religious press suggested that women were not treated fairly by society. It was far from becoming a full-fledged discourse on women's rights, such as that being formed south of the border, but George W. Bungay did speak of 'The Rights of Women,' 'inalienable' ones that had been 'shamefully disregarded.' Although Canadians might condemn other cultures where women were oppressed, he told the readers of the *Canada Christian Advocate*, in their own country the double standard still operated. 'The rake may dishonour virtue, and yet be a welcome guest' in respectable society; the woman he victimized, though, would become a 'cast-away' for life. Bungay went even further, pointing out that 'woman' was denied both the vote and the same kind of inheritance rights as men. He argued for an understanding of women's oppression that embraced a multitude of factors: fashion; lack of education; the 'mutual tyranny' of brothers and sisters; tyrannical, lazy, domineering, and sometimes drunken husbands; children who were abusive towards their mothers; and the behaviour of many factory owners towards their female employees. Woman, he concluded, must defend her rights.[107] What is interesting about this piece (apart from the fact of its existence in Upper Canada) is that Bungay himself was, in the eyes of his editor, a respected temperance lecturer, not an eccentric or a 'crank.' While Bungay was not the only one to consider the possibility that women were treated unfairly, his was a lone voice in arguing that women were actually 'oppressed' by social, legal, and political institutions. Others might argue that women were badly off, as a result of misfortune in marriage or family life (a poorly chosen mate, for example). Rarely, though, did they address the issue in Bungay's sweeping manner. Nor did they trace women's problems to patriarchal relationships in society.

Although further research that moves into other areas of society in Canada West is necessary in order to evaluate more definitively the construction of womanhood in the 'public' area, the evidence considered above suggests that our notions of 'public' in this period must be weighed carefully. The meaning of the 'public sphere' was not monolithic but instead tended to be fragmented, shifting according to location and time. It could be broken down to encompass different kinds of activities engaged in by different social groups at different times. Political life, as carried out in the legislature or within the confines of the Executive Council, was designated as a masculine realm, one in which 'public men' might be found. Economic life, despite the rise of nineteenth-century laissez-faire liberalism that designated the 'market' as subject to private forces, was perceived somewhat differently when the subject was gender. Many of those who wrote about domesticity used the categories of private and public to distinguish between the home (as a place for women but also for men) and the workplace (as a place where men went to carry out their responsibilities as family breadwinners).

The issue of voluntarism and the place it occupied in Upper Canada complicates this question. Although taken up ostensibly outside the boundaries of the state, voluntary activity rarely was entirely 'private.' Seldom did those who participated in benevolence or charity do so strictly from within the confines of the home. Moreover, activities such as visiting prisons and boarding houses and attending temperance meetings and parades were given public recognition in the pages of the press, and, as we have seen, the language of benevolence drew upon that of domesticity. Voluntarism certainly was concerned with that which Riley has designated the 'social,' the sphere of moral and social improvement. References to the work of women in this sphere often used the term 'woman,' thus glossing over class, racial and ethnic distinctions and tensions.'[108] As I have argued in these last two chapters, the men of Upper Canada and Canada West were also urged to be part of this world. Men, it was proclaimed, must work for their own and society's moral regeneration in young men's groups and temperance societies (to name but a few). And, to judge from the reports in the press, men and women responded to the appeal of voluntarism, albeit in different ways.

Men's participation in voluntary life, though, could not be taken for granted, nor could masculine morality be assumed to be innate; it had to be encouraged and stimulated at an early stage in a man's life. Discussions of youthful masculinity continued in both religious and secular newspapers throughout the 1840s, often accompanied by a certain amount of agonizing about this period in a man's life. In pieces such as 'A Story for Boys,' youthful readers were advised to honour their mothers, as those who did not invariably come to a nasty end.[109] In these stories, the physical risks that boyhood entailed signified the even greater moral risks that they might encounter.[110] Much of this literature, as we have mentioned, was not new. What became more prevalent during the 1840s, especially as the decade drew to a close, was the language of social mobility and striving for 'improvement.'

'Truth and Honesty,' run by The Church in September 1847, told the story of a boy's upward mobility when he displayed the urge for self-improvement.[111] The obverse of this young paragon of virtue was 'The Man of Leisure and the Pale Boy'; this article warned boys and young men of the uselessness of idle lives.[112] However, this discourse of the 'striving young man' was tempered by the need to remember religious principles. 'The Book for Business Men' told an illuminating tale of the life history of a business man. On his deathbed, he spoke of the importance of the Bible during a time when he was 'embarrassed' in business. It gave him, he declared, peace and a way out of his difficulties. The author advised other businessmen not to look to 'news from abroad, or the prices current' but instead to consult the book of God.[113] Those who wished to better themselves must temper their ambition with religiosity and moral principles.

This discourse of youthful male self-improvement culminated in the 1848 Toronto newspaper, The Artisan.[114] Supposedly the 'cheapest' in British America (a subscription cost one dollar per year), this weekly paper was published by Henry C. Grant from September 1848 until early 1849. In February 1849, it was superseded by Grant's *Provincial Telegraph and Commercial and Mechanical Intelligencer*. *The Artisan* focused on the theme of 'honest work' for young men and the problems they might encounter. There was a certain ambiguity surrounding its title, for *The Artisan* ran pieces such as 'The Kings of the Salt,' a poem celebrating those who 'reap and till,' as well as articles addressed to 'Merchants' Clerks.'[115] This latter piece examined the problems of these young men, arguing that 'no class of young persons' was more deserving of sympathy than clerks in 'Canadian mercantile establishments.' However, their problem was not exploitation in the workplace but the 'exclusive spirit' of the town élite that left them marginalized and ostracized from Canadian society. Deprived of a 'homelife' and of any association with their employers' families, these clerks resorted to private or public boarding houses and saw only other clerks. While 'agreeable,' the company of these young men 'cannot produce that humanizing influence upon their minds which the social family circle is capable of,' especially that of the 'virtuous gentle sex.' Thus, 'taught by the example of their employers to look upon the families of mechanics as inferior to them in point of rank (though upon what grounds they would find it difficult to explain),' working long hours, and barred from 'female society,' these young men were in danger of falling into 'snares of vice.' The author concluded by stating that these were arguments made 'from personal observation, in the different towns of Upper Canada, of the evil effects of numbers of young men (not clerks only) of good disposition, respectable education and other personal merits, being thrown together, night after night, in some public house where, unknowing and unknown, habits of dissipation are generated, and the hopes of their relatives and friends are blasted forever.'[116]

Exactly what these 'habits of dissipation' were was not made clear. However, this and other articles touched on a theme common to *The Artisan*: the links between the working world of young men and the home and family. 'Locks of Hair,' a poem that appeared in the December issue, used romantic language to speak of those belonging to the poet's family, his mother, father, sister, and fiancée. The locks represented familial emotional bonds.[117] 'The Two Breakfasts' made the point that a working man could not prosper without an industrious and well-organized wife. Matthews, home from the foundry for breakfast, opens the door to find bad smells, his 'squalling' children, and a slatternly wife (her hair uncombed, her gown unlaced and open at the back, and her boots dirty). The problem could be traced to the fact that she had stayed in bed until the very last minute, bringing a wet and screaming baby down into a kitchen with an unlit fire and the previous night's dirty dishes. Matthews, who had been up since 6 A.M., has to resort to the coffee-house for breakfast, a place he had frequented so often it felt like home. In contrast, Richard Cooper, his next-door neighbour and fellow foundry worker, opens his front door to clean, happy, and affectionate children, a wife ('a tight and trim little body') who always dresses properly, overall cleanliness, and a good breakfast. And, the author concludes, his visit 'to his family every morning sent him back to his work with renewed hope and confidence. The secret of his comfort and good temper lay in his wife's habit of early rising and careful management.' Her attention to lacing and other matters of dress (the 'tight and trim little body') also was important. Female unruliness and lack of 'careful management' of the household were signified by an absence of physical containment.[118]

The Artisan told its readers that it expected working men (the farmer, the mechanic, and the merchant) to improve their understanding of matters outside their homes and workshops. Free trade and the repeal of the navigation laws were especially important. Moreover, as the 'democratic principle' in government spread, the paper told its readers, there was an especial need for people to be 'intelligent and virtuous,' able to be independent of 'political aspirants and selfish demagogues, whose creed is *party* and whose aim is *office*.'[119]

The paper did not advocate a ruthless pursuit of self-improvement for its own sake. While a worthy goal, the point of economic prosperity was to benefit those who gave meaning to masculine endeavours: wives, children, and other family members. Moreover, this discourse of 'self-improvement' did not emanate only from the kind of prescriptive literature we have been describing. Like the Young Men's Societies of the 1830s, the formation of similar groups in the following decade indicated a preoccupation with youthful masculinity.[120] The 'Young Men's Mutual Improvement Society' met at the Toronto Mechanics' Institute in April 1847 to hear a lecture by the Hon. Robert Baldwin Sullivan. On this occasion, Sullivan did not speak on temperance, choosing instead to stress the importance of 'mental cultivation' and 'earnestness.'[121] Not all of the society's events were so solemn: two years later it held a 'festive evening' to which young women were invited.[122]

Although the reports of voluntary societies and the prescriptive literature would appear to bear only a tenuous relationship to the other categories and discourses on gender discussed throughout this chapter – the 'public man' and the 'woman in public' – we must not overlook the sense of process and development that ran through all of this literature. The earnestly improving young man would, with the right guidance, become either the 'public man' (a Robert Baldwin Sullivan) or at least one of those responsible for choosing such dignitaries. Those young women invited to the Young Men's Society dance would mature into those 'ladies' who presented banners, ran bazaars and mission fund-raisers, and rode in the temperance parade carriages. Together, rising above party, patronage, and all other forms of 'selfish interest,' they would become the symbols of the middle class of Canada West.

Epilogue

The discourses of politics, religion, and social morality deployed a number of gendered languages in different contexts. Patriotic and political discourses used languages laden with gendered images and symbols to organize and give meaning to significant events and processes, from the War of 1812 to the formation of political parties. During the war, discussions of loyalty to Upper Canada and the British connection relied heavily on the image of the colony's men defending their families and homes. Masculine protectiveness, especially as personified by General Brock and the Christian soldier, was invoked in order to save the defenceless women and children of Upper Canada from the rapaciousness of the American invaders. This language posed problems for women, as their contributions to the war effort were seldom recognized as the activities of loyal patriots. Those women who performed acts of physical bravery and who did not conform to dominant images of feminine helplessness and passivity were excluded from the official narrative of wartime heroism. Moreover, when questions of rewards for patriotic actions or compensation for wartime losses were discussed, wartime service was constructed as a masculine activity. Women's claims on the colonial state or on the Loyal and Patriotic Society had to be made through their male relatives and did not reflect women's own efforts to support and defend the colony.

In the 1820s and 1830s, debates over matters such as responsible government were conducted in languages that marked out political affairs as masculine preserves. In order to discredit their reform opponents, the conservative press and its supporters defined reformers as excessively emotional and hysterical, qualities that were identified as being womanly. In response, reformers labelled conservatives as effeminate, dependent on patronage, and interested in only the material rewards of political office.

Using many of the elements of eighteenth-century 'Commonwealth' discourse, reformers argued that Upper Canadian politics needed men who were independent and virtuous, qualities reformers believed they themselves possessed. Both parties framed political struggle for power and place as a battle between men; both used languages that relied heavily on images of femininity to discredit each other. While it is clear that some women were concerned with, and involved in, the political turmoil of the 1830s, the languages used to frame political debates had little to say about women's participation in politics.

Religious discourse, on the other hand, used gendered languages in a number of different ways. Methodists suggested that gender relations in both the family and religious and political hierarchies in Upper Canadian society, might be challenged and reworked. Religious choice was the fundamental issue for individuals; the decision to accept one's state of sin and Christ's salvation and love took precedence over accustomed patterns of hierarchy and authority. Thus, the power of an abusive husband or father who stood between a wife or daughter and her saviour could be questioned and, with God's help, overturned. Furthermore, Methodists who wrote about the early itinerants in Upper Canada created a masculine archetype that was a more complex figure than the independent man of reform discourse or the manly protector created in the language of loyalty. The image of the minister combined both strength and emotion, withstanding the physical challenges of his work while being unashamed to weep in public. In the prescriptive material of the evangelical press, the family was seen as an important feature of social structure, one that served as a safeguard against the dangers of excessive individualism that were implicit in evangelicalism. The participation of both men and women in the family was perceived as necessary for the triumph of religion. Religious literature created categories of virtuous womanhood and virtuous manhood, constructing women as wives, mothers, daughters, and sisters, and men as husbands, fathers, sons, and brothers. Discussions of the 'Christian woman' identified her with the home and family and attempted to designate all three as the 'private' realm. Yet it is important to note that the image of the 'Christian man' was given meaning by his relation to the family and that Christian men were expected to take their familial responsibilities into other areas (the workplace, for example). While some evangelicals saw the family as 'woman's domain,' other writers insisted that women must submit to patriarchal governance. The family and gender relations were perceived by Methodists as needing reshaping and constant monitoring, but there was some disagreement over the balance of power in the family. These matters were much clearer in missionary writings and pronouncements concerning the Native peoples of Upper Canada. White Methodist writers agreed that the 'reformation' of the Native home and familial relations was crucial to the missionaries' program of 'civilization.'

The evangelical language of gender also helped shape discourses on manners and moral behaviour in Upper Canada. Using the codes set out by evangelical Protestantism and late-eighteenth- and early-nineteenth-century notions of domesticity and sentiment, those who shaped this discourse engaged in discussions of gender relations within the home, the workplace, and the voluntary association. These writers condemned practices such as drinking and duelling, constructing them as vices practised by weak and vicious men, vices whose chief victims were the unfortunate female relatives of these men. Many of the writers who shaped the discourse on manners and moral behaviour attempted to pinpoint 'essential' manhood and womanhood and then create structures for these archetypes. These structures appeared to ensure that manhood and womanhood would exist as separate categories (the 'private' world of the home as 'woman's world,' for example). However, 'true womanhood' and 'honest manhood' were mutually dependent. The meanings of these categories and images were grounded in family relationships with the opposite sex. Furthermore, the construction of reformed gender relations that took place in the discourse of manners and morality was subject to other contradictions and fissures. While 'honest womanhood' was best found within the home, the influence of other, equally influential categories (class, race, and religion) complicated attempts to confine to the domestic realm both this symbol of feminine virtue and the flesh-and-blood women at whom it was aimed. Moreover, that archetype of honest manhood, the white, Protestant, bourgeois man, was defined as much by his relations with women (as a husband, father, son, and brother) as he was by his occupational identity. Although religious and secular writers were confident that the conflicts inherent in such fragmentation would be overcome through the power of moral principles, tensions and conflicts could not be wished away so easily. These problems were particularly acute when the question of youthful masculinity arose.

By the 1840s, the languages of politics and religion helped shape a code of white, middle-class morality. In political discourse of the 1840s, attempts to create consensus and harmony resulted in the emergence of a different symbol of virtuous manhood in the political realm. The image of the 'public man' was shaped by apprehensions over the rise of political parties and by political writers' desire to ensure that the tumult of the previous decade would not be repeated. The 'public man' rose above 'private' selfishness and personal loyalties in order that he might unite the many factions of Upper Canadian politics and forge them into a unified body, working for the 'common good.' His symbolic counterpart was the woman who worked diligently for the church and the voluntary society, who ran bazaars, sewed banners, and rode in temperance parades.

Not only do the discourses of politics, religion, and social morality indicate the multiple ways in which Upper Canadians constructed the 'public' and the 'private,' they also demonstrate that Upper Canadians' attempts to draw sharp delineations between them were not always successful. As chapters 4 and 5 have argued, discourses around religion, manners, and morality helped shape a place in Upper Canadian society that occupied a middle ground between the sanctity of the home and the rough and tumble of the floor of the legislature. Voluntarism, an ethos in which moral behaviour was promoted and celebrated, might occur in a number of spaces, from the home to the seat of local government. The language of voluntarism, and voluntary activity, involved men and women as husbands and wives, mothers and fathers, and sons and daughters. To a certain extent, it disrupted attempts to divide Upper Canadian society into the tidy 'spheres' of private and public, female versus male. Furthermore, the number of times when other categories (such as class and race) were also deployed in these discourses complicates matters. None of these categories, it should be stressed, appeared in a neat configuration separate from the others. At particular moments, and in particular contexts, one might be more important than others, such as in the discourse of missionaries, in which race and gender were more clearly deployed. At other times, as in the critique of fashionable consumerism and duelling discussed in chapter 4, class and gender might be seen 'at work.' Rather than imposing these categories on the past in a overly rigid manner, we must be sensitive to their historical specificity and the ways in which discourses around them shifted according to time and place.

The political, social, and economic developments of the 1850s – the rise of the 'Clear Grit' movement, the growth of antislavery societies, the subsiding of British immigration, and the development of more extensive transportation and communication systems – demand a more developed study of Canada West than can be provided here.[1] However, it is worth considering, if only briefly, some suggestions about both continuity and change in the gendered languages I have examined. Many of the processes discussed in this book – particularly the conceptualization and organization of the 'social' – were, of course, far from complete by the mid-1850, and the meanings and usages of these languages did not remain static. The image of the public man, for example, continued to suggest a higher moral authority in political life, but it could also be evoked in the anti-Catholic rhetoric that became more common in *The Globe*'s pages by mid-decade. The arbitrary tyranny of ultramontanism (whereby a foreign, unelected power made decisions that affected the liberties of British subjects) was targeted, but the paper also argued that men who supported the Catholic Church were no better than slaves; they had renounced their 'manly independence' to bow to Rome's despotism. Some of this rhetoric, with its suggestion that Catholic clerics (and their political supporters) were unmanly and effeminate, was redolent of 1820s and 1830s reform attacks on churchmen who took money from the state.[2] Yet while attacks on bishops and priests in the previous decades had targeted them as parasites and sycophants because of their financial relationship to the state (whether Anglican or, after 1833, Methodist), the articles of the 1850s were much more clearly focused on the Catholic Church and its effect on 'British manhood.' Later in the century, as J.R. Miller has argued, attacks on the church often focused on the confessional and its potential to disrupt familial harmony by replacing a husband's authority with that of the priest.[3] Earlier in the century, though, devotion to Rome was depicted as 'unmanning' men, denying them their independent status as adult men free of any hidden entanglements. As well, Catholicism robbed them of political virtue and morality because they no longer possessed the free will to act according to their consciences. Such men were the antithesis of public men because they were bound by secret, hidden ties and were no longer able to act in an unencumbered fashion for the good of all.[4] Countries dominated by the Catholic Church, where political and social relations had been perverted by politicians answering to priests, provided particularly clear examples of these dangers.[5] Examples of widespread sexual immorality in Catholic religious orders demonstrated the need for Protestant men's vigilance, although the virtue and superior morality of Protestant women also might be enlisted in resisting Catholicism.[6]

Antislavery rhetoric also deployed the theme of masculine independence from subjugation and tyranny. At times, writers such as Brown made use of the figure of the black man, whose masculine dignity was affronted by the degrading conditions of slavery.[7] But the theme of slavery cannot be seen in isolation or only as it pertained to blacks. For one, there were certain similarities between the images of black slaves who were struggling for freedom and those of the enslaved and degraded Native men and women of missionary discourse. To be sure, the first groups had been enslaved by whites, particularly Americans, a point hammered home by *The Globe* in its antislavery articles.[8] By contrast, in missionary discourses, as chapter 3 has argued, Native culture and lack of 'true religion' were pinpointed as the main agent of Native peoples' problems (although it was sometimes admitted that irreligious whites were also to blame).

Antislavery rhetoric was deployed not only when the fate of Natives or blacks was at stake. It helped illuminate the plight of, and raise sympathy for, these particular groups, suggesting that their differences from those of European descent had been artificially imposed by a wide range of cultural, socio-economic, and political forces. The trope of liberation from servitude was also deployed when distinctions needed to be drawn between Upper Canada and the United States, or when the encroachments of the Catholic Church were perceived as threatening the freedom of Upper Canadians. The language of antislavery was used to reinforce Upper Canada's link to Britain and her traditions of constitutional and religious freedom (particularly that of Protestant churches). Much of this discourse was organized around the figure of the free, British, and Protestant man who had a history of combatting tyranny and absolutism. As such, he would protect Upper Canadian liberties against slave-catchers, priests, republican demagogues; he also would bring Native peoples under his protection and up to his position and would protect the helpless and weak (especially women and children of all races and classes). An ideal to be worked towards (although never completely attained) by men of other races, this image of masculine integrity and morality helped embody the various ways in which certain Upper Canadians helped define and then defend colonial society. It is clear that, just as white women helped define their own identities in abolitionist work, so too did white men.[9]

Black Upper Canadians' constructions of race, gender, and class have received even less attention from historians than those of their white contemporaries.[10] However, the pages of the *Provincial Freeman* provide some hints for future research by historians. The *Freeman*, the first Upper Canadian paper to be co-founded and edited by a black woman, Mary Ann Shadd, emphasized both 'the elevation of the coloured people' and the efficacy of self-help.[11] Some writers believed that elevation should be towards the creation of a black middle class and called for the black community to use strategies that may seem to replicate those of the white colonial middle class, particularly when coupled with the paper's emphasis on respectability through the temperance movement. But we should also consider the differences that a history of slavery might make to narratives of racial and class uplift. Shadd and other black writers supported integration with whites, vehemently denounced those who opposed racial amalgamation as friends of slavery, and pointed to areas of the colony where blacks and whites co-existed happily, but they also insisted that blacks must take responsibility for their own fate. They hoped that whites would support them in their endeavours (particularly white Upper Canadians whose connection to Britain would inspire them), but, given the histories of racism and slavery in Anglo-American communities, many writers in the *Freeman* wanted to stress that blacks must develop their own strengths, both as individuals and as a community. They could not rely solely on the goodwill of British men and women to perform their work for them.[12]

Much of the language of uplift in the *Freeman* relied on phrases such as 'the coloured people,' deploying them in ways that continued the discursive collapsing of relations such as gender and class that we have seen earlier (in the language of political reformers, for example). Yet there were some significant differences in the *Freeman*'s conception of gender relations. Instead of the ridicule and fear apparent in other papers when the American woman's rights movement was discussed, Lucy Stone's Toronto lecture was described enthusiastically. Stone, Shadd informed her readers, had a reputation as a talented woman and orator; even in Toronto, with its 'strong attachment to antiquated notions respecting woman and her sphere so prevalent,' she was greeted with patience and much applause. The St Lawrence Hall was packed, and there were no shouts of 'brigadier' or 'virago.' Shadd was, however, disappointed that so few 'coloured people seized upon the occasion to learn lessons of practical wisdom.'[13] Shadd's own support for woman's suffrage must, of course, have influenced her treatment of Stone; the *Freeman* was one of the very few papers to accept women's right to speak for their rights in public. It is not surprising, then, that Lucy Stone appears as a very different figure than that depicted by *The Globe* in the 1840s.[14] Shadd herself, upon her resignation from the paper's editorship in 1855, wrote an 'Adieu' to her readers that acknowledged the 'difficulties, and ... obstacles such as we feel confident few, if any, females have had to contend against in the same business, except the sister who shared our labors [*sic*] for awhile.' And 'to colored women, we have a word – we have "broken the editorial ice," whether willingly or not, for your class in America; so go to Editing, as many of you as are willing, and able, and as soon as you may, if you think you are ready.' Those women who did not feel ready, Shadd wrote, should assist in other ways, by subscribing to the paper and encouraging their neighbours to do the same.[15] Shadd's comment about facing obstacles unknown to other women in journalism suggests that the configurations of race and gender might have very different meanings for black women (as some historians have argued regarding African-American women).[16]

Furthermore, although much remains to be done on the constructions of white womanhood by black women *or* men in nineteenth-century Ontario, the *Freeman* suggests that some significant differences may have existed from those images shaped by evangelical writers. Black writers called into question the inherent beneficence and moral superiority of white women, particularly mothers. This symbolism was often employed by *The Globe*, in its coverage of the address written by the Toronto Ladies' Association for Relief of Destitute Coloured Fugitives, the paper spoke of the usefulness of 'female influence,' particularly within the family and in education (although Brown also commended the ladies for not sweetening the truth but instead expressing the situation in 'plain speech').[17] To be sure, the *Freeman* commended the appeal of white British women abolitionists who had called upon their American women to work for the abolition of slavery.[18] But, as an article taken from *Lloyd's Newspaper* pointed out, the American women met this appeal with extraordinarily bad grace, so much so that their letter of response might have been written by a man: 'We cannot mistake the masculine stride that distends the petticoats,' wrote the author of 'Mrs America answers Mrs England.' Even if the response was the work of women, they 'pucker their mouths, and with a prolonged, laborious, curtsey' beg English women to look to the behaviour of their own menfolk: in India, Africa, China, Ireland, and towards the British working class. 'With a truly feminine self-denial they swallow their indignation; put down the rising heart with a strong hand, and proceed with the catalogue. Sisters in America are so sisterly towards sisters of Stafford House!'[19] There was little here to suggest women's elevated morality or natural propensity to help the oppressed and downtrodden.

At times, white women were even more directly implicated in the viciousness of slavery, as slaveholders themselves. Such was the lesson of 'Slavery in Baltimore,' which recounted the cruel treatment of a number of slaves by rich owners. One particularly wealthy woman was notorious for her inhumanity. Her coachman died of frostbite after being kept outside on her carriage in bitter weather; another slave, who escaped after similar treatment, was caught by the woman's son and made to run for sixteen miles; yet another woman was left a cripple after falling from a third-storey window (she had fallen asleep while washing windows after being deprived of rest as a punishment). 'Such is the system as administered by the rich, the fashionable, and the aristocratic,' concluded the writer.[20] The viciousness of this women might be attributed to her class for, as we have seen, middle-class writers often targeted men and women of the aristocracy for their callousness towards the poor. The writer did not suggest that 'womanly nature' – or 'maternal feeling' – might mitigate or soften this woman's contempt for the human beings whom she owned and who served her.

The construction of social space, where middle-class men and women mingled in fêtes, bazaars, and soirées, not only continued into the 1850s, but it also became increasingly dependent on the figure of 'the lady' to give this space its special appeal and meaning for middle-class society. Temperance, of course, facilitated the ongoing creation of social space, with its mixed-sex gatherings and parades; so, too, did church bazaars.[21] While fund-raising for the church was probably the least controversial form of voluntary activity for middle-class Protestant women (although we should not discount the possibility of unreported conflicts between the women themselves or with ministers and church elders), 'respectable' women were also involved in other forms of voluntarism. Antislavery work was one such activity; work for the Toronto Magdalen Asylum was another. The asylum's annual report for 1855 stated that one of the institution's most important 'agencies' was the 'periodical visits of the ladies to the Jail,' for it was from this location that the asylum gathered its 'outcasts.' The asylum's managing board was made up of eight men. Two of them were ministers (the Reverends Sanson and Burns), and the other members included men such as James Lesslie and G.W. Allan, individuals who were active in the city's voluntary societies. The asylum also was served by a ladies' committee of thirty-one women (twenty-nine of them married or widowed), with surnames such as Baldwin, Lesslie, Robinson, and Dunlop. Further research would be needed to determine whether or not jail visits to prostitutes were seen as a respectable form of voluntary activity for middle-class women, but the society clearly employed the language of Christian love, the trope of woman's victimization, and the hope of her rescue and uplift. While the ladies of the committee bore witness that licentiousness certainly hardened the heart, they were still 'gratefully received' by those they visited. When appeals were made to Christian love and the gospels were heeded, 'many a weeping eye has given testimony that the springs of sensibility had not wholly been dried up in that moral descent.' According to its annual report, the asylum housed three women in a 'hopeful condition' and had sent one to hospital, where she had died in hope of religion; six women had gone into service, another four were living with their friends, and three had gone to the House of Industry. The report acknowledged that these figures might be small in comparison with rescue work in New York City but insisted that the asylum performed a valuable service. The women in it were friendless and were 'watched for by those monster criminals who keep houses of infamy and live by the ruin and death of women.' (There were, the committee believed, at least ten such houses in Toronto.) The 'most wicked artifices are being constantly employed to supply them with victims'; young, innocent girls, particularly those who were new to the city and looking for work, were enticed to these places where they were then ruined. Here the committee employed a similar discourse to that of the press, although the villains of this piece – the 'monster criminals' – were not given a gender-specific identity, unlike the hardened madams in The Globe's coverage of prostitution. And, in the asylum committee's narrative of rescue, the agents of the salvation of these unfortunate women were other women – middle-class, respectable, 'ladies' – not the representatives of the colonial state.[22]

Although men and women of the mid-nineteenth-century middle class continued to meet to work for temperance, the well-being of religious institutions, or the abolition of slavery and prostitution, we should not let the rhetoric employed in these accounts obscure the power relations that defined and shaped social space.[23] To be sure, women's presence was often seen as essential if these gatherings were to be truly representative of their constituencies; in the case of antislavery work, the independent Ladies' Association appears to have been crucial in keeping the movement financially afloat.[24] But the papers consulted here suggest that there was never unanimous support for women's participation in all voluntary activities or in shaping social space on the same terms as men. In the temperance movement, women rarely spoke of their own accord, and they continued to line the routes as spectators, not as marchers, in the temperance parades (at least until 1855). While their labour within churches was recognized as extremely important, women were excluded from positions of authority in church governance in mainstream Protestant churches. Political dinners continued to be represented as masculine gatherings of 'public men' and their supporters; if women's labour had made those gatherings possible (and I suspect that such was the case), it was conspicuous by the lack of attention it received.[25]

Other kinds of power relations were implicated in determining the meanings of social space. Just as the masculinity of patriotic discourse could not be fully understood without taking images of femininity into account, the trope of 'ladies' in the colonial press of the 1850s was also heavily dependent on images of 'deviant' femininity. Others kinds of womanhood and others kinds of women continued to be represented in the colonial press, and they differed in many ways from the Daughters of Temperance, the organizers of bazaars, or the virtuous rescuers of the Magdalen Asylum's inhabitants. The records of convictions from the Lincoln and Welland county courts, for example, present women as plaintiffs and defendants: Harriet Allan prosecuted Jane Kirkland for assault and damage, Bridget Welsh charged Charles Blake for assault and battery, and Elizabeth Madden took Judy McNamara to court for a breach of a by-law.[26] Four years later, 'Bloody Affray' recounted the story of two women of Hibbert Township who came to blows over a man that both claimed as their husband. Ellen Doyle was arrested for her attack on Mrs Dougherty when the two met in the woods; Doyle cut her husband's first wife's throat with a razor, slashing her 'sinews, veins, and windpipe.' Although Mrs Dougherty was not expected to live, she apparently had won the fight and received an apology from Doyle. The latter was a 'fearful spectacle' upon her arrest, 'being covered with wounds and her clothes saturated with blood.'[27] The press treated this encounter with a certain kind of morbid fascination – and the suggestion that such behaviour was not commonly found among women – but this article, and others like it, made the point that such women were decidedly not 'ladies.'

The category 'lady' did not occur by accident, nor was its use strictly a matter of inherited languages from Anglo-American culture (although certainly that was important). Like virtuous, public manhood, the 'lady' of colonial discourse was shaped and crafted in mid-nineteenth-century Ontario society in several ways, both within the press and in other contexts. As the century wore on, this trope would have increased significance for gender relations in a number of areas – the law, the church, the state, and the workplace – as well as playing an extremely important role in the languages and practices of social reform and feminist activism. For those women who were constructed and represented as 'ladies,' the image would symbolize constraints (in politics, education, and the professions), but it also could be deployed strategically to challenge 'women's sphere.' While white, middle-class, Protestant women might find its legacy ambiguous, configurations of femininity and masculinity had even more serious consequences for other groups of men and women. For Native, immigrant, and working-class women, the trope of the 'lady' might be seen as a badly flawed ideal that had little meaning for their lives. Even so, the category of virtuous womanhood helped shape the social, legal, economic, and political frameworks in which these women lived, while simultaneously creating significant divisions between themselves and those women who sought to create common ground in an ideal of shared womanhood.

Notes

Introduction

1 See Leonore Davidoff and Catherine Hall, *Family Fortunes*.
2 For examples of American material, see Barbara Welter, 'The Cult of True Womanhood'; Carroll Smith-Rosenberg, 'The Female World of Love and Ritual: Relations Between Women in Nineteenth-Century America,' in her *Disorderly Conduct*, 53–76; Nancy Hewitt, *Women's Activism and Social Change*; Mary P. Ryan, *Cradle of the Middle Class*.
3 See, for example, Jacqueline Jones, 'Introduction,' in her *Labor of Love, Labor of Sorrow*; Christine Stansell, *City of Women*; Sylvia Van Kirk, '*Many Tender Ties*.'
4 Nancy F. Cott, *The Bonds of Womanhood*; Lawrence Stone, *The Family, Sex and Marriage in England, 1500–1800* (Harmondsworth: Penguin, 1979); Peter Ward, *Courtship, Love, and Marriage*. For a reassessment of causal factors in the exclusion of women from formal positions of religious authority, see Susan Juster, 'Patriarchy Reborn: The Gendering of Authority in the Evangelical Church in Revolutionary New England,' *Gender and History* 6, no. 1 (April 1994): 58–81.
5 Recent work on nineteenth-century Maritime women, though, has grappled with this issue. See Janet Guildford and Suzanne Morton, eds., *Separate Spheres*.
6 J.K. Johnson, *Becoming Prominent*; Jane Errington, *The Lion, the Eagle, and Upper Canada*; David Mills, *The Idea of Loyalty in Upper Canada, 1784–1850*; William Westfall, *Two Worlds*; Susan E. Houston and Alison Prentice, *Schooling and Scholars*; Bruce Curtis, *Building the Educational State*
7 Beth Light and Alison Prentice, eds., *Pioneer and Gentlewomen*; Katherine M.J. McKenna, 'The Role of Women in the Establishment of Social Status in Early

Upper Canada'; also her *A Life of Propriety*; Gretchen Green, 'Molly Brant, Catherine Brant, and Their Daughters'

8 Marjorie Cohen, *Women's Work, Markets, and Economic Development*

9 Joan Wallach Scott, 'Gender: A Useful Category of Historical Analysis,' in her *Gender and the Politics of History*, 28–50

10 In *Canada Dry*, Jan Noel describes the ideology of separate spheres in temperance literature. Women appeared as mothers, a 'hallowed social role' centred in the home, while men were perceived as breadwinners, part of the competitive marketplace (see her chap. 7, 'Mothers of the Millennium'). See also McKenna, *A Life of Propriety*, especially pt. 3, 'The Transmission of Female Gender Roles'; also Elizabeth Jane Errington, *Wives and Mothers*, for a short discussion of domestic ideology (20–4).

11 Scott, 'Gender,' 42–5

12 Although the American field in particular has seen a huge growth in literature on women and religion, perhaps the best example of an identification of the two is Ann Douglas's *The Feminization of American Culture*.

13 See Linda Kerber, *Women of the Republic*; Ruth H. Bloch, 'The Gendered Meanings of Virtue in Revolutionary America'; Dorinda Outram, 'Le langage mâle de la vertu'; Joan Landes, *Women and the Public Sphere*; Siân Reynolds, 'Marianne's Citizens?' For religion, see Juster, 'Patriarchy Reborn'; Davidoff and Hall, *Family Fortunes*, especially chaps. 1–3; Deborah Valenze, *Prophetic Sons and Daughters*; Christine Krueger, *The Reader's Repentance*.

14 For a review essay of some of this literature, see Colin Read, 'Conflict to Consensus.' For an overview of religious developments in Upper Canada, see John Webster Grant, *A Profusion of Spires*, especially chaps. 2–7.

15 See Denise Riley, *'Am I That Name?'*; also Hanna Fenichel Pitkin, 'Justice: On Relating Private and Public,' for discussions of the identification of women with the 'social' realm.

16 In addition to the work of McKenna and Green, see also Janice Potter-MacKinnon, *While the Women Only Wept*.

17 For an overview of women's activities in religious and benevolent organizations in British North America, see Alison Prentice et al., *Canadian Women*, 103–5; also Katherine McKenna, 'Options for Elite Women in Early Upper Canadian Society'; and Errington, *Wives and Mothers*, chap. 7.

18 See two articles by Joan Kelly in *Women, History, and Theory*: 'The Doubled Vision of Feminist Theory' and 'The Social Relation of the Sexes'; also Natalie Zemon Davis, 'Women's History in Transition.'

19 For selected bibliographical essays that provide an overview of the field, see Eliane Leslau Silverman, 'Writing Canadian Women's History, 1970–82: An Historiographical Analysis,' *Canadian Historical Review* 63, 4 (1982): 513–33;

Margaret Conrad, 'The Re-Birth of Canada's Past: A Decade of Women's History,' *Acadiensis* 12 (1983): 140–62; Gail Cuthbert Brandt, 'Post-Modern Patchwork: Some Recent Trends in the Writing of Women's History in Canada,' *Canadian Historical Review*, 72, no. 4 (Dec. 1991): 441–70. Much of the historical literature on education in nineteenth-century Ontario incorporates gender. See, for example, Alison Prentice, *The School Promoters* (Toronto: McClelland and Stewart, 1977); Curtis, *Building the Educational State*; and Houston and Prentice, *Schooling and Scholars*. For work on teachers that looks at gender specifically, see Alison Prentice, 'The Feminization of Teaching,' in Susan Mann Trofimenkoff and Alison Prentice, eds., *The Neglected Majority: Essays in Canadian Women's History* (Toronto: McClelland and Stewart, 1977), 49–65; Marta Danylewycz, Beth Light, and Alison Prentice, 'The Evolution of the Sexual Division of Labour in Teaching: A Nineteenth-Century Ontario and Quebec Case Study,' *Histoire sociale/Social History* 16, no. 31 (May 1983): 81–109; Marta Danylewycz and Alison Prentice, 'Teachers' Work: Changing Patterns and Perceptions in the Emerging School Systems of Nineteenth- and Early-Twentieth-Century Central Canada,' *Labour/Le Travail* 17 (Spring 1986): 58–80; Alison Prentice, '"Friendly Atoms in Chemistry": Women and Men at Normal School in Mid-Nineteenth-Century Toronto,' in David Keane and Colin Read, eds., *Old Ontario*, 285–371.

20 Scott, 'Gender,' 31
21 Joan W. Scott, 'Experience,' 26
22 Ibid., 33
23 Elizabeth Spelman, *Inessential Woman*, 185
24 Linda Kerber, 'Separate Spheres,' 37–8. See also Nancy Hewitt, 'Beyond the Search for Sisterhood'; Joy Parr, 'Nature and Hierarchy.'
25 Kerber, 'Separate Spheres,' 38
26 I would argue that this paradigm exerts less influence, or perhaps is viewed with a more critical eye, in Britain and Canada than in the United States. The tendency has also been pointed out by Guildford and Morton in their discussion of separate spheres as an analytic framework for researching nineteenth-century Maritime women's lives (*Separate Spheres*, 12).
27 Kerber, 'Separate Spheres,' 37
28 Ibid., 17
29 Ellen Carol DuBois and Vicki L. Ruiz, 'Introduction,' in DuBois and Ruiz, eds., *Unequal Sisters: A Multicultural Reader in U.S. Women's History* (New York and London: Routledge, 1990), xi–xvi
30 Kerber, 'Separate Spheres,' 39
31 See *Gender and History: Special Issue on Gender, Nationalisms and National Identities* 5, no. 2 (Summer 1993); also Ruth Roach Pierson, *'They're Still*

Women After All': The Second World War and Canadian Womanhood (Toronto: McClelland and Stewart, 1986).

32 Scott, 'Gender,' 45

33 Ibid.

34 The quote is from Joan Hoff, 'The Pernicious Effects of Poststructuralism on Women's History,' *Chronicle of Higher Education* (Oct. 1993): B4. Sentiments similar to Hoff's (although based on an apparently more thorough and nuanced reading of both poststructuralism and gender history) have been expressed by Judith M. Bennett, 'Feminism and History,' *Gender and History* 1, no. 3 (Autumn 1989): 251–72. See also Tania Modleski, *Feminism Without Women: Culture and Criticism in a 'Postfeminist' Age* (New York and London: Routledge, 1991). For a discussion of critiques of gender history in the Canadian context, see Joy Parr, 'Gender History and Historical Practice.'

35 Hoff, 'Pernicious Effects,' B5; Modleski, *Feminism Without Women*, pt. 2, 'Masculinity and Male Feminism'

36 See, for example, the essays in J.A. Mangan and James Walvin, eds., *Manliness and Morality*.

37 Joy Parr, *The Gender of Breadwinners: Women, Men, and Change in Two Industrial Towns, 1880–1950* (Toronto: University of Toronto Press, 1990); Mark Rosenfeld, '"It Was a Hard Life": Class and Gender in the Work and Family Rhythms of a Railway Town, 1920–1950,' *Historical Papers* (1988): 237–79; Steven Maynard, 'Rough Work and Rugged Men: The Social Construction of Masculinity in Working-Class History,' *Labour/Le Travail* 23 (Spring 1989): 159–69; Steven Penfold, '"Have You No Manhood in You?" Gender and Class in the Cape Breton Coal Towns, 1920–1926,' *Acadiensis* 23, no. 2 (Spring 1994): 21–44

38 Mark C. Carnes and Clyde Griffen, eds., *Meanings for Manhood*, 13

39 John Tosh, 'What Should Historians Do with Masculinity?' 184–7

40 Parr, *The Gender of Breadwinners*; Curtis, *Building the Educational State*; Tina Loo, *Making Law, Order, and Authority in British Columbia, 1821–1871* (Toronto: University of Toronto Press, 1994); Ian McKay, *The Quest of the Folk: Antimodernism and Cultural Selection in Twentieth-Century Nova Scotia* (Montreal and Kingston: McGill-Queen's University Press, 1994); Mariana Valverde, *The Age of Light, Soap, and Water: Moral Reform in English Canada, 1885–1925* (Toronto: McClelland and Stewart, 1991); Kay J. Anderson, *Vancouver's Chinatown: Racial Discourse in Canada, 1875–1980* (Montreal and Kingston: McGill-Queen's University Press, 1990). Three of the six authors cited here, though, are not historians: Curtis, Valverde, and Anderson work in historical sociology and geography.

41 A.B. McKillop, 'Culture, Intellect, and Context,' *Journal of Canadian Studies* 24, no. 3 (Fall 1989): 11

42 Loo, *Making Law*, 10

43 For an example of this type of response to poststructuralism and 'language,' see Bryan D. Palmer, 'Response to Joan Scott,' *International Labor and Working-Class History* (hereafter *ILWCH*) 31 (Spring 1987): 14–23. For an analysis of the work of Scott and of Denise Riley that, although critical, points to the benefits of a poststructuralist approach and the limits of the reaction to it, see Mariana Valverde, 'Poststructuralist Gender Historians.'

44 See also Christine Stansell, 'A Response to Joan Scott,' *ILWCH* 31 (Spring 1987): 24–9, and Bryan D. Palmer, *Descent into Discourse*. Although Palmer provides a more nuanced analysis of poststructuralism here than in his earlier reponse to Scott, he is still wary of a focus on language as opposed to historical materialism. Recent debates have also taken place in the pages of *Past and Present* between Lawrence Stone, Patrick Joyce, Catriona Kelly, and Gabrielle Spiegel (nos. 131, 133, and 135), in *Social History*, between David Mayfield, Susan Thorne, Jon Lawrence, Miles Taylor, Patrick Joyce, and James Vernon (May 1992, Jan. 1993, May 1993, and Jan. 1994), and in *American Historical Review* between David Harlan, David A. Hollinger, and Allan Megill (94, no. 3 [June 1989]).

45 Terry Eagleton, 'Marxism, Structuralism, and Post-Structuralism'

46 The problem of context crops up in Riley, *'Am I That Name?'*, which tends to treat the passage of four centuries rather lightly. For a critique of Riley, see Karen Offen, 'The Use and Abuse of History,' *Women's Review of Books*, April 1989, 15.

47 Chris Weedon, *Feminist Practice*, 19–27

48 Mary Poovey, 'Feminism and Deconstruction,' 51

49 Terry Eagleton, *Literary Theory*, 148

50 Ibid., 151

51 Jonathan Culler, *On Deconstruction*, 140, 153–4

52 See Scott's introduction to *Gender and the Politics of History*, 1–11. See also Mary Poovey, *Uneven Developments*; Carroll Smith-Rosenberg, 'Hearing Women's Words: A Feminist Reconstruction of History,' in her *Disorderly Conduct*, 11–52.

53 Culler *On Deconstruction*, 128–9, 134

54 For an example of this approach in intellectual history, see A.B. McKillop, 'So Little on the Mind,' in his *Contours of Canadian Thought* (Toronto: University of Toronto Press, 1987), 18–33.

55 James Vernon, 'Who's Afraid of the "Linguistic Turn"?' 84

56 The purpose of this section is to provide an outline of some of the more significant political, economic, and social features of Upper Canadian history. As with
most historical processes and events, there are debates over most of this material, some of which will be dealt with in the following chapters. For an overview
of the 'founding' of the colony, see Gerald Craig, *Upper Canada*, especially
chaps. 1–3.

57 Ibid., 5; also Peter S. Schmalz, *The Ojibwa of Southern Ontario*, chaps. 5 and 6

58 Craig, *Upper Canada*, 51. For population growth in the 1840s, see J.M.S. Careless, *The Union of the Canadas*, 27, 150; also Douglas McCalla, *Planting the
Province*, 179–80.

59 Craig, 'Economic Growth in the 1820's and 1830's,' chap. 8 in *Upper Canada*;
Careless, *Union*, 27–32; also John McCallum, *Unequal Beginnings: Agriculture
and Economic Development in Quebec and Ontario until 1870* (Toronto: Uni-
versity of Toronto Press, 1980); Douglas McCalla, 'The Wheat Staple and
Upper Canadian Development,' *Historical Papers* (1978): 34–45; also his *The
Upper Canada Trade 1834–1872: A Study of the Buchanans' Business* (Toronto:
University of Toronto Press, 1979); B.G. Wilson, *The Enterprises of Robert
Hamilton: A Study of Wealth and Influence in Early Upper Canada, 1776–1812*
(Ottawa: University of Ottawa Press, 1983).

60 Craig, *Upper Canada*, 17–19

61 Ibid., chaps. 5, 6, and 10–13, for political developments in the 1820s and 1830s.
For a discussion of the Executive Council, see Paul Romney, *Mr Attorney: The
Attorney General for Ontario in Court, Cabinet, and Legislature, 1791–1899*
(Toronto: Osgoode Society, 1986), 5–6.

62 Craig, *Upper Canada*, 262. For the development of 'party' in the 1840s, see
Carol Wilton-Siegel, 'The Transformation of Upper Canadian Politics'; also
Careless, *Union of the Canadas*, especially 119–20.

63 Craig, *Upper Canada*, 16. For a closer look at the Church of England's early
years in Upper Canada, see Curtis Fahey, *In His Name*, chap. 1, 'Establishment
and Survival.'

64 See Grant, *Profusion of Spires*, chaps. 2–4. For controversies over the issues represented by the clergy reserves, see ibid., chaps. 6 and 9; Fahey, *In His Name*,
chaps. 4 and 5; Goldwin French, *Parsons and Politics: The Role of Wesleyan
Methodists in Upper Canada and the Maritimes, 1780–1855* (Toronto: University of Toronto Press, 1962).

65 Careless, *Union of the Canadas*, 194; Fahey, *In His Name*, 270–1

66 The 'university question' came about in 1827 when the Anglican rector of York,
John Strachan, obtained a royal charter for a provincial university at York, to be
called King's College. Student enrolment in arts courses was not limited to
Anglicans, although only Anglicans could enrol in divinity courses or be profes-

sors or college council members. Coupled with the issue of the reserves, the university was a sore spot for other denominations. The problem was partially resolved when Sir John Colborne, the province's lieutenant-governor, 'diverted the available money to the foundation of Upper Canada College, which attracted mainly Anglican students but was not officially linked with the Church of England' (Grant, *Profusion of Spires*, 90).

67 A more extensive bibliography of Methodist missionary work will be given in chapter 3. For other denominations, see Grant, *Moon of Wintertime*, especially chap. 4; Elizabeth Graham, *From Medicine-Man to Missionary*; Schmalz, *The Ojibwa*, 133, 137, 151, 157, 163–4.

68 See, for example, Tony Hall, 'Native Limited Identities and Newcomer Metropolitanism in Upper Canada, 1814–1867,' in Keane and Read, eds., *Old Ontario*, 148–73; Donald B. Smith, *Sacred Feathers*; Donald Harman Akenson, *The Irish in Ontario*; Bruce S. Elliott, *Irish Migrants in the Canadas: A New Approach* (Montreal and Kingston: McGill-Queen's University Press, 1988); Cecil J. Houston and William J. Smyth, *Irish Emigration and Canadian Settlement: Patterns, Links, and Letters* (Toronto: University of Toronto Press, 1990). There has been far less work in labour and working-class history in early-nineteenth-century Ontario, but see, for example, Ruth Bleasdale, 'Class Conflict on the Canals of Upper Canada'; Paul Craven and Tom Traves, 'Dimensions of Paternalism: Discipline and Culture in Canadian Railway Operations in the 1850s,' in Craig Heron and Robert Storey, eds., *On the Job: Confronting the Labour Process in Canada* (Montreal and Kingston: McGill-Queen's University Press, 1986), 47–74; Gregory S. Kealey, 'Work Control, the Labour Process, and Nineteenth-Century Canadian Printers,' in *On the Job*, 75–101.

69 For example, see Paul E. Johnson, *A Shopkeeper's Millennium: Society and Revivals in Rochester, New York, 1815–1837* (New York: Hill and Wang, 1978); Ryan, *Cradle of the Middle Class*; Stuart M. Blumin, *The Emergence of the Middle Class*; Karen Haltunnen, *Confidence Men and Painted Women*; John P. Kasson, *Rudeness and Civility*; Davidoff and Hall, *Family Fortunes*; G.J. Barker-Benfield, *The Culture of Sensibility*. For a critique of arguments concerning the link of domesticity to middle-class formation, see Dror Wahrman, '"Middle-Class" Domesticity Goes Public: Gender, Class, and Politics from Queen Caroline to Queen Victoria,' *Journal of British Studies* 32 (Oct. 1993): 396–432.

70 Allan Greer and Ian Radforth, eds., *Colonial Leviathan*, 6

71 Prentice, *School Promoters*; Curtis, *Building the Educational State*. For an earlier examination of class in Canada West based primarily on quantification, see Michael B. Katz, *The People of Hamilton, Canada West* (Cambridge: Harvard University Press, 1975). McKenna uses the term 'middle-class' to describe the

ideology of domesticity that by mid-century increasingly came to dominate the lives of the Powell family, particularly the women, but her study does not explore the contradictions and complexities involved in defining as 'middle-class' a family that, in many other ways, resembled the 'would-be' colonial gentry (McKenna, *A Life of Propriety*).

72 David G. Burley, *A Particular Condition in Life*, 10

73 Ibid., 11

74 The importance of bourgeois attempts to stake out the moral high ground is discussed in Davidoff and Hall, *Family Fortunes*, especially pt. 1 and Barker-Benfield, *Culture of Sensibility*, chap. 5.

75 Benedict Anderson, *Imagined Communities: Reflections on the Origin and Spread of Nationalism*, rev. ed. (London and New York: Verso, 1991), 77. See also Jürgen Habermas, *The Structural Transformation of the Public Sphere*, 20–21, 59–67.

76 This has been especially true for political history, and two recent works (Mills, *Idea of Loyalty*, and Errington, *The Lion, the Eagle*) make extensive use of newspapers. While to date there is no comprehensive study of the Upper Canadian press, see W.H. Kesterton, A *History of Journalism in Canada* (Toronto: McClelland and Stewart, 1967), 11–24. There are a number of articles that trace the development of the press. See, for example, Carl Benn, 'The Upper Canadian Press, 1793–1814,' *Ontario History* 60, no. 2 (June 1978): 91–114; Ian MacPherson, 'The *Liberal* of St Thomas, Ontario, 1832–1833,' *Western Ontario Historical Notes* 21 (1965): 10–29; J.J. Talman, 'The Newspapers of Upper Canada a Century Ago,' *Canadian Historical Review* 19 (1938): 9–23; W.S. Wallace, 'The Periodical Literature of Upper Canada,' *Canadian Historical Review* 12 (1931): 4–22; Mary McLean, 'Early Parliamentary Reporting in Upper Canada,' *Canadian Historical Review* 20 (1939): 378–91. Many thanks to Paul Rutherford for drawing my attention to this material. As he has argued, the press became a 'force' in British North American politics by the 1830s by the sheer number of writers and publications (Rutherford, *The Making of the Canadian Media* [Toronto: McGraw-Hill Ryerson, 1978], 7). Of course, we must be careful not to overestimate their impact: despite the growth in the number of publications in Upper Canada (from one paper in 1813 to 114 in 1853), our ability to determine circulation figures is limited. What evidence we do have suggests that subscribers were a relatively small group: in 1833, the thirty papers in the province had a combined circulation of 20,000 (Kesterton, *History of Journalism*, 11). We also lack any broad-based studies of literacy or, unlike England and the United States, cultural histories of the transmission of knowledge (see, for example, Richard D. Brown, *Knowledge Is Power: The Diffusion of Information in Early America, 1700–1865* [New York: Oxford University Press, 1989]).

However, as Rutherford and Graeme Patterson have argued, it is likely that
newspapers were passed around and read aloud in homes, churches, taverns, and
workplaces. Certainly these cultural practices were common in late-eighteenth-
century England and, judging from some of Upper Canada's better-known diaries, they continued in the backwoods of the colony (Rutherford, *Making of the
Canadian Media*, 29; Graeme Patterson, *History and Communications: Harold
Innis, Marshall McLuhan, the Interpretation of History* [Toronto: University of
Toronto Press, 1990], 194).

77 For an example of this tendency see Ward, *Courtship, Love and Marriage*. He
states that the 'private papers on which this study rests came from the pens of
quite ordinary folk' who, he argues, cannot be discussed in terms of class
relations since 'working class,' and 'middle class' cannot 'be used with much
precision when discussing social structure and cultural patterns' (6–7). For a
particularly insightful critique of Ward, see Karen Dubinsky's review of *Courtship, Love and Marriage* in *Ontario History* 82, no. 4 (Dec. 1990): 317–20.

1: 'That Manly and Cheerful Spirit'

1 Mills, *Idea of Loyalty*, 25–8; Errington, *The Lion, the Eagle*, 89
2 For discussions of the war, see Morris Zaslow, ed., *The Defended Border*; also
   George Sheppard, *Plunder, Profit, and Paroles*. See also Reginald Arthur
   Bowler, 'Propaganda in Upper Canada.'
3 For the image of Marianne, see Maurice Agulhon, *Marianne into Battle*; for
   American republican motherhood, Linda Kerber, 'The Republican Mother:
   Female Political Imagination in the Early Republic,' in her *Women of the
   Republic*.
4 See Madge Dresser, 'Britannia,' in Raphael Samuel, ed., *Patriotism: The Making
   and Unmaking of British National Identity* (London: Routledge, 1989), 3:26–
   49. Dresser, though, notes the frequency of misogynist treatments of Britannia
   at the hands of both radicals and conservatives (36).
5 Kesterton, *History of Journalism*, 3–8; but for a more detailed look at the press
   in this period, see Benn, 'The Upper Canadian Press,' 91–114.
6 *Upper Canada Gazette*, 21 Aug. 1794
7 H.V. Nelles, 'Loyalism and Local Power: The District of Niagara, 1792–1837,'
   Ontario History 58, no. 2 (June 1966): 98–104
8 *Canada Constellation*, 6 Sept. 1799
9 See, for example, *The Constitution*, 21 March 1837.
10 To date, there is no full-length academic study of John Strachan (1788–1867),
   the schoolmaster, cleric, and Anglican bishop of Toronto, who was often
   depicted by reformers as a key player in the Family Compact. See G.M. Craig,

'John Strachan,' *Dictionary of Canadian Biography* (hereafter *DCB*) (1976), 9:751–66.

11 S.F. Wise, 'Upper Canada and the Conservative Tradition,' in A.B. McKillop and Paul Romney, eds., *God's Peculiar Peoples*, 182

12 Mills, *Idea of Loyalty*, 19. See Errington, *The Lion, the Eagle*, 27, as well as Wise's 'Sermon Literature and Canadian Intellectual History' (3–17) and 'Canadians View the United States: Colonial Attitudes from the Era of the War of 1812 to the Rebellions of 1837' (45–60), both in McKillop and Romney, eds., *God's Peculiar Peoples*, for other discussions of Strachan's *Discourse*.

13 In addition to Mills, Errington, and Wise, others have commented on the *Discourse*, seeing it as either 'adulatory pap' or, at the very least, a 'particularly florid piece of writing' (Robert Fraser, '"Like Eden in Her Summer Dress,"' 18; Fahey, *In His Name*, 115). What is often overlooked in these assessments is that Strachan's piece was part of a larger trend in royal propaganda in Britain that glorified George for his domestic simplicity (Linda Colley, *Britons*, 233).

14 John Strachan, *Discourse*, 21–8, 37–8

15 Ibid., 38

16 For another discussion of the monarch as the 'good father,' see Lynn Hunt, 'The Rise and Fall of the Good Father,' in her *The Family Romance of the French Revolution*.

17 Strachan, *Discourse*, 8–9

18 Ibid., 10–11

19 Ibid., 11

20 The Queen Caroline affair will be discussed in chapter 4, but see Dorothy Thompson, *Queen Victoria*, 5–6.

21 Strachan, *Discourse*, 12

22 Ibid., 13

23 Ibid., 14–15

24 Ibid., 32–3

25 Ibid., 49

26 Ibid., 50

27 Ibid.

28 As quoted in Patrick Brode, *Sir John Beverley Robinson*, 11

29 Ibid., 11. See also the letter from 'A Friend of Peace,' *Kingston Gazette*, 9 Oct. 1810. This reply to the *Discourse* wholeheartedly agreed with Strachan's 'encomium upon those domestic and conjugal virtues' but disagreed with the rector's assessment of the United States.

30 During this period, the *York Gazette*, which published out of York until its

presses were destroyed during the American occupation of the town in 1813, and the *Kingston Gazette* were the only papers that were either published or have survived (Benn, 'Upper Canadian Press,' 99, 109–11).

31 *Kingston Gazette*, 28 Jan. 1811
32 On this aspect of anti-American sentiment, see Errington, *The Lion, the Eagle*, 134–5.
33 *Kingston Gazette*, 28 Jan. 1811
34 Ibid.
35 Ibid., 28 Feb. 1812
36 Ibid., 28 July 1812; also Brock's public 'Proclamation,' 22 July 1812, in E.A. Cruikshank, ed., *The Documentary History of the Campaign upon the Niagara Frontier*, 3:135–8
37 Herbert C.W. Goltz, 'Tecumseh,' *DCB* (1983), 5:795–801
38 Brock to Colonel Proctor, 25 Aug. 1812, in Cruikshank, ed., *Documentary History*, 3:303
39 See ibid. for correspondence: Lieutenant-Colonel Harvey to Colonel Claus, 15 July 1813, 6:236; Sir George Prevost to General Drummond, 17 Feb. 1814, 9:188–9; Lieutenant-Colonel Harvey to Colonel Matthew Elliott, 17 Dec. 1813, 9:23; and Prevost to Drummond, 17 Feb. 1814, 9:188–9.
40 This 'fear' of Natives is discussed in George F.G. Stanley, 'The Indians in the War of 1812,' in J.R. Miller, ed., *Sweet Promises: A Reader on Indian-White Relations in Canada* (Toronto: University of Toronto Press, 1991), 105–24. It is difficult to know what role rumour and conjecture played in constructing narratives of 'native atrocities' among white soldiers, but certainly later histories of the War of 1812 made use of this theme, particularly in recounting the Battle of Beaverdams (see Cecilia Morgan, '"Of Slender Frame and Delicate Appearance": The Placing of Laura Secord in Narratives of Canadian Loyalist History,' *Journal of the Canadian Historical Association* 5 (1994): 210).
41 John Richardson as quoted in Matilda Edgar, *Ten Years of Upper Canada*, 174. See also Dr William Dunlop, *Recollections of the War of 1812*, 77–8.
42 This is not to argue, of course, that British and American military leaders were unaware of Native peoples' reasons for participating (Stanley, 'The Indians in the War of 1812,' 109–10).
43 For the attitudes of former American colonists towards Native peoples, see Sheppard, *Plunder, Profit, and Paroles*, 121–9.
44 *Kingston Gazette*, 28 Feb. 1812
45 Ibid., 28 Jan. 1811
46 Ibid., 18 Sept. 1813. See also Lieutenant-Colonel Mahlon Burwell to Colonel Talbot, 21 May 1813, in Cruikshank, ed., *Documentary History*, 5:239, and Prevost's public 'Proclamation' of 1814 concerning the burning of Lewiston,

Black Rock, and Buffalo in retaliation for the razing of Newark in Cruikshank, 9:112–16.

47 *Kingston Gazette*, 18 Sept. 1812

48 Ibid., 28 July 1812

49 Ibid., 18 Feb. 1812

50 Ibid., 3 March 1812

51 *York Gazette*, 4 July 1812

52 Sheaffe, 'Militia District Orders,' 1 Nov. 1812, in Cruikshank, ed., *Documentary History*, 4:174

53 See, for example, the *York Gazette*, 18 Dec. 1813; 4 Jan. 1814; 1 Feb. 1814; 1 March 1814; 20 Aug. 1814; also Sheaffe's speech to the legislature, 8 March 1813, in Cruikshank, ed., *Documentary History*, 5:90–2.

54 *Kingston Gazette*, 20 April 1813

55 John Strachan, *Sermon Preached at York*, 2 Aug. 1812, 6–12

56 For a discussion of Strachan's military record, see George Sheppard, '"Deeds Speak?"' 215.

57 *Kingston Gazette*, 20 April 1813

58 W.W. Weekes, 'Civil Authority and Martial Law in Upper Canada,' in Zaslow, ed., *Defended Border*, 193

59 *Kingston Gazette*, 7 Nov. 1812

60 Cruikshank, ed., *Documentary History*, 4:114–16

61 *Upper Canada Gazette*, 6 Aug. 1818; 21 Oct. 1824; *The Examiner*, 5 Aug. 1840; *British Colonist*, 25 July 1840

62 See Morgan, '"Of Slender Frame and Delicate Appearance."'

63 *Kingston Gazette*, 20 April 1813

64 Colley, *Britons*, 261

65 Certainly such would be the case for élite women from families such as the Jarvises, Powells, Ridouts, Boultons, and Cartwrights, whose husbands, fathers, brothers, sons, and other relatives would likely be in the militia. For a study of the Powell family, see McKenna, *A Life of Propriety*.

66 Mary Agnes Fitzgibbon, 'A Historic Banner,' *Transactions of the Women's Canadian Historical Society of Toronto* 1 (Feb. 1896): 20

67 *War of 1812 Losses Claims*, Dept. of Finance, Upper Canada

68 Drummond to Prevost, 16 July 1814, in Cruikshank, ed., *Documentary History*, 1:60; Mrs Hannah Janoway to her sister-in-law at Fort George, 14 Sept. 1814, ibid., 2:230–1; William H. Merritt's personal note, 8 July 1813, ibid., 6:208–10. See also Brian Leigh Dunnigan, 'Military Life at Niagara, 1792–1796,' in Richard Merritt, Nancy Butler, and Michael Power, eds., *The Capital Years: Niagara-on-the-Lake, 1792–1796* (Toronto: Dundurn Press, 1991), 67–102. The wives of both officers and soldiers, Dunnigan states, were at the Niagara garri-

son; the latter received rations and did laundry. The military authorities also took pains to regulate 'unattached women,' being fearful in 1793 that they would bring a '"malignant disorder"' into the garrison (93).

69 Adjutant-General E. Baynes, 'General Orders,' 14 July 1813, in Cruikshank, ed., *Documentary History*, 6:235–6

70 Ibid., 4:229

71 Ibid., 6:99

72 Ibid., 98

73 *Montreal Gazette*, 20 April 1813, cited in Cruikshank, ed., *Documentary History*, 6:116–18

74 *Montreal Gazette*, 7 Nov. 1812

75 Janice Potter-MacKinnon, *While the Women Only Wept*, 45–51

76 *Kingston Gazette*, 20 April 1813

77 Ibid., 7 Nov. 1812

78 Ibid., 1 Feb. 1814

79 Ibid., 9 Oct. 1813

80 George W. Spragge, ed., *The John Strachan Letter Book*, 18–19. See also 'An Act to Amend the Militia Act,' 6 Oct. 1812, in Cruikshank, ed., *Documentary History*, 6, and Merritt's personal notes regarding the American advance on Niagara, ibid., 5:261.

81 *Kingston Gazette*, 19 Sept. 1812

82 Ibid., 7 Nov. 1812

83 Captain J.H. Holland to Major Deane, 31 May 1814, in Cruikshank, ed., *Documentary History*, 1:21; 'General Order,' issued by Adjutant-General C.K. Gardner, 2 July 1814, ibid., 37; and Drummond to Lord Bathurst, 10 July 1814, ibid., 52. Sheppard also discusses both élite and popular opposition to attacks on private property (*Plunder, Profit, and Paroles*, 93–4).

84 See, for example, Prevost's proclamation on the burning of Newark, which dealt at great length on the iniquities of American conduct concerning private property, in contrast to British troops' behaviour, and fulminated about the treatment of the 'four hundred helpless women and children' of Newark, thereby collapsing the two issues (*Kingston Gazette*, 1 Feb. 1814). It is worth remembering that married women were generally unable to own property in the colony, nor did they generally have legal rights concerning their children's custody (Constance Backhouse, *Petticoats and Prejudices*, chaps. 6 and 7).

85 Hamilton Craig, 'The Loyal and Patriotic Society of Upper Canada'; Sheppard, *Plunder, Profit, and Paroles*, 66–8, 177–81

86 Loyal and Patriotic Society, *Report*, 3, 375–8

87 Ibid., 9, 26–8; Loyal and Patriotic Society, *Explanation of the Proceedings*, 33–5

88 Loyal and Patriotic Society, *Report*, 26–8

89 Ibid., 76–304. Given the available sources, it is difficult to explain the anomaly of 1816. It is possible that a greater awareness of the society's work led to this increase in the number of female applicants. The society seems to have been faster in disbursing its funds than was the government in settling its war losses claims.

90 Ibid., 226–304

91 Ibid., 237

92 Ibid., 201

93 Ibid., 104

94 Ibid., 113

95 Errington, *The Lion, the Eagle*, 191

96 Akenson, *Irish in Ontario*, 134

97 Ibid., 135–8

98 *York Gazette*, 10 Feb. 1816

99 Anne Powell received such a grant as a daughter of a Loyalist (McKenna, *A Life of Propriety*, 224), as did, it seems, other single women.

100 *Kingston Gazette*, 28 June 1818

101 Potter-MacKinnon, *While the Women Only Wept*, 148–51

102 *Kingston Chronicle*, 5 March 1819

103 *Niagara Gleaner*, 4 July 1835

104 *Kingston Chronicle*, 11 July 1823

105 David Thompson, *A History of the Late War*, vi

106 Ibid., 102 For a much less reverential examination of the war, especially with regard to the British, see Dunlop, *Recollections of the War of 1812*.

107 Robert Gourlay, *Statistical Account of Upper Canada*, 1:571–2

108 Ibid., 579–80

109 Ibid., 576. For a discussion of the effects of the war on Gourlay's supporters, see Sheppard, *Plunder, Profit, and Paroles*, 196.

110 Mills, *Idea of Loyalty*, particularly chaps. 5–7

111 For civic humanism and republicanism, see J.G.A. Pocock, *The Machiavellian Moment*.

112 A glance at the biographical sketches in Johnson's *Becoming Prominent* shows that various well-known reformers had records of militia service: John Rolph (223), Charles Duncombe (188), and William Warren and Robert Baldwin (171–2).

113 For an analysis of militia service in Upper Canada, see ibid., 68–79.

114 Potter-MacKinnon, *While the Women Only Wept*, 137–46

115 See McKenna, 'The Role of Women,' for a study of élite women's exercise of social power and their indirect political influence.

2: Ranting Renegades and Corseted Sycophants

1 For some of the central arguments concerning the meanings of British law and justice in this colonial context, see Paul Romney, 'From the Types Riot to the Rebellion'; also his 'Very Late Loyalist Fantasies.' See also Blaine Baker, 'The Juvenile Advocate Society,' and '"So Elegant a Web."'

2 Mangan and Walvin, eds., *Manliness and Morality*; Carnes and Griffen, eds., *Meanings for Manhood*; Michael Roper and John Tosh, eds., *Manful Assertions*

3 This literature is voluminous. See Kerber, *Women of the Republic*; Bloch, 'Gendered Meanings of Virtue'; Paula Baker, 'The Domestication of Politics.' For France, see Jane Abray, 'Feminism in the French Revolution,' *American Historical Review* 80, no. 1 (Feb. 1975): 43–62; Outram, 'Le langage mâle de la vertu'; Landes, *Women and the Public Sphere*; Reynolds, 'Marianne's Citizens?' For Britain, see Dorothy Thompson, 'Women and Nineteenth-Century Radical Politics'; Barbara Taylor, *Eve and the New Jerusalem*; Anna Clarke, 'The Rhetoric of Chartist Domesticity.'

4 For an analysis of public male power in the nineteenth century, see Michael Grossberg, 'Institutionalizing Masculinity: The Law as a Masculine Profession,' in Carnes and Griffen, eds., *Meanings for Manhood*, 133–51, and, for a more theoretical examination, Jeff Hearn, *Men in the Public Eye*. Recent historical work has begun to address this issue; see, for example, Michael D. Pierson, '"Guard the Foundation Well": Antebellum New York Democrats and the Defense of Patriarchy,' *Gender and History* 7, no. 1 (April 1995): 25–40.

5 Scott, *Gender and the Politics of History*, 39

6 For Collins, see H.P. Gundy's entry in the *DCB* (1987), 6:164–6.

7 S.F. Wise, 'Tory Factionalism: Kingston Elections and Upper Canadian Politics, 1820–1836,' and 'Upper Canada and the Conservative Tradition,' both in McKillop and Romney, eds., *God's Peculiar Peoples*

8 'Court' and 'country' rhetoric will be discussed more fully on p. 77. For Romney's arguments about these categories, see 'From the Rule of Law to Responsible Government,' 92–4.

9 Carroll Smith-Rosenberg, 'Dis-Covering the Subject of the "Great Constitutional Discussion,"' 845

10 For Robert Gourlay, see the entry by S.F. Wise, *DCB* (1976), 9:330–6; also Lois Darroch Milani, *Robert Gourlay, Gadfly*.

11 Barry Wright, 'Sedition in Upper Canada,' 29

12 *Upper Canada Gazette*, 4 Feb. 1819

13 Ibid., 21 Jan. 1819

14 Ibid.

15 *Kingston Chronicle*, 29 Jan. 1819
16 *Upper Canada Gazette*, 11 March 1819
17 Ibid., 21 Jan. 1819. Such dialogues between two or more characters were a favoured form of political exposition in the press.
18 *Niagara Spectator*, 29 July 1819. Presumably Stuart meant the 1804 provincial Sedition Act, which allowed the government to arrest and imprison anyone whose speech and activities were perceived as creating disaffection and who had been in the colony for less than six months and had not taken the oath of allegiance. Those arrested under the act had to prove their own innocence (Craig, *Upper Canada*, 98). For a discussion of sedition trials in Upper Canada, see Wright, 'Sedition in Upper Canada.'
19 *Niagara Gleaner*, 5 Aug. 1819
20 *Kingston Chronicle*, 29 Jan. 1819
21 *Niagara Spectator*, 29 July 1819
22 On the image of John Bull, see Jeanine Surel, 'John Bull,' in Raphael Samuel, ed., *Patriotism*, vol. 3. For a different interpretation of John Bull, see Miles Taylor, 'John Bull and the Iconography of Public Opinion in England, c. 1712–1929,' *Past and Present* 134 (Feb. 1992): 93–128.
23 *Upper Canada Gazette*, 20 July 1820
24 Gerald Bloch, 'Robert Gourlay's Vision of Radical Agrarian Reform'
25 Gourlay to Thomas Clark, *Kingston Gazette*, 31 March 1818
26 Gourlay to 'The Traveller,' ibid., 21 Aug. 1818
27 Gourlay's address to Niagara residents, reprinted ibid., 19 May 1818
28 Gourlay, open letter to the public, ibid., 12 May 1818
29 Ibid.
30 Ibid.; Gourlay's address to Niagara residents, reprinted ibid., 19 May 1818
31 For an analysis of masculinity that explores the concept as a negative identity that defines itself against emotionality and connectedness, see Victor Seidler, *Rediscovering Masculinity*, 7. Ruth Salvaggio, in *Enlightened Absence*, argues that Enlightenment thought consistently represented the 'other' as feminine.
32 Gourlay, *Kingston Gazette*, 3 March 1818; Gourlay to 'The Traveller,' ibid., 22 Aug. 1818; Gourlay, ibid., 12 May 1818; Gourlay, letter to the editor, *Niagara Spectator*, 8 July 1818; also the Petition to the Crown from the inhabitants of Upper Canada, reprinted in the *Kingston Gazette*, 2 June 1818
33 Gourlay, letter to editor, *Niagara Spectator*, 8 July 1818
34 Ibid.
35 Gourlay, *Kingston Gazette*, 12 May 1818
36 'Publicola,' ibid., 30 June 1818
37 Gourlay, ibid., 12 May 1818
38 Gail C. Campbell, 'Disfranchised but not Quiescent'

39 *Kingston Gazette*, 19 May 1818. See Potter-MacKinnon, *While the Women Only Wept*, 103–9, 148–52, for discussions of Loyalist women's use of the language of female helplessness in their petitions.

40 'Front Page Exchange,' *Weekly Register and Upper Canada Gazette*, 25 Jan. 1823

41 See Olivia Smith, *The Politics of Language*, 20, for a discussion of the hegemonic effects of Johnson's *Dictionary*.

42 'Front Page Exchange'

43 See also the letters between the 'Post Boy' and 'Mrs Eliza Freebottom' in the *Niagara Spectator*, 11 and 18 June 1818, and 'Always Something New' in the *Niagara Gleaner*, 31 Aug. 1833. Salvaggio, in *Enlightened Absence*, examines the ways in which 'woman' personified hysteria and excess in the works of writers such as Swift; see also Poovey, *Uneven Developments*, chap. 2, for nineteenth-century medical equations of women with instability.

44 *Weekly Register and Upper Canada Gazette*, 24 Feb. 1825

45 Ibid., 7 July 1827

46 *Kingston Chronicle*, 31 Jan. 1829

47 *Niagara Gleaner*, 6 Nov. 1824. For a biographical sketch of William Lyon Mackenzie, the Scottish printer, reform advocate, member of the Legislative Assembly, and mayor of Toronto, see the entry by Frederick H. Armstrong and Ronald J. Stagg, in the *DCB* (1976), 9:496–510.

48 *Patriot and Farmers' Monitor*, 31 May 1833. The paper was also fond of identifying reformers as the faction of the 'knife, firebrand, and bludgeon.'

49 Collins may also have been referring to the tradition of eighteenth-century aristocratic whiggism as well to the Whigs of British parliamentary reform in the early 1830s. For the eighteenth century, see J.G.A. Pocock, 'The Varieties of Whiggism' in *Virtue, Commerce, and History*.

50 *Canadian Freeman*, 23 Jan. 1832

51 Ibid., 17 May 1832. The 'gingerbread medal' was a gold medal, worth $250, that had been given to Mackenzie by his York constituents after his re-election to the assembly in January 1832. He had stood in this by-election after being expelled from the assembly by the tory majority. Calling it a 'gingerbread medal' devalued the tribute and made it seem childish and ephemeral.

52 Ibid., 29 Nov. 1832. James Small, a moderate reformer, stood against Mackenzie in this election. See the entry by Frederick H. Armstrong *DCB* (1976), 9:724–5.

53 *Canadian Freeman*, 29 Aug. 1833. For a study of Joanna Southcott and her religious movement, see James K. Hopkins, *A Woman to Deliver Her People*.

54 Mackenzie's son James was born in 1814 in Alyth, Scotland. He was cared for by his grandmother, Elizabeth Mackenzie. In 1822 James and Elizabeth emi-

grated to Upper Canada to join Mackenzie, and James worked as an apprentice in his father's printing shop (Colin Read and Ronald J. Stagg, eds., *The Rebellion of 1837 in Upper Canada*, 497). While the circumstances of James's birth were not seized upon by his father's enemies, Mackenzie was accused of beating and abusing his son in order to upset Elizabeth (*Canadian Freeman*, 7 Oct. 1830). For the eighteenth-century radical John Wilkes, see John Brewer, *Party Ideology and Popular Politics at the Accession of George III* (Cambridge: Cambridge University Press, 1976).

55 *Niagara Gleaner*, 10 Nov. 1832
56 *Patriot and Farmers' Monitor*, 12 and 23 Sept. 1834
57 Ibid., 23 Jan. 1835
58 'The New Bow Wow,' by 'A Double-Nosed Setter,' *Colonial Advocate*, 22 March 1832
59 *United Empire Loyalist and Upper Canada Gazette*, 26 May 1827
60 *Kingston Chronicle*, 1 Feb. 1822
61 This letter was reprinted in the *Patriot and Farmers' Monitor*, 14 June 1833
62 *Weekly Register and Upper Canada Gazette*, 18 Nov. 1824, 24 Feb. 1825
63 *Patriot and Farmers' Monitor*, 17 May 1833
64 These occasions were covered more extensively in the late 1830s and 1840s by the Upper Canadian press, a development that will be discussed more extensively in chapter 4. It is possible, however, that the *Patriot* was also satirizing temperance societies, of which it strongly disapproved, whose meetings received widespread coverage in other papers at that time.
65 Samuel P. Jarvis, *Statement of Facts*, 9. The Types Riot is discussed more fully in Chris Raible's *Muddy York Mud: Scandal and Scurrility in Upper Canada* (Creemore, ON: Curiosity House, 1992). Mackenzie's 'Patrick Swift' columns, coupled with his accusation that Jarvis had murdered John Ridout in an 1817 duel, angered Jarvis. Accompanied by a number of his peers (including Charles and Raymond Baby and Henry Sherwood), Jarvis wrecked the *Advocate*'s office and threw the type cases into Toronto harbour.
66 Raible, *Muddy York Mud*, 14
67 Caroline Robbins, *The Eighteenth-Century Commonwealthman*; H.T. Dickinson, *Liberty and Property*; Pocock, *Machiavellian Moment*, also his 'The Varieties of Whiggism.'
68 This description of 'country' rhetoric is necessarily reductionist. For a more complex and nuanced analysis, see Pocock, 'Varieties of Whiggism.'
69 'When Bad Men Conspire and Good Men Must Unite,' *Colonial Advocate*, 7 May 1829
70 'The Editor's Address to the Public,' ibid., 18 May 1824
71 Collins's attacks on Mackenzie, Egerton Ryerson, and Jesse Ketchum were an

exception, although Collins's position vis-à-vis other reformers was an ambivalent one.

72 Graeme Patterson, 'Studies in Elections,' 429
73 *Colonial Advocate*, 29 Dec. 1825
74 'To the Electors of Members of Assembly,' ibid., 18 May 1824
75 Ibid., 8 Nov. 1832
76 Ibid.; also, in the same paper, letter from 'A Friend to Liberty,' 3 Jan. 1833; 'To the Electors of Upper Canada,' 8 July 1824; 'Appeal to the People of Upper Canada,' 9 Sept. 1830; 'To the Mechanics and Labourers of Toronto,' 20 March 1834. Report of York Constitutional Meeting, *Canadian Freeman*, 21 Aug. 1828; 'Another Triumph for the People,' ibid., 25 Sept. 1828
77 'A Friend to Liberty,' *Colonial Advocate*, 3 Jan. 1833
78 'Address of the Markham Township Meeting to William Lyon Mackenzie,' ibid., 6 Feb. 1834
79 'To the Electors of Members of Assembly,' ibid., 18 May 1824. Reynolds 'Marianne's Citizens?' (110), Outram, 'Le langage mâle' (125), and Landes, *Women of the Public Sphere* (147) all point to French republicans' equation of *ancien régime* absolutism with effeminacy and women's power in government.
80 Mackenzie, letter to John Beverley Robinson, *Colonial Advocate*, 3 June 1824; 'On the State of the Colony,' ibid., 10 Jan. 1828; Resolutions of Yarmouth public meetings, ibid., 3 April 1834; Editorial, ibid., 9 Aug. 1834; Editorial, ibid., 24 Sept. 1835; Appendix F, 'Independence!' in Colin Lindsey, *The Life and Times of William Lyon Mackenzie*, 2:358–62
81 'Address to Independent Electors of County of York,' *Colonial Advocate*, 8 Nov. 1832
82 Editorial, ibid., 18 July 1833
83 'Address of the Markham Township Meeting,' ibid., 6 Feb. 1834
84 Robert Davis, *The Canadian Farmer's Travels*, 10, 95
85 'Address of the Markham Township Meeting,' *Colonial Advocate*, 6 Feb. 1834; Resolutions of the Yarmouth, Whitby, Bertie, and Ancaster public meetings, ibid., 3 April 1834
86 See Iain McCalman, *Radical Underworld*, 141–7, for the use of 'priest' as an insult in radical circles. It was also used by the conservative press in Upper Canada, but with different connotations.
87 *The Constitution*, 22 Feb. 1837
88 'Persecution!' *Colonial Advocate*, 20 Dec. 1837
89 *The Constitution*, 2 Aug. 1836
90 Ibid., 12 July 1837
91 McCalman, *Radical Underworld*, 205–11
92 *Colonial Advocate*, 3 Nov. 1831

93 Ibid., 6 Sept. 1834
94 Ibid., 3 Nov. 1831
95 Ibid., 18 May 1826
96 Ibid., also 25 May 1826
97 Ibid., 4 July 1836
98 For discussions of women, the family, and the French and American Revolutions, see Landes, *Women and the Public Sphere*, 147–8; Kerber, *Women of the
   Republic*, 269–88; and Bloch, 'Gendered Meanings,' 46–7.
99 'To the Electors of Members of Assembly,' *Colonial Advocate*, 18 May
   1824
100 'Dr. Charles Duncombe's Report on the Subject of Education Made to the
    Parliament of Upper Canada, February 25, 1836,' *Journals of the Legislative
    Assembly*, 12th Parliament, 2nd Session
101 Carol Pateman, *The Sexual Contract*, 70
102 'The Declaration of the Reformers of the City of Toronto to their Fellow
    Reformers in Upper Canada,' 2 Aug. 1837, reprinted in Lindsey, *Life and
    Times of William Lyon Mackenzie*, 344
103 Baker, 'Domestication of Politics,' 624–5; Kerber, *Women of the Republic*, 37–
    41; Bloch, 'Gendered Meanings,' 45–6
104 Dorothy Thompson, 'The Women,' in her *The Chartists*
105 Lynn Hunt, *Politics, Culture, and Class*, 12
106 We lack a truly comprehensive analysis of reformers' political philosophies,
    but see Romney, 'From the Rule of Law to Responsible Government.' For
    their involvement in voluntarism, see Sean T. Cadigan, 'Paternalism and Poli-
    tics.'
107 'A Friend to Liberty,' *Colonial Advocate*, 3 Jan. 1833
108 Addresses of Markham, Yarmouth, Whitby, Bertie, and Ancaster public meet-
    ings, ibid., 3 April 1833
109 Ibid., 3 Jan. 1833
110 In fact, I would argue that they had more in common with Chartism as seen by
    Gareth Stedman Jones, 'Rethinking Chartism,' in his *Languages of Class*, than
    with Sean Wilentz's republican artisans of New York City (*Chants Demo-
    cratic: New York City and the Rise of the American Working Class, 1788–1850*
    [New York: Oxford University Press, 1984]).
111 See David Mills, 'The Controversy over Legitimate Opposition: Reform Loy-
    alty before the Rebellion,' in his *Idea of Loyalty*.
112 For discussions of this shift, see ibid., 103–8; R.A. MacKay, 'The Political Ideas
    of William Lyon Mackenzie;' J.E. Rea, 'William Lyon Mackenzie.' Generally,
    Pocock's observation (in 'Varieties of Whiggism,' 275, 308–9) that British radi-
    calism's republican rhetoric was 'amputated' by the American Revolution, and

that its central tenet became that of democracy instead, could, I would argue, be applied to much of Upper Canadian reform.

113 Mills, 'Controversy over Legitimate Opposition,' 7–8

114 Edward Said, *Orientalism*, 3. For an analysis that examines the cultural, racial, and gender dimensions of Western use of 'the East' in language and art during the nineteenth century, see Joanna de Groot, '"Sex" and "Race."'

115 'Report of Meeting for Gore District Inhabitants,' *Colonial Advocate*, 28 March 1832

116 Said, *Orientalism*, 12

117 Addresses of Markham, Yarmouth, Whitby, Bertie, and Ancaster public meetings, *Colonial Advocate*, 3 April 1833

118 Ibid., 5 Feb. 1835. For the 'Norman Yoke,' see Christopher Hill, *Puritanism and Revolution* (London: Panther, 1968), 58–125.

119 'The Declaration of the Reformers of the City of Toronto,' 2 Aug. 1837, reprinted in Lindsey, *Life and Times of William Lyon Mackenzie*, 334–44

120 *The Constitution*, 11 Oct. 1837

121 *Mackenzie's Gazette*, 17 April 1838

122 *Colonial Advocate*, 22 Feb. 1834

123 For example, see ibid., 19 Feb. 1835; *The Constitution*, 21 May 1837.

124 See Allan Greer, 'La république des hommes'; also '"The Queen Is a Whore!"' in his *The Patriots and the People*. See also Greer's historiographically oriented discussion, '1837–8: Rebellion Reconsidered.'

125 St Thomas *Liberal*, as quoted in *The Constitution*, 30 Aug. 1837

126 *The Constitution*, 22 Nov. 1837

127 *Mackenzie's Gazette*, 17 April 1838

128 Ibid., 12 May 1838

129 Ibid., 4 Aug. 1838

130 Ibid.

131 Ibid.

132 Ibid., 12 May 1838

133 Ibid., 19 Sept. 1838

134 Ibid., 23 June 1838

135 Ibid., 26 May 1838; 1 Sept. 1838; 10 Nov. 1838

136 'To the Men of the Home District,' *Patriot and Farmers' Monitor*, 10 Nov. 1838

137 Ibid., 8 Dec. 1837

138 A clear example of this argument may be found in Craig, *Upper Canada*, 249.

139 Samuel Thompson, *Reminiscences of a Canadian Pioneer*, 118. Joseph Hilts, in his *Experiences of a Backwoods Preacher*, 22, recalled a similar experience,

although interestingly it was his father and older family members who talked him out of his support for the rebellion.

140 See Barbara Corrado Pope, 'Revolution and Retreat, 215–36, for an examination of the conservative use of home, religion, and family in this period.

141 *Kingston Chronicle and Gazette*, 23 Feb. 1839

142 Ibid., 9 March 1839

143 See Jon P. Klancher, *The Making of English Reading Audiences*, 77, for a discussion of the multiple meanings of signs in the popular press, especially the notion of the 'the crowd.'

144 Mary Gapper O'Brien, *Journals*, 32–3, 40–1, 52, 126–8, 268–74.

145 Amelia Harris's letters are reprinted in Read and Stagg, eds., *The Rebellion of 1837 in Upper Canada*, 323.

146 Benjamin Wait and Maria Wait, *Letters from Van Dieman's Land*, 289–90

147 Ibid., 300–8, 319

148 Ibid., 313–15

149 This point is argued most forcefully by Dorothy Thompson in her analysis of the decline in upper-class women's political influence in the early to mid-nineteenth century ('Women, Work, and Politics in Nineteenth-Century England').

3: Familial Celebrations

1 Other sources, both published and manuscript, were consulted, such as the *Canada Christian Advocate, Evangelist, Christian Messenger, Christian Recorder, Christian Sentinel and Anglo-Canadian Churchmen's Magazine*, as well as a number of journals, letters, and missionary records (see bibliography). However, the *Christian Guardian* provides the most consistent coverage from 1829 onwards; the other Methodist publications did not start until the 1840s. Furthermore, although we know very little about Methodism's role at a more popular level, there is a relatively extensive body of secondary literature on the Methodists (much of which will be referred to below) to provide context.

2 See Grant, *Profusion of Spires*, 45–72, for a discussion of the spread of Methodism in Upper Canada and the effects of the War of 1812 on the church.

3 A number of reasons might explain this distinction, particularly the fact that the Baptist Church structure was less centralized and therefore may have been less of a target compared to that of the Methodists. Baptists were also concentrated in the southwestern section of the province and, after the War of 1812, apparently had far less contact with the Baptist Church in the United States; there were also fewer Baptists than Methodists in the colony. Unlike Methodists, they could perform marriages, a right that Methodist ministers did not

secure until 1831 after eight attempts were made in the legislature from 1802 on (ibid., 31, 44–5, 58, 88, 224). In contrast, in the Maritimes, Baptists overtook the Methodists numerically and were more influential; George Rawlyk has argued that this occurred because Maritime Methodists rejected the legacy of their First Great Awakening and the radicalism associated with it (*Canada Fire*, 19–20).

4 For discussions of the development of Methodism's 'respectable' status, see Westfall, *Two Worlds*, 45; also Neil Semple, 'The Quest for the Kingdom.' It could, of course, be argued that Wesleyan Methodism, particularly from the early 1830s on, played a critical role in this process as it attempted to sever Methodist connections to reform and radicalism. For a study of the Baptist Church's suppression of female equality as it attempted to enter mainstream American society, see Susan Juster, *Disorderly Women*.

5 Grant, in *A Profusion of Spires*, 109–10, suggests that the Methodists were particularly effective in bringing about both Christianization and acculturation, although see Carol Devens, *Countering Colonization*, 47–55, 60–6, for a more sceptical assessment.

6 Grant, *A Profusion of Spires*, 103. The first religious periodical in the colony was Strachan's *Christian Recorder*. The transmission of evangelical beliefs and thought in Upper Canada through media such as the press has not received much attention from historians, but it seems that very few other denominations published as consistently and as many different papers as did Methodists (partly because of the different kinds of Methodist churches that were formed during this period). The *Christian Guardian*, as well as being long-lived, published a wider spectrum of secular news than many of the other Methodist papers I have examined. A study similar to that of Susan O'Brien's work on the significance of publishing in eighteenth-century evangelicalism would be helpful (see her 'Eighteenth-Century Publishing Networks in the First Years of Transatlantic Evangelicalism,' in Mark A. Noll, David W. Bebbington, and George A. Rawlyk, eds., *Evangelicalism: Comparative Studies of Popular Protestantism in North America, The British Isles, and Beyond, 1700–1990* [Oxford: Oxford University Press, 1994], 38–57).

7 See, for example, Davidoff and Hall, *Family Fortunes*, especially pt. 1 and chap. 10.

8 Noel, *Canada Dry*, 104. I do not want to suggest that the study of religion be conducted on a narrow denominational basis (a strategy that would only continue the '"unacknowledged quarantine"' from which Canadian religious history is beginning to be lifted), merely to stress the logistical and intellectual reasons for this study's focus on Methodism. See Ruth Compton Brouwer, 'Transcending the "Unacknowledged Quarantine": Putting Religion into English-Canadian Women's History,' *Journal of Canadian Studies/Revue d'études canadiennes* 27, no. 3 (Fall 1992): 47–61.

9 See, for example, French, *Parsons and Politics.*

10 Grant, *Profusion of Spires*, 94–100

11 Rawlyk, *Canada Fire*, 138

12 Nancy J. Christie, '"In These Times of Democratic Rage and Delusion,"' 19

13 Ibid., 42–3

14 Ibid.; also Curtis Fahey points to this belief (*In His Name*, 14–15, 27, 89–90).

15 *Upper Canada Gazette*, 23 May 1793

16 *Kingston Gazette*, 19 May 1812

17 Although the presence of Jesse Ketchum, the well-known Upper Canadian tanner, philanthropist, and supporter of reform, on a board made up of the colony's élite may be surprising, it is worth remembering that Ketchum attended the Anglican Church when it was the only one in York. In the words of his biographer, he was 'no narrow sectarian' and was involved in a variety of voluntary groups and projects (see the entry by Lilian F. Gates in the *DCB* [1976], 9:422–4).

18 *Kingston Gazette*, 11 Jan. 1817. For a discussion of the British and Foreign Bible Society in British North America, see Judith Fingard, '"Grapes in the Wilderness"'; Fahey, *In His Name*, 26–7.

19 *Kingston Chronicle*, 15 Dec. 1826

20 Ibid., 2 May 1829

21 Ibid., 28 May 1831

22 Ibid.

23 Ibid., 11 June 1831. Their exchange went on through June and most of July; by 6 August 1831, 'One of the People' had turned to Presbyterian doctrine, though with considerably less vehemence.

24 *United Empire Loyalist and Upper Canada Gazette*, 27 Jan. 1827. For an illuminating study of the Reverend Thaddeus Osgood's career as an evangelical worker, see W.P.J. Millar's 'The Remarkable Rev. Thaddeus Osgood.'

25 Thomas Dalton (1782–1840), an English businessman who came to Upper Canada in 1817, founded the *Patriot* in 1829 in Kingston, moving himself and the paper to York in 1832. At first a weekly, the paper became a semi-weekly in 1833 and grew to become 'the most influential conservative newspaper in the province.' Although Dalton had been a supporter of Gourlay, a political acquaintance of Mackenzie, and a friend of the Bidwells, he became increasingly conservative after a stint in the legislature. This shift was expressed most clearly in his editorials and his attacks on both American Methodists and Lower Canadians (see the entry by Ian R. Dalton in the *DCB* [1988], 7:223–31).

26 *Patriot and Farmers' Monitor*, 7 Feb. and 13 March 1832

27 Ibid., 17 Jan. 1832

28 Ibid., 6 Sept. 1833

29 Ibid.

30 Ibid., 20 May 1832

31 Ibid., 6 May 1832

32 Ibid., 31 Jan. 1834

33 For a brief discussion of the conceptions of unleashed female sexuality in seventeenth- and eighteenth-century religious thought, see Davidoff and Hall, *Family Fortunes*, 170.

34 *Patriot and Farmers' Monitor*, 10 April 1832

35 Ibid.

36 Ibid.

37 Ibid., 27 Feb. 1832. For a biographical study of Joanna Southcott, the leader of a millenarian sect in late-eighteenth- and early-nineteenth-century England, see Hopkins, *A Woman to Deliver Her People*.

38 *Patriot and Farmers' Monitor*, 10 April 1832

39 Ibid., 25 Jan. 1833; 1 Nov. 1833; 8 Nov. 1833

40 Ibid., 1 May 1832

41 David Mills makes considerable use of the *Patriot and Farmers' Monitor* in his discussion of 'moderate Toryism' of the 1830s (*Idea of Loyalty*, chap. 5). See also Craig, *Upper Canada*, 217, who argues that in its opposition to England's disallowance of the colony's banking legislation in 1834, the paper spoke for both the 'business community in the capital and, as it turned out, for nearly everyone in the province as well.'

42 *Christian Guardian*, 29 Feb. 1832

43 Ibid., 15 May 1833

44 Ibid., 12 June 1833

45 On Egerton Ryerson's political and social striving for respectability, especially with regard to the reform movement, see Mills, *Idea of Loyalty*, chap. 4; also Westfall, *Two Worlds*, 68–78.

46 *Christian Guardian*, 25 Jan. 1832

47 Elizabeth Gillian Muir, *Petticoats in the Pulpit*, 122–8

48 Davidoff and Hall, *Family Fortunes*, 108–18, 130–48

49 Valenze, *Prophetic Sons and Daughters*, especially chap. 3, 'The Call for Cottage Religion and Female Preaching.' There is a large and growing body of work on women, gender, and evangelicalism in the United States. See, for example, Mary P. Ryan's *Cradle of the Middle Class*, also her *Empire of the Mother*; Cott, *Bonds of Womanhood*; Barbara Leslie Epstein, *The Politics of Domesticity*; Hewitt, *Women's Activism and Social Change*; Juster, 'Patriarchy Reborn.'

50 Some of the more recent work in English Canada has focused on women and missionary work. See, for example, Ruth Compton Brouwer, *New Women for God: Canadian Presbyterian Women and India Missions, 1876–1914* (Toronto:

University of Toronto Press, 1990); also Katherine Ridout, 'A Woman of Mission: The Religious and Cultural Odyssey of Agnes Wintemute Coates,' *Canadian Historical Review* 71, no. 2 (June 1990): 208–44. Although we still know much less about the meaning of religion for working-class women, see Lynne Marks, 'Working-Class Femininity and the Salvation Army: "Hallelujah Lasses" in English Canada, 1882–1892,' in Veronica Strong-Boag and Anita Clair Fellman, eds., *Rethinking Canada: The Promise of Women's History*, 2nd ed. (Toronto: Copp Clark Pitman, 1991).

51 Marguerite Van Die, *An Evangelical Mind*, 25
52 George A. Rawlyk, *Ravished by the Spirit*, 119–32
53 Grant, *Profusion of Spires*, 45; Rawlyk, *Canada Fire*, 102
54 Westfall, *Two Worlds*, 54
55 Rhys Isaac, *The Transformation of Virginia*, 263–5
56 Ibid., 263–4; Grant, *A Profusion of Spires*, 59
57 George F. Playter, *The History of Methodism in Canada*, 25 Roblin was expelled from the House in 1810 because of his position as a Methodist preacher (Johnson, *Becoming Prominent*, 128).
58 Playter, *History of Methodism*, 160
59 For an interpretation that portrays early settlers as self-interested, 'atomistic' individuals, see Akenson, *Irish in Ontario*, especially chap. 2, 'Leeds and Lansdowne Township in the Loyalist Era, 1787–1816.'
60 Valenze, *Prophetic Sons and Daughters*, chaps 3 and 4
61 Anson Green, *The Life and Times of the Reverend Anson Green*, 49–50
62 See Davidoff and Hall, *Family Fortunes*, 108–10, on the importance of family religion to evangelicals, especially in 'doctrines of manliness'; see also Michael Gauvreau, *The Evangelical Century*, 45–8, on the lack of an *elaborate* body of doctrine in early Methodism in British North America.
63 Rawlyk, *Canada Fire*, 109
64 Nathan Bangs as quoted in John Carroll, *Past and Present*, 21
65 Carroll, *Case and His Contemporaries*, 40
66 Ibid., 39
67 Douglas, *Feminization of American Culture*, 42
68 Carroll, *Past and Present*, 215
69 For a discussion of the split led by Ryan that resulted in the formation in 1828 of the independent Canadian Methodist Episcopal Church, with William Case as its superintendent, see Grant, *Profusion of Spires*, 75.
70 Carroll, *Past and Present*, 51–4
71 Such was the fate of the Reverend John Dempster, whose health was a constant problem (Carroll, *Case*, 3:57; 4:292–3). However, the Upper Canadian Methodists appear to have had little time for the 'sickliness' attributed by Douglas to the

Congregational and Unitarian clergy of her study; certainly robust physicality was much admired in religious discourse (Douglas, *Feminization of American Culture*, 88–9).

72 For a study of the changing nature of the ministry in New England, see Donald M. Scott, *From Office to Profession*; for dissenting ministers in England during this period, see Davidoff and Hall, *Family Fortunes*, 118–23.

73 See, for example, the letters and reports of the Anglican minister Adam Elliott in *The Stewart Missions*, ed. William Waddilove; extracts from Reverend Charles Taylor Wade's journal, printed in *The Church* from 1837 to 1838; and letters from Reverend G.C. Street, *The Church*, 19 Oct. 1839, 1 Feb. 1840.

74 Carroll, *Case*, 3:57

75 For a discussion of the 'Bushman,' the archetype of frontier masculinity in Australia, see Marilyn Lake, 'The Politics of Respectability'; for America, see Carroll Smith-Rosenberg, 'Davy Crockett as Trickster: Pornography, Liminality, and Symbolic Inversion in Victorian America,' in her *Disorderly Conduct*, 90–108.

76 Carroll, *Case*, 3:295

77 See Donald Yacovone, 'Abolitionists and the "Language of Fraternal Love,"' in Carnes and Griffen, eds., *Meanings for Manhood*, 85–95, for a discussion of male friendships, particularly in the Garrisonian wing of the abolition movement.

78 Gauvreau, 'Protestantism Transformed,' 51–2

79 See ibid., 48–50, for a discussion of this belief. It is most forcefully stated by E.P. Thompson, who argues that 'Methodism is permeated with teaching as to the sinfulness of sexuality' (*The Making of the English Working Class*, 407) and goes on to state that 'joy was associated with sin and guilt' (409). In *Greenbank*, W.H. Graham depicts Methodism as forbidding all aesthetic pleasure (72).

80 Carroll, *Past and Present*, 100

81 Carroll, *Case*, 2:341

82 Ibid., 3:239

83 Playter, *History of Methodism*, 55

84 Although Westfall, in *Two Worlds*, 80, argues that, by the mid-nineteenth century, the 'old revivalist had become an evangelical romantic,' and that Carroll's work can be viewed as an indication of this trend, the works consulted here indicate earlier developments. Tinges of romanticism also may be seen in some literature on parenting and especially motherhood. For romantic influences in English literature on domesticity, see Davidoff and Hall, *Family Fortunes*, 157–61, 189, 191–2.

85 Carroll, *Case*, 2:341

86 For tributes to women who offered hospitality to preachers, see Carroll, *Past and Present*, 47, and Playter, *History of Methodism*, 53–4. The phrase 'mother in Israel' was used most often in obituaries as a way of commending those who 'showed exemplary courage and devotion to the cause.' Women who provided either spiritual nurturance or hospitality and aid in mission areas might have this title bestowed on them (Valenze, *Prophetic Sons and Daughters*, 35–6).

87 See Brouwer, *New Women for God*, 112, 173, on the importance of missionary wives.

88 Muir, *Petticoats in the Pulpit*, 128. Muir argues that women teachers working at missions such as Grape Island or at the Grand River received approximately 75 per cent of a man's salary: £29 5s. per annum for a non-Native woman as compared with £37 10s. to £40 for a non-Native man (127).

89 Carroll, *Case*, 2:98

90 Ibid., 181

91 Ibid., 140

92 Muir, *Petticoats in the Pulpit*, 128. Quaker women preachers, who travelled to Canada from communities in the United States and England, might leave husbands and children at home and travel in mixed company. See Leslie Gray, ed., 'Phoebe Roberts' Diary of a Quaker Missionary Journey to Upper Canada,' *Ontario History* 42, no. 1 (Jan. 1950): 7–46.

93 Carroll, *Past and Present*, 114

94 Ibid., 235

95 Carroll, *Case*, 4:174–5 and 226–7

96 Rose Family Correspondence, Samuel Rose letters, 1831–39, Samuel Rose to John Rose, 26 April 1831

97 Ibid., 24 Nov. 1831

98 Ibid., Samuel Rose to his father, 24 Nov. 1831

99 Ibid., Samuel Rose to John Rose, 26 April 1831; 20 Nov. 1832; 20 Sept. 1839

100 Scott, 'The Crisis of the Pastoral Clergy,' chap. 7 in *From Office to Profession*

101 Seidler, *Rediscovering Masculinity*, 7; Rotundo, 'Manhood in America,' 135–6

102 Carroll, *My Boy Life*

103 Ibid., 82

104 Ibid., 229, 238–80

105 Hilts, *Experiences of a Backwoods Preacher*, 23–6

106 For a discussion of youthful nineteenth-century male culture, see E. Anthony Rotundo, 'Boy Culture: Middle-Class Boyhood in Nineteenth-Century America,' in *Meanings for Manhood*, 15–36.

107 Gauvreau, *Evangelical Century*, 6

108 Ibid., 45

109 Ibid., 45–56

110 Westfall, *Two Worlds*, 46–7, 64

111 For women and religious associations, see, for example, Ryan, 'The Era of Association: Between Family and Society, 1825–1845,' chap. 3 in *Cradle of the Middle Class*; Davidoff and Hall, *Family Fortunes*, 419–36; Hewitt, *Women's Activism*; Lori D. Ginzberg, *Women and the Work of Benevolence*. For Canada, somewhat later in the century, see Wendy Mitchinson, 'Canadian Women and Church Missionary Societies: A Step Towards Independence,' *Atlantis* 2 (Spring 1977): 57–75.

112 For example, see the *Christian Guardian*, 5 Dec. 1829; 20 April 1836.

113 Ibid.

114 Ibid., 11 Jan. 1837; see also 'Female Piety,' *Canada Christian Advocate*, 8 May 1845.

115 *Christian Guardian*, 28 April 1841; also 'For What Is a Mother Responsible?' *Canada Christian Advocate*, 4 Sept. 1845

116 *Christian Guardian*, 8 April 1835

117 Ryan, *Empire of the Mother*, 17–18

118 Ibid., chap. 4

119 *Christian Guardian*, 29 Feb. 1832; Letter to the Editor, James Jackson, Hamilton, *Christian Messenger*, 2 Dec. 1844

120 *Christian Guardian*, 1 Nov. 1837; 'Family Prayer,' *Canada Christian Advocate*, 8 June 1847; 'To Young Married People,' *Canada Christian Advocate*, 18 Dec. 1845

121 *Christian Guardian*, 26 Dec. 1829; 16 Jan. 1830

122 Ibid., 23 Jan. 1833

123 'To Young Married People,' *Canada Christian Advocate*, 18 Dec. 1845

124 *Christian Guardian*, 19 March 1834

125 Ibid., 23 Oct. 1830

126 *Canada Christian Advocate*, 19 May 1846

127 Ibid., 13 Nov. 1849

128 For a discussion of landladies and lodging, see Leonore Davidoff, 'The Separation of Home and Work? Landladies and Lodgers in Nineteenth- and Twentieth-Century England,' in Sandra Burman, ed., *Fit Work for Women* (New York: St Martin's Press, 1979).

129 *Canada Christian Advocate*, 23 Jan. 1845

130 Ibid., 20 Nov. 1845

131 *Christian Messenger*, 1 Nov. 1844

132 *Canada Christian Advocate*, 19 May 1846

133 *Church*, 17 July 1841

134 Ibid., 6 Jan. 1838

135 Westfall, 'Order and Experience: The Religious and Cultural Roots of Protestant Ontario,' chap. 2 in *Two Worlds*

136 See Ryan for a discussion of the deathbed as a 'pulpit' in evangelical literature (*Cradle of the Middle Class*, 87–8).

137 See the discussion of temperance literature in chapter 5.

138 *Christian Guardian*, 23 Jan. 1830

139 Ibid., 19 June 1839

140 *Canada Christian Advocate*, 20 Feb. 1845

141 *Christian Guardian*, 30 March 1842

142 Ibid., 30 April 1831

143 Ibid., 23 June 1841

144 In his letter to the *Guardian* describing a revival at Upper Canada Academy (the forerunner to Victoria College), the academy's principal, Matthew Richey, saw young women and men's conversions as taking different forms. Young women were surrounded by 'pious female friends' and, although they might undergo tumultuous 'wrestling,' the presence of friends and family was extremely significant. In contrast, young men were described by Richey as experiencing conversion in solitude (21 March 1838). For a discusson of gender-based differences in conversions, see Marguerite Van Die, '"A Woman's Awakening."'

145 For Episcopal and Wesleyan Methodist missionary work with the Native people of Upper Canada, especially the Ojibwa, see Grant, *Moon of Wintertime*, 75–95; Schmalz, *The Ojibwa*, 51–75; and Smith's biography of Peter Jones, the Native Methodist missionary, *Sacred Feathers*.

146 Cott, *Bonds of Womanhood*, 130–2

147 *Christian Guardian*, 28 May 1834

148 Ibid., 'Heathen Females – Licentiousness,' 11 May 1836; 'Missions – Paganism,' 17 Jan. 1838; 'Missions – Paganism,' 4 April 1838

149 Ibid., 17 Jan. 1838

150 Barker-Benfield, *Culture of Sensibility*, 266–79

151 See, for example, Playter, *History of Methodism*, 249, 268; also William Case's letter to Reverend Emory concerning work at the Credit mission, reprinted in the *Colonial Advocate*, 4 Jan. 1828.

152 *Christian Guardian*, 14 Aug. 1830

153 Ibid., 12 June 1833. Spelman's *Inessential Woman* provides a most stimulating analysis of the explicit and implicit intersections of gender, race, and class in Western feminist thought.

154 See Schmalz, *The Ojibwa*, 145–79, for a discussion of attempts to turn the Ojibwa into farmers. See also Sarah Carter, 'Two Acres and a Cow: "Peasant" Farming for the Indians of the Northwest, 1889–1897,' in J.R. Miller, ed., *Sweet Promises*, 353–82.

155 I would like to thank Sylvia Van Kirk for reminding me of this point. See also Carol Devens, *Countering Colonization*, 47–55.

156 John West, a chaplain with the Hudson's Bay Company, whose trips throughout British North America and the United States were supported by the Church Missionary Society, observed of the Mississaugas at the Credit that 'the neat apparel of some of the women affords a pleasing comment on the change which has taken place in their husbands and fathers' (*The Substance of a Journal*, 304).

157 While I would argue that we should not romanticize gender relations in Native societies as Edenic, gender differences did not automatically lead to gender inequalities. See Devens, *Countering Colonization*, 34–5; also Karen Anderson, *Chain Her by One Foot: The Subjugation of Native Women in Seventeenth-Century New France* (New York and London: Routledge, 1991). Gender, the state, and Native policy are discussed briefly in Lykke de la Cour, Cecilia Morgan, and Mariana Valverde, 'Gender Regulation and State Formation in Nineteenth-Century Canada,' 173–5.

158 *Christian Guardian*, 27 Nov. 1830. Similar comments, although not as clearly focused on women's role, were made by 'B' for the *Kingston Chronicle*, 28 Nov. 1829.

159 *Christian Guardian*, 13 March 1830; also *Kingston Chronicle*, 5 March 1831

160 *Christian Guardian*, 27 Nov. 1830

161 Ibid., 4 Feb. 1835. See Smith, *Sacred Feathers*, 110, for a somewhat different, possibly second, encounter between these two. The similarities between Methodists' disapproval of Native peoples' 'adorning' themselves and Victorian discourses that focused on working-class women's dress are quite striking. See Mariana Valverde, 'The Love of Finery.'

162 *Christian Guardian*, 21 March 1838

163 Evelyn Brooks-Higginbotham, 'African-American Women's History,' 260–1

164 Devens, in *Countering Civilization*, 47–8, argues that, during the nineteenth century, Ojibwa women were largely absent from missionaries' accounts of resistance and opposition to their work, but that these women converted infrequently. I would add that this issue – at least with regard to the Ojibwa of southern Ontario – warrants much closer attention from historians of gender, religion, and Native–white relations.

165 *Christian Guardian*, 6 Nov. 1830; 5 Nov. 1831

166 Ibid., 7 Oct. 1835

167 George Copway, *Recollections of a Forest Life*, 32, 41

168 Schmalz, *The Ojibwa*, 131–9; Smith, *Sacred Feathers*, 162–72

169 *Kingston Chronicle and Gazette*, 16 Dec. 1840; *Niagara Gleaner*, 13 July 1833

4: Manners, Mores, and Moral Behaviour

1 Kasson, *Rudeness and Civility*, 3
2 Ibid., 44, 53–7, 128–36. See also Halttunen, *Confidence Men and Painted Women*.
3 Halttunen, *Confidence Men*, xiv, 34–5, 60, 155–6
4 Kasson, *Rudeness and Civility*, 3
5 Barker-Benfield, *Culture of Sensibility*
6 According to Mary Lu MacDonald, the seducer was a more popular figure than the seductress with male writers of fiction in the Canadas (*Literature and Society in the Canadas*, 231).
7 *Upper Canada Gazette*, 18 Jan. 1800
8 Ibid., 29 May 1823
9 *Kingston Gazette*, 6 June 1812
10 Ibid., 23 Oct. 1810
11 *York Gazette*, 13 Dec. 1809
12 *Weekly Register and Upper Canada Gazette*, 6 Nov. 1823
13 Salvaggio, *Enlightened Absences*, 28; also Londa Schiebinger, 'Skeletons in the Closet: The First Illustrations of the Female Skeleton in Eighteenth-Century Anatomy,' in Catherine Gallagher and Thomas Laqueur, eds., *The Making of the Modern Body: Sexuality and Society in the Nineteenth Century* (Berkeley: University of California Press, 1987), 72
14 *Kingston Gazette*, 25 Dec. 1810
15 *Weekly Register and Upper Canada Gazette*, 11 March 1824
16 *Kingston Gazette*, 11 Feb. 1817
17 Ibid., 21 July 1812
18 *Colonial Advocate*, 12 July 1834
19 *Canadian Freeman*, 29 Nov. 1832
20 *Niagara Chronicle*, 7 Jan. 1846
21 *Kingston Gazette*, 6 Jan. 1811
22 For example, see the *Upper Canada Gazette*, 'Miscellaneous,' 24 Aug. 1820.
23 Davidoff and Hall, *Family Fortunes*, 155
24 See Gauvreau, *Evangelical Century*, 45–56.
25 *Christian Guardian*, 5 June 1830
26 Ibid., 20 Aug. 1834
27 Barker-Benfield acknowledges that women were expected to 'internalise male wishes' far more than men did women's (*Culture of Sensibility*, 194). However, he does not explore the ways in which sensibility's identification of women as vulnerable and victimized tended to deny middle-class women a range of emotional responses, including rage.

28 *Christian Guardian*, 12 June 1830

29 Ibid., 20 July 1831

30 Although common to many of the newspapers examined here, the theme of romantic love was especially popular in the *Kingston Chronicle and Gazette*, which by 1842 was running stories that featured women either seeking, or as the objects of, romance. The majority of these tales were from British or American periodicals.

31 *Christian Guardian*, 19 July 1837. Similar concerns were expressed in the *Christian Messenger*, as in 'The Pious Father's Prayer,' 1 Sept. 1845.

32 Light and Prentice, *Pioneer and Gentlewomen*, 8. Light and Prentice's arguments are, admittedly, generally taken from material that was published and distributed in the mid-nineteenth century and that looks at household advice to women; this might account for the clearer focus on women that they found. However, it is important that we not overlook the larger context and relationships of these women's lives (that of wives and mothers) and the ways in which the colonial press helped construct this context.

33 *Christian Guardian*, 5 Dec. 1829

34 *Kingston Gazette*, 12 Feb. 1811

35 *Christian Guardian*, 11 Sept. 1830

36 Ibid., 23 July 1831, 23 Nov. 1836

37 *Colonial Advocate*, 7 Oct. 1824. See Grant, *Profusion of Spires*, 108, for a very brief discussion of evangelical objections to such amusements.

38 For a discussion of this view of women in American society, see Halttunen, *Confidence Men*, 59–60.

39 *Kingston Gazette*, 18 Aug. 1812. The fact that the colony was facing invasion by the United States when this piece was run may have influenced the choice of analogy of 'Poor Robert.'

40 *Christian Guardian*, 17 July 1839; also 'Love to a Mother,' *Christian Messenger*, June 1846; 'For What Is a Mother Responsible?' *Canada Christian Advocate*, 4 Sept. 1845

41 'A Few Words to Young Men,' *Christian Guardian*, 5 July 1837; 'Dangers of Young Men,' ibid., 19 July 1837

42 For discussions of the rural idyll and conceptions of the city as a site of vice, see Davidoff and Hall, *Family Fortunes*, 28–9, and Stansell, *City of Women*, especially chap. 4, 'Places of Vice: Views of the Neighborhoods.'

43 For Caldicott, see the entry by Margot H.C. Meikleham, *DCB* (1976), 9:112–13. For Lesslie, see the entry by J.M.S. Careless, *DCB* (1982), 11:516–19.

44 *Christian Guardian*, 11 Jan. 1832

45 Ibid., 18 Sept. 1835

46 *Kingston Gazette*, 14 Jan. 1812

47 See 'History and Present State of Education in Upper Canada,' *Christian Recorder*, 1, no. 2 (April 1819); also Richard Cockrel, *Thoughts on the Education of Youth* (Newark, 1795).

48 For a discussion of gender and education in Upper Canada, see Houston and Prentice, *Schooling and Scholars*, 14–16.

49 *Christian Guardian*, 5 Dec. 1829

50 'Youth's Department,' ibid., 13 Nov. 1830; 'Value of Character to Young Men,' ibid., 6 Nov. 1839; 'Self-Improvement,' *Christian Messenger*, Oct. 1846

51 See above, chap. 3, 126–8.

52 *Canada Christian Advocate*, 25 May 1847

53 *Christian Guardian*, 2 March 1836

54 *Christian Guardian*, 26 April 1837

55 Ibid., 19 Dec. 1829; 'Pretty Hands,' *Canada Christian Advocate*, 26 May 1846

56 *Christian Guardian*, 5 July 1837; 'A Rich Young Man,' *Canada Christian Advocate*, 24 Oct. 1848

57 See Halttunen, *Confidence Men*, 98–101, for a discussion of American evangelical ambivalence towards 'politeness.'

58 *Kingston Gazette*, 13 Nov. 1810

59 *Kingston Chronicle*, 5 Dec. 1824

60 See, for example, 'The Fair Defended,' *Kingston Gazette*, 28 Jan. 1812; also 'A Finished Coquette,' *Upper Canada Gazette*, 16 Jan. 1811.

61 *Colonial Advocate*, 14 June 1832

62 *Christian Guardian*, 14 Aug. 1830

63 Ibid., 20 Nov. 1830. As J.G.A. Pocock notes, credit was often symbolized by a 'female and hysterical' figure in early-eighteenth-century political language (*Virtue, Commerce, and History*, 235).

64 *Christian Guardian*, 22 Oct. 1831

65 Ibid., 30 May 1832

66 Ibid., 23 July 1831; 'If We Only Had a Piano!' *The Church*, 6 March 1846

67 See Ryan, *Empire of the Mother*, 31–50, for a discussion of the rise of periodicals such as *Godey's Lady's Book* in America, publications that told women where purchases might be made. Even these magazines, though, warned women to steer clear of the fashionable life. See also Halttunen, *Confidence Men*, 70–89.

68 *Christian Guardian*, 13 Nov. 1830. For a discussion of the more 'prosaic' household manuals and columns of New England, see Ryan, *Empire of the Mother*, 19–30.

69 'Getting into Society,' *Christian Guardian*, 26 April 1837

70 See Davidoff and Hall, *Family Fortunes*, 18–35; Ryan, *Cradle of the Middle Class*, especially chap. 4; Blumin, *Emergence of the Middle Class*, especially chaps. 3–5.

71 Davidoff and Hall have pointed out that, 'gender and class always operate together, that consciousness of class always takes a gendered form.' But 'the articulation of class and gender is never a perfect fit' and may produce myriad tensions (*Family Fortunes*, 13).

72 See Blumin, *Emergence of the Middle Class*, 9–13, 240–57, for a discussion of middle-class consciousness, especially with regard to the difficulty of applying this concept to American society.

73 Noel, *Canada Dry*, 104; also Grant, *Profusion of Spires*, 108

74 *Kingston Gazette*, 16 Oct. 1810

75 *Kingston Chronicle*, 14 Jan. 1832

76 *Kingston Chronicle and Gazette*, 20 July 1842

77 *Christian Guardian*, 11 Sept. 1830

78 Ibid., 26 June 1833

79 *Colonial Advocate*, 11 July 1824

80 *Christian Guardian*, 18 April 1838

81 Ibid., 22 Aug. 1832

82 Carroll, *Past and Present*, 57

83 Playter, *History of Methodism in Canada*, 268

84 *Niagara Gleaner*, 13 February 1830

85 *Christian Guardian*, 12 June 1833

86 Ibid., 14 June 1837

87 Ibid., 28 Aug. 1833

88 Noel, *Canada Dry*, 101

89 For discussions of the temperance movement that posit a clearer link between it and women's activism, see Epstein, *Politics of Domesticity*, especially chap. 5, 'The Woman's Christian Temperance Union and the Transition to Feminism.' For Canada, see Wendy Mitchinson, 'The WCTU: "For God, Home and Native Land": A Study in Nineteenth-Century Feminism,' in Linda Kealey, ed., *A Not Unreasonable Claim: Women and Reform in Canada, 1880s–1920s* (Toronto: Women's Press, 1979), 151–68, and, most recently, Sharon Anne Cook, *'Through Sunshine and Shadow': The Woman's Christian Temperance Union, Evangelicalism, and Reform in Ontario, 1874–1930* (Montreal and Kingston: McGill-Queen's University Press, 1995).

90 Ryan, *Empire of the Mother*, 37–8. In her assessment of this literature, the 'patriarchal household' of New England had disappeared by the 1840s (43), but in this regard Upper Canadian literature more closely resembled that of England, where the definition of male and female 'responsibilities' was more ambiguous (Davidoff and Hall, *Family Fortunes*, 117). Rather than seeing concepts of 'women's influence' as simply superseding older notions of male familial leadership, it may be more fruitful to see this as a site of negotiation and

tension in Upper Canadian discourses, given that different viewpoints were offered on whose 'domain' the family really was.

91 'Cautions of Young Men,' *Christian Guardian*, 23 July 1831; 'The Inebriate,' *Canada Christian Advocate*, 1 May 1845

92 *Christian Guardian*, 26 June 1833

93 Halttunen, *Confidence Men*, chap. 1, 'The Era of the Confidence Man.' In '"Taste Not; Touch Not; Handle Not"' James M. Clemens argues that temperance literature and activism were mostly aimed at plebeian and working-class men and women. While I would not deny that these groups were frequent targets of temperance literature, I would suggest that perhaps Clemens overlooks temperance efforts to portray alcohol's potential to cross lines of class and status.

94 *Patriot and Farmers' Advocate*, 23 Aug. 1833

95 Ibid., 24 May 1832

96 Cadigan, 'Paternalism and Politics,' 334–8

97 Ibid., 336

98 Samuel Jarvis, *Statement of Facts*, 10–11

99 'Rowdyism,' *British Colonist*, 24 Feb. 1846; 'Tom and Jerryism,' *Patriot and Farmers' Advocate*, 17 Nov. 1840

100 *Weekly Register and Upper Canada Gazette*, 19 Sept. 1822

101 Edward Allan Talbot, 'Recreational Violence,' in Richard M. Reid, ed., *The Upper Ottawa Valley to 1855* (Ottawa: Champlain Society, Carleton University Press, 1990), 59–60. See Elliott J. Gorn, '"Gouge and Bite, Pull Hair and Scratch": The Social Significance of Fighting in the Southern Backcountry,' *American Historical Review* 90, no. 1 (Feb. 1985): 18–43.

102 Donna Andrew, 'The Code of Honour and Its Critics'

103 *Upper Canada Gazette*, 4 Jan. 1800

104 William Renwick Riddell, 'The First Attorney-General of Upper Canada,' 421–2; also his *The Duel in Early Upper Canada*, 3–5.

105 Riddell, *Duel in Early Upper Canada*, 4. Although it is not entirely clear if the code was exactly the same from country to country, a fair duel appears to have been one in which participants fired from the same distances, gave equal warning of their intentions to fire, were armed with the same type of weapon, and so forth. For a more detailed discussion of duelling in Upper Canada, see Cecilia Morgan, '"In Search of the Phantom Misnamed Honour": Duelling in Upper Canada,' *Canadian Historical Review* 76, no. 4 (Dec. 1995): 529–562.

106 See Riddell, *Duel in Early Upper Canada*, 5–9, 10–14, for the duel between Samuel Jarvis and Thomas Ridout in which the latter was killed, as well as the John Wilson–Robert Lyons duel over Lyon's insult to Elizabeth Hughes,

whom Wilson married afterward. See also Edward MacLeod Shortt, *The memorable duel at Perth*, and Josephine Phelan, 'A Duel on the Island.'
107 V.G. Kiernan, *The Duel in European History*, 8
108 For international literature on the meanings of bodies in this period, see Thomas W. Laqueur, 'Bodies, Details, and the Humanitarian Narrative,' in Lynn Hunt, ed., *The New Cultural History*, 176–204. Dorinda Outram's *The Body and the French Revolution* is particularly helpful in attempting to understand the public, political meanings of bodies.
109 *Upper Canada Gazette*, 11 Jan. 1800
110 Ibid., 26 June 1813
111 Rev. W. Taylor, *A Testimony Aganist Duelling*, 7–9
112 Ibid., 18
113 *Kingston Chronicle and Gazette*, 12 March 1836
114 *York Gazette*, 26 June 1813
115 Ibid.
116 *Kingston Gazette*, 11 Jan. 1818
117 Davidoff and Hall, *Family Fortunes*, 21
118 Kiernan, *Duel in European History*, 327
119 *Weekly Register and Upper Canada Gazette*, 25 Oct. 1823
120 *Church*, 11 March 1844; *Christian Guardian*, 8 Sept. 1847
121 Kiernan, *Duel in European History*, 327
122 *Weekly Register and Upper Canada Gazette*, 23 July 1823
123 Davidoff and Hall, *Family Fortunes*, 397–403; Pocock, *Virtue, Commerce, and History*, 234–9
124 *Patriot and Farmers' Monitor*, 6 Sept. 1833
125 See the comments in chapter 2 on Mackenzie's untidy appearance.
126 Cadigan, 'Paternalism and Politics,' 335
127 Ibid., 336–7; Noel, *Canada Dry*, 148–51
128 Mackenzie was particularly fond of making this point about the Bank of Upper Canada (see, for example, *Constitution*, 7 June 1837). See de la Cour, Morgan, and Valverde, 'Gender Regulation and State Formation,' for a discussion of what historians might look at in examining gender and state formation; also Curtis, *Building the Educational State*.
129 The 'Queen Caroline affair' began when George brought a divorce action against his wife in the House of Lords, which led to a trial in which 'her supposed misdeeds' were exposed 'to the inquisitive eyes and ears of the expanding literate public' (Davidoff and Hall, *Family Fortunes*, 150). Caroline became a popular figure with the country's radicals, a symbol of 'wronged womanhood' pitted against the government's moral degradation. George was forced to drop the case when the bill was passed with a very small majority. Nine

months after the trial, Caroline died (Davidoff and Hall, 151–5). See also Thompson, *Queen Victoria*, 7–14.

130 *Upper Canada Gazette*, 16 Nov. 1820

131 Davidoff and Hall, *Family Fortunes*, 153

132 I do not want to suggest that this relationship was so simple and straightforward that it involved the conscious design and implementation of gendered policies by bureaucrats after reading the morning papers! As de la Cour, Morgan, and Valverde have argued, 'the regulation of gender by the state is seldom carried out consciously and directly: rather, it takes place in a helter-skelter manner and through complicated relations to other types of regulation' ('Gender Regulation and State Formation,' 164). But if we understand the process of state formation in British North America as having been informed by the cultural and social norms and relationships of these men, most of whom were of European descent and middle-class, then it should not be too surprising that the gendered languages I have outlined might be particularly influential.

133 *Kingston Chronicle*, 14 Jan. 1825. For a brief discussion of some of these groups, see Light and Prentice, *Pioneer and Gentlewomen*, 8, 181–90.

134 *Kingston Chronicle*, 4 May 1827

135 For example, see 'Temperance at Niagara,' *Christian Guardian*, 10 April 1844. This tendency was more pronounced in the 1840s. See Noel, *Canada Dry*, 98–102, for the growth of women's temperance groups and activities.

136 *Kingston Chronicle*, 14 Jan. 1827, 4 May 1827, 14 Jan. 1832; *Christian Guardian*, 14 Aug. 1830

137 Although most pronounced in the Methodist press, examples of this womanly benevolence occasionally appeared in the Anglican press. See, for example, 'The Eleventh Annual Report of the Quebec Diocesan Committee of the S.P.C.K.,' *Christian Sentinel* 3, no. 3 (May/June 1829): 141–7, esp. 145–6.

138 See Laura Wexler, 'Tender Violence: Literary Eavesdropping, Domestic Fiction, and Educational Reform,' in Shirley Samuels, ed., *The Culture of Sentiment: Race, Gender, and Sentimentality in Nineteenth-Century America* (New York and Oxford: Oxford University Press, 1992), 15. Wexler's argument is about nineteenth-century interracial American boarding schools, and it is intended to apply to Natives, blacks, the working class, and immigrants; her observations concerning the relationships between sentimentalism (in which the private home was posited as the 'apotheosis of nuture') and imperialism are particularly relevant to the colonial society of Upper Canada (15–17). See chapter 3 above.

139 This concept will be explored further in chap. 5. See Denise Riley for a discussion of the identification of the 'social' with women, especially in early- to mid-nineteenth-century Western society ('*Am I That Name?*' 47–55).

140 Although the growth of domesticity as a dominant ideology has often been identified with better (since less brutal and violent) relations between men and women, nevertheless it should be recognized that domesticity often required considerable emotional sacrifices of women. Ruth Perry, in 'Colonizing the Breast,' is attentive to these power relations in her examination of the construction of 'motherhood' within the discourse of domesticity.

5: Party, Parades, and Bazaars in the 1840s

1 See Careless, *Union of the Canadas*, especially chaps. 1–7; William Ormsby, *The Emergence of the Federal Concept in Canada;* Ian Radforth, 'Sydenham and Utilitarian Reform,' in Greer and Radforth, eds., *Colonial Leviathan;* Wilton-Siegel, 'The Transformation of Upper Canadian Politics.'

2 For discussions of the reserves and the question of religious voluntarism in this period, see Westfall, 'The Alliance of Church and State,' chap. 4 in *Two Worlds;* Grant, 'Affairs of State,' chap. 9 in *Profusion of Spires;* Fahey, 'The Seeds of Independence,' chap. 7 in *In His Name.*

3 Westfall, in *Two Worlds*, 68–81, argues that Methodism underwent expansion and consolidation during the mid-nineteenth century. During this process, revivalism became 'tempered' as a new code of respectability was formed to which 'good works' were integral. While in general agreement with his argument, I believe it is worth noting that these changes may have been more common in certain areas of mid-nineteenth-century Ontario, such as the southern and central regions, than others, Fahey is more concerned with political and internal developments in Anglicanism than with the social and cultural issues discussed here, but see 'A House Divided,' chap. 8, in *In His Name.*

4 Noel, *Canada Dry;* F.L. Barron, 'The American Origins of the Temperance Movement in Ontario'; Clemens, '"Taste Not; Touch Not; Handle Not"'

5 Careless, *Union of the Canada*, 150–3; Bruce Curtis, 'Class Culture and Administration: Educational Inspection in Canada West,' in Greer and Radforth, eds., *Colonial Leviathan*, 103–33; Curtis, *Building the Educational State*

6 See chapter 1, 52–3

7 *British Colonist*, 29 March 1838

8 Craig, *Upper Canada*, 249–51

9 *British Colonist*, 22 March 1838, 11 Oct. 1838; *Patriot and Farmers' Monitor*, 30 Oct. 1838, 15 Nov. 1838

10 *British Colonist*, 4 Oct. 1838. See Careless, *Union of the Canadas*, 153–5; Schmalz, 'Early Reserves,' chap. 7 in *The Ojibwa.*

11 The *Patriot and Farmers' Monitor* liked to remind its readers of past treachery,

especially with regard to Egerton Ryerson. See its editorial on Ryerson, 11 Dec. 1838, and 'Mr. Egerton Ryerson,' 28 Feb. 1840.

12 *Patriot and Farmer's Monitor*, 12 Feb. 1841

13 *The Church*, 10 Dec. 1847, 21 Jan. 1848. Having been granted amnesty, Mackenzie returned to the province in 1850.

14 Mills, *Idea of Loyalty*, 127–31 Brown's writings in *The Globe* spoke of both the British connection and the importance of Canadian patriotism. For a discussion of Brown's ideology as expressed in his journalism, see Careless, 'Reform Journalist,' in *Brown of the Globe*.

15 There is some disagreement as to what 'responsible government' meant and when it had been attained in the colonial context. Wilton-Siegel identifies specific events as 'landmarks' in its development (the resignation of the Executive Council over the Secret Societies Bill in 1844 and the 1849 Rebellion Losses Bill, for example) and also points to the importance of processes such as the acceptance and development of political parties ('Transformation of Upper Canadian Politics,' 95–7, chap. 3).

16 While Wilton-Siegel takes into account the controversy that the notion of 'party' stirred up, she tends to overlook the significance of the symbolism of party in the early years of the decade. See also Mills on the acceptance of party ('Loyalty and the Idea of Party in the 1840s,' chap. 7 in *Idea of Loyalty*); Phillip Buckner, *The Transition to Responsible Government*, 262–74.

17 *British Colonist*, 28 Aug. 1839

18 *Patriot*, 11 Sept. 1840

19 *Kingston Chronicle and Gazette*, 12 Oct. 1844

20 For a discussion of political patronage in this period, and the way in which reformers learned to manipulate it, see Wilton-Siegel, 'Transformation of Upper Canadian Politics,' 283; also S.J.R. Noel, 'Canada West,' in his *Patrons, Clients, Brokers*.

21 *Patriot*, 23 Oct. 1842

22 *British Colonist*, 6 Oct. 1846

23 *Globe*, 9 July 1844; 'Toronto Election,' ibid., 15 Oct. 1844; 'The Administration and Their Supporters,' ibid., 31 July 1847; *British Colonist*, 23 Jan. 1844; 9 Feb. 1844; *Patriot*, 8 Dec. 1840, 27 Feb. 1844, 30 Aug. 1844

24 *Globe*, 9 July 1844

25 *Examiner*, 14 July 1841. The newspaper publisher Francis Hincks (1807–85) is even better-known as a major player in the 'brokerage' politics of this decade, one who helped shape the reform coalition with Lower Canadians (Noel, *Patrons, Clients, Brokers*, 140–5). See William Ormsby's entry on Hincks, *DCB* (1976), 9:406–16.

26 'To the Electors of the Third Riding of York,' *Examiner*, 5 Oct. 1842; see also 'Politics,' ibid., 20 March 1844

27 *British Colonist*, 31 March 1841
28 Ibid., 3 Feb. 1841
29 Ibid. For Buchanan, see the entry by Douglas McCalla, *DCB* (1987), 11:125–31.
30 'Political Portrait Gallery,' *Globe*, 1 Sept. 1847
31 See Bruce Curtis, *True Government by Choice Men?* for a discussion of state attempts to inculcate such values, particularly through the educational inspectorate.
32 'Political Portrait Gallery,' *Globe*, 18 Aug. 1847
33 Ibid. These themes continued into the next decade. See, for example, 'The Morality of Public Men,' *Globe*, 1 Oct. 1855
34 David Ouellette, 'Hugh Scobie,' *DCB* (1985), 8:789–91
35 *British Colonist*, 21 Feb. 1844
36 Ibid., 12 March 1844
37 Ibid., 9 Feb. 1844
38 Ibid., 17 March 1841
39 Ibid., 12 March 1844
40 Careless, *Brown of the Globe*, 63
41 *Globe*, 22 Oct. 1844
42 'Electors of Canada West,' ibid., 22 Oct. 1844; 'The Waterloo Demonstration,' ibid., 16 June 1849
43 *Patriot and Farmers' Monitor*, 14 June 1844
44 Ibid., 30 Aug. 1844
45 *British Colonist*, 31 March 1841
46 Ibid., 10 March 1841
47 Ibid., 26 Dec. 1843
48 *Globe*, 15 Oct. 1844
49 For waged work in Upper Canada and Canada West, see Joy Parr, 'Hired Men: Ontario Agricultural Wage Labour in Historical Perspective,' *Labour/Le Travail* 15 (Spring 1985): 91–103; Bleasdale, 'Class Conflict on the Canals.' See also Paul Craven, 'The Law of Master and Servant in Mid-Nineteenth-Century Ontario,' in David H. Flaherty, ed., *Essays in the History of Canadian Law* (Toronto: University of Toronto Press, 1981), 1:175–211. For Native men and the colonial state, see Schmalz, *The Ojibwa*, chaps. 6–8.
50 *British Colonist*, 3 Feb. 1841
51 See chapter 4, 180–1.
52 As did the school inspectors examined by Curtis, *True Government*, particularly 8–9 and chap. 5, 'The District Inspectoral Corps.'
53 John Garner, *The Franchise and Politics in British North America*, 155–60. Garner argues that women's exclusion was a result of votes cast by women for the conservative James Webster in 1844, in Halton County. His reform opponent,

James Durand, protested the election. According to Garner, the reform government of 1849 remembered this incident when consolidating the election laws (159).

54 de la Cour, Morgan, and Valverde, 'Gender Regulation and State Formation," 184. See also Curtis, *True Government*, 192.

55 *Christian Sentinel* 1, no. 1 (Jan./Feb. 1827)

56 Mary P. Ryan, *Women in Public*, 39–43

57 *British Colonist*, 17 Feb. 1841

58 'The Governor-General's Visit to Toronto,' *British Colonist*, 27 April 1842; 'Arrival of His Excellency the Governor-General,' ibid., 19 Oct. 1847; 'Public Dinner to James Smith,' *Globe*, 29 Jan. 1846

59 They were also used to her advantage in securing her accession to the throne. See Thompson, *Queen Victoria*, 23–30.

60 *British Colonist*, 17 Feb. 1841

61 This argument has been made by Mark Francis, in *Governors and Settlers*, 56.

62 I cannot agree with Francis's argument that there was no theatrical component to these ceremonies (since there were no actor-audience distinctions and they were not performed onstage) and that they were not marked by displays of enthusiasm or pleas for support (*Governors and Settlers*, 70). His analysis overlooks the coverage of these events by the press. It also takes a very narrow view as to what ceremonial power might be intended to encompass. For an analysis of public banquets in America that is attentive to gender, see Ryan, *Women in Public*, 19; also Bonnie Huskins, 'Banquets, Ox Roasts, Institutional Repasts and Tea and Coffee Soirees: Toward a Typology of Public Feasting in Mid-Victorian Saint John and Halifax,' paper presented to the Canadian Historical Association's 73rd annual conference, Calgary, June 1994.

63 *Globe*, 16 June 1848. For a satirical look at such an event, see 'The Sarnia Dinner,' ibid., 16 July 1853.

64 Mills, *Idea of Loyalty*, 124–5; Wilton, '"A Firebrand among the People"'

65 de la Cour, Morgan, and Valverde, 'Gender Regulation and State Formation,' 164

66 *Kingston Chronicle*, 14 Jan. 1825, 4 May 1827; *York Weekly and Upper Canada Gazette*, 11 Feb. 1821

67 *Kingston Chronicle*, 14 Nov. 1829

68 *Kingston Chronicle and Gazette*, 14 May 1842

69 Ibid.

70 *Christian Sentinel* 11, no. 3 (May/June 1829)

71 *Church*, 29 March 1844

72 See, for example, 'St. Andrew's Church, Toronto,' *British Colonist*, 25 Jan. 1843; ibid., 26 April 1844; ibid., 20 March 1846; *Church*, 26 Feb. 1842; ibid., 6 Jan.

1843; 'Toronto Sunday Schools' Clothing Fund,' ibid., 25 July 1845; 'Cooksville Soiree,' *Christian Guardian*, 9 April 1845.

73 Westfall, 'Epics in Stone: Placing the Sacred in a Secular World,' chap. 5 in *Two Worlds*. For a discussion of Irish Catholic women's fund-raising activities in Toronto, see Brian P. Clarke, *Piety and Nationalism: Lay Voluntary Associations and the Creation of an Irish-Catholic Community in Toronto, 1850–1895* (Montreal and Kingston: McGill-Queen's University Press, 1993), 82–9.

74 Karen Halttunen argues that bourgeois parlours constituted a 'third social sphere' between the public space of the urban street and the private back rooms of a house. Parlours, she states, were 'cultural podiums' for women, who were charged with the responsibility of enforcing the rules of 'polite social intercourse' (*Confidence Men*, 59–61).

75 The *British Colonist*, for example, reported a bazaar held at the Toronto City Hall (26 April 1844).

76 F.K. Prochaska, however, in his discussions of the fund-raising bazaars for the Anti-Corn Law League in England, does not see a connection between women's involvement in these activities and any political interest on their part (*Women and Philanthropy*, 62–4).

77 See, for example, 'An Indian Burial,' *Church*, 28 March 1845; also 'Opening of the Mohawk church on the Bay of Quinte,' ibid., 16 Aug. 1844.

78 This phrase comes from Laura Wexler, 'Tender Violence: Literary Eavesdropping, Domestic Fiction, and Educational Reform,' in Samuels, ed., *Culture of Sentiment*, 17.

79 See, for example, *Christian Guardian*, 6 May 1835.

80 *Church*, 28 Aug. 1841

81 For attitudes towards the Irish, especially Irish Catholics, see Peter A. Russell, *'Here We Are Lairds Ourselves'*, 120–2, 170–2.

82 *Niagara Chronicle*, 17 July 1844

83 Bleasdale, 'Class Conflict on the Canals,' 272

84 Except, of course, in writings on religion and domesticity.

85 *British Colonist*, 26 April 1844

86 *Christian Guardian*, 19 Sept. 1849, 9 Nov. 1842, 9 April 1845; *Evangelist*, Feb. 1848; 'Hamilton Mission,' ibid., Oct. 1848

87 *Evangelist*, April 1851

88 *Christian Guardian*, 10 April 1848

89 For the Daughters of Temperance, see Noel, *Canada Dry*, 101.

90 *Examiner*, 27 Oct. 1841

91 *Canada Christian Advocate*, 28 May 1850

92 See chapter 4.

93 *Canada Christian Advocate*, 9 July 1850 Extensive coverage of temperance

parades in the 1850s may be found in *Canadian Son of Temperance*: see, for example, 26 Feb. 1851; 'Don Mills Soiree,' 29 Nov. 1851; 'Oshawa Cadets,' 19 April 1853; 'Soirees! Soirees! Soirees!' 19 April 1853.

94 Ryan, *Women in Public*, 36. A similar point is made by Bonnie Huskins, 'The Ceremonial Space of Women: Public Processions in Victorian Saint John and Halifax,' in Guildford and Morton, eds., *Separate Spheres*, 153–4.

95 The 'mayoress' was the wife of the mayor. Catherine (Darby) Gurnett married George, who served two terms as mayor of Toronto, in 1841. She was his second wife and survived her husband who died suddenly of a stroke in 1861.

96 'The Banner,' 10 Aug. 1848, Ephemera Collection, Baldwin Room, Metropolitan Toronto Reference Library.

97 This is Ryan's description of women in public during the 1840s and 1850s (*Women in Public*, 37).

98 *Christian Guardian*, 6 Dec. 1846

99 See J. Jerald Bellomo, 'Upper Canadian Attitudes Towards Crime and Punishment, 1832–1851,' *Ontario History* 64, no. 1 (1972): 11–26. The Irish, according to Bellomo, 'consistently comprised over thirty per cent of the prison population, and an even higher proportion of the women prisoners' (13). See also John Weaver, 'Crime, Public Order, and Repression: The Gore District in Upheaval, 1832–1851,' *Ontario History* 78 (Sept. 1986): 178–201.

100 Constance Backhouse traces the career of an Irish prostitute, Mary Gorman, who was in and out of Toronto jails throughout the 1860s and 1870s. Although to date no comparable work has been done for the period studied here, the number of Irish women's names that appear in the press suggest that Mary Gorman was not unique (*Petticoats and Prejudice*, 229–41).

101 See Gregory S. Kealey, 'Orangemen and the Corporation: The Politics of Class During the Union of the Canadas,' in Victor L. Russell, ed., *Forging a Consensus: Historical Essays on Toronto* (Toronto: University of Toronto Press, 1984), 44–5. See also Huskins, 'Ceremonial Space of Women,' 153.

102 Huskins, 'Ceremonial Space of Women'

103 'Always Something New,' *Niagara Gleaner*, 31 Aug. 1833; 'The Male Sex Alone Adapted to the Chief Command in Society,' *British Colonist*, 9 March 1842; 'A Daughter's Love,' *Christian Guardian*, 3 Nov. 1847

104 *British Colonist*, 1 Nov. 1850

105 *Church*, 26 Nov. 1847

106 *Globe*, 1 Dec. 1847

107 *Canada Christian Advocate*, 15 Oct. 1847. G.W. Bungay was an agent for Temperance Unions throughout Canada West in the 1840s and appears to have been a popular and effective speaker (Noel, *Canada Dry*, 114).

108 Riley, *'Am I That Name?'* 47–55

109 *Church*, 15 Jan. 1847
110 See, for example, 'The Brave Boy,' *Canada Christian Advocate*, 26 June 1849; 'The Cabinet,' *Evangelist*, Aug. 1851.
111 *Church*, 10 Sept. 1847
112 Ibid., 21 Nov. 1845
113 *Canada Christian Advocate*, 26 Dec. 1848
114 Edith Firth, *Early Toronto Newspapers, 1793–1867* (Toronto: Baxter, 1961), 21
115 *Artisan*, 12 Oct. 1848
116 Ibid.
117 Ibid., 7 Dec. 1848
118 Ibid., 23 Nov. 1848
119 Ibid., 7 Dec. 1848
120 'Young Men's Association,' *British Colonist*, 1 Dec. 1846; 'Young Men's Mutual Improvement Society,' ibid., 13 April 1847; 'Toronto Young Men's Mutual Improvement Society,' ibid., 9 Jan. 1849. It is quite possible that these were different manifestations of what was essentially the same organization.
121 Ibid., 13 April 1847
122 Ibid., 9 Jan. 1849

Epilogue

1 For political developments in the 1850s and 1860s, see Careless, *Union of the Canadas*; also Careless, ed., *The Pre-Confederation Premiers: Ontario Government Leaders, 1841–1867* (Toronto: University of Toronto Press, 1980). For antislavery movements, see Allen P. Stouffer, *The Light of Nature and the Law of God*, and, for discussions of demographic and other socio-economic developments, see Douglas McCalla, 'The Province at Mid-Century,' pt. 3 in his *Planting the Province*.
2 'The Roman Organ,' *Globe*, 1 July 1851. See also 'William Lyon Mackenzie on Endowments,' *Globe*, 30 April 1853.
3 As J.R. Miller points out, not only was the church seen as intervening in the husband-wife relation, Catholicism was perceived as a particularly misogynistic religion that denigrated marriage through its insistence on priestly celibacy and that 'destroyed the family by brutalizing and corrupting its heart, the wife and mother.' See 'Anti-Catholicism in Canada: From the British Conquest to the Great War,' in Terence Murphy and Gerald Stortz, eds., *Creed and Culture: The Place of English-Speaking Catholics in Canadian Society, 1750–1930* (Montreal and Kingston: McGill-Queen's University Press, 1993), 34–5.
4 'The Liberality of Priestcraft,' *Globe*, 24 Sept. 1853; 'Letter from Peter Prayer,' ibid., 9 Aug. 1853

5 'Mariolatry,' ibid., 18 June 1855. The *Globe*'s editorial for 4 September 1853 discussed mob attacks on Protestant evangelicals in Ireland that had been instigated by priests. See also Miller, 'Anti-Catholicism,' 35, for a discussion of the use of these examples of Catholic domination.

6 'Transubstantiation,' *Canadian Son of Temperance*, 9 Dec. 1854. Miller, 'Anti-Catholicism,' 32, has pointed out that transubstantiation was a favourite target of anti-Catholics. 'Woman's Liberty and Virtue – Nunneries,' *Canadian Son of Temperance*, 5 Oct. 1853; see also 'The Beast Biting, with Intent to Kill,' *Christian Guardian*, 4 Dec. 1855.

7 Stouffer, *Light of Nature*, 109. In the *Globe*, see 'Slavery Not So Bad as People Think!' 11 March 1851; 'The Elgin Association,' and 'A Host of Negroes,' 25 Sept. 1851; 'Anti-Slavery Society in Hamilton,' 22 March 1853; 'Pro-Slavery in a Church!' 24 Sept. 1853; 'Slave Decoys at St. Catharines,' 1 Sept. 1855.

8 See, for example, 'Beauties of Practical Republicanism,' *Globe*, 11 Jan. 1851.

9 See Vron Ware, 'An Abhorrence of Slavery: Subjection and Subjectivity in Abolitionist Politics,' in her *Beyond the Pale*.

10 Although see, for example, Robin Winks, *The Blacks in Canada* (New Haven: Yale University Press, 1971); C. Peter Ripley, *The Black Abolitionist Papers*, vol. 2, *Canada, 1830–1865* (Chapel Hill: University of North Carolina Press, 1986); Peggy Bristow, Dionne Brand, Linda Carty, Afua P. Cooper, Sylvia Hamilton, and Adrienne Shadd, *'We're Rooted Here and They Can't Pull Us Up': Essays in African Canadian Women's History* (Toronto: University of Toronto Press, 1994); Shirley J. Yee, 'Gender Ideology and Black Women as Community-Builders in Ontario, 1850–70,' *Canadian Historical Review* 75, no. 1 (March 1994): 53–73.

11 Shadd, a member of a free black family from Delaware, had come to Canada in 1850, settling in Windsor and opening a school with money from the American Missionary Association. She quickly became involved in antislavery societies and in 1852 published *A Plea for Emigration*, which offered information on Canada West for African Americans who wanted to move north. A year later, Shadd founded the *Provincial Freeman*, inviting a prominent member of the African-Canadian community, Samuel Ringgold Ward, to serve as editor. But it appears that this was a task Ward performed in name only; in 1854, when the paper moved to Toronto for one year, Ward's name no longer appeared on the masthead. Shadd continued to edit the paper with the help of her sister, Amelia, until 1855, just before she returned to southwestern Ontario to set up business in Chatham. The Reverend William Newman became the *Freeman*'s editor, with Shadd devoting herself to the business of selling subscriptions and lecturing throughout the United States. She returned to the United States in 1863 and, apart from visits to Canada in 1866 and 1881, spent the rest of her life there. For

further biographical information on Shadd (or Shadd Cary), see Peggy Bristow, '"Whatever You Raise in the Ground You Can Sell It in Chatham": Black Women in Buxton and Chatham, 1850–65,' in Bristow et al., *'We're Rooted Here'*, 105–22; also Jim Bearden and Linda Jean Butler, *Shadd: The Life and Times of Mary Shadd Cary* (Toronto: NC Press, 1977). For Ward, who was the son of escaped slaves and who had been a Congregational minister, teacher, temperance activist, and editor in New York state, and who was a fund-raiser and lecturer for the Anti-Slavery Society of Canada, see Stouffer, *Light of Nature*, 120–9.

12 See, for example, the *Provincial Freeman*'s editorial, 'Introductory,' 24 March 1853; also 'Our Tour,' ibid., 23 July 1854; and the letter from 'Moses,' ibid., 24 April 1853.

13 'Lectures,' ibid., 17 March 1855

14 See my discussion of the press's coverage of woman's rights, 213–14.

15 'Adieu,' *Provincial Freeman*, 30 June 1855

16 These differences are a theme addressed throughout Jacqueline Jones's, *Labor of Love, Labor of Sorrow*.

17 'American Slavery,' *Globe*, 11 Jan. 1853

18 This appeal was apparently sponsored by the Duchess of Sutherland; see Stouffer, *Light of Nature*, 125–6.

19 'Mrs America answers Mrs. England,' *Provincial Freeman*, 24 March 1853

20 'Slavery in Baltimore,' ibid., 30 June 1855

21 'Soirees! Soirees! Soirees!' *Canadian Son of Temperance*, 19 April 1853; 'Knox Church Bazaar,' *Globe*, 1 Jan. 1851

22 'The Magdalen Asylum – Annual Meeting,' *Globe*, 28 May 1855

23 See Stouffer, *Light of Nature*, 119–20, 125–6, 128, and 189, for discussions of antislavery work by women in this period.

24 Ibid.

25 See, for example, 'The Zorra Demonstration!' *Globe*, 15 Oct. 1853; 'The Berlin Dinner,' ibid., 24 July 1853; 'The Election,' *Niagara Chronicle*, 15 July 1853.

26 'Schedules of Convictions,' *Niagara Chronicle*, 4 Dec. 1851

27 'Bloody Affray,' *Niagara Mail*, 13 June 1855; see also 'Frailty Thy Name is Woman,' which was coverage of a similar clash (with less horrific results) between two women in Allegheny, New York (*Niagara Chronicle*, 26 Aug. 1853).

Bibliography

ABBREVIATIONS

AHR, *American Historical Review*
BR, Baldwin Room, Metropolitan Toronto Reference Library
CHR, *Canadian Historical Review*
HP, Canadian Historical Association *Historical Papers*
MQUP, McGill-Queen's University Press
OH, *Ontario History*
OUP, Oxford University Press
PAO, Public Archives of Ontario
UCA, United Church Archives
UCP, University of Chicago Press
UTP, University of Toronto Press
UWO, Regional Collection, D.B. Weldon Library, University of Western Ontario

PRIMARY SOURCES

Newspapers

The Artisan 1848 (Toronto)
British Colonist 1837–50 (Toronto)
Canada Christian Advocate 1845–50 (Cobourg and Hamilton)
Canada Constellation 1799–1800 (Newark)
Canadian Freeman 1824–34 (York)
Canadian Son of Temperance and Literary Gem 1851–54 (Toronto)
Christian Guardian 1829–55 (York/Toronto)

Christian Messenger 1844–47 (Montreal)
Christian Recorder 1819–21 (York)
Christian Sentinel and Anglo-Canadian Churchmen's Magazine 1827–30
The Church 1837–50 (Toronto)
Colonial Advocate 1824–37 (Queenston and York)
The Constitution 1836–37 (Toronto)
The Evangelist 1848 and 1851 (Toronto)
The Examiner 1840–50 (Toronto)
The Globe 1844–55 (Toronto)
Kingston Gazette 1810–18; renamed *Kingston Chronicle* 1819–32; *Kingston Chronicle and Gazette* 1833–45 (Kingston)
Mackenzie's Gazette 1838–39 (Rochester)
Niagara Chronicle 1836–53 (Niagara)
Niagara Gleaner 1819–37 (Niagara)
Niagara Herald 1801–03, 1837–50 (Niagara)
Niagara Mail 1855 (Niagara)
Niagara Spectator 1817–19 (Niagara)
Patriot and Farmers' Monitor 1832–44 (Kingston and Toronto)
Provincial Freeman 1853–57 (Chatham and Toronto)
Upper Canada Gazette 1793–1806; renamed *York Gazette* 1807–16 (as a result of the destruction of the press during the War of 1812, the paper was not published from April 1813 until late 1814) *Upper Canada Gazette* 1817–20; *York Weekly and Upper Canada Gazette* 1821; *Weekly Register and Upper Canada Gazette* 1822–25; *United Empire Loyalist and Upper Canada Gazette* 1826–28 (Newark and York)

Manuscript Collections

Department of Finance, Upper Canada. *War of 1812 Losses Claims*. PAO
Graham, C.H. 'Correspondence of, with and in Connection with Refugees from the 1837 Rebellion, 1837–1842.' UWO
Kilbourne, Payne Kenyon. 'The History and Antiquities of the Name and Family of Kilbourn.' Grover Genealogical Collection. UWO
Rogers Family Papers, 1829–36. PAO
Rose Family Correspondence, 1831–39. PAO
Smith, Samuel. Diaries, 1821–54, PAO
Stark, Mark Young. Personal Papers, General Correspondence, 1723–1899. UCA
Tidey Papers. John Tidey's Diary, 1839–45. UWO
Wright, Captain E. Diary, 1835. UWO

Published Material

Bangs, Nathan. *A History of the Methodist Episcopal Church*. Vols. 2–4. *1793–1840*. New York: Carlton and Porter, 1838. UCA

Boulton, D'Arcy. *Sketch of His Majesty's Province of Upper Canada*. 1805. Reprint, Toronto: Baxter, 1961. PAO

Carroll, John. *Case and His Contemporaries*. Vols. 1–5. Toronto: Samuel Rose, 1867–77

– *My Boy Life, presented in a succession of True Stories*. Toronto: William Briggs, 1882

– *Past and Present, or a description of persons and events connected with Canadian Methodism for the last 40 years*. Alfred Dredge, 1860

Carruthers, J. *Retrospect of 36 Years' Residence in Canada West: being a Christian Journal and Narrative*. Hamilton, 1861

Cooney, Robert. *The Autobiography of a Wesleyan Methodist Missionary*. Montreal: E. Pickup, 1856

Copway, George. *Recollections of a Forest Life; or, the Life and Travels of Kah-ge-ga-gah-bowh, or George Copway, Chief of the Ojibway Nation*. London: C. Gilpin, 1851. PAO

Cruikshank, E.A. *The Documentary History of the Campaign upon the Niagara Frontier, 1812–1814*. Vols. 1–9. Welland, ON: Lundy's Lane Historical Society, 1896–1908

Davis, Robert. *The Canadian Farmer's Travels in the United States of America*. Buffalo, 1837. BR

Duncombe, Dr Charles. 'Dr. Charles Duncombe's Report on the Subject of Education Made to the Parliament of Upper Canada, February 25, 1836.' *Journals of the Legislative Assembly*, 12th Parliament, 2nd Session. PAO

Dunlop, Dr Wm. *Recollections of the War of 1812*. 1846. Reprint, Toronto: Historical Publishing Co., 1908

Edgar, Matilda. *Ten Years of Upper Canada in Peace and War 1805–1815; Being the Ridout Letters*. Toronto: Wm. Briggs, 1890

Fairley, Margaret, ed. *The Selected Writings of William Lyon Mackenzie, 1824–1837*. Oxford: OUP, 1960

Firth, Edith. *The Town of York, 1815–1834*. Toronto: Champlain Society, 1966

– *The Town of York, 1793–1815*. Toronto: Champlain Society, 1962

Gourlay, Robert. *Statistical Account of Upper Canada*. Vols. 1 and 2. London: Simpkin and Marshall, 1822

Gray, Hugh. *Letters from Canada, Written During a Residence There in the Years 1806, 1807, and 1808*. London: Longman, Hurst, Rees, and Orme, 1809. PAO

Green, Anson. *The Life and Times of Anson Green*. Toronto: Methodist Bookroom, 1877

Hall, Francis. *Travels in Canada and the United States, in 1816 and 1817*. London: Longman, Hurst, Rees, Orme, and Brown, 1818. PAO

Harris, J.H. *A Sermon preached at St. James' Church, York; on Sunday March 17, 1833, in aid of the Sunday School Society for the Diocese of Quebec*. PAO

Henderson, J.L.H., ed. *John Strachan: Documents and Opinions*. Toronto: McClelland and Stewart, 1969

Hilts, Joseph H. *Experiences of a Backwoods Preacher or, facts and incidents culled from 30 years of ministerial life*. Toronto: Methodist Mission Rooms, 1892. AO

Hopper, Jane Agar. *Old-Time Primitive Methodism in Canada, 1829–1884*. Toronto: William Briggs, 1904. UCA

Jarvis, Samuel P. *A Contradiction of the Libel published in the 'Canadian Freeman' of the 28th February, 1828, under the signature of 'A Relative.'* York, 1828

– *Statement of Facts, Relating to the Trespass, on the Printing Press, in the Possession of Mr. William Lyon Mackenzie, in June 1826*. York: Robert Stanton, 1828

Lindsey, Colin. *The Life and Times of William Lyon Mackenzie*. Vols. 1 and 2. Toronto, 1862

Loyal and Patriotic Society of Upper Canada. *Explanation of the Proceedings of the Loyal and Patriotic Society of Upper Canada*. Toronto: Robert Stanton, 1841

– *The Report of the Loyal and Patriotic Society of Upper Canada*. Montreal: William Gray, 1817

Macdougall, P.L. *Correspondence between F.H. Vane, P.L. Macdougall, and Robt. Abraham, relative to an affair of honour*. St Johns, 1849

Machar, Agnes Maule. *The Story of Old Kingston*. Toronto: Musson Book Co., 1908

Mackenzie, William Lyon. *Catechism of Education*. York: Colonial Advocate Press, 1830. BR

– *Mackenzie's Own Narrative of the Rebellion with Notes Critical and Explanatory Exhibiting the Only True Account of What Took Place at the Memorable Siege of Toronto in the Month of December 1837*. Toronto: Rous and Mann Ltd., 1937. PAO

– *A New Almanack for the Canadian True Blues, With Which is Incorporated the Constitutional Reformers' Textbook*. York: Colonial Advocate Press, 1834. BR

– *Observations on the State of Representation of the People of Upper Canada in the Legislature of that Province*. York: 1832. Lindsey Papers, Literary Works, PAO

– *Sketches of Canada and the United States*. London: Effingham Wilson, 1833. BR

Meacham, A.G. *A Compendious History of the Rise and Progress of the Methodist Church*. Hallowell, 1832

O'Brien, Mary Gapper. *The Journals of Mary Gapper O'Brien, 1828–1838*, edited by Audrey Saunders Miller. Toronto: Macmillan, 1968

Playter, George F. *The History of Methodism in Canada; with an account of the rise and progress of the work of God among the Canadian Indian tribes and occasional notices of the civil affairs of the province.* Toronto: Anson Green, 1862

Phillips, Rev. T. *A Loyal Sermon.* 23 April 1826. PAO

Radcliff, Thomas, ed. *Authentic Letters from Upper Canada.* 1833. Reprint Toronto: Macmillan, 1953

Read, Colin, and Ronald J. Stagg, eds. *The Rebellion of 1837 in Upper Canada.* Ottawa: Champlain Society, Carleton University Press, 1985

Richardson, John. *Major Richardson's Major-General Sir Isaac Brock and the 41st Regiment*, edited by T.B. Higginson. 1846. Reprint, Burks Falls, ON Old Rectory Press, 1976

Riddell, William Renwick. *The Duel in Early Upper Canada.* 1935. AO
– 'The First Attorney-General of Upper Canada: John White, 1792–1800.' *OH* 23 (1926): 413–33
– 'The Solicitor-General Tried for Murder.' In *Upper Canada Sketches: Incidents in the Early Times of the Province*, 24–32. Toronto: Carswell: 1922

Rorke, Richard. *Forty Years in the Forest, reminiscences as from the pen of a backwoodsman, 1820–1868*, edited by Phyllis Knight Armstrong. Tottenham, ON: Tecumseth and West Gwillimbury Historical Society, 1987

Ryerson, Egerton. *Civil Government – the late Conspiracy: A Discourse.* Toronto: 1838. Preached at Kingston, 31 Dec. 1837. PAO
– *Wesleyan Methodism in Upper Canada: a sermon Preached Before the Conference of Ministers of the Wesleyan Methodist Church in Canada.* Toronto, 1837. PAO

Select Committee of the Legislative Assembly of Upper Canada. 'Report of the Select Committee on the Proceedings of the Loyal and Patriotic Society, in relation to certain Medals.' *Appendix to the Journal of the House of Assembly of Upper Canada*, 5th session, 13th Parliament, 1839–40. Vol. 1. Toronto: W.J. Coates, 1840

Shortt, Edward MacLeod. *The memorable duel at Perth.* 1930. Pamphlet 75. PAO

Sissons, C.B. *Egerton Ryerson, His Life and Letters.* Vol. 1. Toronto: Clarke, Irwin, 1937

Spragge, George W., ed. *The John Strachan Letter Book: 1812–1834.* Toronto: Ontario Historical Society, 1946

Stevens, Abel. *The Life and Times of Nathan Bangs, D.D.* New York: Carlton and Porter, 1863. UCA
– *The Women of Methodism: its Three Foundresses, Susanna Wesley, the Countess of Huntingdon, and Barbara Heck; with Sketches of their female Associates and*

Successors in the Early History of the Denomination. New York: Carlton and Porter, 1869. UCA

Strachan, John. *Discourse on the Character of King George the Third Addressed to the Inhabitants of British America.* Montreal: Nahum Mower, 1810

– *Sermon Preached at York Before the Legislative Council and House of Assembly.* 2 Aug. 1812. PAO

Taylor, Rev. W. *A Testimony Against Duelling: a Sermon Preached in the United Secession Church, Montreal, August 1838.* Montreal: Campbell and Beckett, 1838. BR

Thompson, David. *A History of the late war between Great Britain and the United States of America; with a Retrospective view of the causes from whence it originated.* Niagara, 1832. Reprint Toronto, 1845. BR

Thompson, Samuel. *Reminiscences of a Canadian Pioneer for the Last Fifty Years.* Toronto: Hunter Rose, 1884. PAO

Waddilove, William, ed. *The Stewart Missions; a Series of Letters and Journals, Calculated to Exhibit to British Christians, the Spiritual Destitution of the Emigrants Settled in the Remote Parts of Upper Canada.* London, 1838. PAO

Wait, Benjamin, and Maria Wait. *Letters from Van Dieman's Land.* Buffalo: A.W. Wilgas, 1843. PAO

Weld, Isaac. *Travels Through the States of North America, and the Provinces of Upper and Lower Canada, During the Years 1795, 1796, and 1797.* London: John Stockdale, 1799. PAO

Wells, W.B. *Canadiana: containing sketches of Upper Canada, and the Crisis in its political affairs.* London: C & W Reynell, 1837. PAO

West, John. *The Substance of a Journal during a Residence at the Red River Colony, British North America; and Frequent Excursions Among the North West American Indians.* London: L.B. Seeley, 1827. PAO

Withrow, W.H. *Barbara Heck, 1734–1804: a Tale of Early Methodism.* Toronto: William Briggs, 1895. UCA

SECONDARY SOURCES

Books

Agulhon, Maurice. *Marianne into Battle: Republican Imagery and Symbolism in France, 1789–1880.* Trans. Janet Lloyd. Cambridge: Cambridge University Press, 1981

Akenson, Donald Harman. *The Irish in Ontario: A Study in Rural History.* Montreal and Kingston: MQUP, 1984

Backhouse, Constance. *Petticoats and Prejudice: Women and Law in Nineteenth-Century Canada*. Toronto: Women's Press, 1991

Ban, Joseph D., and Paul R. Dekar, eds. *In the Great Tradition: Essays on Pluralism, Voluntarism, and Revivalism*. Valley Forge, PA: Judson Press, 1986

Barker-Benfield, G.J. *The Culture of Sensibility: Sex and Society in Eighteenth-Century Britain*. Chicago: UCP, 1992

Barkun, Michael. *Crucible of the Millenium: The Burned-Over District of New York in the 1840s*. Syracuse, NY: Syracuse University Press, 1986

Blumin, Stuart M. *The Emergence of the Middle Class: Social Experience in the American City, 1760–1900*. New York: Cambridge University Press, 1989

Brod, Harry, ed. *The Making of Masculinities: The New Men's Studies*. Boston: Allen and Unwin, 1987

Brode, Patrick. *Sir John Beverley Robinson: Bone and Sinew of the Compact*. Toronto: UTP, 1984

Buckner, Phillip. *The Transition to Responsible Government: British Policy in British North America, 1815–1850*. Westport, CT: Greenwood Press, 1985

Burley, David G. *A Particular Condition in Life: Self-Employment and Social Mobility in Mid-Victorian Brantford, Ontario*. Montreal and Kingston: MQUP, 1994

Careless, J.M.S. *Brown of the Globe*. Vol. 1. *The Voice of Upper Canada, 1818–1859*. Toronto: Macmillan, 1959

– *The Union of the Canadas: The Growth of Canadian Institutions, 1841–1857*. Toronto: McClelland and Stewart, 1967

Carnes, Mark C. *Secret Ritual and Manhood in Victorian America*. New Haven and London: Yale University Press, 1989

Carnes, Mark C., and Clyde Griffen, eds. *Meanings for Manhood: Constructions of Masculinity in Victorian America*. Chicago: UCP, 1990

Cawardine, Richard. *Transatlantic Revivalism: Popular Evangelicalism in Britain and America*. Westport, CT: Greenwood Press, 1978

Clark, S.D. *Church and Sect in Canada*. Toronto: UTP, 1948

– *Movements of Political Protest in Canada, 1640–1840*. Toronto: UTP, 1959

Cohen, Marjorie. *Women's Work, Markets, and Economic Development in Nineteenth-Century Ontario*. Toronto: UTP, 1988

Colley, Linda. *Britons: Forging the Nation, 1707–1837*. New Haven: Yale University Press, 1992

Cott, Nancy. *The Bonds of Womanhood: 'Woman's Sphere' in New England, 1780–1835*. New Haven: Yale University Press, 1977

Craig, Gerald. *Upper Canada: The Formative Years, 1784–1841*. Toronto: McClelland and Stewart, 1963

Culler, Jonathan. *On Deconstruction: Theory and Criticism After Structuralism.* London: Basil Blackwell, 1982

Curtis, Bruce. *Building the Educational State: Canada West, 1836–1871.* London, ON: Althouse Press, 1988

– *True Government by Choice Men? Inspection, Education, and State Formation in Canada West.* Toronto: UTP, 1992

Davidoff, Leonore, and Catherine Hall. *Family Fortunes: Men and Women of the English Middle Class, 1780–1850.* Chicago: UCP, 1987

Dawe, Brian. *'Old Oxford is Awake!' Pioneer Settlers and Politicians in Oxford County, 1793–1853.* Toronto: Ontario Historical Society, 1980

Devens, Carol. *Countering Colonization: Native American Women and Great Lakes Missions, 1630–1900.* Berkeley: University of California Press, 1992

Dickinson, H.T. *Liberty and Property: Political Ideology in Eighteenth-Century Britain.* London: Methuen, 1979

Douglas, Ann. *The Feminizaton of American Culture.* New York: Anchor Press, 1988

Dunham, Aileen. *Political Unrest in Upper Canada, 1815–1836.* Toronto: McClelland and Stewart, 1963

Eagleton, Terry. *Literary Theory: An Introduction.* Minneapolis: University of Minnesota Press, 1983

Epstein, Barbara Leslie. *The Politics of Domesticity: Women, Evangelism, and Temperance in Nineteenth-Century America.* Middletown, CT: Wesleyan University Press, 1981

Errington, Elizabeth Jane. *Wives and Mothers, Schoolmistresses and Scullery Maids: Working Women in Upper Canada, 1790–1840.* Montreal and Kingston: MQUP, 1995

Errington, Jane. *The Lion, the Eagle, and Upper Canada: A Developing Colonial Ideology.* Montreal and Kingston: MQUP, 1987

Fahey, Curtis. *In His Name: The Anglican Experience in Upper Canada, 1791–1854.* Ottawa: Carleton University Press, 1991

Foucault, Michel. *Discipline and Punish: The Birth of the Prison.* New York: Pantheon Books, 1978

Francis, Mark. *Governors and Settlers: Images of Authority in the British Colonies, 1820s-1860s.* London: Macmillan, 1992

Garner, John. *The Franchise and Politics in British North America, 1755–1867.* Toronto: UTP, 1968

Gauvreau, Michael. *The Evangelical Century: College and Creed in English Canada from the Great Revival to the Great Depression.* Montreal and Kingston: MQUP, 1991

Gay, Peter. *The Bourgeois Experience: Victoria to Freud*. Vol. 1. *Education of the Senses*. Vol. 2. *The Tender Passion*. Oxford: OUP, 1984, 1988

Ginzberg, Lori D. *Women and the Work of Benevolence: Morality, Politics and Class in the Nineteenth-Century United States*. New Haven: Yale University Press, 1990

Graham, Elizabeth. *From Medicine-Man to Missionary: Missionaries as Agents of Change Among the Indians of Southern Ontario, 1784–1867*. Toronto: UTP, 1975

Graham, W.H. *Greenbank: Country Matters in Nineteenth-Century Ontario*. Peterborough: Broadview Press, 1988

Grant, John Webster. *Moon of Wintertime: Missionaries and the Indians of Canada in Encounter Since 1534*. Toronto: UTP, 1984

– *A Profusion of Spires: Religion in Nineteenth-Century Ontario*. Toronto: Ontario Historical Studies Series, 1988

Greer, Allan. *The Patriots and the People: The Rebellion of 1837 in Rural Lower Canada*. Toronto: UTP, 1993

Greer, Allan, and Ian Radforth, eds. *Colonial Leviathan: State Formation in Mid-Nineteenth-Century Canada*. Toronto: UTP, 1992

Guildford, Janet, and Suzanne Morton, eds. *Separate Spheres: Women's Worlds in the Nineteenth-Century Maritimes*. Fredericton: Acadiensis Press, 1994

Gunn, J.A.W. *Beyond Liberty and Property: The Process of Self-Recognition in Eighteenth-Century Political Thought*. Montreal and Kingston: MQUP, 1979

Habermas, Jürgen. *The Structural Transformation of the Public Sphere: An Inquiry into a Category of Bourgeois Society*, translated by Thomas Burger with the assistance of Frederick Lawrence. Cambridge: MIT Press, 1989

Haltunnen, Karen. *Confidence Men and Painted Women: A Study of Middle-Class Culture in America, 1830–1870*. New Haven: Yale University Press, 1982

Harrison, J.M.C. *The Second Coming: Popular Millenarianism, 1780–1850*. New Brunswick, NJ: Rutgers University Press, 1979

Hearn, Jeff. *The Gender of Oppression: Men, Masculinity, and the Critique of Marxism*. New York: St Martin's Press, 1987

– *Men in the Public Eye*. London: Routledge, 1992

Hewitt, Nancy A. *Women's Activism and Social Change: Rochester, New York, 1822–1872*. Ithaca: Cornell University Press, 1984

Hopkins, James K. *A Woman to Deliver Her People: Joanna Southcott and English Millenarianism in an Age of Revolution*. Austin: University of Texas, 1982

Houston, Susan E., and Alison Prentice. *Schooling and Scholars in Nineteenth-Century Ontario*. Toronto: UTP, 1988

Hufton, Olwen. *Women and the Limits of Citizenship in the French Revolution*. Toronto: UTP, 1992

Hunt, Lynn. *The Family Romance of the French Revolution*. Berkeley: University of California Press, 1992
– ed. *The New Cultural History*. Berkeley: University of California Press, 1988
– *Politics, Culture, and Class in the French Revolution*. Berkeley: University of California Press, 1984
Isaac, Rhys. *The Transformation of Virginia, 1740–1790*. Chapel Hill: University of North Carolina Press, 1982
Johnson, J.K. *Becoming Prominent: Regional Leadership in Upper Canada, 1791–1841*. Montreal and Kingston: MQUP, 1989
Jones, Gareth Stedman. *Languages of Class: Studies in English Working-Class History, 1832–1982*. Cambridge: Cambridge University Press, 1982
Jones, Jacqueline. *Labor of Love, Labor of Sorrow: Black Women, Work and the Family, From Slavery to the Present*. New York: Vintage Books, 1985
Juster, Susan. *Disorderly Women: Sexual Politics and Evangelicalism in Revolutionary New England*. Ithaca: Cornell University Press, 1994
Kasson, John P. *Rudeness and Civility: Manners in Nineteenth-Century America*. New York: Hill and Wang, 1990
Keane, David, and Colin Read, eds. *Old Ontario: Essays in Honour of J.M.S. Careless*. Toronto: Dundurn Press, 1990
Kelly, Joan. *Women, History, and Theory: The Essays of Joan Kelly*. Chicago: UCP, 1984
Kerber, Linda. *Women of the Republic: Intellect and Ideology in Revolutionary America*. Chapel Hill: University of North Carolina Press, 1980
Kiernan, V.G. *The Duel in European History: Honour and the Reign of Aristocracy*. Oxford: OUP, 1988
Klancher, Jon P. *The Making of English Reading Audiences, 1790–1832*. Madison: University of Wisconsin Press, 1987
Krueger, Christine L. *The Reader's Repentance: Women Preachers, Women Writers, and Nineteenth-Century Social Discourse*. Chicago: UCP, 1992
LaCapra, Dominick. *History and Criticism*. Ithaca: Cornell University Press, 1985
– *Rethinking Intellectual History: Texts, Contexts, and Language*. Ithaca: Cornell University Press, 1985
Landes, Joan B. *Women and the Public Sphere in the Age of the French Revolution*. Ithaca: Cornell University Press, 1988
Light, Beth, and Alison Prentice, eds. *Pioneer and Gentlewomen of British North America 1713–1867*. Toronto: New Hogtown Press, 1980
MacDonald, Mary Lu. *Literature and Society in the Canadas, 1817–1850*. Lewiston, NY: Edwin Mellon Press, 1992
Malmgreen, Gail, ed. *Religion in the Lives of English Women, 1760–1850*. Bloomington: Indiana University Press, 1986

Mangan, J.A., and James Walvin, eds. *Manliness and Morality: Middle-Class Masculinity in Britain and America*. Manchester: Manchester University Press, 1987

McCalla, Douglas. *Planting the Province: The Economic History of Upper Canada, 1784–1870*. Toronto: Ontario Historical Studies Series, 1993

McCalman, Ian. *Radical Underworld: Prophets, Revolutionaries and Pornographers in London, 1795–1840*. Cambridge: Cambridge University Press, 1988

McKenna, Katherine M.J. *A Life of Propriety: Anne Murray Powell and Her Family, 1755–1849*. Montreal and Kingston: MQUP, 1994

McKillop, A.B., and Paul Romney, eds. *God's Peculiar Peoples: Essays on Political Culture in Nineteenth-Century Canada*. Ottawa: Carleton University Press, 1993

McLoughlin, William G. *Revivals, Awakenings, and Reform: An Essay on Religion and Social Change in America, 1607–1977*. Chicago: UCP, 1978

Milani, Lois Darroch. *Robert Gourlay, Gadfly*. Ottawa: Ampersand Press, 1971

Mills, David. *The Idea of Loyalty in Upper Canada, 1784–1850*. Montreal and Kingston: MQUP, 1988

Muir, Elizabeth Gillian. *Petticoats in the Pulpit: The Story of Early-Nineteenth-Century Methodist Women Preachers in Upper Canada*. Toronto: United Church Publishing House, 1991

Noel, Jan. *Canada Dry: Temperance Crusades Before Confederation*. Toronto: UTP, 1995

Noel, S.J.R. *Patrons, Clients, Brokers: Ontario Society and Politics, 1791–1896*. Toronto: UTP, 1990

Obelkevich, James. *Religion and Rural Society: South Lindsey, 1825–1875*. Oxford: Clarendon Press, 1976

Ormsby, William. *The Emergence of the Federal Concept in Canada, 1839–1845*. Toronto: UTP, 1969

Outram, Dorinda. *The Body and the French Revolution: Sex, Class and Political Culture*. New Haven: Yale University Press, 1989

Palmer, Bryan D. *Descent into Discourse: The Reification of Language and the Writing of Social History*. Philadelphia: Temple University Press, 1990

Pateman, Carole. *The Sexual Contract*. Stanford: Stanford University Press, 1988

Pleck, Elizabeth, and Joseph Pleck. *The American Man*. Englewood Cliffs, NJ: Prentice-Hall, 1980

Pocock, J.G.A. *The Machiavellian Moment*. Princeton: Princeton University Press, 1975

– *Virtue, Commerce, and History: Essays on Political Thought and History*. Princeton: Princeton University Press, 1985

Poovey, Mary. *Uneven Developments: The Ideological Work of Gender in Mid-Victorian England*. Chicago: UCP, 1988

Potter-MacKinnon, Janice. *While the Women Only Wept: Loyalist Refugee Women in Eastern Ontario*. Montreal and Kingston: MQUP, 1993

Prentice, Alison, Paula Bourne, Gail Cuthbert Brandt, Beth Light, Wendy Mitchinson, and Naomi Black. *Canadian Women: A History*. Toronto: Harcourt Brace Jovanovich, 1988

Prochaska, F.K. *Women and Philanthropy in Nineteenth-Century England*. Oxford: OUP, 1980

Rawlyk, G.A. *The Canada Fire: Radical Evangelicalism in British North America, 1775–1812*. Montreal and Kingston: MQUP, 1994

-, ed. *The Protestant Experience in Canada, 1760–1990*. Burlington, ON: Welch Publications, 1990

- *Ravished by the Spirit: Religious Revivals, Baptists, and Henry Alline*. Montreal and Kingston: MQUP, 1984

Rea, J.E. *Bishop Alexander Macdonell and the Politics of Upper Canada*. Toronto: Ontario Historical Society, 1974

Read, Colin. *The Rising in Western Upper Canada, 1837–1838: The Duncombe Revolt and After*. Toronto: UTP, 1982

Riley, Denise. *'Am I That Name?' Feminism and the Category of 'Women' in History*. Minneapolis: University of Minnesota Press, 1988

Robbins, Caroline. *The Eighteenth-Century Commonwealthman*. Cambridge: Harvard University Press, 1961

Roper, Michael, and John Tosh, eds. *Manful Assertions: Masculinities in Britain since 1800*. London: Routledge, 1991

Russell, Peter A. *'Here We Are Lairds Ourselves': Attitudes to Social Structure and Mobility in Upper Canada, 1815–1840*. Lewiston, NY: Edwin Mellon Press, 1990

Ryan, Mary P. *Cradle of the Middle Class: The Family in Oneida County, New York, 1790–1865*. Cambridge: Cambridge University Press, 1981

- *The Empire of the Mother: American Writing About Domesticity, 1830–1860*. New York: Harrington Press, 1985

- *Women in Public: Between Banners and Ballots, 1825–1880*. Baltimore: Johns Hopkins University Press, 1990

Said, Edward. *Orientalism*. New York: Pantheon Books, 1978

Salvaggio, Ruth. *Enlightened Absence: Neoclassical Configurations of the Feminine*. Chicago: University of Illinois Press, 1988

Samuel, Raphael, ed. *Patriotism: The Making and Unmaking of British National Identities*. Vol. 3. *National Fictions*. London: Routledge, 1989

Samuels, Shirley, ed. *The Culture of Sentiment: Race, Gender, and Sentimentality in Nineteenth-Century America*. Oxford: OUP, 1992

Schmalz, Peter. *The Ojibwa of Southern Ontario*. Toronto: UTP, 1991

Scott, Donald M. *From Office to Profession: The New England Ministry, 1750–1850*. Philadelphia: University of Pennsylvania Press, 1978

Scott, Joan Wallach. *Gender and the Politics of History*. New York: Columbia University Press, 1988

Seidler, Victor J. *Rediscovering Masculinity: Reason, Language, and Sexuality*. London: Routledge, 1989

Sheppard, George. *Plunder, Profit, and Paroles: A Social History of the War of 1812 in Upper Canada*. Montreal and Kingston: MQUP, 1994

Shevelow, Kathryn. *Women and Print Culture: The Construction of Femininity in the Early Periodical*. London: Routledge, 1989

Shiach, Morag. *Discourse on Popular Culture: Class, Gender and History in Cultural Analysis, 1730 to the Present*. Oxford: Basil Blackwell, 1989

Sklar, Kathryn Kish. *Catharine Beecher: A Study in American Domesticity*. New Haven: Yale University Press, 1973

Smith, Donald B. *Sacred Feathers: The Reverend Peter Jones (Kahkeqaquonaby) and the Mississauga Indians*. Toronto: UTP, 1987

Smith, Olivia. *The Politics of Language, 1791–1819*. Oxford: OUP, 1984

Smith-Rosenberg, Carroll. *Disorderly Conduct: Visions of Gender in Victorian America*. New York: OUP, 1985

Spelman, Elizabeth. *Inessential Woman: Problems of Exclusion in Feminist Thought*. Boston: Beacon Press: 1988

Stansell, Christine. *City of Women: Sex and Class in New York, 1789–1860*. Chicago: University of Illinois Press, 1987

Stouffer, Allen P. *The Light of Nature and the Law of God: Antislavery in Ontario, 1833–1877*. Montreal and Kingston: MQUP, 1992

Sturrock, John, ed. *Structuralism and Since: From Levi-Strauss to Derrida*. Oxford: OUP, 1979

Taylor, Barbara. *Eve and the New Jerusalem: Socialism and Feminism in the Nineteenth Century*. London: Virago Press, 1984

Thompson, Dorothy. *The Chartists*. London: Temple Smith Press, 1984

– *Queen Victoria: Gender and Power*. London: Virago Press, 1990

Thompson, E.P. *The Making of the English Working Class*. Harmondsworth: Penguin, 1980

Valenze, Deborah. *Prophetic Sons and Daughters: Female Preaching and Popular Religion in Industrial England*. Princeton: Princeton University Press, 1985

Vance, Norman. *The Sinews of the Spirit: The Ideal of Christian Manliness in Victorian Literature and Religious Thought*. Cambridge: Cambridge University Press, 1985

Van Die, Marguerite. *An Evangelical Mind: Nathanael Burwash and the Methodist Tradition in Canada, 1839–1918*. Montreal and Kingston: MQUP, 1989

Van Kirk, Sylvia. *'Many Tender Ties': Women in Fur Trade Society, 1670–1870*. Winnipeg: Watson and Dwyer, 1980

Ward, John Manning. *Colonial Self-Government: The British Experience, 1759–1856*. Toronto: UTP, 1974

Ward, Peter. *Courtship, Love, and Marriage in Nineteenth-Century English Canada*. Montreal and Kingston: MQUP, 1990

Ware, Vron. *Beyond the Pale: White Women, Racism, and History*. London: Verso, 1992

Westfall, William. *Two Worlds: The Protestant Culture of Nineteenth-Century Ontario*. Montreal and Kingston: MQUP, 1989

Weedon, Chris. *Feminist Practice and Poststructuralist Theory*. Oxford: Basil Blackwell, 1987

White, Hayden. *The Content of the Form: Narrative Discourse and Historical Representation*. Baltimore: Johns Hopkins University Press, 1987

– *Tropics of Discourse: Essays in Cultural Criticism*. Baltimore: Johns Hopkins University Press, 1978

Zaslow, Morris, ed. *The Defended Border: Upper Canada and the War of 1812*. Toronto: Macmillan, 1964

Articles

Alcoff, Linda. 'Cultural Feminism Versus Post-Structuralism: The Identity Crisis in Feminist Theory.' *Signs* 13, no. 3 (Spring 1988): 404–36

Alexander, Ruth M. '"We Are Engaged as a Band of Sisters": Class and Domesticity in the Washingtonian Temperance Movement, 1840–1850.' *Journal of American History* 75, no. 3 (Dec. 1988): 763–85

Andrew, Donna. 'The Code of Honour and Its Critics.' *Social History* 5, no. 3 (Oct. 1980): 409–34

Baker, G.B. 'The Juvenile Advocate Society, 1821–26: Self-Proclaimed Schoolroom for Upper Canada's Governing Class.' *HP* (1985): 74–101

– '"So Elegant a Web": Providential Order and the Rule of Secular Law in Early-Nineteenth-Century Upper Canada.' *University of Toronto Law Journal* 38 (1988): 184–205

Baker, Paula. 'The Domestication of Politics: Women and American Political Society, 1780–1920.' *AHR* 89, no. 3 (1984): 620–47

Barron, F.L. 'The American Origins of the Temperance Movement in Ontario, 1828–1850.' *Canadian Review of American Studies* 2, no. 2 (Fall 1980): 131–50

Bleasdale, Ruth. 'Class Conflict on the Canals of Upper Canada in the 1840s.' In *Pre-Industrial Canada, 1760–1849*, edited by Gregory S. Kealey and Michael S. Cross, 100–38. Toronto: McClelland and Stewart, 1982

Bloch, Gerald. 'Robert Gourlay's Vision of Radical Agrarian Reform.' In *Canadian*

Papers in Rural History, edited by Donald Akenson, 2:110–28. Gananoque, ON: Langdale Press, 1982

Bloch, Ruth H. 'The Gendered Meanings of Virtue in Revolutionary America.' *Signs* 13, no. 11 (Autumn 1987): 37–58

Brooks-Higginbotham, Evelyn. 'African-American Women's History and the Meta-language of Race.' *Signs* 17, no. 2 (Winter 1992): 251–74

Burns, R.J. 'God's Chosen People: The Origins of Toronto Society, 1793–1818.' *HP* (1973): 213–28

Cadigan, Sean T. 'Paternalism and Politics: Sir Francis Bond Head, the Orange Order, and the Election of 1836.' *CHR* 72, no. 3 (Sept. 1991): 319–47

Campbell, Gail. 'Disfranchised but not Quiescent: Women Petitioners in New Brunswick in the Mid-Nineteenth Century.' *Acadiensis* 28, no. 2 (Spring 1989): 22–54

Christie, Nancy. ' "In These Times of Democratic Rage and Delusion": Popular Religion and the Challenge to the Established Order.' In *The Canadian Protestant Experience, 1760–1990*, edited by George A. Rawlyk, 9–47. Burlington, ON: Welch Publishing, 1990

Clarke, Anna. 'The Rhetoric of Chartist Domesticity: Gender, Language, and Class in the 1830s and 1840s.' *Journal of British Studies* 31 (Jan. 1992): 62–88

Clemens, James M. '"Taste Not; Touch Not; Handle Not": A Study of the Assumptions of the Temperance Literature and Temperance Supporters in Canada West Between 1839 and 1859,' *OH* 64, no. 3 (Sept. 1972): 142–60

Craig, Hamilton. 'The Loyal and Patriotic Society of Upper Canada and Its Still-Born Child: The "Upper Canada Preserved" Medal.' *OH* 52, no. 1 (1960): 31–52

Cross, Michael S., and Robert Fraser. '"The Waste that Lies before Me": The Public and Private Worlds of Robert Baldwin.' *HP* (1983): 164–83

Davis, Natalie Zemon. 'Women's History in Transition: The European Case.' *Feminist Studies* 3, nos. 3/4 (Spring–Summer 1976): 83–103

de Groot, Joanna. '"Sex" and "Race": The Construction of Language and Image in the Nineteenth Century.' In *Sexuality and Subordination: Interdisciplinary Studies of Gender in the Nineteenth Century*, edited by Susan Mendus and Jane Rendall, 89–128. London: Routledge: 1989

de la Cour, Lykke, Cecilia Morgan, and Mariana Valverde. 'Gender Regulation and State Formation in Nineteenth-Century Canada.' In *Colonial Leviathan: State Formation in Mid-Nineteenth-Century Canada*, edited by Allan Greer and Ian Radforth, 163–91. Toronto: UTP, 1992

Eagleton, Terry. 'Marxism, Structuralism, and Post-Structuralism.' *Diacritics* (Winter 1985): 2–12

Fingard, Judith. '"Grapes in the Wilderness": The Bible Society in British North America in the Early Nineteenth Century.' *Histoire sociale/Social History* 5, no. 9 (April 1972): 5–31

French, Goldwin S. 'Egerton Ryerson and the Methodist Model for Upper Canada.' In *Egerton Ryerson and His Times*, edited by Alf Chaiton, 45–58. Toronto: Macmillan, 1978
– 'The Evangelical Creed in Canada.' In *The Shield of Achilles*, edited by W.L. Morton, 16–34. Toronto: McClelland and Stewart, 1968
Gauvreau, Michael. 'Beyond the Half-Way House: Evangelicalism and the Shaping of English Canadian Culture.' *Acadiensis* 20, no. 2 (Spring 1991): 158–77
– 'Protestantism Transformed: Personal Piety and the Evangelical Social Vision, 1815–67.' In *The Canadian Protestant Experience, 1760–1990*, edited by George A. Rawlyk, 48–97. Burlington, ON: Welch Publishing, 1990
Green, Gretchen. 'Molly Brant, Catherine Brant, and Their Daughters: A Study in Colonial Acculturation.' *OH* 83, no. 3 (Sept. 1990): 179–206
Greer, Allan. '1837–8: Rebellion Reconsidered.' *CHR* 76, no. 1 (March 1995): 1–18
– 'La république des hommes: les Patriotes de 1837 face aux femmes.' *Revue d'histoire de l'Amérique française* 44, no. 4 (printcmps 1991): 507–28
– 'The Sunday Schools of Upper Canada.' *OH* 68 (Sept. 1975): 169–84
Gunderson, Joan. 'Independence, Citizenship, and the American Revolution.' *Signs* 13, no. 11 (Autumn 1987): 59–77
Hewitt, Nancy A. 'Beyond the Search for Sisterhood: American Women's History in the 1980s.' In *Unequal Sisters: A Multicultural Reader in U.S. Women's History*, edited by Ellen Carol DuBois and Vicki L. Ruiz, 1–14. New York: Routledge, 1990
Kerber, Linda K. 'Separate Spheres, Female Worlds, Woman's Place: The Rhetoric of Women's History.' *Journal of American History* 75, no. 1 (June 1988): 9–39
Lake, Marilyn. 'The Politics of Respectability: Identifying the Masculinist Context.' *Historical Studies* 22, no. 86 (April 1986): 116–31
MacKay, R.A. 'The Political Ideas of William Lyon Mackenzie.' *Canadian Journal of Economics and Political Science* 3, no. 1 (Feb. 1937): 1–22
McKenna, Katherine M.J. 'Options for Elite Women in Early Upper Canadian Society: The Case of the Powell Family.' In *Historical Essays on Upper Canada: New Perspectives*, edited by J.K. Johnson and Bruce G. Wilson, 401–23. Ottawa: Carleton University Press, 1989
– 'The Role of Women in the Establishment of Social Status in Early Upper Canada.' *OH* 83, no. 3 (Sept. 1990): 179–206
Millar, W.P.J. 'The Remarkable Rev. Thaddeus Osgood: A Study in the Evangelical Spirit in the Canadas.' *Histoire sociale/Social History* 19 (May 1977): 59–76
Outram, Dorinda. 'Le langage mâle de la vertu: Women and the Discourse of the French Revolution.' In *The Social History of Language*, edited by Peter Burke and Roy Porter, 120–35. Cambridge: Cambridge University Press, 1987
Parr, Joy. 'Gender History and Historical Practice.' *CHR* 76, no. 3 (Sept. 1995): 354–76

- 'Nature and Hierarchy: Reflections on Writing the History of Women and Children.' *Atlantis* 11, no. 1 (Fall 1985): 39–44
Patterson, Graeme. 'An Enduring Canadian Myth: Responsible Government and the Family Compact.' In *Interpreting Canada's Past*. Vol. 1, *Before Confederation*, edited by J.M. Bumstead, 230–47. Oxford: OUP, 1986
Perry, Ruth. 'Colonizing the Breast: Sexuality and Maternity in Eighteenth-Century England.' *Journal of the History of Sexuality* 2, no. 2 (Oct. 1991): 204–34
Phelan, Josephine. 'A Duel on the Island.' *OH* 69, no. 4 (Dec. 1977): 235–38
Pitkin, Hanna Fenichel. 'Justice: On Relating Private and Public.' *Political Theory* 9, no. 3 (Aug. 1981): 327–52
Poovey, Mary. 'Feminism and Deconstruction.' *Feminist Studies* 14, no. 1 (Spring 1988): 51–65
Pope, Barbara Corrado. 'Revolution and Retreat: Upper-Class French Women After 1789.' In *Women, War, and Revolution*, edited by Carol R. Berkin and Clara M. Lovett, 215–36. New York: Holmes and Meier, 1980
Rea, J.E. 'William Lyon Mackenzie: Jacksonian?" In *Canadian History Before Confederation*, edited by J.M. Bumsted, 332–42. Georgetown, ON: Irwin-Dorsey, 1972
Read, Colin. 'Conflict to Consensus: The Political Culture of Upper Canada.' *Acadiensis* 19, no. 2 (Spring 1990): 169–85
Reynolds, Sîan. 'Marianne's Citizens? Women, the Republic, and Universal Suffrage in France.' In *Women, State, and Revolution: Essays on Power and Gender in Europe since 1789*, edited by Sîan Reynolds, 102–22. Amherst: University of Massachusetts Press, 1986
Romney, Paul. 'A Conservative Reformer in Upper Canada: Charles Fothergill, Responsible Government and the "British Party," 1824–1840.' *HP* (1984): 42–62
- 'From the Rule of Law to Responsible Government: Ontario Political Culture and Origins of Canadian Statism.' *HP* (1988): 86–119
- 'From the Types Riot to the Rebellion: Elite Ideology, Anti-legal Sentiment, Political Violence, and the Rule of Law in Upper Canada.' *OH* 79 (1987): 113–44
- 'Reinventing Upper Canada: American Immigrants, Upper Canadian History, English Law, and the Alien Question.' In *Patterns of the Past: Interpreting Ontario's History*, edited by Roger Hall, William Westfall, and Laurel Sefton MacDowell, 78–107. Toronto: Dundurn Press, 1988
- 'Very Late Loyalist Fantasies: Nostaligic Tory "History" and the Rule of Law in Upper Canada.' In *Canadian Perspectives on Law and Society: Issues in Legal History*, edited by W. Wesley Pue and Barry Wright, 119–47. Ottawa: Carleton University Press, 1988
Rotundo, E. Anthony. 'Romantic Friendships: Male Intimacy and Middle-Class Youth in the Northern United States, 1800–1900.' *Journal of Social History* 23, no. 1 (Fall 1989): 1–25

Scott, Joan Wallach. 'Deconstructing Equality-Versus-Difference: Or, the Uses of Poststructuralist Theory for Feminism.' *Feminist Studies* 14, no. 1 (Spring 1988): 33–50
– 'Experience.' In *Feminists Theorize the Political*, edited by Judith Butler and Joan W. Scott, 22–40. New York: Routledge, 1992
– 'On Language, Gender, and Working-Class History.' *International Labor and Working-Class History*, no. 31 (Spring 1987): 1–13
Semple, Neil. 'The Quest for the Kingdom: Aspects of Protestant Revivalism in Nineteenth-Century Ontario.' In *Old Ontario: Essays in Honour of J.M.S. Careless*, edited by David Keane and Colin Read, 95–117. Toronto: Dundurn Press, 1990
Sheppard, George. '"Deeds Speak?" Militiamen, Medals, and the Invented Traditions of 1812.' *OH* 82, no. 3 (Sept. 1990): 207–32
Smith, Allan. 'The Myth of the Self-Made Man in English Canada, 1850–1914.' *CHR* 54, no. 2 (1978): 189–219
Smith-Rosenberg, Carroll. 'Dis-Covering the Subject of the "Great Constitutional Discussion," 1786–1789.' *Journal of American History* 79, no. 3 (Dec. 1992): 841–73
Thompson, Dorothy. 'Women and Nineteenth-Century Radical Politics: A Lost Dimension.' In *The Rights and Wrongs of Women*, edited by Juliet Mitchell and Ann Oakley, 112–38. Harmondsworth: Penguin, 1976
– 'Women, Work, and Politics in Nineteenth-Century England: The Problem of Authority.' In *Equal or Different: Women's Politics, 1800–1914*, edited by Jane Rendall, 57–81. London: Basil Blackwell, 1987
Toews, John E. 'Intellectual History After the Linguistic Turn: The Autonomy of Meaning and the Irreducibility of Experience.' *AHR* 92 (1987): 879–907
Tosh, John. 'What Should Historians Do with Masculinity? Reflections on Nineteenth-Century Britain.' *History Workshop* 38 (Autumn 1994): 179–202
Valverde, Mariana. 'The Love of Finery: Fashion and the Fallen Woman in Nineteenth-Century Social Discourse.' *Victorian Studies* 32, no. 2 (Winter 1989): 168–88
– 'Poststructuralist Gender Historians: Are We Those Names?' *Labour/Le Travail* 25 (Spring 1990): 225–36
Vernon, James. 'Who's Afraid of the "Linguistic Turn"? The Politics of Social History and Its Discontents.' *Social History* 19, no. 1 (Jan. 1994): 81–97
Welter, Barbara. 'The Cult of True Womanhood, 1820–1860.' *American Quarterly* 18 (1966): 151–74
Wilton, Carol. '"A Firebrand Amongst the People": The Durham Meetings and Popular Politics in Upper Canada.' *CHR* 75, no. 3 (Sept. 1994): 346–75
Wright, Barry. 'Sedition in Upper Canada: Contested Legality?' *Labour/Le Travail* 29 (Spring 1992): 7–57

Theses and Unpublished Papers

Bowler, Reginald Arthur. 'Propaganda in Upper Canada: A Study of the Propaganda Directed at the People of Upper Canada During the War of 1812.' MA thesis, Queen's University, 1964

Fraser, Robert. '"Like Eden in Her Summer Dress": Gentry, Economy, and Society, Upper Canada, 1812–1840.' PhD thesis, Department of History, University of Toronto, 1979

Hall, Anthony J. 'The Red Man's Burden: Land, Law, and the Lord in the Indian Affairs of Upper Canada, 1791–1858.' PhD thesis, Department of History, University of Toronto, 1984

Kewley, Arthur E. 'Mass Evangelism in Upper Canada Before 1830.' ThD thesis, Emmanuel College, Victoria University, 1960

Patterson, Graeme. 'Studies in Elections and Public Opinion in Upper Canada.' PhD thesis, Department of History, University of Toronto, 1969

Rotundo, E. Anthony. 'Manhood in America: The Northern Middle Class, 1770–1920.' PhD thesis, Brandeis University, 1982

Van Die, Marguerite. '"A Woman's Awakening": Evangelical Belief and Female Spirituality in Mid-Nineteenth-Century Canada' Paper presented to the 70th annual conference of the Canadian Historical Association, 1991

Wilton-Siegel, Carol. 'The Transformation of Upper Canadian Politics in the 1840s.' PhD thesis, Department of History, University of Toronto, 1984

Index

STUDIES IN GENDER AND HISTORY

General editors: Franca Iacovetta and Craig Heron